الإجماع

The Doctrine of Ijma' in Islam

A Study of the Juridical Principle of Consensus

Ahmad Hasan

Qadeem Press

Qadeem Press

Qadeem Press Edition
Breathing Life into Forgotten Pages
www.qadeempress.com

Reprinted by Qadeem Press in 2026

Find our titles on your favourite online bookstore using the keyword 'Qadeem Press'

Contents

Preface

Recent researches in Islamic law and jurisprudence have opened up new horizons and, therefore, much work can be done in this field. One feels that since the formation of the orthodox schools of law, there has been a great development in legal theory, doctrine, and norms. Most of these doctrines and schools have been obviously influenced by the historical process. And this is natural. No law in any society, even in a religious one, is ever stagnant. It develops with the development of society. Islamic law, although authoritative, is not rigid by nature. It does not, of course, change very rapidly. Its development is very slow and imperceptible. To reconstruct a society in the context of changing conditions it is essential that its law should be constantly revised by means of fresh interpretations. A vigorous search, deep and extensive study, and re-examination of the legal material would be conducive to the formulation of the guidelines for further development.

To acquaint oneself with the origins of Islamic law one must go back to its early legal manuals. The early phase has been surveyed to some extent; there, however, remains much work to be done. The classical period remained almost unexplored, although it is rich in legal literature. The various aspects of legal theory, important legal doctrines, legal maxims, legal devices, a comparative study of the principles of the four orthodox schools, a comparison between the Sunni and the Shi'i law, and a study of classical legal thought and philosophy may constitute some important topics of future research. The study of law in different modern Muslim countries with their changing societies is also a subject of inquiry.

In the field of Islamic jurisprudence, a good deal of work has to be done. Some doctoral dissertations produced in recent decades are a welcome contribution to the subject. Dr. M.Z. Madina's unpublished thesis on the classical doctrine of consensus, submitted to the University of Chicago in 1957, is a fine piece of research. The Islamic Research Institute has a master plan aiming at producing scholarly works on various topics of Islamic studies. The present work is a part of this program.

The work has been prepared with the materials available in the library of the Institute. I also benefited from the libraries at Lahore and Karachi during my short stay there. I could not refer much to the periodicals for want of their back issues in the library.

I am deeply indebted to Dr. Rashid Ahmad Jullundhri, the present Director of the Institute, for taking a keen interest in the book and expediting its publication. I owe profound thanks to Professor Mazheruddin Siddiqi, who guided me on some difficult problems and edited the manuscript. I am also grateful to all my colleagues for their assistance to me in the preparation of this work.

Ahmad Hasan

Note On Transliteration

The system of transliteration of Arabic words adopted in this series is the same as has been employed by the editors of the Encyclopaedia of Islam, new edition with the following exceptions: q has been used for k and j for dj, as these are more convenient to follow for English-knowing readers than the international signs. The use of *dh*, *gh*. *kh*, *sh*, and *th*, with a subscript dash, although it may appear pedantic, has been considered necessary for the sake of accuracy and clearer pronunciation of letters peculiar to Arabic and Persian. As against the Encyclopaedia. *Tā' marbūtah* has throughout been retained and shown by the ending *h* or *t*, as the case may be. This was also found necessary in order to avoid any confusion.

Introduction

Islamic jurisprudence is originally based on the Qur'ān, the Sunnah, *Ijmā'* (consensus), and *Qiyās* (analogy). These are the basic sources of law, apparently autonomous and separated from each other. The main sources are the Qur'ān and the Sunnah, *Ijmā'*, and *Qiyās* are, in fact, subsidiary principles. They are generally applied when the original sources are silent on a certain question. These sources do not form watertight compartments, as the tradition shows. They are closely interrelated and carry the same spirit of revelation: the Qur'ān is the word of God; the Sunnah is its commentary, explanation, and its application in practice, though sometimes it carries only the spirit and import of the Qur'ānic teaching; *Ijmā'* is based on evidence derived from either of them; *Qiyās* requires an original basis. Hence Islamic law is described as divine law.

Islamic law portrays the *I'lān* of the Qur'ānic prescriptions through a process of reasoning and individual interpretation. Viewed from this standpoint, the whole body of traditional law is an outcome of the exercise of personal opinion and individual reasoning. In this sense the phenomenon becomes subjective; and the four sources may better be called the basis of law, as personal opinion and approach are involved in the process. But this product of the human mind has been granted sanctity by means of an infallible *Ijmā'*.

So much about the four principles. Let us discuss the significance of *Ijmā'*. This important doctrine played a vital role in the integration of the Muslim community. In its early phase, it manifested itself as a general average opinion, a common feeling of the community, and as a binding force of the body of law against unsuccessful and stray opinions. In the classical period, it developed with its complex theory and ramifications. It became a decisive authority in religious affairs. All religious doctrines were standardized through *Ijmā'*. Its rejection was considered heresy, indeed sometimes tantamount to unbelief. On account of its loose machinery, it can hardly be compared with the institution of the church. Nevertheless, the classical theory treats it as carrying the same force and spirit. Ultimately it became the hallmark of orthodoxy, i.e. Sunnism.

Ijmāʿ in its early stages was parochial, i.e. the *Ijmāʿ* of Medina, Kufa, Basra, and Syria. Al-Shāfiʿī almost rejected the *Ijmāʿ* of the scholars because of its parochial nature and because it involved personal opinion. He recognized only the *Ijmāʿ* of the community on the essentials of religion. He substantiated his standpoint on the basis of some traditions that were adopted later by the jurists. With the development of its theory in the medieval period, there appeared three types of attitudes, viz. that which upheld the classical theory in toto; that which partially recognized it with reservations; and that which rejected it outright. Orthodoxy could hardly convince its opponents because of the divergence of opinion on many points in the theory itself.

In this study, our inquiry begins with the post-Shāfiʿī period. The early period has been explored, of course not finally, by Professor Schacht in "*The Origins of Muhammadan Jurisprudence*", and by myself in my earlier work. Hence questions of the early concept and development of *Ijmāʿ*, its position in the legal schools, its early usage, and al-Shāfiʿī's treatment of it have not been dealt with in greater detail. The classical theory of *Ijmāʿ* largely differs from its early concept and usage. One can hardly find its definition in the early legal texts, although the term has been frequently used there.

The first three chapters of this treatise are introductory studying the social and political role of *Ijmāʿ* and its authority. The following chapters present a detailed analysis of its classical theory, i.e. its definition, competence, period, jurisdiction, subject matter, and other relevant questions. The point of view held by the opponents of *Ijmāʿ* has been discussed in a separate chapter. The last two chapters deal with its comparative study and with the emerging trends in *Ijmāʿ*.

The present study poses some important questions for further inquiry of this doctrine in the context of the present-day situation. How this principle should be applied in the changing Muslim society of our day is a big question to answer.

Chapter I: *Ijmāʿ*: An Integrating Force in The Muslim Community

The Qurʾān repeatedly calls the Muslims an *ʾUmmah* (community).[1] This appellation, i.e. the *ʾUmmah*, by its very definition, presupposes unity, integration, and solidarity, not only in external organization but also on the ideological plane. The Qurʾān does not mean by this nomenclature a nominally united group united externally but split up internally. It exhorts the Muslims to remain united and to keep away from schism and disagreement.[2] The Prophet after his arrival at Medina formed for political purposes a larger community which consisted of the Jews as well.[3] This larger community was short-lived and the non-Muslims were eventually excluded from the Islamic community. Now the solidarity of the Islamic community rests on certain fundamentals which can be broadly categorized into law, dogma, and rituals. These formal institutions give an external shape to the community.

The process of integration of the *ʾUmmah* commenced after the migration of the Prophet to Medina. The community secured its standing in its integrated form at Medina. The first step taken by the Prophet in respect of integration was the exclusion of the non-Muslims from the community after they had violated the pacts concluded with them. Simultaneously, the institution of brotherhood (*Muʾākhāt*) united the Muslims in a single whole. The Qurʾān talks of the Muslim brotherhood as a blessing from God.[4] On a certain occasion when a blood feud arose between the tribes of Aws and Khazraj, the Qurʾān soothed their hostile feelings by calling the believers brothers.[5] Since there was no ideological disagreement

---

[1] Qurʾān 2:143; 3:110; 21:92; 23:52.
[2] Qurʾān 3:103, 105.
[3] *Ibn Hishām*, *Sīrat al-Nabī*, Cairo: *Maṭbaʿah Ḥijāzī*, n.d. II, 119-23.
[4] Qurʾān 3:103; 15:47.
[5] Qurʾān 49:10.

among the Muslims during the time of the Prophet, such as appeared in later times, this ideological cohesion was a vital binding force. The Qur'ān repeatedly talks of the Muslim Brotherhood and exhorts them to cooperate with each other.[6] This moral teaching of the Qur'ān for external and internal unity gave new momentum to the integration of the community. The ideological cementing force during the time of the Prophet was the Qur'ān and the Sunnah.

The need of integration was actually felt when, during the caliphate of Abū Bakr, a number of tribes refused to pay *Zakāt* to the state. Abū Bakr took the situation seriously and decided to fight with them. He wanted to preserve the state of religion as it stood during the Prophet's time. The non-payment of *Zakāt* was very serious for Abū Bakr, but ʿUmar and some other Companions viewed the situation from a different angle. As the people were neo-Muslims, they wanted to treat them with leniency. ʿUmar is reported to have remarked: "How do you fight with the people while the Prophet has said: I have been commanded to fight with people until they utter 'there is no God but Allah'. When they utter this credo, they save their lives and property from me except for what is due to it." But Abū Bakr did not agree with him. He is reported to have replied: "By God, I shall fight with a man who separates what the Prophet had united".[7] There are different versions of Abū Bakr's reply to ʿUmar, and his determination to fight with such people is of capital importance for the purpose of inquiry as to how the legal definition of a Muslim developed in later history. ʿUmar seemingly desired to save the community from disintegration, and wanted to include in it the persons who refused to pay *Zakāt*. According to him, violation of an obligatory duty could be tolerated for a more important reason. Hence, he quoted the tradition which gives the legal

---

[6] Qur'ān 5:2; 9:11; 33:5.

[7] Al-Bukhārī, *Al-Jāmiʿ al-Ṣaḥīḥ*, Leiden, 1908, IV, 421, 443 (*Kitāb al-Iʿtiṣām*).

definition of a Muslim. But to Abū Bakr, putting the community on a solid basis and following the practice of the Prophet's time were more important than integration. Abū Bakr regarded the discontinuation of the previous practice as a deterioration of religion (*Naqṣ fil-Dīn*). This model practice (Sunnah) in the later ages proved to be the unifying force of the community prior to the emergence of the principle of *Ijmāʿ*. ʿUmar changed his stand and ultimately agreed with Abū Bakr. Abū Bakr gave battle to these tribes and brought them to submission.[8] From this, we conclude that in the early days of Islam ideological integration was emphasized even at the cost of some Muslim tribes. And this was achieved through adherence to the model practice. From this model practice (Sunnah) in the long run there emerged divergent sects in Islam. The radical group as well as the moderate one claimed to be the followers of the model practice. The moderate group ultimately distinguished itself from others by its appellation *Ahl al-*Sunnah *wal Jamāʿah.*

After the demise of the Prophet, it was not possible to extend the prophetic Sunnah per se in the changed circumstances. Hence the Sunnah assimilated in its ambit some other elements not originally coming from the Prophet. It contained local customs, the practices of the Muslims, and the legal rules framed by the political authorities during the early centuries. So long as the Sunnah in its wider concept conformed to that of the Prophet and the practice of the Muslims remained pure and continuous, it was taken as the Sunnah of the Prophet. The practice of the Muslims during the time of the first four Caliphs was comparatively pure and continuous. One finds nominal differences in the fields of law and dogma. Hence the practice of the first four Caliphs is considered normative

---

[8] Ibn Kathīr, *Al-Bidāyah Wal-Nihāyah*, Cairo: Maṭbaʿah al-Saʿādah, 1932, VI, 311 f; ʿAlī al-Muttaqī, *Kanz al-ʿUmmāl*, Hyderabad, Deccan: *Maṭbaʿah Dāʾirat al-Maʿārif al-Niẓāmiyyah*, 1312 A.H., III, 142.

practice, being a part of the prophetic Sunnah. These Caliphs are generally known as *A'immat al-Hudā* (leaders of guidance). Although the latter appellation owes its origin to a tradition of the Prophet, it marks a distinction between the early Caliphs and their successors, i.e. Umayyads and ʿAbbasids. With the emphasis of al-Shāfiʾī on the prophetic traditions the wider concept of the Sunnah was narrowed, and eventually identified with the traditions recorded in the well-known collections of *Ḥadīth*. Still, the concept of the Sunnah of the first four Caliphs and the Sunnah of the Companions survived in the medieval period. Now until the time of al-Shāfiʾī there existed three channels to ascertain the model practice, (1) prophetic traditions, (2) the traditions of the first four Caliphs, and (3) the practice of the Companions on record.

With the movement of the compilation of traditions, the *Ḥadīth* literature swelled in the third century of the Hijrah. This gave rise to the problem of conflict between the well-known and solitary traditions. The *Ḥadīth* collections contained mostly the isolated traditions which did not coincide with the practice. The collections of *Ḥadīth*, however, prevailed over the well-known traditions which represented the established practice of the Muslims. The domination of *Ḥadīth* in different fields resulted in the justification of law, dogma, and rituals on the basis of *Ḥadīth*. Al-Ashʾarī, the eponym of the moderate school, sums up the orthodox tenets by saying, "This is the epitome of the beliefs of *Ashab al-Ḥadīth wal-Sunnah*," and at another place, he remarks: "This is what is followed by *Ahl al-Ḥadīth wal*-Sunnah."[9]

After the emergence of disagreement in the community, the moderate group called themselves *Ahl al*-Sunnah *wal-Jamāʿah*, *Ahl* al-

---

[9] Al-Ashʿarī, *Maqālāt al-Islāmiyyīn*, Cairo: Maṭbaʿat al-Nahḍah al-Miṣriyyah, 1950, 1, 320.

Sunnah *wal-Istiqāmah*, and *Aṣḥāb al-Ḥadīth wal*-Sunnah.[10] These appellations indicate the role played by *Ḥadīth* in uniting the community. The term current during the Prophet's time as a symbol for the unity of the community was *Ṣalāt* (prayer). Hence the phrase *Al-Ṣalātu Jāmiʾah* frequently used in the time of the Prophet and during the early caliphate to assemble people for any important social problem.[11] The terms *Ahl al-Ṣalāh* and *Ahl al-Qiblah* were, therefore, reserved to refer to the whole community comprising even the heretics who claimed to be Muslims. But it is surprising that the community was never called *Ahl al-Qurʾan*, although the basic unifying force throughout the ages was the Qurʾān. The reason is, we presume, that the Qurʾān was never applied in its pure literal form. Its application remained subject to interpretation. It was interpreted in the light of the Sunnah (*Ḥadīth*), on the basis of *Raʾy* (considered opinion), and in the context of beliefs and doctrines of different sects. It was eventually decided by the Sunnis during the third century of the Hijrah that the Qurʾān would be interpreted on the basis of its obvious meaning.[12]

Through the efforts of al-Shāfiʾī and later on of Ahmad b. Hanbal orthodoxy took its stand on *Ḥadīth. Al-Ashʾari* uses the term *Ahl-al-Ḥadīth* for the group which takes its stand on *Ḥadīth.* The word Sunnah in this appellation points to the moderate school which follows the practice of the Prophet through *Ḥadīth. Al-Ashʾarī* calls the groups which differed with orthodoxy *Ahl al-Bidʾah, Ahl al-ahwaʾ*, and *Ahl al-Zaygh wal-Taḍlīl.* He applies these terms to the *Murjiʾah,*

---

[10] *Ibid.*, 145, 147.

[11] Al-Bukhārī, *Al-Jāmiʿ al-Ṣaḥīḥ* (Kusūf, 3, 8, 19); Muslim, *Ṣaḥīḥ* (Kusūf 4, 20 and Fitan, 120); Abū Dawūd, *Sunan* (Malahim, 11); Ahmad b. Hanbal, Musnad, Cairo, 1313 A.H., 1, 14; 11, 161, 175, 191; IV, 89; V, 299; VI, 89.

[12] Al-Ashʿarī, *al-Ibānah*, Hyderabad, Deccan: Maṭbaʿah Jamʿiyyat Dāʾirat al-Maʿārif al-ʿUthmāniyyah, 1948, p. 11.

Khawārij, Muʿtazilah, and *Shīʾah*[13]. The *Muʿtazilah* laid stress on the well-known Sunnah. They refused to recognize the solitary traditions not known and practiced among Muslims. Their attitude towards *Ḥadīth* is pretty clear from the works of *al*-Shāfiʿī, *al-Jāḥiz*, and *al-Khayyat*. Refuting the isolated traditions advanced by the Shīʾah in support of their stand, *al-Khayyat* replies to al-Rawandi, "This is because that the Sunnah of the Prophet is well-known (*Maʾrūfah*), transmitted by the community at large. Whoever reports an isolated tradition which contradicts his (Prophet's) Sunnah, his falsehood will be known to all and his report shall be rejected.[14] Even the early Shīʾah did not accept a tradition contradictory to the Qurʾān and to the consensus of the Muslims.[15] The Khawārij too looked askance at the isolated traditions. This is obvious from their criticism on *Ḥadīth* in Ibn Qutaybah's *Taʾwīl Mukhtalif al-Ḥadīth*. With this background in view, the reason can be easily discerned for the appellation *Ahl al-Ḥadīth wal*-Sunnah applied by al-Ashʾari to the right wing.

So far, our hypothesis shows that the doctrine of the Sunnah was the unifying force in the community prior to *Ijmāʿ*. Although the term *Ijmāʿ* was recurrently used in the early Islamic literature of the first and the second century in its non-technical or semi-technical sense, it did not carry the same force of authority as the term Sunnah did. For this, there are two reasons. First, the Sunnah was a concept already recognized in the pre-Islamic Arabian social order. If anything appeared as a Sunnah in the society, it had a psychological appeal at least to those who were conversant with it. Moreover, the significance of this institution was already known to the Arabs. Secondly, it had the support of the Qurʾān at its back. The Qurʾān emphasized obedience to the Prophet. Sunnah was,

---

[13] *Ibid.*, p. 8; Al-Ashʿarī, *Maqālāt*, 11, 149, 152.

[14] Al-Khayyāṭ, *Al-Intiṣār*, Cairo: Maṭbaʿah Dār al-Kutub al-Miṣriyyah, 1925, p. 135.

[15] Al-Kulini, *al-Kafi*, Tehran: Al-Maktabah al-Islāmiyyah, 1382 A.H., I., 169.

therefore, an authoritative force for unifying the community. Things attributed to the Prophet had to be followed by the Muslims. If they were rejected, this was not because they were Sunnah, but because of some defect or weakness in their transmission or attribution to the Prophet. We have shown elsewhere that roughly until the middle of the second century of the Hijrah Sunnah and *Ijmāʿ* were so close to each other that both these terms were used interchangeably, rather sometimes identified.[16]

With the break in the established practice after the orthodox caliphate, a state of chaos appeared in different spheres. Differences arose in almost every legal problem; the community was divided into several theological sects. This resulted in the division of the Sunnah. Since *Ijmāʿ* could not replace disagreement. al-Shāfiʿī was correct in his criticism on this principle. It appears that the principle of *Ijmāʿ* was utilized to save the community from chaos. The Sunnah and *Ijmāʿ* were henceforth separated. The Sunnah became synonymous with *Ḥadīth* and *Ijmāʿ* now became a term of reference. The concept of *Ijmāʿ* developed with the emergence of the majority group (*Ahl al*-Sunnah) vis-à-vis different theological sects. The majority group claimed to be the followers of the right and ideal practice. Hence the Sunnah became a part of their appellation. At this stage, the institution of *Jamāʿah* was stressed, as the extremists were declared heretics by the majority group.

From al-Shāfiʿī's discussions on the problem of *Ijmāʿ* and solitary traditions,[17] it appears that orthodoxy justified their stand on the basis of traditions. But when different sects quoted traditions in support of their viewpoint, and this created a chaotic state of affairs with the increasing *Ḥadīth* literature, the moderate group receded

---

[16] Ahmad Hasan, *The Early Development of Islamic Jurisprudence,* Lahore: Islamic Research Institute, 1970, p. 169.
[17] Al-Shāfiʿī, Kitāb al-Umm, Cairo, Būlaq, 1321 A.H., VII, Treatise "*Ijmaʿ al-ʿIlm*".

and again had recourse to *Ijmāʿ*. The titles *Ahl al-Ḥadīth*, *Ahl al-*Sunnah, and *Ahl al-Ijmāʿ* now became identical. During the third century, we find emphasis on *Jamāʿah*. Ahmad b. Hanbal, who completed the work of al-Shāfiʿī, divides the whole community into three groups with respect to prayer (*Ṣalāt*). First, he groups together *Khawārij*, *Rawāfid*, and *Ahl al-Bidʾah*. This group, he remarks, despises prayer in congregation and regards the Muslims as heretics. Second, he refers to people devoted to ease and pleasure holding ignoble assemblies of drinking and evil deeds. The third group is *Ahl al-Jamāʿah* who attends the prayer in congregation in the mosques regularly. This group, according to him, is the best of all.[18] By *Ahl al-Jamāʿah* Ibn Hanbal does not refer only to the people who say their prayer in congregation, but presumably, he means the moderate group. The term *Ahl al-Jamāʿah* is the second phase of the development of the appellation *Ahl al-*Sunnah. We come across this term in an epistle of Abū Hanifah addressed to ʿUthman al-Batti, who levelled the charge of *Irja* at him. Abū Hanīfah refuting this charge replied: "Let it be known that the best of things that you should learn yourself and teach people is the Sunnah. You should know the people who have learned it of necessity. As regards the title *al-Murjiʾah*, it may be remarked that it is no sin if a group believes in moderation (*ʾAdl*). The people of innovation (*Ahl al-Bidʾah*) have applied this term to the moderate group. But they are, in fact, *Ahl al-ʾAdl wa Ahl al-*Sunnah (people of the middle-of-the-road and followers of the established practice). The antagonists have applied this term (*Murjiʾah*) to them."[19] This shows that *Ahl al-*Sunnah and *Ahl al-Bidʾah* were earlier divided. *Ahl al-Bidʾah* represented the left wing comprising all those groups which opposed orthodoxy.

---

[18] Ahmad b. Hanbal, *al-Risālah al-Saniyyah*, (in *Majmūʿah al-Ḥadīth al-Najdiyyah*), Qatar: Maṭābiʿ al-ʿUrūbah, 1383 A.H., p. 468.

[19] Maḥmūd al-Ḥasan, *Muʿjam al-Muṣannifīn*, Beirut, 1344 A.H., II, 196.

The concept of *Jamāʿah* in the context of the integration of the community emerged for the first time in the first century of the Hijrah. The year 41 A.H., when Muʿawiyah became the caliph after his compromise with al-Hasan bin ʿAlī, is known as *ʿĀm al-Jamāʿah* (the year of unity).[20] The reason for this seems to be that the dual caliphate was henceforth abolished and the conflict between ʿAlī and Muʾawiyah now came to an end. Although politically this year was the beginning of integration, al-Jahiz (d. 255 A.H.) portrays it as the beginning of schism, absolutism, and kingship.[21] The term *ʾĀm al-Jamāʿah* indicates that the community was absolutely disgusted with the internecine wars and it needed both internal and external solidarity. It is important to note that soon after the death of the Prophet emphasis was laid on the solidarity of the community. Disagreement resulting in chaos and anarchy was avoided as far as possible. Ibn Masʾūd and Abū Dharr are reported to have said four *Rakʿāt* of prayer even during the journey at Minā following the caliph ʿUthman who prayed four *Rakʿāt*. They disagreed in principle with ʿUthman who departed from the established rule of saying two *Rakʿāt* of prayer during journey. When they were asked why they prayed four *Rakaʾat* despite their disagreement, they replied, "Disagreement is evil," and "disunity" is worse."[22] ʿUthman is said to have detained the chiefs of the Quraysh in Medina lest perversion (*fitnah*) and dissension (*Wahn*) should spread among the

---

[20] Al-Jāḥiẓ, *al-Nābitah* (*Risalah fi Bani Umayyah*), Cairo, 1937, p. 94; Charles Pellah, *The Life and Works of Jahiz*, Eng. tr. D.M. Hawke, London: Routledge & Kegan Paul, 1969, p. 84.

[21] *Ibid.*

[22] Abū Dāwūd, (*Manāsik*); al-Haythami, *Majmaʿ al-Zawāʾid*, Cairo: Maktabah al-Qudsi, 1353 A.H., V, 216.

community.[23] Unity (*Jamā'ah*) was called blessing and separation (*furqah*) punishment. [24]

The rise of the heretical sects in Islam was the result of the political upheaval since the time of 'Uthman. This reached its climax during the reign of 'Alī. The external disunity was thus redeemed by the movement of *Jamā'ah*. We shall discuss presently how *Ḥadīth* literature accelerated this movement by laying emphasis on adherence to the majority or *Jamā'ah*. The internal disagreement or the ideological chaos was removed by the dominating concept of the Sunnah. The title *Ahl al*-Sunnah *wal-Jamā'ah*, which represents the moderate and majority group, emerged as a via media out of radical trends. To establish this *modus vivendi*, law and theology cooperated with each other. The doctrine of *Taqlīd* (conformity) conserved the legal heritage of the first three centuries with the process of systematization. The development of orthodox theology pioneered by Ahmad bin Hanbal and accentuated by al-Ash'arī standardized the dogma of Islam. In this process of standardization, the doctrine of *Ijmā'* which must have been derived from the concept of *jumā'ah* played a paramount role. Although the term *Ijmā'* was in currency in pre-Islamic Arabia, it gained momentum in its technical form, emerging as an authoritative force, with the emergence of disagreement in Islam. Orthodoxy was identified with *Ahl al-Ijmā'* in its culminating phase of development.[25] The force of *Ijmā'* can be imagined from the fact that even the left-wing justified their views by referring to *Ijmā'* and excommunicated their opponents on its basis.[26]

---

[23] Al-Tabari, *Ta'rīkh al-Umam wal-Mulūk*, Cairo: *Al-Maṭba'ah al-Ḥusayniyyah*, 1336 A.H., V, 134.

[24] Ahmad b. Hanbal, *Musnad*, IV, 278, 375.

[25] Ibn Hazm, *Al-Iḥkām fī Uṣūl al-Aḥkām*, Cairo: Maṭba'ah al-Sa'ādah, 1347 A.H., IV, 128.

[26] Al-Khayyāṭ, *op. cit.*, pp. 163, 164.

The civil wars which resulted in the emergence of the concept of *Jamāʿah* are known as *fitnah* in history. This is termed *Fitnah Ṣamma, ʿamyaʾ* and sometimes *Bakmā* (deaf, blind, and dumb schism) in *Ḥadīth* literature.[27] The word *fitnah* and its adjectives have been presumably derived from the Qurʾānic verse, "And they supposed there should be no trial (*Fitnah*); but blind they were, and deaf. Then God turned towards them; then again blind they were, many of them, and deaf."[28] It is reported that Ibn ʿUmar was once asked about the meaning of *fitnah*. Quoting the Qurʾānic verse, "And fight them until there is no persecution, and religion is only for Allah,"[29] he remarked: "Do you know what *fitnah* is? The Prophet was fighting with the infidels (so that they might embrace Islam and might not return to their religion). The return to their religion was known as *fitnah* and not the battle that you are fighting for worldly hegemony."[30] This shows that these civil wars were very serious in the eyes of the people, and they took them as the perversion of the community. But Ibn ʿUmar held a different view of the civil wars and disillusioned people by giving a new interpretation of *fitnah*. The report, however, indicates that there was confusion in the minds of people as to the meaning of *fitnah*. The concept of *Jamāʾah* seems to be a reaction against the rise of schism (*fitnah*) in Islam. The *Ḥadīth* literature supports our hypothesis. Nearly all the collections of *Ḥadīth* which belong to the third century of the Hijrah contain chapters on *fitnah*. The main theme of these chapters is the prediction of the rise of sects and the disintegration of the community. The traditions about *fitnah* lay emphasis on the

---

[27] Abū Dāwūd, *Sunan*, (Kitâb al-Fitan).

[28] Qurʾān 5:71.

[29] Qurʾān 2:193.

[30] Al-Bukhārī, *al-Jāmi al-Ṣaḥīḥ* (Fitan, 16).

solidarity of the community. All these traditions of the Prophet were quoted by orthodoxy in support of their stand.[31]

The predictory traditions concerning the rise of sects in Islam and adherence to the community (*Jamāʿah*) are copious. It will lead us far afield if we quote them in toto. We, therefore, analyze some relevant and important traditions in this context. The Prophet is reported to have said, "The people of the Book before you were divided into seventy-two groups. And this community will be divided into seventy-three groups. Seventy-two of them will go to hell, and only one of them will enter paradise. This single group is the *Jamāʿah*."[32] This tradition has different versions. The most important and interesting is the one which tells that only *Ahl al-*Sunnah *wal-Jamāʿah* will receive salvation. This version also defines *Ahl al-*Sunnah *wal-Jamāʿah* as the followers of the Prophet and his Companions.[33] The occurrence of the title *Ahl al-*Sunnah *wal-Jamāʿah* in this tradition is astonishing. This shows how the moderate group justified their school and even their title on the basis of *Ḥadīth*. Earlier we have shown the development of this title and concluded that orthodoxy stands on the traditions of the Prophet. This is illustrated by the remarks of al-Asfaraīnī (d. 741 A.H.), "There is no sect out of so many sects in the community more obedient to the Prophet and more attached to his Sunnah than these people (moderate group). This is why they are called *Ashāb al-Ḥadīth* and their title is *Ahl al-*Sunnah *wal-Jamāʿah.*[34] Another tradition runs: "Disagreement will appear after me. If you find a man who separates himself from the community or designs to shatter the practice of the community of Muhammad, kill him, whoever he may be. This is because Allah's

---

[31] Cf. Fazlur Rahman, *Islamic Methodology in History*, Lahore: Central Institute of Islamic Research, 1965, p. 53 f.
[32] Ibn Mājah, *Sunan*, Lucknow, 1315 A.H., p. 296 (*Abwāb al-Fitan*).
[33] Al-Shahrastānī, *Kitāb al-Milal Wal Nihal*, Cairo: Maktabah al-Azhar, 1910, 1, 7.
[34] Al-Asfarāʾīnī, *al-Tabṣir fil-Din*, Cairo: Maktabah al-Khānjī, 1955, p. 167.

hand is upon the community (*Jamaʿah*), and Satan goes with a man who disassociates himself from the community."[35] Such traditions predict the aftermath of the civil wars when the community fell a prey to deep disagreement and required total integration. This situation does not permit the slightest difference of opinion from the views generally held by the community, and constitutes an overemphasis on integration.

The concept of strict adherence to the *Jamāʿah* gave rise to the idea of the infallibility of the agreed decisions of the community. The following tradition gives sanction to this notion: "My community will not agree on an error. When you see disagreement, you should follow the overwhelming majority."[36] This tradition is a basis for the justification of the principle of *Ijmāʿ*.

The emphasis on *Jamāʿah* in medieval Islamic society for the sake of the stability of the *ʾUmmah* leads to the disparagement of the individual. This gave a setback to the individual thought. Alongside of adherence to the *Jamāʿah* we find also stress on unquestioning allegiance to the amir. Strict adherence to the *Jamāʿah* coupled with obedience to the amir left no freedom for the individual. This was done as a makeshift but subsequently, it became permanent. The following tradition illustrates the point in question: Hydhayfah b. al-Yaman reports, "People used to ask the Prophet about good, but I used to ask him about evil for fear of getting it". I said, "O Prophet of Allah, we were in ignorance and evil, Allah brought this good for us; will there be any evil after this good?" He said, "Yes." I said, "Will there be good after that evil?" He said, "Yes, there will be *dakhan* (dinginess)." I asked, "What is this *dakhan* (dinginess)?" He replied, "People will follow the Sunnah other than mine, and lead a life without guidance; you will find in them good and evil." I asked, "Will

[35] Al-Nasāʾī, *Sunan* (Kitāb al-Muḍarabah).
[36] Ibn Majah, *Sunan*, (Abwāb al-Fitan).

there be evil after good?" He said, "Yes, people will invite to the gates of hell. One who responds to them will be thrown in it." I said, "O Prophet of Allah, tell me their qualities." He replied, "They will be from our group, and will speak our language." I said, "What do you adivse me to do if I get them?" He said, "Follow the community (*Jamā'ah*) of the Muslims and their leader." I said, "If they have no community and leader, what should I do?" He replied, "Leave all the sects, even you take shelter in the root of a tree until you die in the same condition."[37]

Another tradition goes: "If any of you finds his leader doing some work detestable to him, he should tolerate it patiently. This is because he who separates himself from the community (*Jamā'ah*) by a span will die the death of ignorance."[38] The Prophet laid emphasis on obedience to the amir to protect the community from chaos.

Since the Umayyads and 'Abbasids could not maintain the standards established by the Prophet, the masses were not satisfied with their behaviour. Hence the term "Sunnah of the rightly-guided Caliphs" indicates the distinction between the practice of the first four Caliphs and that of the later Caliphs. The following tradition emphasizes obedience to the first four Caliphs: "I advise you to fear Allah and to obey the leader, even if he is a negro slave. One who survives me shall see profound disagreement. You should then follow my Sunnah and the Sunnah of the rightly-guided Caliphs. Hold fast to it and follow it to the last letter. You should desist from following new practice, because every new practice is innovation (heresy) and every innovation is error."[39]

Although the tradition in question does not name the rightly guided Caliphs, it is generally interpreted as referring to the first four

---

[37] Walī al-Dīn al-Khaṭīb, *Mishkāt al-Maṣābīḥ*, Delhi, 1350 A.H., p. 461 (Kitāb al-Fitan).
[38] Al-Bukhari, *Al-Jāmi' al-Ṣaḥīḥ*(Kitāb al-Fitan).
[39] Abū Dawud, *Sunan*, (Kitāb al-*Sunnah*).

Caliphs. It seems that the term *Al-Khulafāʾ al-Rāshidūn* must have gained currency during the third century of the Hijrah, because it is not traceable in the Islamic literature of the first two centuries. The title might have been derived from this tradition.

One concludes from the preceding analysis that emphasis was laid equally on adherence to the Sunnah and the *Jamāʿah*. In other words, Sunnah and *Jamāʿah* at one stage became identical. And this was natural because the majority group grew out of the radical schools and identified their views with the Sunnah. Therefore, it has been well said in a tradition that abandonment of the Sunnah is tantamount to separation from the *Jamāʿah*.[40] Further, the Sunnah in the last stage was identified with 'the pure practice of the Prophet, *Jamāʿah* with the 'group of the adherents of truth, even though in a minority' and *furqah* with the 'group of the followers of falsehood, even though in a majority.'[41] A leader was considered indispensable for the unity of the community. The absence of a leader in the community was regarded as the 'death of ignorance.[42] Obedience to the tyrant and unjust rulers was tolerated so long as they were regular in saying their prayers.[43]

The question of the definition of *ummat al-Islam* (the Islamic community) is a corollary to the concept of *Jamāʿah*. It also involves the problem of excommunication (*Takfīr*). It was introduced probably to establish the orthodox standards in different spheres vis-à-vis the standards of the opponents. Al-Shafii emphasized strict allegiance to the community. But he did not lay down any definition of the *ʾUmmah*. During the second century of the Islamic era the theological sects arose, as is evident from al-Shāfiʿī's use of the term *Ahl al-Kalām*, and also from Abū Hanīfah's letter to ʿUthman al-Batti.

---

[40] Ahmad b. Hanbal, *Musnad*, II, 229, 506.
[41] ʿAlī al-Muttaqī, *Kanz al-ʿUmmāl*, I, 96.
[42] Ahmad b. Hanbal, *Musnad*, IV, 96.
[43] *Ibid.*, 1, 275; Muslim, *Ṣaḥīḥ*, (Kitāb al-Imārah) pp. 62-63.

Moreover, the term *Ahl al-'Adl wal-Tawhīd* in this letter indicates the emergence of the moderate group. But the standard definition of the *'Ummah* is not traceable until the death of al-Shāfi'ī (204 A.H.). The reason may be that the doctrinaire aspect of Islam in its systematic form was in evolution and the process was developing. As a result of the emergence of the various theological sects the question of the definition of a Muslim and that of the community arose. The definition of the community (*Jamā'ah*) perhaps owes its origin to the *Jamā'ah* of the prayer. Ahmad b. Hanbal tells us that the *Khawārij, Rawafid,* and *Ahl al-Bid'ah* (innovators) did not offer their prayer together with the rest of the Muslims in their mosques, and they held them heretics, rather separate from the community.[44] Besides, the *Azāriqah*, a sect of the Khawārij, regarded the territory of the Muslims as dār al-kufr. They had their own separate camps which they called *Dār al-Islām*. It was obligatory, according to them, on a *Khariji* to migrate to their camp, because one who lived with the Muslims in their territory was an unbeliever (*Kāfir*) in their eyes.[45] Such trends of separation must have paved the way for defining the *'Ummah* of Islam.

We do not find any standard definition of the *'Ummah* before 'Abd al-Qahir al-Baghdadi (d. 429 A.H.). We come across, of course, sporadic statements regarding the definition of the community. Al-Jahiz refutes the charges of the Shī'ah of his time that Abū Bakr was an unbeliever. He tells them: "You agree with us on the point that he (Abū Bakr uttered the credo of Islam, ate the flesh of the legally slaughtered animal, and exhibited Islam Therefore, according to the established rule, it is essential to regard him as a Muslim on the basis of our agreement upon his obvious belief. "[46]

---

[44] Ahmad b. Hanbal, *al-Risālah al-Saniyyah*, p. 468.

[45] Al-Ash'arī, *Maqālāt*, pp. 195, 162; M. Watt, *Islam and the Integration of Society*, London: Routledge & Kegan Paul, 1961, p. 100.

[46] Al-Jahiz, *al-'Uthmaniyyah*, Cairo: *Dar al-Kitāb al-'Arabi*, 1955, pp. 245-46.

Whether a Muslim becomes an unbeliever by committing a grave sin was a serious problem. It seems that *Ijmāʿ* was already reached before the time of al-Ashʿari on the point that Muslims do not become an unbelievers by committing a grave sin. Al-Ashʿarī regards a Muslim who commits a grave sin as a believer. He considers this belief an article of faith of the moderate group (*Ahl al-Ḥadīth wal-*Sunnah).[47] He remarks that there are two viewpoints concerning a man who commits a grave sin. One holds him to be an unbeliever, while the other regards him as an unrighteous (*Fasiq*). The former is the view of the Khawārij and the latter of *Ahl al-Istiqāmah* (the moderate group). According to him, no one before Wāṣil bin ʿAṭā' held that a Muslim who commits a grave sin is neither a believer nor an unbeliever. Further, he remarks that since Wāṣil separated himself from the community by making such a statement and opposing the *Ijmāʿ* on the definition of a Muslim, he was called Muʿtazili. Again, he says that all the Muslims agree that a sinner from among the *Ahl al-salah* (people of the prayer) is either a believer or an unbeliever. The agreement of the Muslims on this point excommunicates him (*Wāṣil*) and his opinion stands rejected.[48] The term *ʾUmmah*, however, was not sharply defined by al-Ashʿari. The *Ahl al-Qiblah* and the *Ahl al-salah*, according to him, constitute the *ʾUmmah*. It comprehends both the moderate and the extreme groups.

The definition of the *ʾUmmah* of Islam crystallized during the time of al-Baghdadi (d. 429 A.H.). He records the definitions of the *ʾUmmah* as given by al-Kaʿbi (d. 319 A.H.), *al-Karramiyah*, and a group of *Ahl al-Ḥadīth*. He refutes the definitions of these groups and takes his own as the standard one. According to al-Kaʿbī, he observes, the name *millat al-Islām* applies to a man who confesses the prophethood

---

[47] Al-Ashʿarī, *Maqālāt*, 1, 322.
[48] Al-Ashʿarī, *Kitāb al-Lumaʿ*, Beirut, 1953, p. 76.

of Muhammad (peace be upon him) and holds that his teachings are true; let him say anything after this confession. The name *Ummat al-Islām*, according to *al-Karrāmiyah*, is applied to persons who utter the credo (*Kalimah*) of Islam, whether they believe in it sincerely or not. According to a group of an *Ahl al-Ḥadīth*, the term *Ummat al-Islām* stands for the people who believe in the obligatory duties, i.e. offering five daily prayers facing the Kaʿbah. Finally, he puts forth his own definition which represents the beliefs and doctrines of *Ahl al*-Sunnah. The definition says: "What is true, according to us, is that the term *Millat al-Islām* (Islamic community) applies to a man who believes in the temporary existence of the world, oneness of its creator and His eternity, and that He is just, judicious, and rejects the anthropomorphism and the negation of divine epithets, and believes in the prophethood of all His prophets and that of the Prophet Muhammad (peace be upon him), and that he was sent as a Prophet to all and sundry, and that God helps His *Shariʿah*, and that his teachings are true, and that the Qur'ān is the source of the *Shariʿah*, and that observance of five daily prayers, payment of *zakat*, fasting during the month of Ramadan, and the hajj pilgrimage are obligatory duties. One who confesses this is a member of the Islamic *'Ummah*. If one does not confound one's faith with the evil innovation (*Bid'ah*) leading to unbelief, one is a *Muwahhid* (a believer in the unity of God) and a Sunni (moderate)."[49] The above definition clearly reflects the Ashʿarite prejudice because it does not allow an opponent of the orthodox viewpoint to be a member of the community. Nonetheless, al-Baghdadi is not clear about the excommunication of all heretical sects, but he is strict in the case of their leaders. He treats them sometimes on a par with the apostates and occasionally with the Magians.[50]

---

[49] Al-Baghdādī, *al-Farq bayn al-Firaq*, Cairo: *Maktabah Nashr al-Thaqafah al-Islāmiyyah*, 1948, pp. 141-42.

[50] Al-Baghdādī, *Uṣūl al-Din*, Istanbul: Matbaʿah al-Dawlah, 1928, pp. 335-37.

Al-Shahrastani is more logical in his definition than al-Baghdadi. He defines the terms *millah*, *Minhāj*, and Sunnah as follows:-

"Mankind requires association with their fellow beings in order to earn their livelihood and to make preparation for the next world. This association should be established in a form by which solidarity and cooperation may be achieved. By solidarity one can protect one's right; and by cooperation a man can acquire what is not owned by him. The association established in this form is known as *millah*. The particular way which leads to this body (*Hay'ah*) is called *minhaj* (method), *Shari'ah* (pathway), and Sunnah (trodden path). The acquiescence in this Sunnah is termed *Jama'ah*. God says:

﴿لِكُلٍّ جَعَلْنَا مِنكُمْ شِرْعَةً وَمِنْهَاجًا﴾

"To every one of you, we have appointed a right way and an open road" [TMQ Surah Al-Maidah: 48][51]

This definition shows that the terms *minhaj, shir'ah,* and Sunnah are approximately synonymous. The definition also draws a distinction between the *millah* and the *Jamā'ah*. The *Jamā'ah* is the mainstay while the Sunnah and other allied terms are instrumental to the *Jamā'ah*. The link between the Sunnah and the *Jamā'ah* is also clear from the above definition.

With the establishment of the creed through the theologians of Islam, the idea of excommunicating the opponents developed. The definition of a Muslim formulated by orthodoxy became the standard for excommunication. Since orthodoxy stood on *Ijmā'*, the denier of *Ijmā'* in principle was declared heretic.[52] The theologians frequently excommunicated their opponents with the result that

---

[51] Al-Shahrastāni, *op. cit.*, I, 48.
[52] Al-Bazdawī, *Uṣūl al-Bazdawī*, Karachi: Nūr Muhammad Karkhanah Tijarat Kutub, 1966, pp. 245-47.

the study of scholastic theology became a point of dispute. Numerous tracts were written in favour of as well as in opposition to the study of this science.[53]

Al-Ghazali (d. 505 A.H.) expressed his vehement opposition to the frequent excommunication of the Muslims. Disbelief, according to him, means belying the teaching of the Prophet. He thinks that Jews, Christians Hindus, and atheists are unbelievers because of their disbelief in the Prophet of Islam and also in the prophets before him. Explaining the seriousness of excommunication, he asserts that if a Muslim is declared *kāfir*, he becomes eligible for condemnation to death and residing eternally in the hellfire. Al-Ghazālī thinks that disbelief can be known through textual evidence (Naṣṣ) or by analogy. He does not regard the persons who interpret Islam allegorically as unbelievers, provided they follow the rules of allegory (*Qānūn al-Ta'wīl*). He contends that there seems no reason to declare the allegorists unbelievers because every sect of Islam has recourse to it. As regards the essentials of Islam, al-Ghazālī presumes that one who changes the external meaning in toto without furnishing any proof is necessarily an unbeliever. It seems, however, that he was very careful in excommunicating the Muslims. He has left a valuable counsel concerning excommunication which we reproduce literally: "You should deter yourself as far as possible from excommunicating the people of *Qiblah* (*Ahl al-Qiblah*) so long as they utter, 'there is no god but Allah, Muhammad is the apostle of Allah' without contradicting it. Contradiction means to think it lawful that the Prophet can tell a lie with reason or without reason.

---

[53] Al-Ashʿarī, *Risālah Istihsān al-Khawḍ fī ʿIlm al-Kalām*, Hyderabad, Deccan, 1344 A.H.; Ibn Qudamah, *Taḥrīm al-Naẓar fī Kutub Ahl al-Kalām*, London: Luzac & Co. Ltd., 1962.

Excommunication is signally hazardous while silence has no danger."[54]

The doctrines of Islam are based on three sources, namely continuous and well-known tradition (*Tawātur*), isolated tradition (*Khabar al-Wāḥid*), and consensus (*Ijmāʿ*). On who rejects the doctrines based on *Tawātur* (continuous practice and report) is an unbeliever according to al-Ghazāli', while one who denies solitary reports is not a kafir (unbeliever). As regards rejection of the doctrines based on *Ijmāʿ*, he observes that it is not disbelief because the fact that *Ijmāʿ* is an authority by itself is disputed. Moreover, he raises the same objections to *Ijmāʿ* as al-Shāfiʿī had done before him. He thinks it is difficult to know whether a point in question was agreed upon by Muslims. Finally, he remarks that a man who opposes *Ijmāʿ* which is not yet established in his opinion is an ignoramus and erroneous, but not unbeliever. He, therefore, cannot be excommunicated.[55]

Al-Ghazali does not accept the definition of a Muslim furnished by the Sunni theologians as the standard one. He shows his abhorrence to the schoolmen who narrowed the mercy of God and confined it to the theologians alone. He enunciates his own definition of a Muslim which seems to be more reasonable than those furnished by his predecessors. He remarks: "What is clearly true is that one who believes firmly in the teaching of the Prophet and the content of the Qur'ān is a believer (*Al-Muʿmin*), no matter if he is ignorant of the evidence. Rather the belief based on theological evidence is fairly weak; strong is the belief of the masses which they imbibed in childhood through continuous transmission (*Tawātur*)."[56]

---

[54] Al-Ghazāli, *Al-Tafrīqah bayn al-Islām Wal-Zandaqah* (in Majmūʿah al-Rasāil) Bombay, n.d., pp. 4, 8, 12-14.
[55] *Ibid.*, pp. 14-16.
[56] *Ibid.*, pp. 16-18.

The term *Ijmāʿ* in its etymological sense shows that its concept must have emerged when disagreement raised its head in Islam. A brief discussion of its semantics will prove our presumption. The root meaning of *Ijmāʿ* is 'to collect', 'bring together' 'gather up', 'assemble', 'congregate', 'muster, or 'draw together'. The term has been derived probably from the Arabic idiom أجمعت النهب I collected together from every quarter the camels taken as spoils from the people to whom they belonged, and drove them away). It signifies simply 'the driving of camels together.[57] Abū Dhuwayb, a Hudhali poet, is generally quoted by the lexicographers in support of the meaning of the word *Ijmāʿ*. He says:

فَكَأَنَّهَا بِالْجِزْعِ بَيْنَ تَبَايُعٍ وَأُولَاتُ ذِي الْعَرْجَاءِ نَهْبٌ مُجْمَعُ

(The wild ass and her mates seemed below in the hollow vale of Nubayi' and the ravines that lead to the Dhu'l-ʿArjāʾ steep, a fresh plundered herd of camels).[58]

The Arabic idiom أجمعت النهب is an appropriate example to indicate the meaning of *Ijmāʿ*. The phrase means an open ground in which people are assembled, and they are not separated from each other lest they should go astray. The ground is, therefore, called *Mujmiʾah* because it unites them together.[59] The word *Ijmāʿ* is also used for binding the teats of a she-camel together with a tie.[60] This shows that the term carries the root meaning of uniting separate things.

---

[57] E.W. Lane, Arabic-English Lexicon, London, 1863, pt.1455(s.v. جمع)

[58] Al-Mufaḍḍal al-Ḍabbī, *Al-Mufaḍḍaliyyāt*, Cairo: Dar al-Maʿarif, n.d. p. 432; Eng. tr. Charles James Lyall, English translation of the *Mufaddaliyat*, Oxford 1918, 11, 357.

[59] Ibn ManṢūr, *Lisān al-ʿArab* (s.v. جمع)

[60] Lane, *op. cit.*, (s.v. جمع)

Besides, the term has another meaning. It means 'composing and settling a thing which has been decomposed (and unsettled), as an opinion which one determines, resolves or decides upon. Therefore, it stands for determining, resolving, or deciding an affair so as to make it firmly settled (after it had been unsettled in the mind), or after considering what might be its issues or results, and saying at one time 'I shall do this', and at another time, 'I will do this.' Hence the phrase, أجمعت الأسر or أجمعت على الأمر I determined, resolved, or decided the affair).[61] The Qur'ān used the word *Ijmāʿ* in this connotation.[62] The term carries both meanings, i.e., unity and determination. The early scholars utilized it for the systematization of the affairs of the community after a period of chaos, and for upholding the established and agreed practice. The term, however, owes its origin to the pre-Islamic Arabic idioms. Whether the term *Ijmāʿ* was borrowed from the Stoics, as Professor Simon Van den Bergh presumes,[63] is a difficult question to answer. It seems that this concept emerged in Islam as a socio-political necessity, for such social institutions are universal in different cultures and religions. This will occupy us in a separate chapter.

Conformity (*Taqlīd*) and consensus (*Ijmāʿ*) went hand in hand since the gate of *Ijtihād* was closed. Rather conformity proved to be an integral factor in bringing about the operation of *Ijmāʿ* as a regulating and binding force in medieval Islamic society. It is difficult to pinpoint the period of the closure of the gate of *Ijtihād* and the domination of *Taqlīd*. It is, however, certain that personal allegiance in different regions of legal activity started since the

---

[61] *Ibid.*

[62] Qur'ān 20:64.

[63] Simon Van den Bergh, *Averroes Tahāfut al-Tahāfut*, London: Luzac & Co; 1945, II, 205, 206; Joseph Schacht, *The Origins of Muhammadan Jurisprudence*, Oxford, 1959, pp. 6, 10, 18.

second century of the Hijrah.[64] This is the period when the early schools of law were in the process of formation. These trends culminated in the strict personal conformity during the fourth century of the Hijrah. The door of *Ijtihād* was not closed down all of a sudden. But this was done by slowing down the creative thinking and original legal activity. We find some clues in the legal manuals of the fourth century of the Hijrah about how conformity permeated Islamic jurisprudence. Abu'l-Hasan al-Karkhi (d. 340 A.H.) produced a tract on the principles of Hanafi law. In this tract, he lays down the following rules: "Any Qur'ānic verse which contradicts the opinion of our masters' will be construed as having been abrogated, or the rule of preference will apply thereto. It is better that the verse in question be interpreted in such a way that it conforms to their opinion." Further, he remarks: "Any tradition which contradicts the opinion of 'our masters' will be construed as having been abrogated, or it will be deemed that the tradition in question contradicts some other parallel tradition (which coincides with the opinion of the masters). The argument will, therefore, be based on the parallel tradition (which conforms to the opinion). Or, if there is no parallel tradition, the rule of preference will be applied as was done by 'our masters'. In case the rule of preference is not applicable, the tradition will be interpreted in such a way that it harmonizes with their opinion."[65] These two principles formulated by al-Karkhi, an eminent authority on Hanafi law, reflect the trend of the legal activity during the fourth century of the Hijrah. The opinion of the masters (i.e. jurists) was in the process of transformation into *Ijmā*ʿ the only mainstay for decisions. As a result of this conformistic attitude toward Islamic law, the Qur'ān and the Sunnah of the Prophet began to be interpreted in the light of the

---

[64] Schacht, *op. cit.*, pp. 6, 10, 18.

[65] Al-Karkhi, *Risālah al-Karkhī*, (in *Al-Dabūsī, Ta'sīs al-Naẓar*), Cairo: al-Matbaʿah al-ʿArabiyyah, n.d. pp. 84-85.

decisions of the masters (early jurists) and not independently. The Iraqi jurists, who were noted for their dynamism in legal thinking in the early period, began to think on law in terms of conformity in medieval period. But it should be remembered that these early authorities are themselves reported to have been opposed to the conformity (*Taqlīd*) in legal matters.[66]

Al-Tabari (d. 310 A.H.), in his *Ikhtilāf al-Fuqahā,* describes the disagreement of the early jurists, e.g. Abū Hanifah Mālik, Al-Awzāʿī, and al-Shāfiʿī on legal problems. But for the point on which they are agreed he uses the word *Ijmāʿ* (agreed). It is for the first time that the term *Ijmāʿ* is markedly used for the agreement of a definite number of the jurists whose names are known. Mālik uses this term in Al-Muwaṭṭaʾ' frequently for the general agreement of the jurists or people of Medina. The same practice is noticeable in al-Shāfiʿī and his contemporary jurists. It is, however, clear that agreement and disagreement were coeval, rather agreement grew out of disagreement. At a later date when law was standardized, disagreement was ruled out, and agreement became the standard. Still, at this stage of *Taqlīd* we find some jurists during the fourth century of the Hijrah differing with the early jurists. For instance, Abū Hanifah, Abū Yūsuf, and al-Shaybanī agree that the eating of spiny-tailed lizard (*al-dabb*) is unlawful.[67] Al-Tahawi discusses this problem at full length and refutes the arguments of al-Shaybani in his *Sharh maani'l-Athār.*[68] But this creative and independent thinking is rarely seen in the medieval period. Henceforth limited *Ijtihād* within the framework of a specific school of law began and independent *Ijtihād* came to an end in the legal sphere. *Ijmāʿ* recognized the authority of the four Sunni schools of law and

---

[66] Ibn Qayyim, *I'lām al-Muwaqqiʿīn*, Delhi: Ashraf al-Matābi, 1313 A.H., 1, 219; al-Muzani, *Makhtasar* (on the margin of *Kitāb al-Umm*), Cairo, 1321 A.H., I, 2.
[67] Al-Tahawi Mukhtaṣar al-Ṭaḥāwī, Cairo, 1370 A.H., p. 439.
[68] Idem, *Sharḥ Maʿānī al-Āthār*, Deoband, n.d., I, 260-63.

rejected the validity of the remaining early schools. Any opinion other than that of the four schools of law became a solitary opinion carrying no weight. Conformity provided sustenance for *Ijmāʿ*. Henceforth *Ijmāʿ* became the basis of religion, as was truly remarked: *Ijmāʿ* is the strap and support of the *Shariʿah* and to it the *Shariʿah* owes its authenticity."[69] This sort of rigidity resulted in the reaction against *Taqlīd*. Ibn Hazm (d. 456 A.H.), Ibn Taymiyah (d. 727 A.H.), Ibn Qayyim (d. 751 A.H.), and al-Shawkāni (d. 1250 A.H.) expressed vehement opposition to *Taqlīd* and laid great stress on independent *Ijtihād*.

Despite their vital role played both by conformity and by consensus in respect of integration in various spheres, unsuccessful individual opinions could not be totally eliminated. Further, disagreement did exist among the four orthodox schools of law. Hence disagreement among the community was considered as sacrosanct as agreement. This religious sanctity to disagreement was given by a tradition of the Prophet, "The disagreement of my community is a blessing."[70]

---

[69] Al-Juwayni, *Al-Burhān fī Uṣūl al-Fiqh*, Ms. 714, Dār al-Kutub al-Miṣriyyah, fo. 192; Al-Bazdawī, *op. cit.*, p. 247.

[70] Al-Suyūṭī, *Al-Jāmiʿ al-Ṣaghīr* Cairo: Mustafa al-Babi al-Halbi, 1954, 1, 13; al-ʿAzizi, Ahmad b. Nūr al-Din, *al-Siraj Munir*, Cairo, I, 170; *Al-ʿAjlūnī, Kashf al-Khafā'*, Cairo: Maktabah al-Qudsi, 1351, A.H., I, 64. For a detailed discussion on this tradition see Tamanna ʿImadi, *Ikhtilafi ummat rahmat hay ya kih zahmat*, Karachi: Ta manna Academi, n.d., pp. 42-62.

Chapter II: The Political Role of *Ijmāʿ*

The question of *Ijmāʿ* in the context of politics arises primarily in law-making. Legislation in Islam is a crucial problem. The difficulty lies indeed in determining the person in whom sovereignty resides. Sovereignty technically means a 'final adjustment-center', the 'authority of the last word'.[1] "Sovereignty is not the same," says Barker, as general State-authority, or puissance-publique: it is the particular sort of State-authority which is the power, and the right, of ultimate decision".[2] Besides, sovereignty is confined to the legal sphere in its operation. It does not decide every case which comes to it, but it moves within the legal orbit. "It is not a capricious power of doing anything in any way: it is a legal power of settling finally legal questions in a legal way."[3] Being legal by its nature it does not extend its authority to the areas which do not require any legal control.[4] The transcendental concept of God in Islam entails that sovereignty should rest with God alone. This has been increasingly stressed in the theological literature of the classical period. The Islamic legal theory also provides a basis for this proposition. The Qur'ān is the primary source of law. The other three sources, i.e. the Sunnah, *Ijmāʿ*, and *Qiyās* have been stamped with the revelatory character. The Sunnah was identified with *Ḥadīth*[5] which is said to have been the latent revelation (*Waḥy Khafī*) to the Prophet. *Ijmāʿ* is infallible according to a well-known tradition. *Qiyās* derives its value from these sources; hence it is indirectly infallible. The mechanism underlying these sources of law is an extension of the divine

---

[1] Barker, Ernest, *Principles of Social and Political Theory*, London: Oxford University Press, 1961, p. 60

[2] *Ibid.*, p. 60.

[3] *Ibid.*, pp. 60-61.

[4] *Ibid.*, p. 60.

[5] Schacht, Joseph, *The Origins of Muhammadan Jurisprudence*, Oxford, 1959, p. 77 f.

revelation the only source of law which can be recognized as infallible beyond doubt. This sort of methodology at work in law-making in Islam is the result of the idea of supremacy of God not only in the legal sphere but also in every field. This is why Islam is presented as a comprehensive way of life covering and controlling all acts of a Muslim. The five legal values (*Al-Aḥkām al-Khamsah*) are an obvious proof of the concept of the omnipotence of God in Islam. The idea of the legal supremacy of God seems to have developed through scholastic theology as well as jurisprudence. This is more or less reflected in the doctrine of the caliphate.

Sovereignty, according to modern political theory, has been divided into an ultimate and an immediate one. The ultimate sovereign is the constitution, while the immediate sovereign is the law-making body.[6] The same is true of the Islamic political theory. God is sovereign in the Islamic state in the sense that no law enacted by the people shall contradict the obvious teaching of the Qur'ān, the word of God. As such, the Qur'ān will exercise a check on the will of the people. The Qur'ān functions as a sort of constitution by its values and spirit. But it is noteworthy that God or the Qur'ān does not make the law. It is the people who make the law. The immediate sovereign is, therefore, the community at large. Since the whole community cannot function as a law-making body, the people who represent the community will serve as the immediate sovereign. The law enacted by a legislative body is either accepted or rejected by the will of the community at large in the long run. This is known as the *Ijmā'* of the community.

In Islam, one is faced with a serious question of whether law is the "revealed will of God, a divinely ordained system preceding and not preceded by the Muslim state, and controlling and not controlled by

[6] Barker, Ernest, *op. cit.*, p. 61 f.

the Muslims society, "[7] or it is a developing phenomenon adapting itself to the changing social conditions. It appears from the classical Islamic legal theory that law in Islam is an ordained system which already exists in the form of *Fiqh* literature. This radical and inert approach to the problem met with violent opposition from the legal modernism. As a result of this opposition, there arose the idea of *Ijmāʿ* modernism - a mechanism advocated by the modernists in Islam for legislation.[8] The bitter opposition to the classical legal theory by the modernists, in almost all Muslim countries today, is the result of the stagnation of the *Shariʿah* law. This reaction to the orthodox stand is so extreme that it seeks to bring under strictly historical study not only *Fiqh* and Sunnah of the Prophet but also the Qurʾān,[9] which is the main source of the Islamic legal theory. The radical attitude towards reformation in the sphere of law is but natural because the reaction to extremism results in extremism. But radicalism is not the solution to the problem. Another solution that the teachings of Islam should be bifurcated into two categories, mutable and immutable, is not feasible. In this case, the question still remains as to who will determine these categories objectively. There are some points which, in all probability, may fall under both categories.

The Qurʾān aims at building Islamic society on the basis of morality and justice, and not strictly on legal foundations. Hence its emphasis on ethics and not on law. This is also the reason why the Qurʾān does not furnish the structure of the Islamic state in detail. The legal element in the Qurʾān is, therefore, scantier than the moral one. Indeed, the Qurʾān tends to bring about a community characterized

---

[7] Coulson, N.J., *A History of Islamic Law*, Edinburgh: Islamic Surveys-2, 1964, pp. 1-2.
[8] Binder, Leonard, *Religion and Politics in Pakistan*, Berkely and Los Angeles, 1961, p. 34 f.
[9] Fazlur Rahman, The Impact of Modernity on Islam, *Islamic Studies*, V, 2 (June, 1966), p. 127.

by faith and morality. It is important to note that the institution of the state in Islam is subservient to the community. It is an organ of the community and not an institution sui generis. The purpose of establishing the state (i.e. *imāmah*) in Islam, as stated by the medieval Muslim political thinkers, is to maintain the law and order, to defend the faith, and to protect the community from schism.[10] Whether the state (*Imāmah*) in Islam is necessary on rational or religious grounds is a point in dispute.[11] This institution however can be defended on a functional basis. In modern times it is not possible to organize the community on the pattern of the one constituted by the Prophet. It is worthy of note that after the outbreak of civil wars and the spread of schism in Islam, great emphasis was laid on solidarity and integrity of the community. This resulted in the idea of unquestioning obedience to the ruler whosoever he might be. Al-Nawawi (d. 676 A.H.), observes: "These traditions persuade (Muslims) to hear and obey their rulers in all circumstances. Their purpose is to keep the Muslims united, because disagreement leads to the corruption of their religious and temporal affairs."[12] Al-Ghazālī,[13] Ibn *Jamā'ah*,[14] and some medieval traditionists[15] justified the rule of usurpers and tyrants on a religious basis for fear of anarchy and civil disturbance. People were allowed to resist the oppressive rulers or to depose them only in

---

[10] Al-Ghazālī, *Al-Iqtiṣād fil-I'tiqād*, Cairo: Maṭba'ah Ḥijāzī, n.d. pp. 105-106; al-Mawardi, *Al-Aḥkām al-Sulṭāniyyah*, Cairo: Al-Maṭba'at al-Maḥmūdiyyah al-Tijāriyyah, n.d. p. 3; Ibn Khaldūn, *Muqaddimah*, Beirut: Al-Maṭba'ah al-Adabiyyah, 1900, pp. 190-91; cf. G.E. von Grunebaum, Islam, London: Routledge and Kegan Paul, Ltd; 1961, pp. 127-29.

[11] G.E. von Grunebaum, Islām, pp. 131-132, n. 11.

[12] Al-Nawawī, *Sharah Sahih Muslim*, Delhi, 1376 A.H., 11, 124.

[13] Al-Ghazāli, *Al-Mustazhīrī*, Leiden: Brill, 1956, p. 77.

[14] Quoted in Erwin I.J. Rosenthal, *Political Thought in Medieval Islam*, Cambridge, 1958, p. 43 ff.

[15] Al-Nawawī, *Sharh Sahih Muslim*, II, 125; Ibn Ḥajar al-'Asqalānī, *Fath al-Bāri*, Cairo, 1329 A.H., XIII, 5, 29.

case they were guilty of unbelief.[16] This culminated in quietism and acquiescence and ultimately undermined popular sovereignty, democratic spirit, and freedom of the individual in the community. The tyrannical rulers in the medieval period made use of the doctrine of passive obedience for their selfish ends. The question of choice between an unjust Muslim ruler and a just non-Muslim ruler was raised at a time when the community lacked the rulers of competence and character. The incompetent persons held sway in the political sphere. This is the reason why the Muslims because of their passive attitude towards the tyrants and despots could not bring about a revolution which could uproot the evil elements at the helm of affairs and build a just and healthy society headed by worthy persons. Here we quote a relevant portion from the reported speech of Muʿadh b. Jabal which he made before the ruler of Syria:

"If your sovereign is Hercules, our sovereign is God who created us. Our leader is one of us; if he implements among us the teaching of our religious Book (i.e. the Qurʾān), and the Sunnah of our Prophet, we shall have him over us. But if he goes against it, we shall depose him. If he commits theft, we shall amputate his hand; if he commits adultery, we shall flog him. If he abuses any of us, he will abuse him as he (the leader) did. If he injures him, he will retaliate upon him. He will not hide himself from us, nor will he be self-conceited. He will not reserve for himself the booty which God bestowed on us. He is a person as good as we are."[17]

This speech of Muʿadh reflects the individual freedom and popular sovereignty in the early days of Islam. It also sheds light on the gradual decadence of the freedom of the individual and the development of autocracy in Islam.

---

[16] Ibn Hajar al-ʿAsqalāni, *Fatḥ al-Bārī*, XIII, 5; Al-Bazdawī, *Kitāb Uṣūl al-Dīn*, Cairo, 1963, pp. 190-91; G.E. von. Grunebaum, Islam, p. 112.
[17] Al-Azdi, Muhammad b. ʿAbd Allah, *Futūḥ al-Shām*, Calcutta, 1854, pp. 104-105.

Orthodoxy, of course, played a capital role in respect of integrating the community at one stage, but this temporary situation should have been allowed to lapse. That the ruler derives his authority from the people became a theoretical concept in the medieval period. With the decline of the *Shūrā* system after the orthodox caliphate the theory of the 'divine right of kings' is clearly reflected in the body politic of the medieval times. The orthodox caliphate displayed a normative character of the community state, yet it has become a utopia for the Muslims since along. There is a great urge for the establishment of an Islamic state on the pattern of the orthodox caliphate the only model state for Muslims. But is this feasible in the existing circumstances, especially when the community has been politically divided into a number of national states? It is remarkable that the orthodox caliphate had its own merits and character. The Prophet through his grim struggle and moral teaching produced persons of competence and model character. The orthodox caliphate was run by such persons. But as soon as the community lost its moral fiber, the caliphate fell into decay. Now there seem to be two alternatives before Muslims. They should either produce persons having talent and caliber by launching a movement if the state is to be run necessarily on the lines of the orthodox caliphate, or it should be patterned on the constitutional states with the flexible law of changing societies. In both cases, particularly in the latter case, the question of legislation will naturally arise. And this should be done through the mechanism of *Ijtihād* and *Ijmāʿ*.

The role of *Ijmāʿ* in politics can be noticed for the first time in the election of Abū Bakr. This was not *Ijmāʿ* in its technical sense.[18] The election of Abū Bakr was justified later on the basis of *Ijmāʿ* at the

---

[18] Ahmad Hasan, *The Early Development of Islamic Jurisprudence*, Lahore: Islamic Research Institute, 1970, pp. 156-57.

time when the question of the validity of his caliphate was raised. Umar was fully conscious of the fact that Abū Bakr was not elected with the unanimous consent of the community. Besides the disagreement of the Anṣār and Banū Hāshim, there were people who resented the election of Abū Bakr because it was effected in haste and as a measure of emergency on the suggestion of 'Umar. He alluded to this fact in his speech saying:

"I have heard that someone said, "If 'Umar were dead I would hail so-and-so. Don't let a man deceive himself by saying that the acceptance of Abū Bakr was an unpremeditated affair (*Faltah*) which was ratified. Admittedly it was that, but God averted the evil of it. There is none among you to whom people would devote themselves as they did to Abū Bakr. He who accepts a man as ruler without consulting the Muslims, such acceptance has no validity for either of them: they are in danger of being killed."[19]

Abū Bakr was, in fact, elected initially by a few Muslims who were present on the occasion. This election was ratified by the people in general the next day. Yet it took time for the election of Abū Bakr to be recognized by the community at large. This seems to be the reason why some Muslim theologians do not stipulate the *Ijmā'* of the community for the election of a caliph. The consent of even one member of *Ahl al-hall wal-'Aqd* (people of losing and binding) is sufficient for the validity of the caliphate. They contend that Abū Bakr after his election at Medina started to enforce his orders and did not wait for the spread of this news to the people living in far-flung areas. But none objected to his executive activities.[20] It is striking to note that the people who originally proposed and elected Abū Bakr were considered *Ahl al-hall wal 'aqd* at a later date. From

[19] Ibn Hishām, *Sīrat al-Nabī*, Cairo: Maṭba'ah Ḥijāzī, n.d. IV, 338; A. Gaillaume, *The Life of Muhammad*, London: Oxford University Press, 1955, p. 585.
[20] Al-Juwaynī, 'Abd al-Malik, *Kitāb al-Irshād*, Cairo, 1950, p. 424; al-Baghdadi, *Uṣūl al-Din*, Istanbul, 1928, pp. 280-81.

this, it follows that Abū Bakr was elected earlier by a few eminent responsible persons, and ultimately it was ratified by the community. This might be the starting point of the idea of *Ahl al-hall wal-aqd* in the body politic of Islam.[21] Although the term appeared in Islam in the early fourth century of the Hijrah,[22] the electoral college constituted by 'Umar to elect his successor was a forerunner of this institution. This electing body was known as *Ahl al-Shūrā*. But no such body was formed to elect the fourth caliph. The surviving members of this body were largely responsible for the election of 'Alī as a caliph. They are mentioned in history as *Baqiyyat al-Shūrā* (the surviving members of the consulting committee).[23] 'Alī is reported to have been elected by the popular consent,[24] It is worthy of note that the nomination of 'Umar by Abū Bakr carries the consent of some responsible persons because it is said that Abū Bakr consulted them before his nomination.[25] As such, the early four Caliphs were elected by the people themselves directly or indirectly. During the Umayyad and 'Abbāsid periods the caliphs were nominated by their predecessors as heir apparent. Yet they had to seek the 'consent of the people' by taking the oath of allegiance by force and coercion. From the foregoing one can conclude that the

---

[21] Judaism has a parallel term 'binding and loosing'. This is available in Christianity too. The terms 'binding' and 'loosing' were originally rabbinical technical terms denoting "forbidding and 'authorizing' a practice or an opinion. These were first used by Christ bestowing the power of binding and losing upon St. Peter and all the apostles. Cf. Mathew 16:19 (Enc. of Religion and Ethics, articles 'Binding and Loosing' and 'Infallibility'). It is doubtful whether the term *Ahl al-hall Wal-'Aqd* in Islam was influenced by such foreign terms.

[22] This term was used in the political context for the first time by Al-Ash'arī, *Kitāb al-Ibanah*, Hyderabad, Daccan, 1948, p. 79; Muhammad Khalid Mas'ud, Tārikh Islām mayn ahli hall wa'aqd kā taṣuwwur (Urdu), *Fikro Naẓar*, I, 7, 8 (Jan., Feb. 1964), pp. 55-59.

[23] Ibn Qutaybah, *Al-Imāmah Wal-Siyāsah*, Cairo: Matba'ah Mustafa Muhammad, n.d. I, 29, 30, *possim.*

[24] Al-Tabari, *Ta'rīkh al-Umam wal-Mulūk*, Cairo, 1336 A.H., V, 152-154; *Ibn Sa'd, al-Ṭabaqāt al-Kubrā*, Beirut: Där Ṣadir, 1957, III, 31.

[25] Al-Tabari, *op. cit.*, IV, 51.

consent of the people was deemed necessary, though sometimes it was only in name, to validate the caliphate.

Ijmāʿ in Islam is an informal activity and there is no definite and approved apparatus to ascertain the will of the community. It owes its origin to the principle of mutual consultation (*Shūrā*) prescribed by the Qurʾān. The root meaning of the term is to "extract honey from the small hollow in the rock in which it had been deposited by the wild bees," or "to gather it from its hives and from other places."[26] The term Shūrā is an antithesis of *Fawḍā.* This is best illustrated by the two Arabic idioms أمرهم شورى بينهم (their affairs are settled by mutual consultation) and أسرهم فوضى بينهم (their affairs are chaotic among them).[27] *Shūrā* is, therefore, a collective endeavour for seeking an objective truth. It is important to note that the Prophet was asked by the Qurʾān to consult his Companions in the affairs concerning the community.[28] The classical commentators have expressed several reasons for this commandment. The most significant of them is that the Prophet was advised to do so in order that the people might follow him in their affairs after his death.[29] Whatever may be the purpose of this commandment, it appears that the Prophet followed this principle to rule out absolutism from the body politic of Islam. This seems to be the reason why he consulted the Companions on many occasions, and people sometimes even disagreed with him.[30] Moreover, the Prophet is reported to have

---

[26] Edward Lane, *Arabic-English Lexicon*, London, 1863 (s.v. شور)

[27] *Ibid*., (s.v. شور)

[28] Qurʾān 3:159.

[29] Al-Tabari, *Jāmiʿ al-Bayān ʿan Taʾwīl Āyat-Qurʾān*, Cairo: Dār al-Maʿārif, (ed. Shakir), n.d. VII, 345-46.

[30] Ibn Hishām, *Sīrat al-Nabī*, II, 259-60.

exhorted the Muslims to practice mutual consultation.[31] He pointed out the qualities of a consultant[32] which denote the significance of this principle in his eyes. The principle of *Shūrā* was not new for the Muslims, because this process was in vogue at Dar al-Nadwa in pre-Islamic Arabia. The Qur'ān also mentions the term nādi,[33] concourses of the pagan Arabs, which signifies their democratic character.[34]

The orthodox caliphate is distinguished by the fact that it derived its authority from the will of the people. These early Caliphs are reported to have conducted the affairs of the state by consulting the intelligent and responsible persons. It is said that Abū Bakr had not allowed 'Umar to go outside Medina with the Muslim army.[35] This he did because he was in need of persons having a sound opinion and acumen in the affairs of the state. In case he was asked about

---

[31] For example, a tradition goes: If your leaders are generous, and your affairs are settled by mutual consultation, the surface of the earth is better for you than its bottom. *Al-Timridhī al-Jami* (Abwāb al-Fitan-78)
The traditions on *Shūrā* are copious in the classical collections of *Ḥadīth*.

[32] A tradition goes: The consultant should be trustworthy (*Abū Dāwūd, Sunan, Kitāb al-Adab*-114).

[33] Qur'ān 96:17.

[34] It would seem strange to attribute democracy to the pagan Arabs. The chieftain in their tribal system wielded supreme power and had the upper hand in most affairs, yet it is certain that the chieftain used to consult the responsible members of the tribe before he arrived at a certain decision. In certain respects, he was *primus inter pares*. Besides, the Arabs had a desire to be led by a man of opinion and talent. They held that the leadership of stupid persons was no leadership. The believed that their tribe could prosper if its leader was a competent person; and their existed cooperation between him and the members of the tribe. They similarised a tribe with a tent having posts and pegs. This indicates the importance of cohesion in the tribe and cooperation between the chieftain and the members. What we call 'democratic' is their spirit of mutual consultation, cooperation, and aspiration for a 'good leader'. S.M. Husain (ed.), *Nukhbah min Kitāb al-Ikhtiyārayn*, Delhi, 1938, pp. 1921; W.M. Watt, What is Islam, London, 1968, p. 72.

[35] Abū Bakr is said to have taken permission from Usāmah, the leader of expedition, to detain 'Umar with him for his assistance. Al-Tabari, *Ta'rīkh al-Umam wal-Mulūk*, III, 212.

some legal questions which he did not know, he never hesitated to consult the people in public.[36] Examples can be quoted copiously to show that these early Caliphs consulted the people on disputed points on the pulpit and on the occasion of Hajj. They are reported to have held discussions with the Muslims about sending expeditions for territorial conquests.[37] People had full liberty to express their opinions on important matters of the state. Liberty of criticism and freedom of opinion were the main features of the orthodox caliphate. ʿUmar's discussion with the people on the question of distributing the lands of Iraq among the army is a well-known fact of history. It is reported that the discussion was animated and prolonged for many days. Since the point in question involved a departure from the earlier practice, ʿUmar had to face a grim opposition in this matter.[38] But since consultation with the community at large was not possible frequently, the early Caliphs used to consult the 'people of opinion and confidence'. This body known as *Ahl al-Shūrā* at that time was termed *Ahl al-hall wal-aqd* in the medieval period.

The council of *Shūrā* was functioning as a legislative body during the orthodox caliphate. It represented the community, though not formally by holding general elections. This process is reminiscent of the representative government. From this one can roughly conclude that the early caliphate in Islam was the government of the people because the caliph conducted the important matters of the state by consulting the people or their representatives. It was a government of the people in the sense that the caliphs were elected by the consent of the people. But, whether the people of the *Shūrā* represented the community is a point in question. The members of this body might have been nominated on the basis of merit, but the

---

[36] Malik, *Al-Muwaṭṭa'*, Cairo: Dār Iḥyā' al-Kutub al-ʿArabiyyah, 1951, II, 513.
[37] Al-Azdi, *Futūḥ al-Shām*, pp. 1-5, 37, *passim*.
[38] Abū Yūsuf, *Kitāb al-Kharāj*, Cairo, Būlaq 1302 A.H., pp. 13-15.

procedure was not as strictly formal as in the modern democratic states. Every person has a dominant will in addition to the general will. This dominant will represent directors in a corporation, government in a state, and pressure groups in a society. The early Caliphs might have had their confidence in the elite of the community and consulted them from time to time. Whenever some important problem was brought to Abū Bakr, he is reported to have called on the Muhajirūn and the Anṣar and invited particularly 'Umar, Uthman, 'Alī, 'Abd al-Rahman b. 'Awf, Mu'adh b. Jabal, Ubayy b. Ka'b, and Zayd b. Thabit for the consultation. These persons pronounced verdicts on legal questions during the caliphate of Abū Bakr, and the people relied on them in respect of their legal opinions. These were called the 'people of opinion' and 'people of understanding' (*Ahl al-Ra'y* and *Ahl al-fiqh*). Abū Bakr generally followed the opinion agreed upon by them.[39] 'Umar's opposition to the sending of expedition against those who refused to pay *Zakāt* during the caliphate of Abū Bakr is a famous historical event. The learned persons (*qurra'*), according to a report, constituted the state council during his caliphate of 'Umar. It included the youth as well as the aged.[40] Consultation with the scholars and intelligent persons was a general practice during the orthodox caliphate[41] until the rise of schism and the outbreak of civil wars. Since the procedure of mutual consultation was informal, we do not find its details in history. It appears from the tone of the early caliphate that the caliph had his final say in the affairs of the state, though he consulted the people of opinion. The opinion of the consultants was not binding on him. The method of mutual consultation in a sense aimed at eliciting public opinion and enlightening the point under

[39] Ibn Sa'd, *op. cit.*, II, 350.

[40] Al-Bukhari, *al-Jami' al-Ṣaḥīḥ*, Leiden, 1908, IV, 443-44 (*Kitāb al-I'tiṣām*).

[41] *Ibid.*

discussion. Yet the final decision lay in the hands of the caliph. Generally, he followed the majority opinion.

With the abolition of the system of *Shūrā*, Muʿawiyah sought to integrate the community by introducing the system of appointing heir apparent. The Umayyad and the ʿAbbasid caliphs had their own advisers, but they were not necessarily the representatives of the people. The leadership was henceforth divided into political and religious groups. The people had no confidence in the caliphs in religious matters. This gave rise to a rift between the scholars (*ʿUlema*) and the political leaders. The rulers sometimes consulted the scholars, yet generally, there was little understanding between the two.[42] The scholars were sometimes exploited by the rulers for their political purposes. The scholars had the dominating will in the community since the time the people lost their trust in the rulers. Consequently, *Ijmāʿ* was defined as the 'agreement of the scholars'. This is why the scholars have been identified with the *Ahl al-Ḥall wal-ʾAqdʾ* by some jurists on the plea that they derive the rules of law from the original sources.[43] Above all, the *Ijmāʿ* of the community came in question whether it meant the agreement of the scholars or the agreement of the people. (To this we shall return in due course). As such, the scholars as a pressure group won the confidence of the people through their religious leadership. This is how there came into being a special class of *ʿUlema* in the community. Their predominant influence on the will of the community in modern times should be seen in the historical perspective.

The Qurʾān asks the Muslims to obey those in authority (*Aulī al-Amr*)'[44] in addition to obeying God and the Prophet. The verse in question is reported to have been revealed on the occasion of a

---

[42] Cf. Watt. W. M. *op. cit.*, pp. 126-28, 135.

[43] Al-Qarāfī, *Sharḥ Tanqīḥ al-Fuṣūl*, Cairo: Al-Maṭbaʿah al-Khayriyyah, 1306 A.H., p. 141; al-Rāzi, *Mafātīḥ al-Ghayb*, Cairo: Al-Maṭbaʿah al-Khayriyyah, 1308 A.H., III, 245.

[44] Qurʾān 4:58.

quarrel between ʿAmmar b. Yasir and Khalid b. al-Walid who was the leader of an expedition sent by the Prophet to some place outside Medina.[45] The term 'those in authority' has been interpreted by the commentators in various manners. According to them, it means leaders, commanders of the expeditions, scholars and jurists, the Companions of the Prophet, Abū Bakr and ʿUmar, and the sultan.[46] Al-Tabari is of the view that the correct meaning of the term is the rulers and the political authorities, for the Prophet is reported to have asked the Muslims, according to a number of genuine traditions, to obey the political leaders (*Aʾimmah*).[47] It should be noted, however, that the term *Aulī al-Amr* cannot be construed exclusively as political authorities because the Qurʾān uses the same term in the following verse in a different context:

"When there comes to them a matter, be it of security or fear, they broadcast it; if they had referred it to the Messenger and to those in authority among them, those of them whose task is to investigate would have known the matter. And but for the bounty of God to you, and His mercy, you would surely have followed Satan, except a few.[48]

In this verse, the Qurʾān means by this term the people of supreme talent and wisdom who could derive knowledge from the matter referred to them. Moreover, in the lifetime of the Prophet, there was no political authority other than the Prophet himself to whom the Qurʾān could refer. The term, however, may include rulers as well as other authorities at different levels. The verse in question is the basic authority oft-quoted by the Muslim political thinkers to substantiate obedience to the rulers- no matter if they be usurpers and tyrants. According to the medieval thinking, there is a general principle relating to obedience to the political authorities. It says

---

[45] Al-Tabarī, *Jāmiʿ al-Bayān ʿan Taʾwīl Āy al-Qurʾān*, VIII, 489-90.
[46] *Ibid.*, pp. 497-502.
[47] *Ibid.*, p. 502.
[48] Qurʾān 4:83.

that Muslims should remain loyal to the rulers so long as they command in accordance with the teachings of Islam. But people should not obey them if they command in contravention to the rules of the *Sharīʿah.* In support of this principle ʿUmar b. ʿAbd al-ʿAzīz is reported to have said in a speech: "One should not obey the command of a creature if it involves disobedience to God. ."[49] This dictum is sometimes quoted. in the form of a prophetic tradition.[50] That the people should go about their business and be loyal to the rulers until they command them to act in disobedience to God is a concept which is supported by a number of traditions of the Prophet, but it gained ground during the period of absolutism and autocracy in the medieval period. This culminated at a later date in the doctrine that no rebellion against an unjust ruler is valid, for this would lead to anarchy and disintegration.[51]

Let us now return to the question of legislation. It is an admitted fact that legislation after the Prophet was the function of the community at large. Since the whole community could not work together practically, the institutions of the caliph, *Shūrā*, the people of binding and loosing, and finally legislative assemblies in Muslim states representing the community came into existence. In the present situation with the emergence of modern Muslim national states, the scope of legislation has been further narrowed down because the law enacted in one Muslim state cannot be enforced in other states. As such, the community has been divided into several independent small units in respect of legislation. Therefore, the question of legislation by the community at large for the community at large does not arise. The question, however, remains to be answered whether the people in general in a Muslim state have

---

[49] ʿAbd Allah b. al-Hakam, *Sīrat ʿUmar b. ʿAbd al-ʿAzīz*, Cairo, 1927, p. 40.

[50] Ahmad b. Hanbal, *Musnad*, 1313 A.H., V, 66, and I, 275; Muslim, *Ṣaḥīḥ*, (Kitāb al-Imārah, 62-63).

[51] Al-Bazdawī, *op. cit.*, p. 192.

their participation in *Ijmāʿ*, or *Ijmāʿ* means the consensus of the people of binding and loosing. It may be pointed out that the point in question among the classical jurists is disputed. Some hold that *Ijmāʿ* represents the agreement of the scholars exclusively.[52] Hence the division of *Ijmāʿ* into the consensus of the community and that of the scholars. This division, of course, crystallized in al-Shāfiʿī (d. 204 A.H.) who criticized the *Ijmāʿ* of the scholars vigorously.[53] The great stress laid on the *Ijmāʿ* of the scholars in the medieval period might have been a reaction to his bitter criticism on this principle. It seems to be the fact that the concept of *Ijmāʿ* must have emerged originally as the consensus of the community at large. With the rise and dominance of the class of scholars in the community, the *Ijmāʿ* of the community received a setback.

The early Caliphs legislated on a number of points through the process of *Shūrā* (*Ijtihād* and *Ijmāʿ*). ʿUmar can be quoted extensively for illustration in this context. But on certain points, his judgment could not become the law because it was given by him in his individual capacity. The questions that were discussed in the council of *Shūrā* or generally accepted by the Companions could win the legal status.[54] This we notice during the formative period when the principle of *Ijmāʿ* was an ongoing and forward-looking process. When this principle became retrospective and was utilized to preserve the heritage of Islam, the participation of the masses in *Ijmāʿ* was discouraged.[55] Nevertheless, as there was no escape from the consent of the community at large, al-Ghazali devised a curious

---

[52] Al-Āmidī, *al-Ihkam fi Usui al-Ahkām*, Cairo, Matbaʿah al-Maʿārıf, 1914, 1, 322, 325.
[53] Al-Shāfiʿī, *Jimāʿ al-ʿIlm*, Cairo: Maṭbaʿah al-Maʿārif, 1940, p. 52.
[54] The opinion of ʿUmar and Ibn Masʿud about *Tayummum* may serve as an illustration for the point in question. Such stray opinions were neglected even if they were held by a caliph. Al-Bukhari, *Al-Jāmiʿ al-Ṣaḥīḥ*, Tayummum-7; al-ʿAyni, *ʿUmdat al-Qārī*, Istanbul, 1310 A.H.: II, 192; Ibn Qudāmah, *al-Mughnī*, Cairo: Där al-Manär, 1367 A.H., 1, 257.
[55] Al-Āmidī, *op. cit.*, p. 325.

method of 'killing two birds with one stone'. He holds that the consensus of the learned is tantamount to the consensus of the community. The masses which constitute the bulk of the community readily recognize the agreement of the scholars on a certain point. This is because the truth lies in the agreement of the people of binding and loosing. The masses cannot differ with the scholars. He seeks to prove this proposition by an illustration. If an army selects a group of persons having a sound opinion as their arbiter for concluding the treaty of peace with the inhabitants of a citadel, and they conclude peace on certain conditions, this agreement of the arbiter would be considered the agreement of the whole army. Likewise, the consensus of the scholars represents the consensus of the people.[56] The analogy drawn by al-Ghazali is not correct because the people of opinion in the army were deputed by the army. But in the case of *Ijmāʿ*, the scholars are not deputed by the people. They command supremacy over the people by virtue of their learning and insight in religious matters. The scholars, therefore, do not represent the people with their consent. Nonetheless, the role of the scholars cannot be ignored, in the process of *Ijmāʿ*. They create public opinion on a disputed issue by pronouncing their individual views. The *Ijma* emerges out of the clash of these divergent opinions in the form of a general practice. The individual or opinion carries no weight unless it is generally accepted by the people and affirmed by the whole community. Professor H.A.R. Gibb explains *Ijmāʿ* as "vox populi, the expressed will of the community not as measured by the counting of votes or the decisions of councils at any given moment, but as demonstrated by the slowly accumulating pressure of opinion over a long period of time."[57]

---

[56] Al-Ghazālī, *Al-Mustaṣfā*, Cairo: Matbaʿah Mustafa Muhammad, 1937, 1, 115.
[57] Gibb, H.A.R. *Modern Trends in Islam*, Chicago, Illinois, 1950, p. 11.

In fine, *Ijmāʿ* in a sense encompasses the whole religious structure in Islam. We have shown in the previous chapter how it was introduced as a binding force in the Muslim community. Yet its role in the sphere of politics is exclusively significant because it is a substitute now for the revelation or for the Prophet's verdict to determine the veracity of the fresh legal content. *Ijmāʿ* is undoubtedly an instrument of legislation, but it is not the agreement of a few persons. It starts, of course, from the opinion of a few, but culminates in the agreement of the whole community. As such, the decisions made by the legislative assemblies and the enactments enforced by them may constitute the law of the land. But it is difficult to call them *Ijmāʿ* unless the legal enactments win the sanction of the will of the whole community. There is no alternative but to enact the laws by the legislative bodies because *Ijmāʿ* takes a long time to evolve. *Ijmāʿ* in the long run would be responsible for retaining a law or rejecting it. The representative bodies like the council of *Shūrā* and the body of scholars in the medieval period, or the legislative assemblies in modern Muslim states, are intrinsically important bodies, for one cannot know the immediate agreed opinion of the community without such organizations. But their enactment should be considered as tentative *Ijmāʿ*.

Since *Ijmāʿ* is the conscience of the community, it must ultimately have the consent of the community. The *Ijmāʿ* of the scholars would, therefore, be accepted as a transitory stage to reach the ultimate goal (i.e. the will and conscience of the community) and not as the last word. It is astonishing to note that the *Ḥadīth* 'my community will not agree on an error' was interpreted in the classical period to mean 'the scholars of my community will not agree on an error'. The reason given for this interpretation is that the masses receive the knowledge of Islam from the scholars and they are, therefore, subservient to them.[58] Fakhr al-Din al-Rāzī seeks to give the scholars, whom he calls *Ahl al-Ijmā'*, superiority over the rulers. He contends that obedience to *Ahl al-Ijmā'* is obligatory beyond doubt, whereas obedience to the rulers is not obligatory because they may command what is unjust. Moreover, the activities of the rulers and political authorities receive sanction from the verdicts of the scholars. The scholars, in his opinion, are leaders of the rulers. Al-Rāzí puts his whole force to prove that the term *Aulī al-Amr* in the Qur'ān means "the scholars."[59] This points to the dominance of the class of the scholars over the will of the community in the medieval period.[60] The dominance of the rulers in the political sphere on the one hand, and that of the scholars in the religious sphere on the other, paralyzed the will of the people in the Muslim community. The process of *Ijmā'* (i.e. will and conscience of the community), therefore, came to a standstill.

---

[58] Al-Shāṭibī, *Kitāb al-I'tiṣām*, Cairo, 1914, III, 137.

[59] Al-Rāzi, *Mafātīḥ al-Ghayb*, III, 242-43.

[60] Cf. W.M. Watt, *Islamic Political Thought*, Edinburgh (Islamic Surveys-6), 1968, pp. 74, 76, 102.

Chapter III: The Argument for The Authority of *Ijmāʿ*

Religion at the stage of its maturity requires a discipline which maintains it. The embryonic and formative phases of religion are undoubtedly important in as much as it owes its birth and growth to them. Yet the final stage of development gives it the perfect shape which survives until its end. Religion, of course, takes its roots from early stages and culminates in a full-grown tree with a deep-rooted and mighty system. This sort of discipline strengthens its foundations, constitutes its mainstay, and gives it a lasting form. This formative discipline is the basic authority in religion, responsible for accepting, rejecting, and assimilating the extraneous elements. This authority, visible or invisible, stands high in every religion. This is a pivotal point around which the whole machinery of religion revolves. Religion can hardly stand without such an authority. This authority in Islam is the *Ijmāʿ* of the community. In the light of these prefatory remarks, one can understand the statements made by the classical legal thinkers about the significance of the doctrine of *Ijmāʿ*. Al-Bazdawī (d. 482 A.H.) observes: "One who rejects the doctrine of *Ijmāʿ* rejects the religion at large. This is because the orbit of all the fundamentals of religion and their returning point is the *Ijmāʿ* of Muslims.[1] "Al-Sarakhsi (d. 490 A.H.) remarks that one who denies the validity of *Ijmāʿ* seeks indirectly to demolish religion per se."[2] ʿAbd al-Mālik al-Juwayni (d. 478 A.H.) makes the *Shariʾah* dependent on *Ijmāʿ* by saying: "*Ijmāʿ* is the strap and support of the *Shariʿah* and to it the *Shariʿah* owes its authenticity".[3] Al-Qarafi (d. 684 A. H.) holds that *Ijmāʿ* is anterior in respect of decisiveness to the other three sources

[1] Al-Bazdawī, *Kanz al-Wuṣūl ilā Maʿrifat al-Uṣūl*, Karachi, 1966, p. 247.

[2] Al-Sarakhsi, *Uṣūl al-Sarakhsī*, Cairo, 1372 A.H., I, 296.

[3] Al-Juwayni, *Al-Burhān fī Uṣūl al-Fiqh* Ms. 714-Uṣūl, Dar al-Kutub al-Miẹriyah, Cairo, fo. 192.

of law, namely the Qur'ān, Sunnah, and *Qiyās.*[4] It should be noted that such an important doctrine of Islam has been subject to a ceaseless controversy since its inception with respect to its religious sanction. The opponents of *Ijmāʿ* raised serious objections to its legitimacy. We shall discuss them in due course.

Ijmāʿ has been justified on the basis of the Qur'ān, Sunnah, and reason. The jurists almost agree that the Qur'ānic verses, which are adduced to justify *Ijmāʿ*, do not clearly prove its authority. The traditions of the Prophet have been quoted copiously in its support. These traditions constitute an evidence, according to the jurists, more explicit and potent than the Qur'ānic verses.[5] Efforts were also made to substantiate *Ijmāʿ* on the basis of reason alongside of the traditional sanction. A formal religious justification was thus provided for this doctrine *fait accompli.*

I

It appears that *Ijmāʿ* was legalized earlier on the basis of *Ḥadīth* and later on the basis of the Qur'ān. But almost all the classical jurists hold that the procedure was reversed. It is generally believed that al-Shāfiʿī justified the doctrine of *Ijmāʿ* for the first time on the basis of the Qur'ānic verse 4:115. This assumption is untenable because al-Shāfiʿī discusses *Ijmāʿ* s at length but nowhere he refers to the Qur'ān. He establishes its legitimacy on the basis of the prophetic traditions. The extant works of al-Shāfiʿī and of the early jurists before him show that *Ijmāʿ* was not justified on the basis of the Qur'ān until his time, i.e. during the first two centuries of the Hijrah. It is difficult to trace, for lack of information, the person who justified *Ijmāʿ* for the first time on the basis of the Qur'ān.

---

[4] Al-Qarafi, *Shark Tanqih al-Fuṣūl*, Cairo, 1306 A.H., p. 146.

[5] Al-Ghazālī, *al-Mustaṣfā*, Cairo, 1937, I, 111-12; Al-Āmidī, *al-Ihkām fi Uṣūl al-Ahkām*, Cairo, 1914, I, 312-13.

Al-Shaybāní (d. 189 A.H.) seems to be the first jurist who justified yma on the basis of a tradition. Discussing the question of tarawih prayer (an additional supererogatory prayer offered in congregation at night during Ramadân) he remarks that this prayer is lawful because the Muslims have agreed on it and considered it good. Further, he substantiates the authority of the agreement of Muslims by quoting a tradition from the Prophet: "Whatever the believers consider good is good in the eyes of God, and whatever they consider evil is evil in His eyes.[6] This tradition was later on reported as a statement of ʿAbd Allah b. Masʿūd and not as a statement of the Prophet.[7] The tradition cited by al-Shaybānī is a part of his (Ibn Masʿūd's) lengthy statement which runs as follows:

ʿAbd Allah b. Masʿūd said: "God looked into the hearts of His servants. He found the heart of Muhammad (peace be upon him) the best of all; He chose it for Himself and sent him with His message Again, he looked into the hearts of his servants after the heart of Muhammad. He found the hearts of his Companions the best of all. He, therefore, chose them as the ministers of His Prophet. They will fight for (the defence of) his religion. Whatever the Muslims consider good is good in the eyes of Allah, and whatever they consider evil is evil in the eyes of Allah."[8]

This tradition has also been recorded by al-Sarakhsi in a different context as a saying of the Prophet. He justified *Ijmāʿ*, inter alia, on its basis. The tradition goes: "The Prophet was asked about the leaven (*khamirah*) which people give and take from each other. He replied: "Whatever the Muslims consider good is good in the eyes of

---

[6] Al-Shaybani, *Al-Muwaṭṭaʾ*, Lucknow: Matabaʿah Yūsufi, 1925, pp. 111-12.

[7] Ahmad b. Hanbal, Musnad, Cairo, 1313 A.H., I, 379; al-ʿAjlūni, Ismail b. Muhammad, *Kashf al-khafa*, Cairo, 1325 A.H., II, 188.

[8] See Comments of various traditionists on this tradition in the annotations of al-Shaybanis *Muwatta'* by ʿAbd al-Hayy, p. 112.

Allah, and whatever they consider evil is evil in the eyes of Allah."[9] One can hardly make out the meaning of this tradition grafted in the statement of Ibn Masʿūd. It has no relevance to the former portion of the statement. The other version mentioned by al-Sarakhsi is, of course, important, for it shows the context in which the tradition was pronounced. This tradition cannot, however, be generalized because customs contrary to the teachings of the Qurʾān and Sunnah can be legalized on the basis of this authority. This should be interpreted in a restricted sense. Al-Shaybanī does not discuss the question of *Ijmāʿ* by itself. We, therefore, fail to understand whether he was familiar with the traditions quoted by al-Shāfiʿī in its support, particularly with the tradition 'my community will not agree on an error' cited later on by the jurists. It seems, that the idea of the 'infallibility' of the practice or consensus of Muslims was in existence in al-Shaybanis time. The tradition quoted by him is clear evidence of this presumption.

The notion of the infallibility of the consensus of the Muslim community further developed during the latter half of the second century of the Hijrah. Al-Shāfiʿī cites a number of traditions from the Prophet to prove the authority of *Ijmāʿ*. The common theme of these traditions is adherence to the community. Here we quote the relevant portion of these traditions:

The heart of a Muslim shall never harbour vindictive feelings against three: sincerity in working for God; faithfulness to Muslims; and conformity to the community of believers their call shall protect (the believers) and guard them from (the Devil's) delusion.

---

[9] Al-Sarakhsi, *op. cit.*, I, 299.

"Only those who seek the pleasure of Paradise will follow the community, for the Devil can pursue one person, but stands far away from two..."[10]

Al-Shāfiʿī discusses these traditions at length and arrives at the conclusion that adherence to the community means adherence to the agreed view of the community on legal matters. The traditions in question do not mean physical conformity to the community because there is no use of such a gathering. The believers and unbelievers, the pious and impious, may get together physically, but the gathering of bodies will constitute nothing unless they follow the community in respect of its agreed opinion concerning lawful and unlawful matters. He, therefore, interprets these traditions in clear terms as a direction from the Prophet to follow the agreement of the Muslim community. Concluding he says: "He who holds what the Muslim community holds shall be regarded as following the community, and he who holds differently shall be regarded as opposing the community he was ordered to follow. So, the error comes from separation; but in the community as a whole there is no error concerning the meaning of the Qur'ān, the *Sunna*, and analogy."[11]

From al-Shāfiʿī's emphasis on strict conformity to the community in respect of legal matters, it is clear that at this stage the idea of the 'infallibility' had fairly crystallized. But the concept 'the community cannot agree on an error' was not yet supported by the traditions of the Prophet. We first meet with this notion in the form of al-Shāfiʿīs statement during the course of his reasoning on *Ijmāʿ*.[12] His opponent inquires him about the authority of the consensus of

---

[10] Majīd Khāddūrī (Eng. tr. of *al-Shāfiʿi's Risāla*), Baltimore: Johns Hopkims Press, 1961, pp. 252-53; Cf. Fazlur Rahman, *Islamic Methodology in History*, Labore, 1965, pp. 53, 56, 77.
[11] *Ibid.*, 287.
[12] Schacht, Joseph, *The Origins of Muhammadan Jurisprudence*, Oxford, 1959, p. 91.

Muslims on problems not expressly mentioned in the Qur'ān or reported from the Prophet. He also questions him whether the agreement of Muslims will always stand on the established Sunnah, even if it is not reported as such by the people. Al-Shāfiʿī replies that the point on which people agree and which, according to their statement, is reported from the Prophet, is then really so. But if they do not state that the agreement is based on the Sunnah of the Prophet, its attribution to the Prophet becomes doubtful. Nothing can be ascribed to the Prophet unless one hears clearly from him. Al-Shāfiʿī further says that he recognizes the validity of the consensus of the people. For this, he gives the reason that the people at large cannot ignore the Sunnah of the Prophet, while individuals may do so. Concluding he remarks, "And we know that the people at large cannot agree on what contradicts the Sunnah of the Prophet and on an error."[13] The notion of infallibility of the consensus of the Muslim community put forward by al-Shāfiʿī was supported later by a host of traditions from the Prophet.

II

Let us now discuss the justification of *Ijmāʿ* on the basis of the Qur'ān. We have shown earlier that al-Shāfiʿī did not substantiate *Ijmāʿ* on the authority of the Qur'ān. We discern that this was done in the post-Shāfiʿī period when the doctrine fully developed. We find the Qur'ānic justification of *Ijmāʿ* for the first time in Abū Bakr al-Jaṣṣaṣ (d. 370 A.H.) who might have been influenced by his predecessors in the third century of Hijrah, or he himself argued originally. He cites the following verses in support of *Ijmāʿ*:

---

[13] Al-Shāfiʿī, *al-Risalah*, Cairo: Būlaq, 1312 A.H., p. 65. Majid, Khadduri, *op. cit.*, pp. 285-86., Schacht, *op. cit.*, pp. 90-91.

﴿وَكَذَٰلِكَ جَعَلْنَٰكُمْ أُمَّةً وَسَطًا لِّتَكُونُوا۟ شُهَدَآءَ عَلَى ٱلنَّاسِ وَيَكُونَ ٱلرَّسُولُ عَلَيْكُمْ شَهِيدًا ۗ﴾

"And thus, We appointed you a midmost nation that you might be witness to the people, and that the Messenger might be a witness to you."
[TMQ Surah Al-Baqara: 143]

﴿وَمَن يُشَاقِقِ ٱلرَّسُولَ مِنۢ بَعْدِ مَا تَبَيَّنَ لَهُ ٱلْهُدَىٰ وَيَتَّبِعْ غَيْرَ سَبِيلِ ٱلْمُؤْمِنِينَ نُوَلِّهِۦ مَا تَوَلَّىٰ وَنُصْلِهِۦ جَهَنَّمَ ۖ وَسَآءَتْ مَصِيرًا ﴿١١٥﴾﴾

"And whoso makes a breach with the Messenger after the guidance has become clear to him, and follows a way other than the believers, him We shall turn over to what he has turned to and We shall roast him in Gehenna-an evil homecoming."
[TMQ Surah An-Nisaa: 115]

﴿أَمْ حَسِبْتُمْ أَن تُتْرَكُوا۟ وَلَمَّا يَعْلَمِ ٱللَّهُ ٱلَّذِينَ جَٰهَدُوا۟ مِنكُمْ وَلَمْ يَتَّخِذُوا۟ مِن دُونِ ٱللَّهِ وَلَا رَسُولِهِۦ وَلَا ٱلْمُؤْمِنِينَ وَلِيجَةً ۚ وَٱللَّهُ خَبِيرٌۢ بِمَا تَعْمَلُونَ ﴿١٦﴾﴾

"Or did you suppose you would be left in peace, and God knows not as yet those of you who have struggled, and taken not apart from God and His Messenger and the believers any intimate? God is aware of what you do."
[TMQ Surah At-Tauba: 16]

﴿وَلِلَّهِ مَا فِى ٱلسَّمَٰوَٰتِ وَمَا فِى ٱلْأَرْضِ ۚ وَإِلَى ٱللَّهِ تُرْجَعُ ٱلْأُمُورُ ﴿١٠٩﴾﴾

"You are the best nation raised up for man: you enjoin good and forbid evil and you believe in Alalh." [TMQ Surah Al-'Imran: 109]

﴿وَٱتَّبِعْ سَبِيلَ مَنْ أَنَابَ إِلَىَّ ۚ﴾

"And follow the way of him who turns to Me." [TMQ Surah Luqman: 15]

Al-Jaṣṣaṣ argues on the basis of these five verses cited by the later jurists too. Quoting verse 2:143 he remarks that *Ijmā'* can be justified on the basis of this verse in a twofold way. Firstly, the Muslim community bears the quality of being a midmost nation. The word "*wasat*" literally means upright and equitable. The quality of uprightness, therefore, requires the recognition of the agreed decisions of the community, and the rectitude of its way. Secondly, the judgement of the Prophet is an authority over the community, because he is the bearer of witness to them. On the same analogy the agreement of the community should be an authority over the people.[14]

Advancing the same argument al-Sarakhsi states that the merit of bearing witness to the people is an honour (*karāmah*) bestowed by God on the Muslim community by virtue of its uprightness. The judgement of the community is, therefore, an authority as good as that of the Prophet himself.[15]

Al-Jaṣṣaṣ infers from verse 4:115 that the Qur'ān makes adherence to the way of Muslims binding on people, and forbids them to diverge from it. This proves the authority of their agreement because God commands to follow the truth. The Qur'ān also lays emphasis on holding fast to the way of believers at large, because it threatens those who swerve from their line.

Verse 9:16, according to him, gives the friendship of the Prophet and that of believers an equal degree. From this, he infers that opposing the believers is as serious as opposing the Prophet. Departure from their way is tantamount to the rejection of truth.

---

[14] Al-Jaṣṣāṣ, *Kitāb Uṣūl al-Fiqh*, Ms. 229-Usūl, Dār al-Kutub al-Miṣriyyah, Cairo, fos. 215 b.-217a.

[15] Al-Sarakhsi, *op. cit.*, I, 288-89.

Interpreting verse 3: 109 he remarks that the Qur'ān mentions three important merits of the Muslim community, namely excellence, enjoining good and forbidding evil. If the community agrees on an error, the Qur'ān would never have praised it in terms of these qualities.

On verse 31:15 al-Jaṣṣaṣ comments that the Qur'ān asks to follow a single person from the Muslim community who turns (devoted) to God. But one cannot know such a person definitely. He must form part of the entire Muslim community. Therefore, the agreement of the community also includes the opinion of such a person ordered by God to be followed. The consensus of believers is, therefore, a decision from God.[16]

Al-Ghazālī (d. 505 A.H.) adds a few more verses to substantiate *Ijmāʿ* on the basis of the Qur'ān. These are as follows:

﴿وَمِمَّنْ خَلَقْنَآ أُمَّةٌ يَهْدُونَ بِٱلْحَقِّ وَبِهِۦ يَعْدِلُونَ ١٨١﴾

"And of those We created are a nation who guide by the truth, and by it act with justice." [TMQ Surah Al-Aʿraf: 181]

﴿يَٰٓأَيُّهَا ٱلَّذِينَ ءَامَنُوا۟ ٱتَّقُوا۟ ٱللَّهَ حَقَّ تُقَاتِهِۦ وَلَا تَمُوتُنَّ إِلَّا وَأَنتُم مُّسْلِمُونَ ١٠٢﴾

"And hold you fast to the rope of God all together, and do not scatter." [TMQ Surah Al-ʿImran: 102]

﴿وَمَا ٱخْتَلَفْتُمْ فِيهِ مِن شَىْءٍ فَحُكْمُهُۥٓ إِلَى ٱللَّهِ ۚ ذَٰلِكُمُ ٱللَّهُ رَبِّى عَلَيْهِ تَوَكَّلْتُ وَإِلَيْهِ أُنِيبُ ١٠﴾

"And in whatever you differ, the judgement thereof is with God." [TMQ Surah Ash-Shura: 10]

---

[16] Al-Jaṣṣās., *op. cit.*, fos. 217a-217b.

﴿يَٰٓأَيُّهَا ٱلَّذِينَ ءَامَنُوٓاْ أَطِيعُواْ ٱللَّهَ وَأَطِيعُواْ ٱلرَّسُولَ وَأُوْلِي ٱلۡأَمۡرِ مِنكُمۡۖ فَإِن تَنَٰزَعۡتُمۡ فِي شَيۡءٖ فَرُدُّوهُ إِلَى ٱللَّهِ وَٱلرَّسُولِ إِن كُنتُمۡ تُؤۡمِنُونَ بِٱللَّهِ وَٱلۡيَوۡمِ ٱلۡأٓخِرِۚ ذَٰلِكَ خَيۡرٞ وَأَحۡسَنُ تَأۡوِيلًا ٥٩﴾

"... then if you should quarrel on anything, refer it to God and the Messenger." [TMQ Surah An-Nisaa: 59]

Al-Ghazali also quotes verses 2:143, 3:109 and 4:115 already cited by al-Jaṣṣaṣ. Commenting on these verses he observes that they signify *Ijmāʿ* by their outword meaning. They do not indicate the objective expressly. He regards the justification on the basis of verse 4:115 as the most potent of all the verses, because it obligates the pursuit of the believers' way. Nevertheless, it does not justify *Ijmāʿ* explicitly. He thinks in this verse God threatens a man who opposes the Prophet instead of obeying, helping and defending him. To refrain from opposing the Prophet means the pursuit of the believers' way in helping and defending him and submitting to him by following his commands and prohibitions.[17]

Fakhr al-Din al-Razi (d. 606 A.H.) seeks to establish the legitimacy of *Ijmāʿ* on the basis of the Qur'ānic verse 4:59. We sum up his line of argument presently. God commanded unquestioning obedience to 'those in authority' (*Aulī al-Amr*). The judgement of a person whose obedience is commanded by God must be immune from error. This is because God cannot command to obey a person who is apt to fall into error, for committing an error is prohibited by God Himself. As such, both command and prohibition about the same thing are combined in a single injunction. But never does this happen in divine commandments. It is, therefore, definitely proved that 'those in authority' mentioned in this verse are infallible. Now the merit of infallibility applies either to 'the community as a whole' or to

[17] Al-Ghazāli, *op. cit.*, I, III.

'individuals'. But this cannot apply to the latter because it is prerequisite for obedience to a person that he should be definitely known. Such an individual is generally identified with the 'infallible imam' of the Shīʿah. But it is not possible at present to approach him and receive religious knowledge from him. Hence the term 'those in authority' occurring in the verse definitely means 'people who bind and loose' and they represent the Muslim community.[18] It is evident from this argument that al-Rāzī justifies *Ijmāʿ* on the basis of the doctrine of infallibility. His contention that the person whose unquestioning obedience is commanded by God must be infallible in his judgement is untenable. The merit of infallibility should be restricted to the prophets alone because they are protected from error by revelation from God. But others cannot stand on a par with them. Further, it should be noted that nothing is 'infallible' in this world in the true sense of the term. Terms like 'infallible', 'immune to error' or 'protected' mean confidence in a thing or a person for their respective proper working. Infallibility, thus, is a relatively functional concept. *Ijmāʿ* in this sense shows reliability in the judgement of the 'community at large or of 'those in authority', but not the absolute infallibility, as al-Rāzi presumes. The notion of 'infallibility' emerged as a social necessity for having trust and confidence in an 'authority'. Had there been no confidence in an 'authority' in any sphere, the whole functioning of society would have collapsed.

Al-Āmidī adduces five Qurʾānic verses in support of *Ijmāʿ*. Arguing on the basis of verse 4:115, the locus classicus, to prove *Ijmāʿ* from the Qurʾān, he remarks that God threatened those who follow a way other than that of the believers. Had it not been forbidden; He would never have given the threat of punishment. Further, it is not fair to combine under the same threat both lawful and unlawful things, as

[18] Fakhr al-Din al-Rāzi, *Mafātīḥ al-Ghayb*, Cairo, 1308 A.H., III, 241-42.

it is not fair to combine disbelief, an unlawful act, and eating bread, a permissible act, under the same threat. Hence the pursuit of the way other than that of the believers is as unlawful as opposing the Prophet.[19]

Explaining verse 2:143 he says that the motive underlying the praise of the Muslim community is to validate and give legal sanction to its decisions, and to make them binding on the people just like the decisions of the Prophet. The legitimacy of *Ijmāʿ* carries no other sense except that the judgement of the community is a binding authority.[20]

Commenting on verse 3:109 he says that when the article al is prefixed to a generic noun, it connotes generality of meaning. The verse in question means that Muslims will prescribe all that is good and prohibit all that is evil. When they make a prescription, it is either good or evil. But it cannot be evil, otherwise they must have forbidden it, as envisaged by the general meaning of the verse. If their prescription is good, then its opposite is evil. And this is what is required. Conversely, if they prohibit a thing, it would be either evil or good. It cannot be good, otherwise they must have prescribed it and not prohibited it. If it is evil, then its opposite is good. And that is the objective.[21]

Adducing verse 3:102 he contends that God prohibited disagreement. And opposing agreement (*Ijmāʿ*) means disagreement which is forbidden. *Ijmāʿ* being an authority carries no other significance except debarring its opposition. Elimination of disagreement presupposes agreement.[22]

---

[19] Al-Āmidī, *op. cit.*, I, 286.
[20] *Ibid.* p. 302.
[21] *Ibid.*, p. 306.
[22] *Ibid.*, pp. 309-10.

Explaining verse 4:59 he remarks that consulting the Qur'ān and the Sunnah is necessary when there is a dispute over a certain point. Dispute is a condition for making a reference to these sources. Now if there is no dispute on a certain question agreement will be presupposed there. The authority of *Ijmā'* serves the same purpose.[23]

III

The opponents of *Ijmā'* raised certain objections to the justification of *Ijmā'* on the basis of the Qur'ān. We analyse below their doubts and the answers given by the exponents of *Ijmā'*. First, we take up verse 4:115.

Q. The threat applies to both points as a whole, i.e. to disobedience to the Prophet and to the pursuit of a way other than that of the believers. In this verse the whole is prohibited and not the parts. The prohibition of the whole does not presuppose the prohibition of its constituents severally, just like the prohibition of marrying two sisters together. Hence the argument is not correct.

A. (a) It is not correct to say that the threat applies to the 'whole' and not to the 'parts'. This is because opposition to the Prophet is a sin by itself already admitted by the opponents. Therefore, mentioning the other case, i.e. divergence from believers' way, is redundant, and redundancy cannot be allowed in the word of God.

(b) Suppose the prohibition of divergence from the way of believers is conditioned by opposition to the Prophet. It would mean that the threat does not apply to the former if the latter is not found, and that divergence from believers' way is lawful in the absence of opposition to the Prophet. But this is a false premise. Opposition to *Ijmā'* may not be an error, but surely it is not a right act. An act which

---

[23] *Ibid.*, p. 311.

is not right cannot be absolutely lawful. Therefore, divergence from believers' way falls by itself within the threat.

(c) A third answer may be that the threat of punishment in both cases is due to some cause of evil (*Mafsadah*). The threat is not justified in case there is no cause of evil. Now the cause of evil lies either in the opposition to the Prophet or not. In the former case mention of the opposition to the Prophet is sufficient. In the latter case, it lies in the very divergence from the believers' way. Hence both cases are independent, and the threat applies to them equally.

Q. Divergence from the believers' way is unlawful after the guidance (*hudā*) is manifested because the connected clause is conditional. The general guidance includes the evidence which supports *Ijmāʿ*. It is not something distinguished from *Ijmāʿ*. The pursuit of the believers' way is binding on the basis of evidence and not on the authority of *Ijmāʿ*.

A (a). The prohibition of opposing the Prophet is conditioned by the manifestation of guidance. The word guidance (*huda*) here stands for the knowledge of the unity of God and the prophethood in general, and not for evidence in support of legal matters. This condition is connected only with the opposition to the Prophet and not with the divergence from the believers' way.

(b) By exhorting the pursuit of the believer's way, the Qurʾān seeks to exalt the position of the community. If it is conditioned by the manifestation of guidance, it would be necessary to pursue the guidance, no matter whether it comes from Muslims or non-Muslims. The pursuit of the believers' way is binding not because it involves guidance but because it is a way which they determined and followed after they were fully acquainted with guidance.

Q. The particle *ghayr* may stand for an exception as well as for an adjective. In case it is adjective, 'the way other than that of the believers' means disbelief. Whoever opposes the Prophet while he is a disbeliever no doubt deserves punishment.

A. The particle *ghayr* in this verse does not stand for adjective; otherwise, it would mean that the pursuit of unbelievers' way is prohibited in general. But this is not correct. Further, suppose 'the way other than that of the believers' means unbelievers' way, then it will include all those ways which contradict believers' way. The word *sabil* indicates the behavioural condition of a man which he maintains perpetually in varying circumstances. To follow the way of tradesmen means to follow them in respect of their dress, ethos and habits. The believers' way will therefore apply to the general conduct and way of life as a whole followed by the community, and not to its any particular aspect. Hence the threat in the verse cannot be applied to disbelief alone.

Q. The word 'believers' occurring in the verse means all the believers from the rise of Islam till the day of judgement, and not the believers of a particular age.

A. This can be answered in a twofold way. First, the word 'believers' has been used in its original sense and not figuratively. It stands for a person who believes. It applies to the living persons, and not to the dead or to those who have not been born as yet. Hence it indicates the Muslims of a particular age, applying equally to the present, and the future members of the past, present and the community. Secondly, the verse condemns opposition to the believers' way and exhorts them to pursue it. If it is taken to mean the Muslims of all ages till the day of judgement, the purpose will be defeated.

Q. The word 'believers' includes both the scholars and the masses. But the masses are not competent for *Ijmāʿ*.

A. Granted that the masses are not included in *Ijmāʿ*; nevertheless, the verse in question serves as an authority for the pursuit of the believers' way in general. To exclude a particular group from a word having general meaning requires evidence.

Q. The word *sabil* being singular indicates any sort of way, good or bad.

A. The word, of course, has a general meaning. But here it means a way worthy of Muslims. The verse requires to pursue the believers' way not only positively but also negatively. 'Adherence' to their way means to do what they do and to abstain from what they abstain.

Q. The believers' way may be construed as the infallible imam of the Shī'ah.

A. This raises the question of the existence of infallible *Imām* in each generation. It is difficult to prove his existence in every generation. Above all, the verse in question is general. It should not be construed to mean the leaders (*A'immah*) or a particular group of Muslims which includes an infallible *Imām*. This proposition is untenable.[24]

The opponents proffer the following criticism on verse 2:143:

Q. The verse means that the Muslim community would be upright in the hereafter to bear witness to the fact that the prophets of other communities had given their message to their respective communities.

A. This is not correct for two reasons: First, every community in the hereafter will be infallible. There is no question of committing sin in that world. Secondly, had it been so, future tense should have been used in the verse instead of past tense.

---

[24] *Ibid.*, pp. 286-98; al-Isnawi, *Nihāyat al-Sūl fi sharh minhaj al-wusūl ilā 'ilm al-Uṣūl*, Cairo, n.d., II, 235-36; Abul Husayn al-Baṣri, *Kitāb al-Mu'tamad*, Damuscus, 1965, II, 464-65.

Q. As the object of giving witness is ambiguous, the verse in question cannot serve as an authority.

A. To remove ambiguity it is necessary that the object of witness should be taken in general, so that it may cover everything possible.

Moreover, the quality of uprightness and not of bearing witness constitutes the evidence of *Ijmāʿ*. If the community is proved upright, its judgement will be recognized in all respects.

Q. The verse shows the uprightness of every person of the community including women, children, corrupt people and lunatics. But these persons are not the participants in *Ijmāʿ*.

A. This verse establishes the uprightness of the community as a whole. Therefore, its collective judgement will be an authority. The individuals will be neglected.

Q. The verse in question proves the internal uprightness of the community and not the external.

A. God knows the reality. He cannot describe as just and upright a person who is not just in reality.

Q. The uprightness is restricted to bearing witness. It has no relevance to legal questions.

A. If once their truthfulness is established, then every decision made by them will be taken as right. This is also confirmed by the tradition that 'what the Muslims consider good is good in the eyes of God'.

Q. The verse addresses itself either to the whole community or to the believers present in the age of Revelation. In the former case, the consensus of any generation is not valid. In the latter case, the consensus of the later generations is not valid.

A. Both explanations are untenable. The judgement of the Muslims during the lifetime of the Prophet was not authoritative for most of them died in his lifetime. Now when the Prophet died, how can those Muslims who died in his lifetime bear witness to the people.? But they are competent to bear witness according to this verse; otherwise, there is no use in calling them 'witness to the people'. Therefore, the word 'community' occurring in the verse means the 'community present in every generation'.[25]

Q. The definite article when prefixed to a generic noun does not make it general, as presumed by the exponents of *Ijmāʿ*. Therefore, the verse indicates a particular kind of good and evil but not good and evil in general.

A. It is an admitted fact that the verse in question seeks to exalt the position of the community and to distinguish it from other communities. If the words "good" and "evil" occurring in the verse are construed as a particular type of good and evil, the purpose would be defeated, because every community enjoins all that is good, such as obedience to the Prophet and to the law, and forbids all that is evil, such as abstaining from heresy and rejection of the prophets.

Q. Granted that good and evil mean general good and evil. But this quality was found in the community in the past as is obvious from the verse. This is not found in the present. This quality applies to the believers who existed before the revelation of this verse, and not to those who came afterwards. But it is not possible to know exactly such persons.

A. The verb *kāna* has been used here in its perfect form (*Tāmmāh*) and not as an imperfect verb (*Nāqiṣah*). It denotes the occurrence of an event in the present. It is immediately followed by its predicate.

---

[25] Al-Āmidī, *op. cit.*, 1, 302-6.

Q. The verb *Kāna* may indicate the past and the present, but surely not the future.

A. Imperfect tense indicates both the present and the future.

Q. The quality mentioned in the verse applies to the generation of the Prophet, and not to those who came afterwards.

A. If it gives sanction to the *Ijmāʿ* of the Companions, it surely gives sanction to the *Ijmāʿ* of others too.

Q. The quality applies to each and every person. But obviously, each and every person cannot be followed.

A. The judgment of individuals is no authority. The verse addresses itself to the whole community. Their collective judgment is an authority beyond doubt.[26]

As regards verse 3:102, the opponents contend that the prohibition of disunity does not cover all areas. It prohibits disunity only in the sphere of holding fast to the rope of God. So long as it is not known that the point on which the people of a generation have agreed is related to the area of holding fast to the rope of God, the disunity would not be prohibited. To this question, it is answered that the first sentence in the verse is a command for unity, and the second is a prohibition of disunity in all areas. If these two sentences are not construed as giving separate meanings, then the latter would be construed as confirming the former. But it is worthy of remark that originality constitutes the nucleus of a speech and not its confirmation and emphasis.

Further, it is questioned that the verse prohibits disagreement after the establishment of *Ijmāʿ* and not before it. Every jurist is allowed to follow his own opinion. When the opinions and speculations are

[26] *Ibid.*, pp. 306-9.

divergent, it means that disagreement is commanded by God, and not prohibited. It is replied that the verse surely prohibits disagreement after the establishment of *Ijmāʿ* and forbids opposing it.[27]

About verse 4:59 the opponents contend that in the case of agreement on a certain point, it is not necessary to consult the Qurʾān and the Sunnah. This agreement is either based on the Qurʾān and the Sunnah or not. In the former case, the Qurʾān and the Sunnah are sufficient authorities; there is no need of *Ijmāʿ*. In the latter case, there is a suggestion of establishing the *Ijmāʿ* without evidence. And this is impossible because this would invalidate the *Ijmāʿ*. To this, it is answered that if the evidence is at all necessary for *Ijmāʿ*. that can be furnished by the process of analogy and inference in addition to the Qurʾān and the Sunnah.[28]

Concluding the discussion of the Qurʾānic verses al-Amidī remarks that these verses may be helpful for speculation, and not for positive proof. If *Ijmāʿ* is a decisive doctrine, as it is believed, then arguing from speculative evidence to prove its legitimacy would not be helpful to achieve the end. Speculative evidence is correct according to him who considers *Ijmāʿ* to be a speculative question, open to individual interpretation.[29]

IV

To demonstrate the development of the traditions about *Ijmāʿ* since al-Shāfiʿī onwards one should go through the works on Islamic jurisprudence produced in the third century of the Hijrah. Unfortunately, we have no work in hand on this subject belonging

---

[27] *Ibid.*, pp. 310-11.
[28] *Ibid.*, p. 312.
[29] *Ibid.*, pp. 312-13.

to this period. This is a period when *Ḥadīth* was formally compiled and the six classical collections came into existence. Henceforth *Ḥadīth* came into wide circulation and was increasingly cited by the jurists in support of Islamic doctrines. This is the reason why *Ijmā'* was justified on the basis of *Ḥadīth* continuously in post-Shāfi'ī period. The earliest extant work on jurisprudence after al-Shāfi'ī's Risālah is Kitāb Uṣūl al-Fiqh by Abū Bakr al-Rāzi al-Jassās (d. 370 A.H.). In this work, the chapter on *Ijmā'* opens with his remarks that the jurists agreed on the legitimacy of *Ijmā'* in the early period of Islam and that the doctrine of *Ijmā'* is an authority from God. The previous *Ijmā'* cannot be changed by a subsequent *Ijmā'* in later generations. The source of realizing the authority of *Ijmā'* is the Qur'ān and the tradition (sam) alone, for reason allows that the community can agree on an error, like the Jews, Christians, and others.[30]

Al-Jaṣṣaṣ adduces the following traditions to substantiate *Ijmā'*:[31]

He cites the speech of 'Umar which he made at al-Jabiyah. It contains the tradition of the Prophet which persuades Muslims to hold fast to the community.[32]

"A section of my community will continue to follow the truth. One who feels hostile to them will do no harm until the divine decree comes down."[33]

"My community will not agree on an error."[34]

---

[30] Al-Jaṣṣās, *op. cit.*, fo. 215b.
[31] *Ibid.*, fos., 217-218a.
[32] This tradition has been cited by al-Shāfi'ī to justify *Ijmā'*. In addition, it is found in *Jāmi'* of *Al-Tirmidhī*, Kitāb al-Fitan 7, and Musnad of Ibn Hanbal, I, 26.
[33] Al-Bukhari, *al-Jami' al-Ṣaḥīḥ*, al-I'tiṣām 10; Muslim, *Sahih*, Īmān, 247; Abū Dawūd, *Sunan*, Fitan 1; Ibn Hanbal, *Musnad*, V. 34, 269, 278.
[34] Ibn Majah, *Sunan*, Fitan 8.

"The hand of God is over the community."[35]

"Three things on which the heart of a Muslim will not be stingy: sincerity of action to seek the pleasure of God, well-wishing of authorities, and adherence to the community - their call encompasses them from behind."[36]

"Whoever separates himself from the Muslim community even a span, throws away the tie of Islam from his neck."[37]

Hudhayfah is reported to have asked the Prophet, "What can save me from it (schism)? He replied, "The community of Muslims and their leader."[38]

These are seven traditions cited by al-Jaṣṣaṣ to justify *Ijmāʿ*. Two of them were earlier cited by al-Shāfiʿī. Al-Jaṣṣaṣ mentions in the context of *Ijmāʿ* almost the same traditions which exhort the Muslims to unity. The famous tradition 'my community will not agree on an error' was mentioned in the third century of the Hijrah in the context of integration of the community by Ibn Majah (d. 279 A.H.) and in a different version by al-Tirmdhi (d. 279 A.H.) and by Ahmad b. Hanbal (d. 241 A.H.) in their respective collections. But in the context of *Ijmāʿ*, this tradition appears in al-Jaṣṣaṣ for the first time. It seems that until the time of al-Jaṣṣaṣ the traditions cited by him were not generally mentioned in the context of time. Hence, he closes his discussion of these traditions with the remarks: "These traditions are clear and well known. They have been reported from different quarters. Since they have been reported through tawātūr, it is impossible that they are in totality speculation and falsehood. These traditions were widely known in the time of the Companions

[35] Al-Tirmidhī *Jami*, Fitan 7: Al-Nasāʾī, Sunan, Tahrim 6.
[36] Al-Tirmidhī, *Jamiʿ ʿIlm* 7; Ibn Hanbal, Musnad, IV, 80.
[37] Al-Tirmidhī, *Jamiʿ*, Adab 78.
[38] Al-Bukhari, *Al-Jāmiʿ al-Ṣaḥīḥ*, Fitan 11, Manaqib 25; Muslim, *Sahih*, Amarah 51; Al-Tirmidhī, Fitan 57; Ibn Majah, *Sunan*, Fitan 13.

who justified *Ijmāʿ* on their basis and asked people to follow them. None of these traditions was rejected by them. Traditions having such a standing must be a source of certain knowledge for action."[39] It should be noted that it is a mere surmise to say that the Companions justified the doctrine of *Ijmāʿ* on the basis of these traditions.

To justify *Ijmāʿ* al-Ghazali places his reliance more on traditions than on the Qurʾānic verses. To him, the tradition 'my community will not agree on an error' indicates *Ijmāʿ* more clearly and strongly than the Qurʾānic verses. But these traditions are not *Mutawātir* like the Qurʾān; the Qurʾānic verses are *Mutawātir* but not clear enough to substantiate *Ijmāʿ*. Therefore, he argues from the traditions as follows: A number of traditions have been reported from the Prophet with different versions, all implying the immunity of the community from error. They spread widely in the long run, being reported by reliable Companions like Ibn Masʿūd, Abū Saʿid al-Khudri, Anas b. Mālik, Ibn ʿUmar, Abū Hurayah, Hudhayfah b. al-Yaman and others. Al-Ghazali then cites all such traditions as emphasize the integration of the community and condemn disunity and chaos. These traditions were adduced by al-Jaṣṣaṣ too before him in support of *Ijmāʿ*. He remarks that they remained continuously familiar to all in the generation of the Companions and the Successors to the present day. No one from among the early and classical traditionists rejected them. They were rather accepted both by the exponents and by the opponents of *Ijmāʿ*.[40]

V

---

[39] Al-Jaṣṣāṣ, *op. cit.*, fo. 218a.

[40] Al-Ghazālī *op. cit.*, I, 111.

Al-Ghazali has recorded in *'al-Mustasfā'* the criticism of the opponents of *Ijmāʿ* on the traditions cited above. We summarize these objections presently along with his answers.

Q. How do you argue on the basis of traditions, particularly when these traditions cannot be claimed to have been reported severally by *Tawātur*, and it is already established that solitary traditions do not, entail certain knowledge?

A. We argue on the basis of traditions in a twofold way. First, the Prophet intended by these traditions to exalt the position of the community, and to signify its infallibility. We gained certain knowledge through isolated reports about ʿAlī's bravery, Hatim's generosity, al-Shāfiʿīs's deep knowledge of fight, and al-Hajjaj's oratory. The individual reports about these facts are not *Mutawātir*. One can reject them severally, but not collectively. The same principle applies to the traditions of *Ijmāʿ*. These traditions ensemble provide certain knowledge. Secondly, apart from certain knowledge, we base ourselves on inferential knowledge. These traditions were widespread among the Companions and the Successors. They justified *Ijmāʿ* on their basis and no one differed from them until the day of al-Nazzām. And normally it is impossible that the people, despite their diverse temperaments, ambitions, and approaches in respect of acceptance and rejection, might accept, in successive generations, a thing which was not genuine. Hence the rules derived from solitary traditions survived even in the teeth of opposition and doubt. The justification of *Ijmāʿ* an authority which determines the correct interpretation of the Qurʾān and the established Sunnah on the basis of these traditions implies that there must have been some positive evidence. To prove a definite object by indefinite evidence is still unknown.

The opponents refute the argument advanced al-Ghazali in a three-fold way: by refutation, by interpretation, and by counter-argument from the Qur'ān and the Sunnah. As regards refutation, they ask four questions:

1. It is most probable that someone might have opposed these traditions and rejected them, but his rejection might not have reached us.

2. You argued in support of *Ijmā*ʿ primarily from the traditions, and then you argued from *Ijmā*ʿ to prove the authenticity of the traditions. Suppose people might have agreed on their authenticity; but how is it proved that the question on which they agreed is really valid? Here lies the point in dispute.

3. How do you refute the counter-argument that people might have proved the legitimacy of *Ijmā*ʿ not on the basis of these traditions but on the basis of some other evidence?

4. If the Companions were acquainted with the authenticity of these traditions, why had they not explained it verbally to the Successors in order to eliminate doubt and thus give them a share in their knowledge?

Al-Ghazali answers:

1. The usual practice denies the line of argument. *Ijmā*ʿ is one of the major doctrines of Islam. If anyone had dissented from it, this would have become an abnormal affair, and his dissent must have spread widely. The disagreement among the Companions on the questions of the bloodwit of the fetus, certain unlawful things, and the punishment for drinking was not extinguished; how could the disagreement on such a major source of law be suppressed? How did the dissent of al-Nazzām, despite his little respect and small dignity, become widely known while the dissent of the senior Companions and Successors remained shrouded in obscurity? Reason does not justify this theory at all.

2. Originally, we justify *Ijmāʿ* on the basis of traditions and prove their authenticity by customary norms. It is an admitted fact that no dispute and disagreement ever existed in the past over such traditions. Further, custom debars justification on the basis of doubtful traditions of a decisive source of law, which overarches other decisive authorities, such as the Qurʾān and the Sunnah. We realized the definiteness and authenticity of these traditions by custom and not by *Ijmāʿ*. Again, through custom and practice, we gained the knowledge of a number of important questions, e.g. falsity of the challenge to the Qurʾān and extinction of such a challenge with the passage of time, the voidness of suggestions to appoint the imam' (political leader of the community) by nomination, the dispute over the forenoon prayer (*duhā*), and fasting during Shawwāl. People accepted these questions as they were transmitted to them, and therefore kept silent. If these questions were not so in reality, as they stand today, silence over them would be normally impossible.

3. The opponents themselves prove on the basis of the self-same traditions that opposition to the community is prohibited and that those who separate themselves from the community stand condemned. This implies that they are relevant to *Ijmāʿ*.

4. The Companions realized the infallible character of the Muslim community from the spirit contained in the indications, signs, repeated statements, and dicta of the Prophet. They inferred that evidently the Prophet by these traditions designed to describe the charisma of the community. These indications, taken cumulatively, could not be covered by verbal narration or words. Had they explained them verbally, doubt must have permeated the individual reports. Therefore, they contented themselves with explaining to the Successors a principle that a decisive source of law could not be proved legitimate on the basis of a doubtful tradition, but that it could be recognized as legitimate by custom and usual practice. The

practice was, therefore, more reliable for the Successors than verbal narration.

The opponents again refute the justification of *Ijmā'* on the basis of traditions in a threefold way:

1. The tradition 'my community will not agree on an error' really refers to disbelief and heresy. The Prophet might have, in all probability, intended by this tradition immunity of the entire community from disbelief which might pervade by misinterpretation and scepticism. Further, the word *'khaṭā* occurring in the tradition has not been reported by *Tawātur.* Suppose it has been reported so, still it means error in general, which may be applied to disbelief.

2. By *'khaṭā* may be meant a mistake in bearing witness in the life hereafter, or a mistake in a rule which is supported by a text (Naṣṣ) or a rational argument, and not necessarily a mistake in the individual legal interpretation and analogical reasoning.

3. The word *'Ummah* occurring in the tradition means those who believe in the Prophet since the rise of Islam till the day of judgment. It is admitted that the community if taken in this sense, cannot agree on an error. The agreement of all the members of the community, belonging to the past, present, and future, is infallible. Suppose the members of the community in the past had lived on and disagreed with the *Ijmā'* of the present generation, then *Ijmā'* would never have been valid.

Al-Ghazālī replies:

1. Viewed from an etymological standpoint, the word *dalal* does not connote disbelief. The adjectives *dall* and *dallin* occurring in verses 93:7 and 26:20 respectively mean those who fall into error and not 'disbelievers'. The Arabic idioms *dalla fulan 'an al-tariq* and *dalla sa'yu fulān* mean falling into error. Literally, the tradition indicates the

sublime dignity of the community and distinguishes it from others by this merit. As regards protection from disbelief, God already bestowed this merit on ʿAlī, Ibn Masʿūd, Ubayy and Zayd b. Thabit, according to al-Nazzām himself, because they died on truth (belief). Besides, there were many people who remained immune from disbelief. What is then the distinction of the community? This shows that the Prophet by this tradition meant forgetfulness, error, and falsehood-shortcomings from which individuals cannot be protected, but the community can be protected. This is because the community occupies the infallible position like the Prophet with respect to religious matters. Even in matters not relating to religion, such as fighting, treaty of peace, and building a town, the generality of meaning of the tradition requires infallibility. This is, however, doubtful because infallibility in such matters is also doubtful about the Prophet himself. Reports tell us that once he committed a mistake in his opinion about the fecundation of palm trees. At that moment he reportedly remarked "You are better acquainted with your temporal affairs, and I am better acquainted with your religious affairs."

2. No one of the community has ever drawn such a distinction. If the community is apt to commit an error in a particular area, on the same analogy it can commit it in another area, too. If there is no characteristic feature of the community, then differentiating one community from the other is useless. There must be some evidence of this difference. The Prophet condemned opposing the community and commanded adherence to it. Now if the area of infallibility is not definitely known, adherence to the community would be impossible. This is possible only in case infallibility is taken to mean in general. As for the infallibility in a particular area, it should be noted that it is already found even in a disbeliever, let alone a believer. No one falls into error in respect of each and every

matter. Rather every person is certainly immune from error in one matter or the other.

3. As it is not permissible to say that by the *ʾUmmah* are meant lunatics, children, miscarried fetuses, and fetus, though they belong to the community, likewise it is not permissible to say that by it are meant those who died, and those who are not yet born. But obviously it means people who have the capability of 'agreement and disagreement'. One cannot conceive of agreement and disagreement of non-existent and dead people. It may be noted that the Prophet commanded adherence to the community and condemned dissidence. If by the *ʾUmmah* is meant what the opponents have suggested, then adherence and opposition can be conceived in the life hereafter, and not in this world. It is, therefore, definitely proved that the Prophet by this tradition meant *Ijmāʿ* which can be opposed in this world. This also applies to those who are present in a certain generation. In case they die, the effect of their dissent will survive.

Another way of refuting the justification of *Ijmāʿ* by oral proofs is their counter-argument from parallel Qurʾānic verses and traditions. The opponents cite verses 2:169, 2:217, and 2:188 which prohibit disbelief, apostasy, and false action. They contend that these verses prohibit false actions, in general, and people usually abstain from the prohibited actions. Were it not practically possible, they would not be asked to abstain from them.

To this, al-Ghazalī replies that these verses have been addressed not to the community but to individuals. The prohibition applies to every individual, even though he abstains from these actions. For divine prohibitions, it is not necessary that the prohibited act should happen actually or potentially. God knows well that all kinds of sins would not be committed by all people, still, He prohibited all of them. And nothing can occur against His knowledge. He knew well that He would protect the Prophet from polytheism and ignorance, still, He forbade him in verses 9:65 and 6:35.

The opponents believe that the community at large can fall into error. They offer the following traditions in support of their viewpoint:

1. 'Islam arose as an alien in an atmosphere of unbelief; it will turn alien as it emerged originally.'

2. 'Best of all is my generation, then those who follow, and then those who follow; falsehood will then spread so much so that one will take an oath, though not asked to do so, and one would bear witness, though not required.'

3. 'The last Hour will come over the wicked of my community.

Al-Ghazali answers that these traditions no doubt imply that disobedience and falsehood will spread widely; but they do not mean that not a single follower of the truth will remain in the community. Moreover, these traditions contradict another tradition which says: A section of my people will continue to follow the truth until the decree of God comes and the Antichrist appears. Again, the traditions adduced by the opponents are not as sound and clear as those offered in support of *Ijmāʿ*.[41]

There is another approach to prove the legitimacy of *Ijmāʿ* on the basis of traditions by Abū'l-Ḥusayn al-Baṣrī (d. 436 A.H.). He contends that the Successors en masse believed in the legitimacy of *Ijmāʿ*. There seems no other possible reason for such a belief than the traditions of the Prophet. The community usually agrees on the import of a tradition in case it is authentic. The Successors never agreed on the import of an isolated tradition, which was not authentic. This is because the rule derived from such a tradition was

---

[41] *Ibid.*, 111-14.

subject to their individual interpretation. The argument is countered by the opponents as follows:

Q. We are not aware that the whole body of the Successors had believed in the legitimacy of *Ijmāʿ*. Instead, they are reported to have deviated from the agreement of the Companions on certain legal matters. Suppose they believed in the legitimacy of *Ijmāʿ*, but they might have done so on the basis of the Qurʾānic verses and not on the basis of traditions. They could not believe in the authority of *Ijmāʿ* on the basis of a tradition which was not in itself definitely authentic. This might lead to an error, and the community cannot agree on an error.

A. Is it not possible that they agree on a certain rule by way of analogy and individual interpretation? Rationally speaking, they can agree on a certain point in the presence of many resembling proofs. In such cases, they investigate relevant traditions and agree on the import of the one found most authentic. They can never agree on a tradition not found authentic.

Q. In jurisprudence there exists no precedent of their agreement on the import of the isolated traditions.

A. Why do you suppose that the Successors agreed usually on those traditions that were found authentic? You never denied that the tradition of *Ijmāʿ* was not authentic and that the Successors agreed on its import. The Compansions are reported to have abandoned their personal opinion on certain questions when the authentic traditions were known to them. They changed their view when the traditions of Haml b. Mālik and ʾAbd al-Rahmān b. ʾAwf came to their knowledge. They agreed that a man cannot marry a woman and her aunt together on the basis of a solitary tradition.

Q. They might have agreed on these rules because the traditions were authentic.

A. If they agreed on a certain rule on the basis of traditions, this shows that they had not accepted any uncertain traditions.

Q: tradition? Is it not possible to agree on the import of a certain solitary

A. Sometimes it is possible and sometimes not. We do not maintain that this always happens necessarily.[42]

VI

The word "'*Ummah*" or "*Jamāʿah*" occurring in the traditions of *Ijmāʿ* gave rise to a controversy over its connotation. There is a difference of opinion among the jurists with regard to its identification. According to one point of view, it means the overwhelming majority of Muslims. This interpretation is supported by a number of statements of the Companions. Abū Masʿūd al-Anṣārī is reported to have been asked on the occasion of the assassination of ʿUthman about *fitnah* (schism). He replied, "Adhere to the community because God will not let the community of Muhammad agree on an error. Beware of separation because separation is an error." A similar report has been attributed to Ibn Masʿūd. When al-Husayn was asked about the validity of the caliphate of Abū Bakr, swearing by God he reportedly said, "God will not let the community of Muhammad agree on an error."[43] These reports show the historical context of the tradition 'my community will not agree on an error. On the basis of such reports the word '*Jamāʿah*' or '*Ummah*' has been interpreted as the 'overwhelming majority."

Another interpretation says that the word *Jamāʿah* means the 'body of the scholars and jurists'. In support of this interpretation, it is contended that he who differs from the agreement of the scholars

---

[42] Abul-Husayn al-Basri, *op. cit.*, II, 472-74.
[43] Al-Sharibi, *al-Iʿtiṣām*, Cairo, 1913, III, 136.

dies the death of ignorance. The masses, it is argued, are subordinate to the scholars, because they acquire their knowledge of religion from them. Therefore, it is said conclusively that the tradition 'my community will not agree on an error' means that the scholars of my community will not agree on an error. This interpretation has been attributed to ʿAbd. Allah b. al-Mubarak, Ishaq b. Rāhwayh, and to some other jurists.[44]

A third group construes the word *ʾUmmah* as the 'body of the Companions' on the ground that they are the founders of Islam, and they are the people who cannot agree on an error. This interpretation is substantiated by a number of traditions from the Prophet. One of them says, "The Prophet was once asked to pinpoint the people who will get salvation.

He replied, those who follow the way which I and my Companions follow." Another tradition runs: "Follow my Sunnah and the Sunnah of the rightly-guided Caliphs." This interpretation is also supported by a speech of ʿUmar b. ʿAbd al-ʿAziz (d. 101 A.H.). It says, "The Prophet introduced many Sunnahs (practices) and the political authorities did so after him. Adherence to these Sunnahs amounts to the belief in the Qurʾān, perfect obedience to God, and reinforcement of Islam. Nobody can change or modify them. Whatever contradicts them is not worth consideration. He who seeks guidance from these Sunnahs is on the right path; likewise, whoever seeks help by virtue of them is helped (by God). But he who opposes them follows the path other than that of the believers and God appoints for him that to which he himself has turned and will admit him to hell." From these statements, al-Shatibi concludes that

[44] Ibid., p. 137.

the term '*Jamāʿah*' in the traditions of *Ijmāʿ* means the Companions of the Prophet.[45]

Another opinion says that the word '*Ummah*' or '*Jamāʿah*' stands for 'the Muslim community at large'. The grace of 'infallibility' endowed by God, according to this view, is confined to the Muslim community as a whole and not to any group.[46]

The last interpretation is attributed to al-Tabari. He thinks that the word '*Jamāʿah*' means 'the community of Muslims who are agreed on a political leader. He puts forward a number of traditions to prove that disunity and disagreement are forbidden by the Prophet. He condemns sects like Khawārij who separated themselves from the community. He identifies *Jamāʿah* with the orthodox group which was united by choosing its political leader and by its adherence to the Qur'ān and the Sunnah.[47]

These are various shades of opinion about the meaning of '*Jamāʿah*' and '*Ummah*' which occur in the traditions of *Ijmāʿ*. It is, however, clear that the traditions on the basis of which the principle of *Ijmāʿ* has been substantiated are not definite in their connotation. They may mean *Ijmāʿ* or something else. All of them emphasize integration and condemn chaos and anarchy. Some of them are predictory, and others circumstantial. Therefore, the argument to establish the authority of *Ijmāʿ* is definitely subjective. We doubt whether *Ijmāʿ* can be justified purely on the basis of traditions as the medieval jurists sought to show. We offer the following contention. In the first place, there existed no idea of *Ijmāʿ* as a theoretical doctrine in the early period, let alone in the time of the Prophet. Secondly, the jurists could not determine a definite meaning of the word '*Ummah*' or '*Jamāʿah*' who were to be followed by the Muslims

---

[45] *Ibid.*, pp. 138-39.
[46] *Ibid.*, p. 140.
[47] *Ibid.*, 141-42.

according to the Prophet's command. Thirdly, traditions bearing general meaning cannot be restricted to a particular point of view. Hence, al-Shawkanl refutes the argument to justify *Ijmāʿ* on the basis of the prophetic traditions. All such traditions, according to him, mean that a section of the Muslim community will continue to follow the truth.[48]

VII

We have another important problem relating to the meaning of the words *dalal* and *ʾkhaṭā* which occur in the famous tradition about *Ijmāʿ*. The jurists use both these words interchangeably in this tradition, which implies that they draw no distinction in their meaning. But in the classical collections of *Ḥadīth* it has been reported only with the word *dalal.* We have noticed previously that the opponents of *Ijmāʿ* distinguish dalā! from *ʾkhaṭā.*" They think that *dalal* means disbelief, and *ʾkhaṭā* connotes mistake in individual interpretation. Dalal is an error in faith leading to disbelief and *ʾkhaṭā* is a mistake leading sometimes to a sin and not to disbelief.[49] Both these traditions have not been reported by *Tawātur* and the exponents of *Ijmāʿ* themselves recognize this weakness.[50] Ibn Hazm doubts both the text and the chain of this tradition. He confirms meaning of this tradition by citing various traditions on the subject.[51] Al-Firawzābādī (d. 826 A.H.) remarks that *Ijmāʿ* is certainly a religious authority, but no tradition of the Prophet is sound on this subject.[52]

---

[48] Al-Shawkānī, *Irshād al-Fuhūl*, Cairo, 1347 A. H., p. 69.

[49] Cf. Madina, M. Z. *The Classical Doctrine of Consensus in Islam*, an unpublished Ph. D. Thesis No. 3872, submitted to Deptt. of Political Science, the University of Chicago, pp. 38-48.

[50] Al-Ghazālī, *op. cit.*, 1, 112-113.

[51] Ibn Hazm, *al-Ihkām fi Uṣūl al-Ahkām*, Cairo: Maṭbaʿah al-Saʿādah, 1347 A.H., IV, 130-31.

[52] Majd al-Din al-Firawzābādi, *Sifr al-Saʿadeh*, Cairo, 1347 A.H. p. 146.

It seems that since there was no concept of *Ijmā'* as such in the time of the Prophet, by such traditions he might have predicted the eternity of Islam. The classical jurists, however, utilized these statements of the Prophet to defend *Ijmā'* on traditional grounds. The word *khata'* being more akin in its connotation to the mistake in the individual legal interpretation, they might have used it in place of *dalal*. It is also probable that they might have been influenced by al-Shāfi'ī who uses the word *khata'* instead of *dalal* in his own statement about the infallibility of *Ijmā'*[53] We find a similar statement of Abū Bakr, the first Caliph, who uses the word *dalal* instead of *khafa*. People persistently demanded to replace Usamah, the leader of a military expedition nominated by the Prophet, by any senior member, and to postpone the expedition in view of the grave situation due to apostasy of some Arab tribes. Abū Bakr relentlessly refused their demand by saying, "It is already known to you that there has been a continuous practice of mutual consultation since the time of the Prophet until your own day, in areas not covered by the prescriptions of the Sunnah of the Prophet and the Qur'ān. You gave your opinion, and soon I shall give you my advice. (By mutual consultation) think what is most right, and then act upon it, for God will not let you agree on an error...."[54] Curiously enough, he does not refer to any tradition of the Prophet, but expresses his own conviction about the infallibility of the decision reached by mutual consultation. Here the word *dalal* obviously connotes an error in the judgment and legal interpretation. This shows that *khafa'* and *dalal* can be used interchangeably. But whether the Prophet also intended the same thing by this tradition is doubtful.

---

[53] Al-Shāfi'ī, *op. cit.*, p. 65; Schacht, *op. cit.*, p. 91.

[54] Ibn 'Asākir, *Tahdhīb al-Tārīkh al-Kabīr*, Damuscus, Maṭba'ah Rawḍat al-Shām, 1329 A.H., I, 119.

VIII

We may now return to the justification of *Ijmāʿ* on the basis of human reason. It seems that the attempt to prove its legitimacy on rational grounds starts from al-Shāfiʿī. He contends that people in general cannot ignore the Sunnahs of the Prophet while individuals may do so. Similarly, people, in general, cannot agree on a point which contradicts the Sunnah of the Prophet and on an error.[55] By such statements he attempts to prove the irrationality of the concept of the agreement of the Muslim community at large on an error. This is why he recognizes *Ijmāʿ* on essentials of Islam transmitted from the Prophet by the people in general to the people in general. This he describes as *ʾilm al-ʾammah.*[56] 56 This sort of transmission of legal knowledge, i.e. from the people at large to the people at large, was termed later *Tawātur.* It has been defined as the transmission of legal knowledge from the Prophet by such a large number of people as cannot reasonably agree on falsehood for their huge number and living at different places. The number of obligatory prayers and rates of *Zakāt* are said to have been established on the basis of tawōtur. Reports coming through *Tawātur* are recognized as coming directly from the Prophet. The knowledge acquired through *Tawātur* is certain (*qatʾi*).[57] It is worthy of note that the mechanism of *Tawātur* is a rational phenomenon. The doctrine of *Ijmāʿ* is justified by al-Shafiʿi by the same logic, namely that the Muslim community at large cannot agree on an error.

---

[55] Al-Shafiʿi, *op. cit.*, p. 65.

[56] *Ibid.*, p. 50.

[57] Al-Sarakhsi, *op. cit.*, I, 282-83; Muḥammad Aʿlā al-Thānawī, *Kitāb Kashshāf Iṣṭilāḥāt al-Funūn*, Calcutta, 1862, II, 1471-72. Professor Simon Van den Bergh observes, "In their rules for the reliability of a tradition the theologians seem to be influenced by the rules given by the empiricists (see Galen, subfig. Emp. 51) for the reliability of traditional knowledge...."*Averroes' Tahāfut al-Tahāfut*, London, 1954, II, 16. This conjecture requires some positive evidence.

Al-Sarakhsi also justified *Ijmāʿ* on rational grounds. He contends that the revelation was closed with the death of the Prophet. But the *Shari'ah* is eternal. This implies that the Muslim community at large has been protected by God from committing an error in its collective agreement. In case the Muslim community agrees on an error, this would challenge the eternity of the *Shari'ah*. Further, he argues that there is a difference between the judgment of an individual and the judgment of the whole community. Hence the agreement of the community cannot be compared with the judgement of an individual. Finally, he proves the authority of *Ijmāʿ* by giving an illustration of the judicial judgment in legal matters. A judge gives his personal judgement which is binding on people by all means. From this, he infers that Islam believes in the infallibility of the judgment of a single person in legal cases. *Ijmāʿ* being the agreement of the Muslim community at large should a fortiori be superior to the individual judgment and hence an infallible authority.[58]

Al-Juwayni justifies *Ijmāʿ* rationally in a twofold way. Firstly, he says, we find that the scholars of our generation, despite their large number in the rimland and heartland of the country, agree on a speculative question, though actually their opinion is divided. Keeping this situation in view we realize that their agreement if at all it is reached, cannot be taken to mean that it is in harmony with their beliefs, and proceeds on one and the same line. Such an agreement is usually impossible due to the possibility of the difference of opinion. Even the agreement of intellectuals on a purely rational question, which is considered positive according to the intellectual standards, is impossible, especially when it is dealt with by deep reflective thought. This is due to divergence in the approach of the thinkers. Normally, this is the position of questions relating to positive thinking; what do you think of questions open

---

[58] Al-Sarakhsi, *op. cit.*, 1, 300.

to speculation, where no certainty can be imagined? When it is proved that according to usual practice, their unanimous agreement on a usual speculative question is impossible, and still we find their definite agreement on a certain rule, thereby rejecting no opinion and discarding no point of view, it would be presumed that they must have had some positive evidence in support of the rule, that could not reach us.

Secondly, if the scholars agreed on a speculative question, and they attributed it in clear terms to speculation, this sort of agreement would also be considered a definite authority. This is because we find that in the past ages and in the communities gone by, it has been customary to silence the opponents if they opposed the unanimous agreement. Such opposition to the unanimous agreement was considered heresy, dissidence, and disobedience. They did not take it lightly but condemned opposition to the religious scholars as open deviation from the right path. Their unanimous agreement has reached this point, now characterized by certainty (after agreement), though rationally it was open to speculation (before agreement). When a unanimous agreemnt was added to a speculative rule, the participants in *Ijmāʿ* considdered it a decisive authority, without expressly rejecting speculation. As such, *Ijmāʿ* has been recognized as a definite legal authority through the condemnation of its opponents. The traditions cited in favour of *Ijmāʿ* might have been reported from the Prophet, and the people might have learned them in his own day from their situational context. The Prophet. might have meant to give sanction to *Ijmāʿ* which the people later on realized and practiced. Afterwards, they successively regarded its dictates as certain, but never cared for its verbal narration due to their certainty.[59]

[59] Al-Juwayni *op. cit.*, fos. 192-93.

From the above argument, it is clear that the *Ijmāʿ* of the past generations is justified more on the basis of human reason (*Tawātur*) than by tradition. Al-Ghazālī, like his teacher, follows the same line of argument which we discuss presently.

He seeks to prove the rationality of *Ijmāʿ* on the basis of the principle of *Tawātur*, especially when the *Ijmāʿ* of the past generations is not supported by any evidence. Arguing he remarks that when the Companions agreed on a certain point, they could not evidently agree on an error, as it is denied by usual practice. It seems ordinarily irrational that not a single person from among them could attain the truth. The Successors adhered to their agreement and inveighed against those who opposed it. They looked upon their agreement as positive, and actually, they considered a thing certain which was not really certain. But usual practice denies that they might regard a thing as certain which was not really certain. The followers of the Successors accepted the agreement of their predecessors by the same logic. This argument is criticized as follows:

Q. If the number of the participants in *Ijmāʿ* is less than the number required for *Tawātur*, is it then possible that the Companions and Successors agree on an error, and deliberately tell a lie?

A: The line of argument is not correct. The error stems either from telling a lie or regarding an indefinite thing as definite. The former is not permissible in the case of *Tawātur* (whatever their number might be). The latter is of course possible. The Jews definitely believe in the falsity of the prophethood of Jesus and Muhammad (peace be upon them), though their number exceeds the number required for *Tawātur*. They regard a thing as certain which is not really certain. The number of heretics in the world exceeds the number of *Tawātur*. These heretics made a mistake in regarding a thing as certain which was not really certain. The advocates of this theory should by this logic consider the unanimous agreement of Jews and Christians, who believe in the falsity of Islam, as definitely authoritative. What is then the privilege of the agreement of the community?

Custom and usual practice allow in the case of *Tawātur* to regard a thing as certain, though really it is not certain. Hence it is a necessary condition for *Tawātur* that it should be supported by sensual perception. Ordinarily, it is improbable that people keep silent and submit to a person who makes a decision which overarches the Qur'ān and the Sunnah, which are based on *Tawātur*. His decision is based on *Ijmāʿ*, a doctrine which is established by a speculative and uncertain evidence. Anything which is certain is learned by sensual perception or situational context or by self-evidence. The medium of acquiring its knowledge is one. People agree on the certainty of knowledge acquired by sensual perception. And such a knowledge cannot usually escape the people of *Tawātur*. But a thing which is speculative can be learned by different media. Custom allows that people of *Tawātur* may commit a mistake by their agreement on such a question. This is the point of difference between the two.[60]

Al-Bazdawī justifies *Ijmāʿ* on the basis of human reason. He contends that the Sharf ah will last until the day of judgment because of the finality of the prophethood. As such, the community will continue to follow the truth. This view is supported by a number of traditions. The term '*Ummah*' occurring in the traditions stands for the people who do not follow evil passions and heresy. Now in a period when the revelation has come to an end, it if is permitted in principle that the whole community can agree on an error, the promise of the eternity of the *Shariʿah* would not come true. Hence it became necessary to formulate a principle that the agreement of the

---

[60] Al-Ghazālī, *op. cit.*, I, 114.

community will be infallible by all means. This is indeed a grace from God to protect religion. This must be allowed. because when a judge arrives at a decision on a disputed question by exercising his personal opinion, it becomes binding on the people. The decision of a judge cannot be rejected by any counter-argument. It is superior to the opinions of the jurists. This is to protect judiciary which is an instrument of religion. That a body of persons may perform an act which cannot be performed by individuals is not something curious. Hence *Ijmāʿ* occupied a position like that of a Qurʾānic verse or of a *Mutawātir* tradition entailing action and certain knowledge.[61]

The argument advanced by al-Bazdawī has been challenged by the opponents of *Ijmāʿ*. ʿAbd al-ʿAzīz al-Bukhari (d. 730 A.H.), the commentator of Al-Bazdawī's *Uṣūl,* answers their questions as follows:-

Q. *Ijmāʿ* corresponds to analogy and solitary traditions with respect to action. How does then its extinction entail the extinction of the whole *Shariʿah*?

A. Analogy and isolated traditions are employed to reveal the truth which is hidden in the collective opinions of the jurists. But you presume that truth lies beyond the collective opinions of the jurists on disputed and settled questions. As such, the truth would remain unknown and void. And what is void in itself cannot be adhered to of necessity. Your contention also implies that whatever the jurists brought forth was no *Shariʿah*, rather they acted against the *Shariʾah*. Therefore, the *Shariʿah* of the Prophet, at least to the extent of a particular rule, will be extinguished, if the rule is not revealed by means of *Ijmāʿ*.

Q. We do not accept that this would entail the extinction of the *Shariʿah*. The reason is that if a rule of law was established in the

---

[61] Al-Bazdawī, *op. cit.*, p. 245.

Shari'ah on the basis of a text (Naṣṣ) before *Ijmā'* such as the prescription of five daily prayers, that rule would last till the continuance of the text. *Ijmā'* nowhere comes in the picture to establish the rule. If it was not established in the *Shari'ah* before *Ijmā'*, it means that the text did not contain it. It enunciated only those rules of law which existed at the time of its genesis, and not those which occurred later on. Therefore, discontinuance of that rule would not entail the discontinuance of the *Shari'ah*. Suppose it was enunciated in the text, then extinction of this rule would not entail the extinction of the *Shari'ah* because of the survival of the fundamental laws, just as its non-existence before *Ijmā'* does not entail the non-existence of the Shariah.

A. Really speaking, all the rules of law are legally established before *Ijtihād* (individual interpretation), some on the basis of the texts, and others by their import, spirit, and underlying meaning. Those which are latent are only discovered, and not established, by the process of *Ijtihād*. Analogy only reveals a rule of law and does not establish it. If this is the case, all rules will be supposed to fall within the texts which cause the survival of the *Shari'ah*. Discontinuance of a part of it would surely go against the text. The contention that the discontinuance of a part does not entail the discontinuance of the whole is absurd. The *Shari'ah* embraces the overall teaching of the Prophet, and the 'whole' (i.e. *Shari'ah*) is nullified by the elimination of its part (i.e. a rule of law). The laws of the previously revealed religions were abrogated by this *Shari'ah* (law of Islam). But this abrogation is nothing more than a partial abrogation of their laws. Hence *Ijmā'* of necessity is a decisive source.[62]

The legitimacy of *Ijmā'* has been challenged on the basis of reason too. The critics object that if people are apt to fall into error individually, how is it possible that the community which is

[62] 'Abd al-'Azīz al-Bukhārī, *Kashfal-Asrar*. Istanbul, 1307 A.H., III, 980-81.

composed of individuals is immune from error? This amounts to saying that suppose the individuals are black, but the body composed of them is not black. To this, it has been answered that 'individuals' and 'body' two are separate entities. One is not analogous to the other. This can be illustrated by saying that a body of persons can lift a heavy stone, but the same people cannot lift it individually. The illustration of black individuals and black bodies does not apply to *Ijmāʿ*. It is of course in connect to say that the people individually are erroneous, in a decision agreed upon by them, and the whole body is not erroneous. No such statement has been made about *Ijmāʿ*. Instead, it is pretended that the people may be wrong in their individual opinions when given separately; but when an individual opinion is added to the opinion of the whole community, that is not erroneous. Individuals should be differentiated from the body. People, for instance, may take a particular food on a certain day individually but it is not possible that they all take the same food on the same day. The opponents' statement is just like saying that everyone of a body is wrong, but the whole body on the same point is not wrong. This corresponds to saying that the 'whole' is not black, but 'everybody' of the whole is black. Actually, this is not the position. *Ijmāʿ* can be illustrated by saying that everybody in a particular city may be black, but when they are transferred to another city, they may not be black but white. What is stressed there is the change of position.[63]

Although orthodoxy put its heart and soul in defending *Ijmāʿ* on traditional and rational grounds, it could not convince the opponents. Even some jurists from among the exponents, like al-Jaṣṣaṣ and Al-Bazdawī, doubted the infallible character of the community on the basis of pure human reason.[64] Al-Qarāft is not

[63] Al-Jaṣṣāṣ *op. cit.*, fo 218a; al-Baṣri, *op. cit.*, II, 278-79.
[64] Al-Jassāṣ, op. cit., fo. 215b; Al-Bazdawī, op. cit., p. 244.

convinced of the rational arguments advanced by al-Juwaynī. He criticizes the latter by saying that the doctrine of *Ijmāʿ* stands on the concept of charisma which is clearly established by a good deal of evidence derived from traditional knowledge. It corresponds to the infallibility of the Prophet.[65] Al-Ghazalī, though he strenuously defends *Ijmāʿ* on traditional, rational and factual grounds, seems to be dissatisfied with these arguments. He has recorded in al-Mankhūl his clear-cut verdict that *Ijmāʿ* can be defended only on customary norms. He remarks:

"There is no hope of justifying *Ijmāʿ* on the basis of reason. Authorities based on revelation such as *Mutawātir* traditions and the textual evidence from the Qur'ān do not support it. Substantiating *Ijmāʿ* by *Ijmāʿ* is incoherence. Speculative analogy has no place in the decisive sources. These are the only essential principles of law. There remains no other principle except customary norms (*Masālik al-'Urf*). We might have acquired this doctrine by means of this source. "[66]

Al-Shatibi is aware of the weakness of justifying *Ijmāʿ* on the basis of traditional or rational norms. He gives no importance to reason in this respect. He suggests a novel method, already hinted at by al-Ghazali before him. He thinks *Ijmāʿ* and similar other doctrines should not be justified on the basis of the Qur'ān, traditions, and *Tawātur* severally. These sources should be taken into consideration collectively as a single whole. Human reason would serve as their instrument. We epitomize his argument presently.

Rational proofs in jurisprudence do not constitute evidence by themselves. They are employed in combination with oral proofs or are instrumental to them. Advancing rational arguments in matters

---

[65] Al-Qarafi, *op. cit.*, p. 142.

[66] Al-Ghazālī, *al-Mankhūl min Ta'liqāt al-Uṣūl*, Damuscus: Maktabah Dār al-Fikr, n.d., p. 306.

requiring legislation from the *Shari'ah* is not correct, because reason is not a legislator. One should depend in respect of such questions on proofs derived from traditional norms. But even there, particularly in solitary traditions, as already learned from common usage, certainty is either totally absent, or at least rare. This is obvious in the case of isolated traditions.... As regards *Tawātur*, it depends on speculative premises. A thing depending on speculation must be speculative. Certainty in *Tawātur* actually comes through diverse factors, i.e. divergent viewpoints on language, grammar, and etymology. If these factors are considered severally, certainty is impossible. The most reliable proofs employed here are those which are determined by exploring the overall possible speculative evidence. Such proofs surely entail certainty because collectivity has a force not possessed of by isolation. Hence *Tawātur* entails certainty. Five daily prayers and *Zakāt* are considered obligatory on the same principle.

Keeping the same norms in view people have relied on *Ijmā'*, because it entails certainty and sets aside factors leading to controversy. Consensus, isolated traditions, and analogy owe their authoritativeness to the same principle. The proofs which justify them have actually been derived from innumerable sources, which, though diverse in approach and subject matter, are identical in 'I'lān and meaning. If there are numerous proofs, which support each other, they all collectively entail certainty.

The sources of law are in fact cohesive and interrelated. Hence, they should be treated as a whole. The early jurists could not explain this point with the result that the later jurists started treating each source of law independently. Arguments from the Qur'ān and the traditions severally generated difficulties in reasoning. In fact, there arises no difficulty if these sources are dealt with cumulatively, constituting a single piece of evidence. If the proofs derived from the *Shari'ah* in support of essentials and minutiae are taken together, then no certainty is possible in any rule of law, except when it is combined with human reason. And human reason overlooks the *Shari'ah*. Hence the necessity of cohesion and co-relationship between the proofs derived from the *Shari'ah*.[67]

In the foregoing, we have noticed that *Ijmāʿ* was defended by its exponents on the basis of traditional as well as rational norms. But the argument is never satisfactory. The classical jurists themselves had misgivings about its justification. The theory of *Ijmāʿ*, as it stands, always remained open to criticism. The reason is, as we pointed out before, that the doctrine came into being as a socio-political necessity. In the long run it developed into a consummate religious doctrine. At this stage, *Ijmāʿ* was theorized and acquired religious sanction. Hence arose, like other similar doctrines, differences in the argument for its justification. One may not be fully satisfied with its justification on purely theoretical grounds, but the part it practically played in the religious sphere cannot be gainsaid.

---

[67] Al-Shatibi, *al-Muwafaqat*, Tunis, 1302 A.H. I, 11-13.

Chapter IV: The Classical Definition of *Ijmāʿ*: The Nature of Consensus

To understand the orthodox theory of *Ijmāʿ*, we must discuss its definition in greater detail. It seems that the question of its formal definition was not raised until the time of al-Shāfiʿī, as it is not traceable in his lengthy discussions about *Ijmāʿ*. In this formative period, al-Shafiʿi recognized the *Ijmāʿ* of the community and almost rejected the *Ijmāʿ* of the scholars. But in the classical period, the matter was reversed. The *Ijmāʿ* of the community was reduced to the *Ijmāʿ* of the scholars.[1] The definition, therefore, started with the question of competence for participation in *Ijmāʿ*. The question of defining a doctrine generally comes in the last after it is fully developed. It appears that the doctrine of *Ijmāʿ* was formally defined in the last decades of the fourth century of the Hijrah. Abū Bakr al-Jaṣṣaṣ (d. 370 A.H.) does not give its formal definition. He repeats the same kinds of *Ijmāʿ* as shown by al-Shafiʿī, namely *Ijmāʿ* of the community and *Ijmāʿ* of the scholars. But he terms them *Ijmāʿ ʾal Tawqīf* (consensus by acquaintance) and *Ijmāʿ ʾal istikhrāj* (consensus by inference).[2] One can, however, find the definition in the works of jurisprudence produced towards the end of the fourth century A.H. It is difficult to give precise reasons for not defining this principle for such a long time. As we said before, the question of definition generally arises after the full development of a doctrine. Further, *Ijmāʿ* was identified in the early centuries of Islam with the *Ijmāʿ* of the community at large, and the *Ijmāʿ* of the scholars remained all along a disputed question. But with the fragmentation of leadership in Islam into political and religious fields, the scholars prevailed

---

[1] Al-Shāfiʿī, *Kitāb al-Umm*, (Cairo: al-Matbaʿah al-Amiriyah, Bolaq, 1325 A.H.), VII, 257.

[2] Abū Bakr al-Jaṣṣaṣ, *Kitāb ʾUṣūl al-Fiqh*, MS. Dār al-Kutub al-Miṣriyyah, No. 229-ʾUṣūl, fos. 219b, 220a.

over the religious domain. By this bifurcation of authority, the *Ijmāʿ* of the community was relegated to the background. Henceforth, the *Ijmāʿ* of the scholars dominated the legal sphere, particularly on moot questions, and *Ijmāʿ* of the community was restricted to essentials alone. The word 'Ummah' occurring in the traditions was interpreted in the classical period, inter alia, as the scholars of the community. Hence, *Ijmāʿ* was finally defined as *Ijmāʿ* of the scholars (i.e. the jurists).

We may now discuss the definition of *Ijmāʿ* as enunciated by the classical jurists and the relevant problems. Abu'l Husayn al-Baṣri(d. 436 A.H.) defines it as agreement of a group (*Jamāʿah*) on a certain matter by action or by abandonment.[3] This was later qualified by the condition of *Ijtihād* (independent legal interpretation) and time.[4] Al-Ghazali gives it as agreement of the community of Muhammad (peace be upon him) on a religious point.[5] Definitions, such as pronounced by al-Ghazali, which stipulate the agreement of the whole Muslim community beginning from the rise of Islam till the day of judgement have been severely criticized by the jurists. This is because such an *Ijmāʿ* according to them is not practically possible[6]. Summing up all the definitions given by the jurists in different ages Al-Āmidī has recorded the following definition of *Ijmāʿ*.

---

[3] Abūl-Ḥusayn al-Baṣrī, *Kitāb al-Muʿtamad*, (Damascus: Institute Francais de Damas, 1964), I. 457.

[4] Al-Sarakhsi, *Uṣūl al-Sarakhsī*, (Cairo: Lajnah Ibya' *al-Maʿārif al-Nuʿmāniyyah*, 1372 A.H.), 1, 311.

[5] Al-Ghazālī, *Al-Mustaṣfā*, (Cairo: Al-Maktabah al-Tijārīyah al-Kubrā, 1937), I, 110.

[6] Al-Āmidī, *Al-Iḥkām fī Uṣūl al-Aḥkām*, (Cairo: Maṭbaʿah al-Maʿārif, 1914), I, 281; ʿAbd al-ʿAzīz al-Bukhārī, *Kashf al-Asrār* (Instanbul: Maktabat al-Ṣanāʾiʿ, 1307 A.H.) III, 947; al-Iji, *Sharḥ Mukhtaṣar al-Muntahā*, (Istanbul: Ḥasan Ḥilmī al-Kutubī), I, 123; al-Insawi, *Nihāyat al-Sūl*, (Cairo: Mahmud Tawfīq Kutubi, n.d.), II, 23.

"Agreement of all the people of binding and loosing who belong to the community of Muhammad (peace be upon him), in a certain period of time, on a rule about a certain incidence".

This definition applies in case the masses are excluded from *Ijmāʿ*. But if they are included, the definition would be:

'Agreement of all those who are legally responsible and belong to the community of Muhammad (peace be upon him) in a certain age, on a rule about a certain incidence.'

The definition has five component parts, namely agreement; people of binding and loosing; membership of the Prophet's community; period of time; and moot questions. The word agreement includes consensus by silence. The term 'people of binding and loosing indicates unanimous agreement of the jurists including agreement of the masses. The condition of the 'membership of the Muslim community' implies the exclusion of those who belong to other communities. The phrase 'in a certain period' means the existing community excluding the past and the future members of the community. And finally, the phrase 'on a rule about a certain incidence' includes positive and negative aspects of consensus, and rules about rational and legal questions.[7]

The problem of the definition of *Ijmāʿ* is in fact a necessary corollary to the question of the eligibility for *Ijmāʿ*- a problem discussed by the jurists in greater detail at the early stage of its theoretical development. It is worthy of note that *Ijmāʿ* due to the strict qualifications for its competence was restricted to the consensus of the jurists and the consent of the masses was thereby neglected. Further, there seems a clear contradiction between the very concept of *Ijmāʿ* and its formal definition. *Ijmāʿ* stands on the concept of infallibility of the agreement of the whole community a privilege

---

[7] Al-Āmidī, *op. cit.*, I, 280-82.

bestowed by God on the Muslim community according to the traditions of the Prophet. On the contrary, it has been defined as 'the consensus of the scholars' who, though may represent, constitute a part of the community. This sort of antinomy between the notion and definition of *Ijmāʿ* resulted in the rejection of the very doctrine by its opponents. The total agreement of the scholars hardly exists on points of detail. This definition which developed in the classical period, however, seems tendentious.

For the purpose of discussion, we divide this definition into four broad categories:

Agreement, Competence, Period of time, and the Subject-matter *Ijmāʿ* on religious and non-religious matters.

As for the number of scholars required for the validity of *Ijmāʿ*, it should be noted that the classical theory does not elaborate. A group of jurists maintain that the minimum number of scholars required for *Ijmāʿ* is three.[8] Others hold that the number of scholars required for *Ijmāʿ* must reach the proportion of *Tawātur* (an indefinite number of people who cannot possibly agree upon a falsehood because of their huge number and geographical situation). Both of these views are not recognized by the majority of jurists. They contend that if there is no jurist except one in the community in a certain age and he agrees on a certain opinion about a disputed question, his agreement would be considered *Ijmāʿ*.[9] Al-Sarakhsi refutes this point of view by saying that if a body of competent scholars agrees on a certain point by verbal expression and the rest of the scholars keep silent, then *Ijmāʿ* would be reached. The number of *Tawātur* is a necessary condition for the certainty of a report

---

[8] Al-Maḥallāwī, *Tashīl al-Wuṣūl ilā ʿIlm al-Uṣūl*, (Multan: al-Madrasah al-ʿArabiyyah al-Islamiyah, 1961), p. 171.

[9] ʿAbd al-Malik al-Juwaynī, al-Burhan, MS. No. 714-'usal, Dār al-Kutub al-Miṣriyyah, fo. 195.

because it involves the possibility of truth and falsehood. But *Ijmāʿ* involves no such possibility. It already stands on the concept of infallibility of the community.[10]

ʿAbd al-Mālik al-Juwayni qualifies it by *Tawātur* because there remains no possibility of error in an *Ijmāʿ* based on *Tawātur*. If the number of the participants in *Ijmāʿ* is less than that of *Tawātur*, it may be open to error.[11] To this Al-Āmidī answers that it is inconceivable to establish the legitimacy of *Ijmāʿ* on the basis of human reason. There is no way of proving it except by the oral proofs (*Adillah Samʿīyyah*) based on the Qurʾān and, the Sunnah. The terms 'community' and 'believers' would be applied to the participants in *Ijmāʿ*, even if their number falls very short of *Tawātur*. The oral proofs establish their infallibility and hence adherence to their consensus is binding. This argument has again been challenged by the opponents, and Al-Āmidī has replied in detail.[12]

According to the orthodox view, *Ijmāʿ* is the unanimous agreement of the community or of the scholars. If the whole community or competent scholars agree upon a certain point, this would constitute *Ijmāʿ*". But the disagreement of a single competent scholar invalidates *Ijmāʿ*,[13] A group of jurists differ from this point of view, and maintain that the majority opinion of competent scholars constitutes *Ijmāʿ*.[14] We presently discuss both points of view and the arguments of their supporters.

In favour of the orthodox stand, Al-Āmidī argues in a twofold way. In the first place, the traditions of the Prophet which substantiate

---

[10] Al-Sarakhsi, *op. cit.,* 1, 312.
[11] *Op. cit.,* fo. 195.
[12] Al-Āmidī, *op. cit.,* 1, 358-60; ʿAlī ʿAbd al-Rāziq, *Al-Ijmāʿ fil-Sharīʿah al-Islāmīyah* (Cairo, Dår al-Fikr al-ʿArabi, 1947), pp. 72-73.
[13] Al-Bazdawī, *Kanz al-Wuṣūl ilā Maʿrifat al-Uṣūl,* (Karachi: Nūr Muhammad Kårkhana Tijarat Kutub, 1966), pp. 243-44.
[14] Al-Āmidī, *op. cit.,* I, 336; Al-Ghazālī, *op. cit.,* I, 119.

Ijmāʿ speak of the infallibility of the whole community and not of its part. The word *ʾUmmah* applies to the whole as well as to the majority. And the word majority (*Akhtar*) applies to the 'whole' according to certain Arabic idioms. If the word *ʾUmmah*' applies to the 'whole', then the majority would be included in it. As such, *Ijmāʿ* would be certain allowing no leeway for doubt. If it applies to the majority, it would no doubt constitute *Ijmāʿ* but not with certainty. It would remain doubtful. The reason is that the Prophet by the word *ʾUmmah*' might have meant the entire community and not the majority because the majority does not constitute the 'whole'. Secondly, to differ from the majority opinion has been a practice since the time of the Companions. Moreover, the majority opinion was never imposed upon the community, nor had anyone rejected the minority opinion because of their small number. Truth lies neither in the minority nor in the majority. Both these opinions were tolerated in different cases on the basis of reasoning. For instance, majority of the Companions differed from Abū Bakr's stand to fight with the tribes who refused to pay *Zakāt*. Similarly, the majority had not accepted the opinion of Ibn ʾAbbas about *ʾawl* (increase) case, *Mutʿah* (temporary marriage) and *ribā al-fadl* (interest by excess). It so happened also in a number of cases where Ibn Masʾūd and Zayd b. Arqam rejected the majority opinion. Abū Mūsā al-Ashʾari is said to have held the view that ablution does not become void by sleep. Abū Talhah is reported to have maintained that fast is not nullified by eating hailstone. Had the majority opinion, Al-Āmidī contends, constituted the *Ijmāʿ* of the community, these stray opinions must have been rejected by the community. Indeed, the majority of the Companions criticized such stray opinions by their individual interpretations, but they did not discard them outright. Hence difference of opinion on such points survives until today. Moreover, the minority opinion might sometimes be correct. Abū Bakr's opinion, for instance, to fight with the tribes who refused to pay *Zakāt* prevailed over the community.

In this case, the majority opinion was not accepted.[15] This shows that truth lies in unanimity.

There is also a different line of argument in favour of the orthodox theory of total *Ijmāʿ*. It says that all competent scholars are allowed to interpret law independently. If majority opinion is taken as the *Ijmāʿ* of the community, it presupposes that the rest of the jurists who constitute the minority should follow the opinion of others (i.e. the majority) and set aside their individual opinions. But an individual cannot be forced to conform to the views of others if he has his own point of view on a legal question. Therefore, no *Ijmāʿ* will be valid so long as the minority opinion stands.[16]

Abū Bakr al-Jaṣṣaṣ strongly supports the orthodox theory of total *Ijmāʿ*. He cites the Qurʾānic verses and traditions to show that the majority opinion sometimes can err while the minority is in the right. Correct reasoning, according to him, carries more weight than majority or minority opinion. *Ijmāʿ* stands on correct reasoning. What constitutes *Ijmāʿ* is quality and not quantity. Al-Jaṣṣaṣ also criticizes the arguments adduced by the advocates of majority opinion. They cite the traditions of the Prophet which ask the Muslims to follow the overwhelming majority (*al-Sawād al-Aʿzam*) and to conform to the *Jamāʿah* (i.e. the majority). Answering them he remarks that these traditions point out that Muslims should follow the majority in respect of fundamentals and essentials of the faith and ignore the minority opinion. As regards disputed points, one is free to hold his one's view. If the community agrees on a certain point in respect of the essentials of Islam, and one or two persons differ with the community, the difference of opinion of such a small number is negligible.[17]

---

[15] Al-Āmidī, *op. cit.*, pp. 336-38.
[16] *Ibid.*
[17] Abū Bakr al-Jaṣṣāṣ, *op. cit.*, fos, 228ab.

In support of the orthodox theory of total *Ijmā*ʿ al-Ghazali asserts that infallibility lies in the unanimous agreement of the whole community. If by *Ijmā*ʿ, he contends, is meant the consensus of the majority, it is, in fact. no *Ijmā*ʿ at all. It is really a disagreement on a certain question. In such disputed cases one should refer to the Qurʾān and the Sunnah. One might ask whether by the word ʾ*Ummah*' is meant majority opinion, as a number of Arabic idioms indicate. To this, he replies that those who believe in the generality of meaning take it to mean the whole and not a part of it. Differentiation is not allowed without an evidence and necessity. But those who do not believe in the generality of meaning may construe it as majority opinion. As such, one cannot distinguish between those to whom the word applies and those to whom it does not. This shows that the word ʾ*Ummah*' is taken in the comprehensive sense. Further, it should be noted that the majority is not necessarily in the right. A number of the Qurʾānic verses and traditions indicate that the followers of truth would always remain in minority. Hence there is no alternative but to recognize unanimity for the legitimacy of *Ijmā*ʿ.

One might argue that the *Ijmā*ʿ of the Companions is considered valid even it is opposed by some of them, as Ibn ʿAbbās differed from them on the ʿ*Awl* case. The answer would be that the Companions rejected the opinion of Ibn ʿAbbas on cases such as ʿ*Awl* (increase), Mutʿah (temporary marriage), and *Ribā al-Nasīʾah* (interest on loan). ʿAʾishah rejected the opinion of Ibn Arqam on ʾ*Inah* (double transaction). The opinion of Abū Mūsā al-Ashʿarī that ablution is not nullified by sleep and the opinion of Abū Talhah that fasting does not become void by eating hailstone were rejected. One should not think that the Companions rejected these views because they were isolated opinions. In fact, they contradicted the obvious evidence established on the basis of the Qurʾān and the Sunnah. Suppose their opinions were rejected because of their isolation, but these solitary dissenters also rejected the opinions of the Companions. Hence,

Ijmāʿ could not be reached on these questions because the opinion was divided.

According to al-Ghazali, a conformist (*muqallid*) may follow the majority opinion if there is no other determining factor to adopt an opinion on a moot question. He does not allow an expert in law to follow any opinion except the original evidence.[18]

We may now discuss the question of the validity of *Ijmāʿ* by majority opinion. We summarize presently the arguments advanced by the opponents in favour of the majority opinions. Literally, the word *ʾUmmah* (community) occurring in the tradition of *Ijmāʿ* applies to the majority of Muslims in every generation and not to the community at large. An Arabic idiom goes: Banū Tamim support their neighbour and respect their guest. Here, Banū Tamim stands for the majority of the members of the tribe and not for all members. Similarly, the word *ʾUmmah* stands for the majority. This interpretation is corroborated by a number of traditions, e.g. 'adhere to the overwhelming majority, 'adhere to the community', 'avoid separation, and 'Satan sticks to a single person, but from two he keeps away'. In these traditions the word '*Jamāʿah*' means majority. Secondly, the caliphate of Abū Bakr is grounded in *Ijmāʿ*. It is a historical fact that Abū Bakr was elected by the majority of the Muslims, and not by all and sundry. ʿAlī and Saʿd b. Ubādah dissented from his consensus. If the majority opinion is not taken into consideration for the validity of *Ijmāʿ*, the caliphate of Abū Bakr remains questionable. Thirdly, according to the principles of *Ḥadīth*, reports based on *Tawātur* carry more weight than isolated reports. The same rule applies to *Ijtihād* and *Ijmāʿ*. Fourthly if the dissent of one or two persons prevents the establishment of *Ijmāʿ*, then *Ijmāʿ* will never be reached. This is because total agreement is reached very rarely. In every case of consensus there always remains

---

[18] Al-Ghazālī *op. cit.*, I, 117-18.

opposing minority. Fifthly, *Ijmāʿ* is binding on both the present and future generations. From this, it follows that there must be an opposing minority on whom the *Ijmāʿ* will be binding. Finally, Ibn ʿAbbās is reported to have differed with the Companions on questions of *Ribā* (interest), temporary marriage, and increase (*ʾawl*) in the law of succession. If *Ijmāʿ* is not valid by majority opinion, there will be no *Ijmāʿ* on these questions.

Al-Āmidī refutes all these arguments. He holds that, first, the word ʾUmmah must apply to "the whole" so that it may constitute positive evidence. The tradition 'follow the overwhelming majority' should be construed as "all the people of a generation". Second, the validity of the caliphate is not based on *Ijmāʿ*; it is not correct to contend that unanimous *Ijmāʿ* was not reached on the caliphate of Abū Bakr. Two persons can adequately legitimize allegiance.

Third, the majority can be relied on in the case of traditions and it may entail certain knowledge. But this does not apply to the *Ijmāʿ* reached on a point by exercising *Ijtihād*. What constitutes the authority of *Ijmāʿ* is the total agreement of the community; the majority does not stand for the whole.

Fourth, the argument on the basis of *Ijmāʿ* is valid in case one realizes the unanimous agreement either by verbal expression or by situational context. And this is possible by realizing the majority opinion which serves as an indicator to the total agreement.

Fifth, *Ijmāʿ* is an authority over those who dissent from the agreement after their consent, and over those coming in the future generations. It is not correct to say that if there is no disagreement, there is no *Ijmāʿ*.

Sixth, the Companions did not reject the opinion of Ibn ʿAbbās on the basis of their agreement, but on the basis of their argument. Ibn ʿAbbās, in fact, opposed some clear traditions.

Concluding, Al-Āmidī remarks that the majority opinion may be recognized in the case of traditions, but not in the case of *Ijtihād*, for it is not known on which side the correct evidence lies. One may possibly ignore it by accepting the majority opinion.[19]

Abū Bakr al-Jaṣṣaṣ (d. 370 A.H.) maintains that if the majority of scholars agree by verbal expression on a certain point, and their agreement is disputed among the community, while the minority is silent, then *Ijmāʿ* is definitely established. He contends that it is not practically possible that all persons individually express their consent. Hence, the silence of one, two or a few persons does not count.[20] It is important to note that al-Jaṣṣāṣ does not clearly give his opinion about the validity of *Ijmāʿ* in case it is expressly opposed by the minority. He repeatedly argues that the *Ijmāʿ* by majority opinion is established in case the minority is silent because people generally keep silent when they agree upon a point, provided there is no obstacle in expressing their viewpoint. From this we conclude that he is validating the tacit *Ijmāʿ* and not the *Ijmāʿ* verbally opposed by the minority. At another place, he vehemently refutes the proposition that majority opinion is always right. He adduces numerous examples from history to show that sometimes majority opinion is erroneous and minority opinion is correct.[21] We, therefore, conclude that al-Jaṣṣaṣ supports the theory of total *Ijmāʿ*.

We summarize below the different views of the jurists about the validity of *Ijmāʿ* by majority opinion:

1. The disagreement of even a single competent scholar invalidates *Ijmāʿ*. This is the orthodox point of view.

---

[19] Al-Āmidī, *op. cit.*, I, 336-44.
[20] Al-Jaṣṣāṣ, *op. cit.*, fos. 226b-227a.
[21] *Ibid.*, fo. 228b.

2. If *Ijmāʿ* is reached on a tradition narrated from the early generations, then majority opinion will be recognized. But if it is reached on a question of *Ijtihād*, then the disagreement of a single scholar will be taken into consideration. The truth may be on the side of a single person.

3. Al-Khayyāt (d. ca 300 A.H.) and al-Tabari (d. 310 A.H.) are reported to have validated *Ijmāʿ* by majority opinion. Al-Tabari stipulates *Tawātur* for *Ijmāʿ*.

4. Abū Muhammad al-Juwayni (d. 438 A.H.) thinks that *Ijmāʿ* is valid by the agreement of the majority and the prominent persons. Unanimity cannot be an essential condition for *Ijmāʿ*, because there might be a certain competent scholar in a remote corner of the world who is not known to others. A person might be well versed in law, but not known to his neighbour. Abū Bakr was elected by the majority of the reliable and responsible persons, and not by all and sundry. Even all the people of Medina did not take the oath of allegiance to him.

5. Al-Ṣafi al-Hindi (d. 715 A.H.?) maintains that the *Ijmāʿ* by majority opinion is speculative and not positive.

6. A group of the jurists holds the view that in principle it is preferable to follow the majority opinion, though one is allowed to dissent from it.

7. *Ijmāʿ* on a certain point is not valid by the opposition of two scholars. It is valid if opposed by one.

8. The opposition of three scholars invalidates *Ijmāʿ* and not of two.

9. If the community allows the exercising of *Ijtihād* on some questions, such as the ʿAwl case opposed by Ibn ʿAbbas, then the disagreement will be considered an *Ijmāʿ*. But in case the community

does not allow *Ijtihād* on questions like essentials, the disagreement will not be taken into consideration.

10. Majority opinion constitutes authority (*hujjah*) and not *Ijmā*ʿ.[22]

The anchoring point in the argument in favour of unanimity is that the truth certainly lies in the whole. If the whole is divided, one cannot know for certain where the truth lies. But is total *Ijmā*ʿ possible in practical life? It appears that *Ijmā*ʿ was taken as the agreement based on majority opinion in pre-Shāfiʿī period. But the concept of unanimous *Ijmā*ʿ prevailed since his time onward, as al-Shāfiʿī vehemently attacks in his polemics the arguments in favour of *Ijmā*ʿ based on majority opinion.[23] The orthodox theory of total *Ijmā*ʿ seems to have been influenced by him.

[22] A hawkāni, *Irshād al-Fuhūl*, (Cairo: Salim b. Saʿd, 1347 A.H.), pp. 78-79; al-Jājäl Al-Maḥallī, *Sharḥ Jam' al-Jawāmi*" (Cairo: Muhammad Tawfīq, 1297 A.H.), II, 157-58.
[23] Al-Shāfiʿī, *Jimaʿ al-ʿIlm*, (Cairo: Maṭbaʿah al-Maʿārif, 1940), pp. 56-67.

Chapter V: Competence for *Ijmā*ʿ

The first and foremost condition for competence for *Ijma*ʾ is Islam. The assent or dissent of a non-Muslim is not taken into consideration in *Ijmā*ʿ. For this Al-Āmidī gives the reason that *Ijmā*ʿ is established on the basis of the Qurʾān and the Sunnah (*Adillah Sam*ʾ*īyyah*) which do not indicate the participation of a disbeliever in *Ijmā*ʿ. They imply infallibility of the agreement of the believers alone. Further, the opinion of a disbeliever is not recognized in Islam. Hence his opinion would not be considered in respect of establishing or rejecting a source of the *Shari*ʿ*ah*, When *Ijmā*ʿ is valid without his opinion, his dissent has no value.[1] If a person has been excluded from the community on account of heresy, his opinion will not be considered in *Ijmā*ʿ. Extremists, like Qadariyyah, Khawārij and Rawāfid, are also not eligible for *Ijmā*ʿ.[2] Al-Ghazali adds that if a person is excommunicated, he will not be eligible for *Ijmā*ʿ, even if he prays facing the qiblah and considers himself a Muslim. In case a person is excommunicated on account of his belief in anthropomorphism (*Tashbīh*), he may be disqualified for *Ijmā*ʿ. But this does not prove the falsity of anthropomorphism[3].

While considering the eligibility for *Ijmā*ʿ people have been classified as follows:-

1. Experts in Law (*Mujtahidūn*);

2. Ambiguous intermediary levels (*Awsāt Mutashābihalı*);

3. Persons not legally responsible (*Al-*ʾ*Awāmm al-Ghayr al-Mukallafīn*).

---

[1] Al-Āmidī, *al-Ihkam fi Uṣūl al-Ahkam*, Cairo: Maṭbaʿah al-Maʿārif, 1914, 1, 321.
[2] Al-Jaṣṣāṣ, *Uṣūl Al-Jaṣṣāṣ*, Ms. fos. 223b-224a; Al-Āmidī, *op. cit.*, I, 327.
[3] Al-Ghazālī, *al-Mustasfā*, Cairo; Matbaʿah Mustafa Muhammad, 1937, I, 116.

The first category comprises persons well versed in the interpretation of law. They are generally called *Mujtahidūn* (specialists in law), sometimes *Ahl al-Ra'y wal-Ijtihād* (people of opinion and legal interpretation), *'Ulamā' al-'Ummah* (scholars of the community), *Faqīh* (lawyer) and finally *Ahl al-Ḥall wal-'Aqd* (people of loosing and binding).[4] The second category contains the legally responsible masses (*Al-Wāmm al-Mukallafūn*), a lawyer (*Faqīh*) who is not a specialist in the science of jurisprudence (*Uṣuli*), an specialist in the science of jurisprudence (*Uṣūli*) who is not a lawyer (*Faqīh*), a morally corrupt expert in law (*Mujtahid Fāsiq*), heretic (*Mubtadi'*), a Successor qualified for exercising *Ijtihād* in the generation of the Companions. Under the last category fall children, lunatics and embryos. These are not competent to participate in *Ijmā'*, as they were not intended by the Prophet in his statement "my community will not agree on an error" for want of understanding.[5]

We may now deal with the first two classes severally. A *Mujtahid*, broadly speaking, means a scholar who can interpret the law authoritatively. *Ijtihād* has been defined as spending one's best effort in the pursuit of knowledge about the rules of the *Shari'ah*. It should be noted that every prescript of the *Shari'ah* is not liable to *Ijtihād*.

Any precept of the *Shari'ah* (*Ḥukm Shar'ī*) which has no definite evidence (*Dalīl Qaṭ'ī*) is liable to *Ijtihād* (individual interpretation). A *Mujtahid*, according to al-Ghazāli, should be fully acquainted with the Qur'ān, Sunnah, *Ijmā'* and *Qiyās*. He should also be familiar with the two kinds of sciences, namely preliminary (*Muqaddamān*) and complementary (*Mutammimān*), in order to derive rules from the original sources. The former includes the knowledge of making

---

[4] Al-Bazdawī, *Uṣūl al-Bazdawī*, Karachi, 1966, p. 243; Al-Maḥallī, *Sharḥ Jam' al-Jawāmi"*, Cairo, 1346 A.H., IV, 129; Al-Ghazālī, *op. cit.*, I, 115.
[5] Al-Ghazālī, *op. cit.*, I, 115.

an argument and its conditions. This requires a thorough knowledge of the original sources of the law, and the knowledge of lexicography and grammar to understand the speech of the Arabs. The latter consists of the knowledge of the abrogating and the abrogated verses of the Qur'ān and traditions, and acquaintance with the science of traditions, so as to distinguish between sound and false reports. The knowledge of these eight sciences, especially of traditions, lexicography, and jurisprudence is the basic requirement for the qualification of a *Mujtahid*. The knowledge of theology (Kalam) is not necessary for being a *Mujtahid* because of the Companions and the Successors were not familiar with this science.[6]

A person may fall, according to the classical jurists, either under the category of *Mujtahid* (specialist in law) or of *muqallid* (conformist). There is no other category between the two. Therefore, scholars other than specialists in law would fall under the category of *muqallid*, i.e. the masses (*'Awāmm*). Grammarians, exegetes, traditionists, and theologians are not eligible for *Ijmā'*, because they are not well-equipped to understand the rules of law. It is disputed whether a lawyer who memorizes a large number of subsidiary cases (*Furū'*) falls under the category of *Mujtahid* or not. But a *Uṣūli* (specialist in the principles of law) who is neither acquainted with points of detail or does he memorize them, is not a *Mujtahid*. The correct view is that an *Uṣūli* (expert in the science of jurisprudence) who is familiar with the original sources, their meaning in letter and spirit, the expression of injunctions, and their ratio deserves more to be a *Mujtahid* than a lawyer who only memorizes a number of subsidiary questions. The reason is that such a type of *Uṣūli* has the full ability to understand the rules of law as and when he desires, though he does not learn points of detail by heart; while a lawyer

[6] *Ibid.*, II, 101-105.

who only memorizes points of detail possesses no such capacity. Most of the Companions who participated in *Shūrā*, it is argued, did not memorize points of detail but were well acquainted with the Qur'ān and the Sunnah. The science of subsidiary questions did not come into being in their day.[7]

Uprightness or reliability (*'Adālah*) is another quality for being a *Mujtahid*. Explaining this condition al-Ghazali says that the condition of uprightness or reliability is necessary for the acceptance of the legal opinion of a *Mujtahid*, not for the validity of his *Ijtihād*. The opinion of a corrupt *Mujtahid*, he argues, may not be acceptable to the people.[8] Opinion, is however, divided on the question of accepting the judgement of an innovator (*Mubradi'*) *Mujtahid* in *Ijmā'*:

1. It will be taken into consideration. This view is held by the jurists in general.

2. It will not be considered. This is held by *Ahl al*-Sunnah, Mālik, Al-Awzā'ī, Al-Shaybānī, the traditionsists, Abū Bakr al-Rāzī from the Hanfis, and Al-Qāḍī Abū Ya'lā from the Hanbalis.

3. *Ijmā'* is not reached on his opinion, but on the opinion of the one who is not an innovator. He may oppose the *Ijmā'* reached on the opinion of others. But others are not allowed to follow him.

4. His opinion will be accepted if he does not call others to innovation. In case he does so, his opinion will be ignored. This is maintained by al-Sarakhsi.[9]

Al-Juwayni expresses the opinion that the views of a heretic *Mujtahid* would be ignored if he is excommunicated. But if he is

---

[7] *Ibid.*, I, 115-16.

[8] *Ibid.*, II, 101.

[9] Muhammad Siddiq Hasan Khan, *Huṣūl al-Ma'mūl min 'Ilm al-Uṣūl*, Istanbul, 1296 A.H., p. 72; al-Sarakhsi, *Uṣūl al-Sarakksi*, Cairo, 1954, 1, 311-12.

moderate in his views, his opinion will be considered. In support of his viewpoint, he quotes al-Shāfiʿī who is reported to have accepted the evidence of heretics and not regarded them as morally corrupt.[10]

Al-Jaṣṣaṣ observes that the opinion of a heretic will not be considered in *Ijmāʿ*. He contends that *Ijmāʿ* is a privilege of the community bestowed by God by virtue of its merits, viz. excellence, moderation, and competence for bearing witness. Hence heretics, such as Khawārij, are not included in the community and their opinion does not count.[11]

Al-Āmidī states that the preferable opinion about this question is that *Ijmāʿ* is not valid without the opinion of a heretic *Mujtahid*, because he is one of the participants in *Ijmāʿ* (*Ahl al-hall wal-ʾaqd*). He is included in the community whose total agreement has been declared as infallible. At most he may be impious; but his impiety does not affect his eligibility for exercising *Ijtihād*.[12]

As regards the opinion of an impious *Mujtahid*, al-Saraskhi maintains that if he keeps his impiety secret, i.e. he does not behave immorally in public, his opinion shall be considered in *Ijmāʿ*. But if his depravity is exposed, his opinion shall be rejected. He contends that if an impious Muslim dies, it is generally believed about him that he would not rest eternally in hell. If he can have the privilege of entering the paradise in the next world, he must have this right in this world, too. Hence his opinion shall be considered in *Ijmāʿ*.[13] In support of this view, al-Juwayni argues that an impious *Mujtahid* is not bound to agree with the views of others. If *Ijmāʿ* is reached ignoring his opinions, such an *Ijmāʿ* shall be imperfect. Further, an impious *Mujtahid* is a scholar whose opinion cannot be called

---

[10] Al-Juwayni, *al-Burhan*, fo. 195.
[11] Al-Jaṣṣāṣ, *op. cit.*, fos. 223b-224a.
[12] Al-Āmidī, *op. cit.*, I, 326-27.
[13] Al-Sarakhsi, *op. cit.*, 1, 312.

definitely right or wrong. He is like an absentee from the assembly of jurists who has the right of vote in the assembly. If the impious jurist repents of his moral laxity, he again becomes eligible for giving his opinion in person, just like an absentee who returns to the assembly.[14] These are a few important qualifications of a jurist competent for *Ijmāʿ*. But this is all in theory. What is generally held after the closing of the door of *Ijtihād* is that *Ijmāʿ* is valid on the opinion of the founders of legal schools, such as Abū Hanifah, Mālik, and al-Shāfiʿī and of those who were able to give their individual judgment on a legal issue from the Companions and the Successors.[15]

The competence of the masses and laymen for *Ijmāʿ* is another vexed question. According to al-Bazdawī, this depends on the nature of questions on which *Ijmāʿ* is reached. The ability of *Ijtihād* is not a necessary condition required for all sorts of problems. The agreement of the masses (*ʾammat al-Muslimin*) is necessary alongside of the jurists in questions relating to the fundamentals of religion (*Uṣūl al-Dīn al-Mumahhadah*), such as transmission of the Qurʾān, and essentials of Islam (*ummahāt al-Sharāʾiʾ*). As regards questions requiring individual opinion and analogical inference (*Al-Raʾy wal-Istinbāṭ*), and similar other issues, only people of opinion and those who are able to interpret authoritatively are competent for *Ijmāʿ*. Apart from the masses, even the scholars who are devoid of this quality are not eligible.[16]

Al-Ghazali observes that the *Shariʾah* is divided into questions understood both by the masses (*ʾAwāmm*) and by the scholars (*Khawāṣṣ*), such as five daily prayers, obligatory fasting, *Zakāt* and Hajj pilgrimage and questions understood only by the scholars, such

---

[14] Al-Juwayni, *op. cit.*, fos. 194-95.
[15] Al-Ghazālī, *op. cit.*, I, 115-16.
[16] Al-Bazdawī, *op. cit.*, p. 243.

as detailed rules of prayer and sale, etc. In the former case, *Ijmāʿ* is reached by the agreement both of the scholars and of the masses in harmony with each other. In the latter case, the masses agree that the truth lies in the agreed opinion of the scholars (the people of losing and binding). The scholars do not conceal their disagreement at all. In this way, the masses agree in congruity with the scholars on questions of technical nature. Hence the *Ijmāʿ* of the scholars is called the *Ijmāʿ* of the whole community.

Al-Ghazali then describes a few misgivings about this problem, and answers them.

Q. If a layman dissents from the agreement of the scholars on a certain question, will *Ijmāʿ* be valid without his consent? If so, how is a layman excluded from the community? If not, how is the opinion of a layman taken into consideration in respect of *Ijmāʿ*"?

A. There is a divergence of opinion on this point. A group of scholars holds that *Ijmāʿ* will not be valid because a layman is a member of the community cumulatively or severally (*bil-Jumlah aw bil-Tafṣīl*). Others mention, and that is the correct opinion, that such an *Ijmāʿ* is valid for two reasons. First, a layman is not competent for searching for the truth. He is like a child or a lunatic in respect of the absence of the requisite qualities. In fact, the infallibility of the community means the infallibility of a person of whom it can be conceived that he has the capacity of attaining the truth. Secondly, and more potently, the Companions, in the first generation, agreed that the opinion of a layman would not be considered in *Ijmāʿ*. This is because when a layman gives his opinion on a legal question, he consciously does so by his ignorance. Actually, he himself does not know what he says, and realizes that he is ineligible for assenting to or dissenting from the consensus of the scholars. But this cannot be conceived of a witty layman; he leaves the questions not known to him for one who knows. By dissenting from the consensus of the scholars a layman commits a sin. The masses are required to consult the scholars, and not to give their opinion on legal questions by ignorance.[17]

Ab'ul-Husayn al-Baṣri also thinks the agreement of the masses along with the scholars is necessary on questions spread out (*Muntaṣir*) among the masses and the scholars. As for questions which require *Ijtihād*, there is a difference of opinion about them. One point of view says that the consent of the masses is necessary for the validity of the agreement of the scholars, for it is an authority over the following generation, provided the scholars are followed by the masses in their generation. If they are not followed by the masses of their period, their agreement will not be binding on the scholars of the following generation. The *Ijmā'* of the scholars binding on the following generation is conditioned by the consent of the masses. What is infallible is the agreement of the whole community. It requires the consent both of the masses and the scholars. The privilege was granted to the community at large according to verses 4:115, 3:110, and 2:143. Another opinion says that the agreement of the scholars is an authority over the following generation, whether the masses of their generation follow them or not. The contention goes that the masses are duty-bound to follow the opinion of the scholars which circulates among them. Hence the assent or dissent of the masses is negligible.[18]

Some jurists maintain that the opinion of the masses is not worth consideration in *Ijmā'*. They contend that in the sphere of sciences, the opinion of the scholars of a particular science in a certain generation is considered in respect of that science, and not that of the scholars of other sciences. Further, the masses are not acquainted with the evidence, and an opinion not supported by any

---

[17] Al-Ghazālī, *op. cit.*, I, 115.
[18] Abul Husayn al-Baṣri, *Kitāb al-Mu'tamod*, Damuscus, 1964, II, 481-82.

evidence is erroneous.[19] The jurists, however, agree that if only the masses agree upon a certain point exclusively, having no opinion of the scholars, such a type of *Ijmāʿ* shall not be valid.[20] What is disputed is whether the consent of the masses is a necessary condition for the validity of *Ijmāʿ* reached by the agreement of the scholars alone.

Al-Āmidī states that the assent or dissent of the masses is negligible according to the majority, though the minority takes it into consideration. Al-Baqillānī supports the minority view. Al-Āmidī describes it as the preferable opinion. He thinks this is, however, a question open to *Ijtihād*. In case the *Ijmāʿ* carries the consent of the masses, the decision made on the basis of such an *Ijmāʿ* will be definite (*Qaṭʾī*); if it does not have the consent of the masses, the decision then will be probable (*zanni*). Those who include the masses in *Ijmāʿ* mean by it a lawyer who learns minutiae by heart (*al-Faqīh al-hafiz li ahkam al-Furūʾ*), though he may not be an expert in jurisprudence (*Uṣūlī*). An expert in jurisprudence (*Uṣūli*) who is not a lawyer is included among the participants in *Ijmāʿ* according to those who include a lawyer among them. This is because a lawyer who is not an expert in jurisprudence, and an expert in jurisprudence who is not a lawyer, are more capable and have more legal acumen than an ordinary man.

Those who do not include the masses among the participants in *Ijmāʿ* differ on including a lawyer and expert in jurisprudence. Some consider them competent and others not. Those who consider them eligible look at the ability not generally found in the masses. Those who do not consider them eligible look at the ability of *Ijtihād* found in the eponyms of the four established schools of law, such as Abū

---

[19] Al-Isnawi, *Nihayat al-Sal fi Shark Minhaj al-Usūl*, Cairo: Maṭbaʿah Tawfīq al-Adabiyyah, n.d. I, 259.
[20] Al-Maḥallī, *op. cit.*, II, 156-57.

Hanifah, al-Shāfiʿī, and others, not generally found in ordinary lawyers and experts in jurisprudence.[21]

Al-Āmidī thinks the consent of the masses is essential for the validity of *Ijmāʿ*. The opponents raise certain objections to which he replies:

Q. It is binding on a layman to follow the opinion of the scholars based on *Ijmāʿ*. His dissent is negligible in questions in which he is required to conform to the opinion of the scholars. How can his opinion be worth consideration in *Ijmāʿ*?

A. It is true that a layman should follow the opinions of the scholars in legal matters. But this does not indicate that the opinions of the scholars alone, excluding the opinion of a layman, are a decisive authority over the jurists of the following generation. This is because it may be possible that the authority of their opinion over the scholars of the next generation may be conditioned by the consent of the masses, though the legal opinions of the masses themselves may not be binding on them.

Q. The opinion of the community is an authority on condition that it is supported by some positive evidence proved by reasoning. But a layman has no capacity to think and reason. Hence his opinion should be negligible like that of a child or a lunatic.

A. Reasoning is no doubt necessary for *Ijmāʿ*. But by whom: by a person capable of reasoning or by all persons in general? In the former case, it is admittedly essential; but in the latter case, it is not. The assent of the masses to the *Ijmāʿ* of the arguing scholars may be a condition for its validity, though a layman may not argue himself. The agreement of children and lunatics is not identical with that of the masses. The difference lies in the degree of understanding. It

---

[21] Al-Āmidī, *op. cit.*, I, 322, 325.

restrains children and lunatics from legal responsibility but obligates it to the masses. The analogy of the former cannot be extended to the latter.

Q. The opinion of a layman on a religious question without evidence is definitely erroneous. The agreement or disagreement of such a person carries no weight.

A: It is true that his opinion on a religious point is erroneous. But his agreement may possibly be a condition for the opinion of the scholars to constitute an authority over others.

Q. In the early generation of the Companions, the scholars, and the masses agreed that the assent and the dissent of a layman was negligible.

A. This is merely a conjecture with no proof.

Q. The infallibility of the community is established by means of argumentation for which a layman is not competent. How is then infallibility established in his case?

A. He may not be competent for *Ijtihād*. But his agreement without his argumentation may be a necessary condition for the authority of *Ijmāʿ*.

Q. One cannot conceive of a layman attaining the truth, especially when he gives his opinion without any evidence. His judgment is fallible because infallibility presupposes attaining the truth.

A. A layman may not attain the truth when he gives the opinion in his individual capacity. But what does prevent him from attaining the truth when he agrees with the scholars? Hence one is right to impose the condition of his agreement for the authority of *Ijmāʿ*.[22]

---

[22] *Ibid.*

So far, we discussed the question of the validity of Ijmāʿ of the masses in case the experts in law (*Mujtahidūn*) exist among the people. Now the question remains whether the *Ijmāʿ* of the masses is valid in case no expert in law survives. There is again a difference of opinion on this point. It is valid according to those who take into consideration the *Ijmāʿ* of the masses along with that of the scholars. It is invalid according to those who neglect their opinion in the *Ijmāʿ* of the scholars.[23]

The question still remains whether there can be a generation which has no expert in law (*Mujtahid*). According to some, it is not possible that in any period of time, there exists no *Mujtahid* of independent mind, standing on the evidence from God, and explaining the revelation to the people. The idea of the continuous survival of a *Mujtahid* is supported by a number of traditions. This view is held by the Hanbalis. Others think, as reported by al-Zarkashi from the majority, a generation may remain without a *Mujtahid*. Al-Rāzī, al-Rafiʿi, and al-Ghazālī are said to have held this opinion. Ibn Daqiq al-Idholds the former opinion and calls it the preferable one. Siddiq Hasan Khan also supports him arguing that after compilation of the religious sciences, the later generations are in a better position to exercise *Ijtihād* than their predecessors. Hence there is no question of the non-existence of a *Mujtahid* during any period of time.[24]

---

[23] Al-Sawkani, *Irshad al-Fuhul*, Cairo, 1347 A.H., p. 78.

[24] Ṣiddiq Hasan Khan, *op. cit.*, pp. 184-87.

Chapter VI: Period of Time for *Ijmāʿ*

The period of time for *Ijmāʿ* is another important question relating to the definition. It is disputed whether *Ijmāʿ* is confined to a particular generation or it can be reached in every generation. The majority of jurists recognize the validity of *Ijmāʿ* in every generation. A group of scholars oppose this view and maintain that only the agreement of the Companions is valid. The exponents contend that the purpose of *Ijmāʿ* is to protect the teachings of the *Shariʿah* from error. This is based on the idea that the community exists par excellence by virtue of its quality of commanding what is good and forbidding what is evil. This can be done only by those who exist in every generation and not by those who have passed away.[1] Al-Ghazali observes that the authority of *Ijmāʿ* is established on the basis of the Qurʾān, Sunnah, and reason. These three sources do not differentiate one generation from the other. Therefore, the agreement of the Successors will be deemed an *Ijmāʿ* of the whole community. One who opposes them pursues the way other than that of the believers. Custom and usual practice deny that the truth eludes the Successors when they are in great number (in their agreement).[2]

The opponents contend that the Qurʾānic verses and the traditions which substantiate *Ijmāʿ* were addressed to the people who were present at the moment of revelation in the lifetime of the Prophet. Further, the companions constituted the totality of the believers and the totality of the community (*Kull Al-Muʾminia Wa Kull Al-ʾUmmah*). The Successors and the following generations cannot be called the 'totality of the community'. Hence if a Companion gives his opinion on a certain question and the Successors agree on a rule

---

[1] Al-Sarakhsi, *Uṣūl al-Sarakks*, Cairo, 1954, 1, 320.

[2] Al-Ghazālī, *al-Mustasfā*, Cairo, 1937, I 121-122.

about the same question which contradicts the opinion of the Companion, their *Ijmāʿ* will not be valid. If a companion dies, he is not excluded from the community by his death. But his opinion still stands. As the Successors do not constitute the totality of the believers and the bulk of the community, their agreement on any point will not be considered an *Ijmāʿ*. Suppose it is established by the Qurʾānic verses and the traditions that *Ijmāʿ* of every generation is valid, still, that can be doubted on the following grounds:

1. The agreement reached in the later generations must have been based on some evidence. If this evidence was derived from the clear text of the Qurʾān or *Ḥadīth*, it must have been known to the Companions. There seems no reason why the Companions ignored such a clear ruling. If the evidence is derived from the *Ijmāʿ* on a disputed point, this must be the *Ijmāʿ* of the Companions. If the evidence is derived by analogical reasoning, there must be some original basis for it, too. That basis must be agreed upon by the Companions.

2. The Prophet is reported to have admired the Companions and asked the people to follow them. Further, he also reportedly predicted that falsehood and corruption would prevail in the later generations. Therefore, the agreement of the later generations is not free from error.

3. One can argue on the basis of *Ijmāʿ*, provided one knows the opinion of each and every scholar. And this is true only of the agreement of the Companions, because they are individually known in history, and because they were limited in number and lived in a few towns. Their opinion about a problem can be known more easily than that of the scholars of the later generations.

4. One finds that the agreement of the Companions was reached on a question on which there was no previous agreement, or for which there existed no textual evidence (Naṣṣ). Suppose the agreement of

the Companions on a certain point is not traceable, nor do there exist explicit rulings about that question in the Qur'ān or Sunnah, it means that the Companions regarded that point as disputed. Now if the Successors agree upon the same point declared by the Companions as disputed, it follows that the agreement of the Companions was opposed by the Successors. Again, if one is further allowed to interpret the point in question even after the final agreement of the Successors, the authority of their *Ijmā'* is again shaken. Thus, there is no possibility of reaching an *Ijmā'* on a given point in any generation indefinitely.

5. The past generations of Muslims cannot give their opinion about a given problem and *Ijmā'* is considered incomplete without their opinion. This is because if they had been alive, they would surely have contributed to the solution of the given problem. Now if the Successors arrive at an *Ijmā'* on a certain point, if does not include the opinion of the Companions. How then is the *Ijmā'* of the Successors valid?

6. If the Successors reach an *Ijmā'* on a certain point, and the disagreement of the Companions about that point is not known, the *Ijmā'* is not still final. The reason is that there is always an apprehension that some Companions might have disagreed and that their agreement might not have been reported. Therefore, *Ijmā'* in later generations other than that of the Companions is not in principle feasible.[3]

Al-Āmidī holds that the *Ijmā'* of the scholars in every generation is valid. According to him, this is the preferable opinion. He refutes the arguments of the opponents in detail that we summarize below.

If by *Ijmā'* is meant the agreement of those living at the time of the revelation, it presupposes that *Ijmā'* cannot be reached after the

---

[3] Al-Āmidī, *Al-Iḥkām fī Uṣūl al-Aḥkām*, Cairo, 1914, 1, 328-32.

death of these people because in that case, it would not be the agreement of all those who lived at the time of the revelation. It is also not correct to say that the Successors do not constitute the totality of the believers and the totality of the community. The reason is that according to this theory, the *Ijmāʿ* of the Companions who survived the Prophet cannot be valid, for those who died in the lifetime of the Prophet were included in the totality of the believers and the totality of the community. But the opponents themselves accept the validity of *Ijmāʿ* after the death of the Prophet. This is obviously contradictory. As regards the validity of the agreement of the Successors against the opinion of a Comparison, it should be noted that the question is already disputed among the scholars. The correct opinion may be that if a Companion holds a point of view about a certain question, and the Successors take a decision against it by their consensus, the consensus of the Successors will not be considered the *Ijmāʿ* of the whole community because of the difference of opinion of a Companion. In case they agree on a certain question which was not disputed among the Companions, this would certainly be considered the opinion of all concerned (i.e. general consensus). Similarly, if a Companion gives his opinion and then dies, and the rest of the Companions agree against his opinion on the same question, their *Ijmāʿ* will not be valid. As for their misgivings about the inference of the evidence, the answer would be as follows:

1. The Companions no doubt might have known the evidence, but the incident might not have happened in their day. Hence, they remained non-committal. The Successors, on the other hand, agreed because the incident took place during their generation. They had to search for a solution by all means.

2. The traditional authority which provides sanction to *Ijmāʿ* does not distinguish between one generation and the other.

3. The men of opinion in every generation are well-known and can be recognized easily.

4. If the Companions agreed that a certain question was open to dispute, and it remained disputed among them, the agreement of the Successors on that question would not be valid, for there would be a contradiction between the two agreements. But in case the Companions agreed that a certain point was open to *Ijtihād*, and no *Ijmā*ʿ was reached upon it, whether positively or negatively, then there would be no contradiction if the Successors agree upon any opinion about that question.

5. A living person can give his opinion, but not a deceased. One is not analogous to the other. If a Companion dies, for instance, and he gives no opinion about a question in dispute, the *Ijmā*ʿ of the rest of the Companions shall be valid.

6. The apprehension that the Companion who died might have expressed his opinion but that might not have been reported is far-fetched. Such misgivings are negligible; otherwise, the *Ijmā*ʿ will be impossible.[4]

The *Ijmā*ʿ, according to the orthodox view, is not confined to the generation of the Companions. Nonetheless, their agreement carries much weight in legislation. Since the classical jurists attached supreme importance to their agreement it was sometimes overvalued, as implied from the following statement: "If the eminent Companions differ among themselves on a certain question due to obvious reasons, no one then is allowed to outstrip all the opinions held by them. This is because it is already known that the truth does not lie beyond them (i.e. their opinions).[5] This is an

---

[4] Abid., pp. 332-36.
[5] Al-Jaṣṣās, *Kitāb Uṣūl al-Fiqh*, Ms. Dār al-Kutub al-Miṣriyyah, No. 229-Usūl, fo. 218 b.

exaggeration to the extent that a rule established on the basis of the *Ijmāʿ* of the Companions carries the same value as the rule established on the basis of the Qurʾān and the Sunnah. One who rejects the *Ijmāʿ* of the Companions is supposed to be a disbeliever, just like a person who denies the rule derived from these two sources. It is considered, above all, as decisive as the explicit commandments of the Prophet. Hence its rejection amounts to heresy.[6] Dawūd al-Zahiri, Ibn Hanbal, and Ibn Taymiyah were staunch advocates of this theory. We shall discuss their views in a separate chapter.

Great importance is attached to the *Ijmāʿ* of the first four Caliphs, known as the rightly-guided (*rashidūn*) in history. A group of jurists, like Ibn Hanbal and Abū Khāzim (d. 292 A.H.), are said to have held the view that the *Ijmāʿ* of the first four Caliphs is absolutely binding, and Muslims are not allowed to deviate from it. The opposition of a Companion to their *Ijmāʿ* is not worth consideration. This point of view is justified on the basis of a well-known tradition of the Prophet. It runs: 'Follow my practice (Sunnah) and the practice (Sunnah) of the rightly-guided Caliphs, and stick doggedly to it.[7] It is remarkable that this tradition merely prescribes a qualification and does not define a particular person. This may apply to any caliph who bears the requisite qualification throughout history. Anyhow, the first four Caliphs, being more pious than their followers, have been singled out for strict adherence.

The question of giving a share to the uterine kindred (*dhawuʾl-arhām*) is disputed among the jurists on the basis of the *Ijmāʿ* of the first four Caliphs. The Companions of the Prophet differed on this point. ʿAlī, Ibn Masʿūd, Ibn ʿAbbas, Muʿadh b. Jabal, Abuʾl-Darda, and Abū ʿUbaydah are said to have allowed the uterine kindred to get

---

[6] Al-Sarakhsi, *op. cit.*, I, 318.
[7] Al-Jaṣṣāṣ *op. cit.*, fos. 226 ab; Al-Āmidī, *op. cit.*, 1, 357.

a share from the property of the deceased. Zayd b. Thabit reportedly differed with them. He holds the opinion that the property should go to the government treasury and not to uterine kindred. Following his legal opinion al-Mu'tadid, the 'Abbasid Caliph, deposited the residue in the treasury. On his inquiry, Abū Khāzim (d.292 A.H.), an eminent jurist of his time, pointed out that the residue of the property should be distributed among the uterine kindred. He contended that the first four Caliphs had agreed upon this point. But the Caliph told him that Abū Bakr and 'Umar were reported to have agreed that the residue should go to the government treasury. Abū Khāzim replied that the report was not correct. The Caliph was convinced and announced that the residue of the property deposited in the treasury should be withdrawn, and distributed among the uterine kindred.[8] But the judge, Yūsuf bin Ya'qūb (d. 297A.H.), is said to have disagreed with him and insisted on following the opinion of Zayd b. Thabit. The Caliph neglected his disagreement.[9]

This shows the significance of the *Ijmā'* of the first four Caliphs. The reason why importance is attached to their agreement seems to be that they conducted the government by mutual consultation.

Another important problem is the agreement of the people of Medina. The majority of the jurists maintain that the agreement of the people of Medina exclusively constitutes no authority over those who reach an agreement against them outside Median. According to Mālik, it is an authority and stands for the *Ijmā'* of the Muslim community. There is a cleavage of opinion among the followers of Mālik. Some hold that by it Mālik meant preference of *Ḥadīth* reported by the Medinese to the reports of others. Others

---

[8] Al-Tabari, *Tarikh al-Rusul Wal-Mulūk*, Leiden, 1964, Vi. 2151; Al-Jaṣṣāṣ, *op. cit.*, fos. 226 ab; al-Sarakhsi *op. cit.*, I, 317; idem, al-Mabsif, Cairo, n.d. XXX, 2.

[9] Ibn Kathir, *al-Bidāyah wal-Nihāyah*, Cairo, n.d. XI, 173.

held the opinion that he intended that their agreement was preferable, though opposition to them was allowed. A third point of view goes that by the agreement of the people of Medina is meant the consensus of the Companions. Al-Āmidī regards the majority opinion as preferable. He argues that the evidence which proves the legitimacy of *Ijmā'* comprehends the Medinese as well as others. If others are ignored in respect of *Ijmā'*, the Medinese alone would not constitute the 'totality of the community', and the 'totality of the believers'. Hence their agreement will be no authority.[10]

We find much controversy over this question in al-Shāfi'īs discussion with his Medinese opponents.[11] According to the early Medinese, the agreement of the people of Medina had superiority over an isolated tradition of the Prophet.[12] The consensus of the people of Medina is justified on the basis of the Prophet's traditions which speak of the merit and superiority of Medina. Rationally it is argued that the Companions of the Prophet who lived in Medina were more familiar with his practice than those who lived away from him outside Medina. Further, the practice prevalent in the day of the Prophet was not changed in the later centuries of Islam. Hence it served as a model for others. These and other similar arguments adduced by the early Medinese and the later Mālikī jurists were challenged by al-Shāfi'ī and other classical jurists.[13]

Al-Āmidī dwells on the arguments adduced in favour of the agreement of the people of Medina and replies to them. The exponents cite a number of traditions of the Prophet which speak of the prominence of Medina. Replying to them, Al-Āmidī remarks that

---

[10] Al-Āmidī, *op. cit.*, I, 349.
[11] Al-Shāfi'ī, *Ikhtilāf al-Ḥadīth*, on the margin of K. *al-Umm*, VII, and his treatise *Ikhtilaf Malik.*
[12] Idem, *al-Risalah*, Cairo, 1321 A.H., p. 73.
[13] Al-Shāfi'ī, *K. al-Umm*, VII, 193, 215, 218, 243, 248; al-Sarakhsi, *Uṣūl al-Sarakhsī*, 1. 314; Ibn Hazm, al-Ihkām *fi* Uṣūl al-Ahkâm, IV, 203, 209, 212.

no doubt these traditions indicate the immunity of Medina from evil. They do not, however, show that those who live outside Medina are not immune from evil, nor do they signify that the agreement of the people of Medina to the exclusion of others is an authority. Rationally, the exponents advance three contentions:

1. Medina is the place of immigration of the Prophet. His grave lies there and the Qur'ān was, revealed to him. It is the seat of Islam and the abode of the Companions. Hence it is impossible that the truth escapes the opinions of its people.

2. The people of Medina personally witnessed the revelation and listened to its interpretation. They knew the Prophet more than others. The truth, therefore, should necessarily be confined to them.

3. The transmission of *Ḥadīth* by the narrators of Medina is preferable to that of others. Hence their agreement became an authority over others.

Al-Āmidī replies:

1. The qualities recounted by the exponents, of course, indicate its merits. But they never negate the merit of other places. Mecca occupies an eminent position by virtue of a number of its qualities. But this does not mean that the agreement of the people of Mecca constitutes an authority over others. No one holds such a point of view. All that counts are the scholarship of the scholars and the qualities of interpretation of the experts in law. Places carry no weight in *Ijmāʿ*.

2. The settlement of the Companions at Medina does not show that the scholars, people of binding and loosing, and authorities were found among them alone. The Companions who lived at Medina also spread out in different towns. All of them were equal in respect of thinking and reasoning. The Prophet is reported to have said, "My Companions are like stars, whomsoever you follow, you will receive

guidance." The Prophet did not distinguish one place from the other because places are not effective in *Ijmāʿ*.

3. The reliability of narrating *Ḥadīth* depends on direct listening, on the context of the reported events in the day of the Prophet, and on his presence. As the people of Medina were more acquainted with and nearer to such reported events, their reports were considered more reliable. But *Ijtihād* is exercised by means of thinking (*Naẓar*) and searching (*bahth*) through examining and reasoning (*bil-qalb wal-istidlal*) about a question.

It does not change by the variation of places and distances. Hence the agreement of the people of Mecca and Medina and that of Kufa and Basra constitute no authority over their opponents.[14]

This question was reconsidered by the scholars of the Māliki school, and they interpreted it in a different way. Abu'l-Walid al-Bāji (d. 474 A.H.), an eminent Māliki jurist, holds the view that the consensus of the people of Medina was considered an authority only in those questions that were based on tradition (*Naql*) and not in those based on reasoning. He illustrates this by giving the examples of a call to prayer, measurement (*Ṣāʾ*) used in Medina, and reciting *tasmiyah* (to begin in the name of God) silently in obligatory prayers. He contends that the consensus of Medina is an authority in these cases because Medina was the home of the Prophet, the seat of the caliphate, and the abode of the Companions.[15]

Al-Shawkānī makes an extensive study of this question. He quotes al-Qādi ʿAbd al-Wahhab (d. 422 A.H.) who interprets the consensus of Medina like al-Bāji, but in a more detailed manner. He divides the *Ijmāʿ* of the people of Medina into two major categories, namely (1)

---

[14] Al-Āmidī, *op. cit.*, I, 349-52.

[15] Abul-Walid al-Baji, *al-Ishārah fī Uṣūl al-Fiqh*, Ms. Escorial, Islamic Research Institute Library No. 130 (Photostate), fo. 127 b.

points based on tradition, and (2) points based on reasoning. He further divides the former into three sub-categories, viz., questions approved by the Prophet verbally, such as measurements (*sāʾ and mudd*), call to prayer, and its timings, or approved by his deed, such as the claim for indemnification for a fault in a slave from the property of a seller (*ʾuhdat al-raqiq*), or approved by him tacitly, as the Prophet levied no *Zakāt* on vegetables in Medina. In such cases, *Ijmāʿ* of the people of Medina is an authority. Any rule based on analogical deduction which contradicts the consensus of Medina will not be taken into consideration. The second category is disputed among the Māliki scholars in a threefold way. First, it is neither an *Ijmāʿ*, nor a determining principle (*murajjih*). Secondly, it is not an *Ijmāʿ* but a determining principle. Thirdly, although it is an authority, the opposing viewpoints would also be recognized because they cannot be called unlawful. The first category of *Ijmāʿ* of the people of Medina is decisive (*Qaṭʾī*) because it is based on tradition reported successively since the time of the Prophet by an overwhelming majority of the people of Medina. It has superiority over isolated traditions and rules based on analogical deduction. As for the second category of *Ijmāʿ* of Medina, a tradition will have superiority over this type of consensus in case one conflicts with the other. The majority of the Māliki scholars hold this view.[16]

Orthodoxy, which believes in the theory of 'total *Ijmāʿ*, refuted the arguments advanced in support of the authority of the *Ijmāʿ* of Mecca and Medina, of Basra and Kufa, and of the first four Caliphs.[17] According to the generally accepted view, *Ijmāʿ* is not confined to any particular generation. It can be held in any generation with the qualification that it should represent the whole community.

---

[16] Al-Shawkāni, *op. cit.*, pp. 72-73.

[17] *Ibid.*, p. 73; *ʿAbd al-Razīq, al-Ijmāʿ fil-Sharīʿah al-Islāmiyyah* Cairo, Dar al-Fikr al-ʿArabi, 1947, pp. 70-71.

Some jurists maintain that *Ijmāʿ* is valid after the death of the Prophet and not in his lifetime. They contend that *Ijmāʿ* cannot be valid during his lifetime without including his opinion. If it is included, there is no need of *Ijmāʿ* because his opinion is an authority by itself. others held the view that it is valid provided that the Prophet agrees with the agreement of the Muslims. In case he does not agree, the *Ijmāʿ* will be void.[18] Generally speaking, the jurists have neglected this problem in their discussion of *Ijmāʿ*. They sometimes impose a condition in the definition of *Ijmāʿ* by adding a phrase 'in a generation after the death of the Prophet'. It seems there was no need of *Ijmāʿ* during the time of the Prophet, as his opinion in itself was an authority.

---

[18] Al-Isnawi, *Nihāyah al-Sūl fī Sharḥ Minhāj al-Wuṣūl*, Cairo: Maṣbaʿah al-Tawfīq al-Adabiyah, n.d., II, 232., Al-Maḥallī, *Sharḥ Jamʿ al-Jawāmi*", Cairo, 1297 A.H., II, 156; ʿAlī, ʿAbd al-Razīq, *op. cit.*, p. 87.

Chapter VII: The Subject Matter of *Ijmāʿ*

The subject matter of *Ijmāʿ* is the last problem relating to its definition. Some jurists define *Ijmāʿ* as "agreement on a religio-legal (short) question"; others define it as "agreement on any point whatsoever (*amr or amr mā*)."[1] This shows that there is a difference of opinion amongst the jurists on the jurisdiction of *Ijmāʿ*. The rules of law (*Ahkām*) have been broadly divided into religious (*Dīniyyah*) and non-religious (*ghayr dintyah*).[2] The religious rules have been sub-divided into *Sharʾiyyah* (legal) and *ghayr Sharʾiyyah* (non-legal). The *Sharʾiyyah* rules have been defined as "what cannot be perceived except by the prescription of the law-giver," or "a prescription of God that depends on *sharʾi*.[3] The *sharʾi* injunctions have been explained by Joseph Schacht as follows:

"Anything connected with the canon law, or anything in keeping with it, or legal is called *Sharʾī*. *Sharʾi* is also used in opposition to *Ḥissī* (purely sensible); the former means the outward perceptible actions, which come under the cognizance of law; the latter, all those in which this is not the case and which, consequently, have no significance in the *Shariʾa* (offer and acceptance are, for example, in concluding a contract, *sharʾia,* in other circumstances *Ḥissī*). According to the orthodox view, the *Shariʾa* is the basis (*Manshaʾ*) for the judgment of actions as good or bad, which accordingly can only come from Allah, while according to the Muʿtazila, it only confirms the verdict of the intelligence which has preceded it."[4]

---

[1] Sadr al-Shariʿah, ʿUbayd Allah b. Masʿud, *al-Tawḍīḥ*, Cairo: Matbaʿah Muhammad ʿAli, 1957, II, 41.
[2] Muhammad Aʿla Thanawi, *Kashshāf Iṣṭilāḥāt al-Funūn*, art. din; Macadonald, B.D. art. din, *Shorter Encyclopaedia of Islam*, Leiden, 1961, p. 78.
[3] Sadr al-Shariʿah, *op. cit.*, I, 12; II, 41.
[4] Schacht, J. art. Sharia, *Shorter Enc. of Islam*, *op. cit.*, pp. 524-25.

The injunctions of the *Shari'ah* fall into *'Amaliyyah* (practical), called *Far'iyyah* (derivative), and *I'tiqādiyyah* (dogmatic), called *aṣliyyah* (fundamental).[5] A non-Shar'ī rule is perceived either by sense or by intelligence, and it is sometimes called d*unyawl* (wordly). Thus, the subject matter of *Ijmā'* is divided and sub-divided into the following categories:

1. Religio-legal (*Shar'ī*);

2. Worldly (*dunyawi or ghayr Shar'ī*);

3. Intellectual (*'Aqlī*);

4. Sensible (*Ḥissī*);

5. Customary (*'Urfī*);

6. Etymological (*Lughawī*).

It is unanimously agreed upon by the classical jurists that all questions relating to the *Shari'ah* are covered by *Ijmā'*. The rest are disputed among them. What lies beyond the scope of *Ijmā'* are those questions whose knowledge precedes the *Ijmā'* itself. The legitimacy of *Ijmā'* depends on such questions, as belief in the unity of God and His attributes, in the prophethood, and in the creation of the universe. These and similar other problems are not covered by *Ijmā'*.

We start with the questions on which *Ijmā'* depends. Discussing this problem Abu'l-Husayn al-Baṣrī remarks that the fact that God is all-wise and all-just cannot be decided by *Ijmā'*. Similarly, that Muhammad (peace be upon him) is a Prophet is not the subject of *Ijmā'*. Rather *Ijmā'* itself is based on the belief that God and His Prophet have approved the authority of *Ijmā'*, and a thing which they approve is all correct. Further, the divinity of God and the

---

[5] Al-Taftāzāni, *Sharḥ 'Aqā'id al-Nasafī*, Cairo, n.d. pp. 7-8; Macdonald, D.B., art. I'tikad, Shorter Enc. of Islam, *op. cit.*, p. 189.

prophethood of Muhammad (peace be upon him) are established by their own qualities and not by *Ijmāʿ*. One should learn in the first instance the original basis on which he seeks to prove a thing before learning the thing being proved.[6]

Al-Shīrāzī thinks questions, such as the creation of the universe, knowledge of its creator, his attributes and the question of prophethood do not fall within the scope of *Ijmāʿ*. This is because they take precedence over the knowledge of the Shart ah. Further, *Ijmāʿ* is a legal authority (Dalīl Sharʿī) established on the basis of oral proofs (*Samʾī*). It is not valid to establish on the basis of *Ijmāʿ* a point whose knowledge takes precedence over the *Ijmāʿ* itself, as the truth of the Qurʾān cannot be proved by the Sunnah because the Qurʾān precedes the Sunnah.[7]

Al-Qarafi's (d. 684 A, H.) treatment of this problem is more logical. He contends that *Ijmāʿ* is a branch of prophecy, and prophecy is a branch of divinity-that God has life, knowledge, will, and power. When God chooses a person, say Zayd, as a prophet, this shows that God has a will, because there is no preferential principle to choose Zayd from among the people except His will. This also proves that God has life which is a prerequisite for knowledge and will. These epithets are pre-conditions for prophecy. It is already established that *Ijmāʿ* depends on prophecy, i.e., authorized by the Prophet, and prophecy rests on these epithets of God, and if these epithets again depend on *Ijmāʿ* and are proved by it, this would entail a vicious circle.[8]

---

[6] Abūl-Ḥusayn al-Baṣrī, *Kitāb al-Muʿtamad*, Damuscus, 1965, II, 493-94.
[7] Abū Ishāq al-Shirazi, *al-Lumaʿ fī Uṣūl al-Fiqh*, Cairo; 1325 A.H., pp. 204-205.
[8] Al-Qarafi, *Sharh Tangth al-Fusūl*, Cairo: Al-Maṭbaʿah al-Khayriyyah, 1306 A.H., p. 149; al-Isnawi, *Nihayah al-Sūl*, Cairo, n.d., II, 245.

But al-Qarafī, unlike[9] others, includes the question of the creation of the universe (*Ḥudūth al-ʾĀlam*) in the subject matter of *Ijmāʿ*. He maintains that *Ijmāʿ* does not depend on the creation of the universe except in a far-fetched way. By accepting the theory of eternity of the universe the divine will is negated, for what is eternal cannot be willed. Moreover, it is inconceivable of a voluntary agent to will a creation which he cannot destroy. Suppose had God not created the universe, even then He could have sent a prophet because He had a will. But one might object that for sending a prophet there should exist a person whom He sends as a prophet, and the people to whom He sends him. There would be nothing in case there is no universe. To this he answers that these are external preventives (*Māniʾ Khārijī*); they cannot prevent the will of God substantially from sending a prophet.[10]

Questions strictly related to the *Shariʾah* such as rituals, social transactions, civil and criminal laws, and similar other laws concerning lawful and unlawful, are covered by *Ijmāʿ*.[11] There is a difference of opinion on dogmatics (*Iʾtiqādiyyāt*). The reason is that according to some scholars they are established on the basis of the *Shariʿah*, and according to others they are purely rational questions. The orthodox view is that dogmatics are covered by *Ijmāʿ*.[12] The question of the vision of God is a rational problem according to al-Baṣrī.[13] According to the orthodox view, rational problems are also covered by *Ijmāʿ*.[14]

---

[9] Al-Shirazi, *op. cit.*, p. 205.
[10] Al-Qarāfi, *op. cit.*, p. 49.
[11] Al-Shirāzi, *op. cit.*, p. 204.
[12] Al-Āmidī, *al-Ihkām fi Uṣūl al-Abkam*, Cairo, 1914, I, 406; (al-Shawkānī, *Irshād al-Fuhūl*, Cairo, 1347 A.H., p. 63.
[13] Abūl-Ḥusayn al-Baṣrī, *op. cit.*, II, 494
[14] Al-Āmidī, *op. cit.*, 1, 406.

There is a difference of opinion amongst the classical jurists on the question of whether worldly affairs are covered by *Ijmāʿ*. It seems, however, that *Ijmāʿ* is indifferent to some of them. The theory that scammony is purgative has little to do with *Ijmāʿ*. Rejection of this theory would not amount to heresy. The rejection may be due to ignorance of the effects of medicines. It is immaterial whether people agree on this theory or not.[15]

Questions relating to the equipment of the army, warfare, inhabitation, agriculture, politics, etc. are described as worldly affairs by the jurists. Abd al-Jabbar al-Muʿtazili is said to have held two different opinions on this question: First, *Ijmāʿ* is no authority on such questions as it is not superior to the opinion of the Prophet. His opinion was authoritative in respect of religio-legal affairs (*Ahkām al-Shari'ah*) and not on questions concerning worldly benefits (*Maṣāliḥ al-Dunyā*). He himself used to consult the Companions in matters of war, sometimes following their opinion and sometimes setting it aside. Hence *Ijmāʿ* is no authority on such questions. This point of view is held by a group of scholars, and is said to be the correct opinion. Second, *Ijmāʿ* is an authority on worldly affairs if agreed upon by reliable competent persons (*Ahl al-Ijtihād wal-'Adālah*). This is because that the oral proofs, i.e., the Qur'ān and Sunnah (*Dalā'il Sam'iyyah*) which justify *Ijmāʿ* do not particularize any subject of *Ijmāʿ*. The decision of the Prophet in matters of war was right if he was inspired by the divine revelation. In case it was based on his personal opinion and was erroneous, he did not persist. He was corrected either by the divine revelation or by the suggestion of his Companions. This also applies to the *Ijmāʿ*. If *Ijmāʿ* is once established, there is no possibility of error. The opinion of the Prophet and *Ijmāʿ* are identical in respect of infallibility. This point of view is held by al-Razi, Al-Āmidī, and their

[15] Badr al-Shariʿah, *op. cit.*, II, 41.

followers. This is said to be the soundest and preferable opinion on this question.[16]

Al-Baṣri and al-Shīrāzi do not take *Ijmā*ʿ as an authority on worldly affairs. According to them, the Prophet himself changed his opinion on such questions.[17] Al-Qadi Abd al-Wahhab states that Mālik tends to disallow opposition to the *Ijmā*ʿ reached on war affairs and the rules based on personal opinion. He, however, says that the overall opinion of Māliki jurists is not clear on this question. Mālik's contention may be that generality of religious sanction of *Ijmā*ʿ shows that it is an authority in all areas unconditionally (*mutlaq*). But this is criticized by the opponents who contend that the infallibility of *Ijmā*ʿ is based on oral proofs (which Muslims think from God), while war affairs and rules based on personal opinion Conot belong to this sphere. Hence *Ijmā*ʿ is not an authority on worldly affairs. This is again objected by saying that this amounts to the demolition of a general principle by imposing a condition. *Ijmā*ʿ is an authority applicable to all spheres as is evident from the oral proofs. But by limiting it to a particular area the generality of the principle is eliminated. which is in fact an elimination of the principle itself.[18]

According to the orthodox view, rational questions fall within the jurisdiction of *Ijmā*ʿ.[19] Imam al-Haramayn does not agree with this view. He thinks *Ijmā*ʿ is not applicable to questions relating to reason. This is because, he contends, in rational problems reasoning is based on decisive proofs (*al-Adillah al-Qaṭʿīyah*). When a theory is established by reason, that cannot be refuted by disagreement or confirmed by agreement. Agreement or disagreement is immaterial

---

[16] Al-Āmidī, *op. cit.*, I, 407; ʿAlī ʿAbd al-Razīq, *al-Ijmāʿ fīl-Sharīʿah al-Islāmiyyah*, Cairo, 1947, p. 89.
[17] Abūl-Ḥusayn al-Baṣrī, *op. cit.*, II, 494; al-Shirāzi, *op. cit.*, p. 205.
[18] Al-Qarāfi, *op. cit.*, p. 149.
[19] Al-Āmidī, *op. cit.*, 1, 406-7.

to questions decided by intelligence.[20] Following the same line of argument Ṣadr *Al-Shari'ah* explains that human reason per se entails certainty; it requires no other corroborating factor.[21] This is criticized by al-Taftāzānī who contends that intellectual knowledge is sometimes speculative (*zanni*). It becomes decisive (*Qaṭ'ī*) by *Ijmā'*, such as the question of superiority of the Companions over others and other kind-red dogmatics.[22] It is again refuted by the contention that if a question is decided on the basis of human reason, it is never speculative. Hence there is no need of *Ijmā'*. Further, if a question remains doubtful after being decided by intelligence, this implies that it was not decided by reason but by *Ijmā'*[23] Al-Baṣri, who is a Mu'tazilī, divides religious into legal (*Shar'ī*) and rational (*'aqli*), and believes that both kinds are covered by *Ijmā'*.[24] The articles of faith fall under the religio-legal category (*Shar'ī*); but Ibn Amir al-Hajj expresses the opinion that they are established by reason rather than by *Ijmā'*,[25] Rational questions have been divided into two: first, questions on which *Ijmā'* itself depends, such as establishing the divinity of God and prophethood; second, questions on which it does not depend, such as creation of the universe, unity of God, and His vision in the hereafter. *Ijmā'* is no authority in the former case as shown previously; it is an authority in the latter case.[26]

Questions of purely sensible (*Ḥissī*) nature may relate to the past or to the future. The former are illustrated by the events of life of the Companions and their superiority over others; the latter are

---

[20] Imam al-Haramayn, *Al-Burhān fī Uṣūl al-Fiqh*, Ms. *op. cit.*, io. 203; al-Qarifi, *op. cit.*, p. 151.

[21] Ṣadr al-Sharī'ah, *op. cit.*, II, 41.

[22] Al-Taftāzāni, *Talwih*, Cairo, 1957, II, 41.

[23] Ali Abd al-Raziq, *op. cit.*, pp. 88-89.

[24] Abul-Husayn al-Basri, *op. cit.*, II, 494.

[25] Quoted in Madina, M.Z. *The Classical Doctrine of Consensus in Islam*, Ph.D. Thesis No. 3872, The University of Chicago, p. 160.

[26] Al-Maḥallī, *Sharḥ Jam' al-Jawāmi"*, Cairo, 1297 A.H., II, 167; Ibn al-Humam, *al-Taḥrīr fī Uṣūl al-Fiqh*, Cairo, 1351 Л.H., p. 414.

illustrated by the eschatological questions and portents of the last Hour. According to the generally accepted view, these questions are covered by *Ijmāʿ*. But some classical jurists controvert this view. Ṣadr *Al-Shariʿah* holds the view that *Ijmāʿ* on the sensible relating to the past corresponds to the tradition. This is not the type of *Ijmaʾ* which characterizes the community. *Ijtihād* is not required for such an *Ijmāʿ*. In fact, it falls under the category of traditions (*akhbar*). The sensible questions relating to the future are also not covered by *Ijmāʿ*, because they cannot be known except when pointed out by a person who is acquainted with the unseen. That should be regarded as a tradition reported from a person familiar with the unseen. As such, it corresponds to the *Ijmāʿ* on the sensibles relating to the past.[27] Al-Taftāzānī refutes this argument by saying that sensible questions relating to the future are sometimes established by analogical reasoning, and not by the express words of the Prophet. In such cases *Ijmāʿ* undoubtedly entails certainty.[28] This is again challenged by the counter argument that the exercise of *Ijtihād* is not allowed in sensible questions relating to the future. If they are established on the basis of a clear text, then there is no need of *Ijtihād*. In the case of a clear text, there is no room for *Ijtihād* on such matters.[29]

Questions relating to custom (*ʾUrfī*) are also covered by *Ijmāʿ*. Al-Baṣri remarks that *Ijmāʿ* is reached by word, by action, and by tacit approval. The scholars sometimes keep silent over the practice prevalent among the masses. This implies that the practice has been approved by them tacitly. Their silent approval of an action indicates the goodness of the action. Had it been wrong, they must have expressed their disapproval. Customs are approved or

---

[27] Ṣadr al-Shariʿah, *op. cit.*, II, 41.
[28] Al-Taftāzānī, *op. cit.*, II, 41.
[29] Ali ʿAbd al-Razīq, *op. cit.*, p. 90.

disapproved by the silence of the scholars or by their unanimous action.[30]

Ibn Rushd is of the view that *Ijmāʿ* cannot be established on theoretical (*Naẓariyyāt*) by way of certainty (*ʾAlā Ṭarīqin Yaqīnī*) as it can be established on practicals (*ʾamaliyāt*).[31]

Al-Isnawī observes that the phrase, 'the agreement on any point whatsoever (*Amr min al-Umūr*)' which occurs in the definition of *Ijmāʿ*, comprehends legal questions (*sharʾiyāt*), such as permissibility of commercial transaction, lexicographical questions (*Lughawīyāt*), such as the fact that particle fa signifies order (*taʾqib*), and rational questions (*ʾaqliyāt*) such as the creation of the universe and political matters. It is not restricted to the religious questions alone as the definition shows.[32]

From the controversy over the subject matter of *Ijmāʿ*, it is manifest that *Ijmāʿ* is not confined to religious questions. Its authority is extensible to the non-religious affairs, too.

---

[30] Abūl-Ḥusayn al-Baṣrī, *op. cit.*, II, 479; al-Shawkāni, *op. cit.*, p. 63.
[31] Ibn Rushd, *Kitāb Faṣl al-Maqal*, Leiden, 1959, p. 15.
[32] Al-Isnawi, *op. cit.*, II, 231.

Chapter VIII: *Ijmāʿ* by Silence

Ijmāʿ is reached by verbal expression, by action, and by silence. These questions have been discussed by the classical jurists under *rukn al-Ijmāʿ* (constitutive factor of consensus). *Ijmāʿ* by verbal expression is technically called *ʾAzīmah* (regular), and *Ijmāʿ* by tacit agreement is called *Rukhṣah* (concession). The term *Rukn al-Ijmāʿ* and its division into *ʾAzīmah* and *Rukhṣah* are not traceable before the fifth century A.H. Al-Jaṣṣaṣ touches upon this question, but does not use these terms. It seems that these terms were coined after him. *ʾAzīmah* in the context of *Ijmāʿ* means the agreement of Muslims on the essentials of Islam. The knowledge of this kind of *Ijmāʿ* is possessed both by the scholars and by the masses. It covers the fundamentals of religion, such as prayer, fasting during Ramadan, the Hajj pilgrimage, prohibition of adultery, of usury, and of marrying one's own mother or sister. It also comprises the agreement of the scholars on questions which the masses do not understand. The scholars alone are acquainted with them. They are, for example, the prohibition of marrying a woman and her aunt together, rates of *Zakat* as prescribed by the Prophet, and prohibition of temporary marriage. Both the scholars and the masses are required to possess the knowledge of the essentials of Islam. In the former case, it is presumed that the whole community agrees upon these questions. In the latter case, the agreement of the scholars who represent the community is considered to be the *Ijmāʿ* of the Community. The *Ijmāʿ* on these points was not reached by deliberation in a formal meeting. Their overall recognition both by the masses and by the scholars in the case of essentials is supposed to be the total *Ijmāʿ*. In other words, as there is no dispute over the essentials of Islam, they are thought to have been settled by the community at large.

If the opinion of some scholars on a disputed question spreads widely among the community, and the rest of the scholars accept it by verbal expression, or keep silent, then agreement is reached on that question. This kind of *Ijmāʿ* is known as *Rukhṣah* (concession), and *Ijmāʿ sukūtī* (tacit agreement).[1] Al-Bazdawī maintains that *Ijmāʿ* by silence is valid on two conditions, namely that the opinion of a single scholar or a group of scholars should reach all the remaining scholars, and that the time of consideration of the disputed question should pass away.[2]

Explaining the kinds *ʾAzīmah* and *Rukhṣah*, al-Bukhārī says that the former signifies the regular process of *Ijmāʿ*, for the word *ʾAzīmah* cannotes regularity or originality (*Aṣl*). The latter implies an *Ijmāʿ* reached by some necessity (*Ḍarūrah*), for *Rukhṣah* is based on necessity. The *Ijmāʿ* by silence is called *Rukhṣah* in order that incompetence and impiety may not be attributed to the jurists who kept silent on a matter which required pronouncement of their opinion. A person keeping silent on a question where he should speak is called a dumb Satan.[3]

We may now discuss the arguments of the exponents of the *Ijmāʿ* by silence. Al-Sarakhsi remarks that God has not put the community in hardship. It is not practically possible to hear directly from the scholars of the past, or from each and every scholar of every generation. Spreading out of an individual opinion about a disputed question among the community, and the silence of the rest of the scholars over that opinion will be considered sufficient for the validity of *Ijmāʿ*. This is because it is not lawful for the scholars to keep silent if they dissent from the point of view agreed upon by the community. This also removes the possibility of disagreement if

---

[1] Al-Sarakhsi, *Uṣūl al-Sarakhsī*, Cairo, 1372 A.H. I, 303.

[2] Al-Bazdawī, *Uṣūl al-Bazdawī*, Karachi, 1966, p. 239.

[3] ʿAbd al-ʿAzīz al-Bukhārī, *Kashf al-Asrār*, Constantinople, 1307 A.HH. ПI, 948; ʿAli *Abd al-Raziq, *al-Ijmāʿ fil-Sharīʿah al-Islāmiyyah*, Cairo, 1947, p. 74.

they keep silent; rather the probability of their agreement would be preferred.[4]

Dwelling upon this question Abu'l-Husayn al-Baṣri says that if the opinion of a scholar gains wide publicity in the community, and the rest of the scholars keep silent and do not express their dissent from it, *Ijmāʿ* will be established, provided it is known of necessity that they actually agreed. In case their consent is not known of necessity, it would be seen whether the point in dispute is a question of legal interpretation *Ijtihād*) or not. If it is not so, it will be seen whether the moot question relates to legal obligation (*taklif*) or not. If it is not so, the opinion already published might be erroneous, as the rest of the scholars are not duty-bound to consider such matters (as, for example, ʿAmmar is superior to Hudhayfah). They might have intended to neglect a question that was not worth consideration, and their agreement might have reached on this fact. If the point in question does not involve legal obligation, and the rest of the scholars do not pronounce their dissent, it implies that the opinion is correct. The jurists are legally bound to reject it and express their opinion if it is wrong. Now when this opinion is right, its opposite will be wrong, because this is a matter in which truth lies in one point of view. If the case is not the question of *Ijtihād*, the exponents of this principle argue in the same manner as explained above. But those who believe that every *Mujtahid* is right, differ among themselves on this question. Abū ʿAlī holds the opinion that this will be considered *Ijmāʿ* if the opinion spreads widely and time lapses. Abū Hashim maintains that this is not an *Ijmāʿ* but an authority. Abū ʿAbd Allah is of the view that this is neither *Ijmāʿ* nor authority.[5]

Rejection of tacit agreement starts from the time of al-Shāfiʿī who refutes this theory by saying that no statement or action can be

---

[4] Al-Sarakhsi, *op. cit.*, 1, 305-6; Al-Bazdawī, *op. cit.*, p. 242.
[5] Abūl-Ḥusayn al-Baṣrī, *Kitāb al-Muʿtamad*, Damascus, 1965, II, 532-33.

attributed to a silent person. On this basis, he also rejects the *Ijmāʿ* of the scholars.[6] He is reported to have said that if the majority of scholars pronounce their consent on a legal opinion about a certain problem, *Ijmāʿ* will be reached. This is because so much is practically possible (since pronouncement by each and every scholar is not feasible). Hence silence of the rest of the scholars is considered to be their agreement to prevent the community from falling into hardship. Further, there is no harm if we take the pronouncement of their consent by the majority of scholars on a certain point as a valid *Ijmāʿ*, for minority opinion falls under majority opinion. If the majority of the scholars keep silent over a point of view about a disputed issue, their silence will be regarded as the silence of all. Similarly, if the majority of scholars pronounce their 'approval, their pronouncement will be considered the pronouncement of all. Refuting this line of argument al-Sarakhsi remarks that the silence of the minority is taken as their agreement not because the minority falls under majority, but because it is not lawful for the scholars to keep silent over a point of view about an issue if they disagree. They are duty-bound to pronounce their disagreement and put forward their own point of view if they have any. The point at issue becomes clear if one or two scholars pronounce their standpoint; rather it becomes more manifest if the majority does so. Hence silence of the scholars, whether they are in a minority or majority, over a legal opinion, provided it spreads widely among the community is considered an indication of their agreement.[7] This shows that according to the Hanafīs, majority opinion does not count in tacit agreement. Even the dissent of one competent scholar is sufficient to invalidate *Ijmāʿ* by silence. The main point in the argument in favour of tacit agreement is that silence of the scholars after the

---

[6] Al-Shāfiʿī, *Jimaʿ al-ʿIlm*, *op. cit.*, pp. 56-57; idem, *Ikhtilāf al-Ḥadīth* (on the margin of *Kitāb al-Umm*, *op. cit.*) p. 143.
[7] Al-Sarakhsi, *op. cit.*, 1, 305-6.

lapse of time of consideration indicates their consent, for they were legally bound to pronounce their disagreement.[8]

Al-Ghazali rejects the validity of *Ijmāʿ* by silence. He states that tacit agreement is neither an *Ijmāʿ* nor an authority. This may be permissible if the circumstances indicate that those who kept silent had concealed their consent. He also allows it in case a group of scholars keep silent. He contends that the legal opinion of a jurist is known by his explicit verbal expression which is not subject to any doubt. But silence is doubtful. The following may be the reasons for the silence of a scholar on a moot question:

1. There may be some hidden restraint which prevents him from expressing his opinion and that may not be known to others. The context of his anger coupled with his silence sometimes indicates this position.

2. He may regard the opinion of a scholar as allowable according to his own interpretation (*Ijtihād*), though he himself may differ from him, taking his opinion as erroneous.

3. He may believe that every jurist (*Mujtahid*) is right. Hence, he may not think it at all necessary to reject a point of view on matters of opinion. He may think that answering verbally to a question is a collective duty. He may take the opinion of another scholar as correct, although it may contradict his own interpretation.

4. He may intend by his silence to reject the opinion, but he may wait for a proper occasion. He may not make haste in pronouncing his opinion due to some obstacle in his way and may be waiting for its elimination. In the meantime, he may die or be engaged in some other work distracting his attention from the point in question.

---

[8] *Ibid*, pp. 300-309.

5. He may apprehend that in case of expression, his opinion will be rejected, and thus he will be disgraced. Ibn ʿAbbas, for instance, accounts for his silence over the *ʾAwl* (increase) case by saying that he was afraid of ʿUmar during his lifetime, as he was a man of dignity.

6. He may be considering the matter all the time while he keeps silent. His time of consideration may be prolonged.

7. He may take the rejection of others as sufficient, regarding it as a pronouncement on his behalf. But he may be wrong in this presumption.

Al-Ghazali criticizes the arguments advanced in support of *Ijmāʿ* by silence by its exponents as follows:

Exponents:

Had there been any disagreement in the *Ijmāʿ* by silence, it must have come to the surface. This implies that there was no disagreement.

Al-Ghazali:

The same thing can be said about the agreement, too. What prevents disagreement from coming to the surface prevents agreement as well. This confutes the opinion of al-Jubbaʾi who stipulates a lapse of time for the validity of *Ijmāʿ* by silence. It may be noted that the restraint may continue till the end of the generation.

Those who regard tacit agreement as an authority are also not right, because such an agreement would be an arbitrary opinion. The infallibility of *Ijmāʿ* is, in fact, established by total agreement, and not by arbitrary opinion.

Exponents: It is a well-known fact that whenever the Successors disputed over a question, and an opinion of the Companions, already widely known and approved silently, was reported to them, they never departed from it. This shows that they agreed upon the *Ijmāʿ* by silence.

Al-Ghazāli: Such a type of *Ijmāʿ* was never recognized; rather it remained all along disputed among the scholars. The supporters of tacit Ijmāʿ are well aware that silence is doubtful, and that the opinion of a section of the community constitutes no authority.[9]

The agreement by silence is recognized as an *Ijmāʿ* and authority by Ahmad bin Hanbal, by most of the followers of Abū Hanifah, by some of the followers of al-Shāfiʿī, and al-Jubbaʾi. The classical jurists hold diverse views about the validity of the tacit agreement that we delineate presently.

It is neither *Ijmāʿ* nor an authority. This is held by Dawūd al-Zahiri, al-Murtada, and al-Shāfiʿī. It is contended that *Ijmāʿ* by silence is liable to suspicion.

2. It is an *Ijmāʿ* as well as an authority. This is held by a group of Shāfiʿī jurists, al-Asfarāʾīnī, and also attributed to al-Shafiʿī.

3. It is an authority and not an *Ijmāʿ*. This is maintained by Abū Hashim, al-Ṣayraft, and Al-Āmidī. Al-Ṣafi al-Hindi is reported to have stated that no one maintains the reverse of it. The contention goes that it is not an *Ijmāʿ* because silence is liable to create doubt. But it can be an authority, for it entails speculative knowledge which is accepted as an authority on the basis of traditions.

4. It is an *Ijmāʿ* provided that the generation in which it was reached lapses. This is held by al-Jubbaʾi. (a. 321 A.H.), Ibn Hanbal (d. 241 A.H.), Ibn al-Qattān (d. 359 A.H.), and some followers of al-Shafiʿī. It is argued that the scholars generally pronounce their opinions about novel questions, provided there is no case of dissimulation

[9] Al-Ghazālī, *al-Mustasfā*, Cairo, 1937, I, 121-122.

(*taqiyyah*) after the lapse of time. In the case of dissimulation, they would finish its reasons. A pious scholar pronounces his opinion before a reliable person or his associate if not before a ruler or a person whom he fears. The opinion, however, comes to the surface by all means. Silence, therefore, indicates their consent, especially after the lapse of time.

5. If the tacit agreement is reached on a legal opinion of the scholars (*fatwa*), it will be considered an *Ijmāʿ*. In case it is reached on an edict issued by a ruler, it will not be considered an *Ijmāʿ*. This is held by Ibn Abī Hurayrah (d. 345 A.H.). It is contended that political authorities sometimes issue their edicts against the opinion of the scholars. Hence consensus on their edict does not indicate their consent.

6. The tacit agreement reached on the edict of a ruler is an *Ijmāʿ* if it is issued with the consultation of the scholars. This is held by Abū Ishaq al-Marwazī (d. 340 A.H.) and al-Ṣayrafī (d. 330 A.H.).

7. It is an *Ijmāʿ* in those cases which cannot be redeemed, such as the decision of killing a person, or allowing an unlawful marriage. In other cases, it is an authority but not an *Ijmāʿ*. Al-Zarkashi (d. 794 A.H.) reports this point of view but does not mention the names of its upholders.

8. It is an *Ijmāʿ* in case the scholars who keep silent are in the majority, otherwise not. The argument and its refutation have already been examined.

9. If it was reached in the generation of the Companions, it would be considered an *Ijmāʿ*. It is not *Ijmāʿ* if reached in later generations. In the former case if agreement was reached on cases which could be redeemed, then it is *Ijmāʿ*; otherwise, it would be an authority. It is argued that if there were any difference among them, they would

surely pronounce it, as the truth was confined to their opinions. This is held by al-Mawardi (d. 450 A.H.) and al-Rūyani (d. 505 A.H.).

10. It is valid in those cases which occur frequently and one can look into them. Imam al-Haramaya al-Juwaynī holds this view.

11. Al-Ghazālī holds, as he explains in al-Mankhūl, that agreement by silence is an authority only in two situations: first, the scholars keep silent over a question which is not definite, yet it is proved definite in their very presence, though many other factors refute it; second, they keep silent as the time wears on, and no dissenting opinion comes to the fore over the point in question. On the contrary, if they gather in an assembly and any of them presents his opinion, while others keep silent, that means that they avoided criticism on that point of view, that will not be considered *Ijmā*ʿ, because the question is of speculative nature. On such occasions, etiquette requires that no criticism should be made on the judges and jurists. Here, al-Ghazali regards the tacit agreement as an authority in a special situation. But earlier on we have shown that he recognizes it as an authority, provided the circumstances indicate it.

12. It will be taken as *Ijmā*ʿ in case it was reached before the establishment of the schools of law, and not after them. This is because tacit agreement cannot change any opinion held by a recognized school of law.[10]

If the scholars agree on a certain question by their actions and no one expresses his dissent, the validity of such a type of *Ijmā*ʿ by silence is disputed. According to one point of view, it is valid like the actions of the Prophet, for the infallibility of the actions of the

---

[10] Abūl-Ḥusayn al-Baṣrī, *op. cit.*, II, 533-534; al-Shawakani, *Irshād al-Fuhūl*, Cairo, 1347 A.H., pp. 74-75 al-Qarafi, *Sharḥ Tanqīḥ al-Fuṣūl*, Cairo, 1306 A.H., pp. 144; Al-Āmidī, *al-Iḥkām fī Uṣūl al-Aḥkām*, Cairo, 1914, I, 361-62; Al-Ghazālī, *al-Mankhūl*, Damuscus: Maktabah Dar al-Fikr, n.d. p. 319.

scholars is established by virtue of their agreement like that of the Prophet. Their unanimous actions correspond to the actions of the Prophet in respect of infallibility. Another opinion says that the agreement reached by actions of the scholars will not be taken as *Ijmāʿ*, for the unanimous consensus of the scholars on a certain point by verbal expression or by their actions is impossible, particularly when their number is not known. A third view says that agreement by action is possible. But in this case, the *Ijmāʿ* will indicate the permissibility (*ibāhah*) of an action unless it is proved on the basis of a certain evidence that the action is recommendable or obligatory. Finally, *Ijmāʿ* will not be established by doing an action which stands for articulation (*Bayān*) or ordinance (*Ḥukm*). This view is held by Ibn al-Samʿānī.[11]

If a certain jurist performs an action and the other jurists keep silent when informed about it, their silence will be considered as tacit *Ijmāʿ*, provided the generation in which it took place passes away. This is the opinion of al-Shīrāzī. In case the generation does not lapse, then opinion is divided about its validity. According to one point of view, it is an authority (*Ḥujjah*); and according to another, it is an *Ijmāʿ* and authority. A third opinion says that it is neither *Ijmāʿ* nor authority,[12] But al-Ghazali maintains that such an *Ijmāʿ* is not valid, for the jurists are not infallible in their individual actions. This will apply to them collectively. Nevertheless, he observes that the generally accepted opinion is that such a type of *Ijmāʿ* can be a basis of argument.[13]

We have stated above that controversy over the validity of the tacit agreement started since the time of al-Shāfiʿī, who himself rejected it. Diverse opinions on this question were ascribed to him by the

---

[11] Al-Shawakani, *op. cit.*, pp. 75-76; Al-Ghazālī, *al-Mankhūl*, *op. cit.*, p. 318; al-Shirāzi, *al-Luam*, Cairo, 1325 A.H. p. 206.
[12] Al-Shirāzi, *op. cit.*, pp. 207-209.
[13] Al-Ghazālī, *al-Mankhūl*, *op. cit.*, p. 318.

classical jurists. *Ijmāʿ* by silence has been rejected by the opponents because of its equivocal nature. Al-Jaṣṣaṣ and al-Sarakhsi have dealt with this question in greater detail and sought to refute the counter-arguments. Summing up the arguments, for and against, Al-Āmidī adopts a middle course. The tacit agreement, he says, is a probable authority, and the argument on its basis may be valid outwardly (*Ẓāhir*) and not decisively (*Qaṭʿī*).[14]

[14] Al-Āmidī, *op. cit.*, I, 365.

Chapter IX: The Evidence of *Ijmāʿ*

Although *Ijmāʿ* is an authority by itself, it still requires a supporting evidence for its validity. According to the classical theory, no *Ijmāʿ* is valid without a supporting evidence (*lā Ijmāʿ illā an musianadin*).[1] The evidence derived directly from the Qurʾān or the Sunnah is technically known as *Dalālah* (indicative or decisive evidence); while the one derived from an isolated tradition or by exercising analogy (*Qiyās*) is called *Amārah* (evidence by sign, allusive or speculative evidence).[2]

The notion of a supporting evidence for *Ijmāʿ* appears to have developed towards the end of the fourth century of the Hijrah. Al-Shāfiʿī and al-Jaṣṣās do not touch upon this question. Yet the traces of polemic over this question are noticed during the third century of Islamic era. Muways b. ʿImran (d. circa 250 A.H.), a Muʿtazili jurist, is reported to have held the view that a scholar is legally permitted to pronounce his opinion without producing any evidence because God knows that he will not say anything but right.[3] Besides, al-Nazzām (d. 231 A.H.) defines *Ijmāʿ* in a way which implies that no supporting evidence is necessary for its validity.[4] Such a liberal attitude towards *Ijmāʿ* might have resulted in free thinking in the sphere of law. Hence the condition of supporting evidence was imposed by orthodoxy in order to exercise a check on a resulting anomaly in legal reasoning. It is worthy of note that one marks free thinking in law towards the middle of the second century of the Hijrah in the early schools. Al-Shāfiʿī staunchly attacked the frequent use of *Raʾy* in reasoning because it was not based on any

---

[1] Ibn Human, *al-Taḥrīr fī Uṣūl al-Fiqh*, Cairo, 1351 A.H., p. 411.
[2] Al-Baṣri, *Kitāb al-Muḥammad*, Damuscus, 1964, II, 520.
[3] *Ibid.*, p. 521.
[4] Al-Āmidī, *al-Iḥkām fī Uṣūl al-Aḥkām*, Cairo, 1914, 1, 280.

authority. Analogy (*Qiyās*), according to him, was a correct mode of reasoning in law because it was always based on an original authority. He also condemned the principle of approbation (*Istisḥān*) for the same reason.[5] It appears that the condition of supporting evidence (*sanad*) was imposed for the validity of *Ijmā*ʿ, inter alia, under the influence of al-Shāfiʿī, who laid great emphasis on the asl (original basis) for *Qiyās* (analogy). This theory, though upheld by the majority of the jurists, was challenged by a group of classical jurists, who maintained that *Ijmā*ʿ could be reached without an evidence. It takes place by divine inspiration (*Tawfīq*) and not by instruction and argumentation (*Tawqīf*). In fact, God helps the people to adopt a right opinion without any evidence.[6] We analyze below the arguments, for and against, the theory of evidence.

The exponents of the supporting evidence adduce the following arguments:

1. In the absence of an evidence or authority, one cannot, of necessity, attain the truth.

2. It is generally known that the Prophet used to make all his decisions on the basis of revelation. The Companions were not in a stronger position than the Prophet. When he resorted to an evidence, the Companions should a fortiori do so. Hence the community is also required to give all its judgements on the basis of some authority.

3. If the people are allowed to give judgments without any authority, they will follow the decisions made by individuals. In the long run, individuals will make decisions on the basis of their personal

---

[5] Al-Shafiʿi, *Kitāb al-Umm*, Cairo, 1325 A.H., VI, 205-7; VII, 271-73; idem, *al-Risālah*, Cairo, 1321 A.H. p. 66.

[6] Al-Baṣri, *op. cit.*, II, 520; Al-Āmidī, *op. cit.*, I, 374.

opinions, and the universal agreement will lose its merit and superiority over the individual opinion.

4. Pronouncing an opinion on religious matters without any decisive (*Dalālah*) or speculative (*Amārah*) evidence is erroneous. If people agree on such an opinion, they will, in fact, agree on an error. But this is impossible as that will corrupt the principle of *Ijmāʿ*.

5. If an opinion is not based on some evidence, it cannot be attributed to the lawgiver. As such, it will not be permissible to follow such an opinion.

6. If *Ijmāʿ* is allowed without a supporting evidence, the condition of *Ijtihād* for the competence of *Ijmāʿ* will be meaningless. But this condition cannot be waived, as it has been recognized by the universal consensus.[7]

The arguments advanced in favour of supporting evidence are refuted by counter-arguments as follows:

1. It is admitted that if there is no evidence in support of a rule, and the community does not agree on it, God may possibly direct them to the right path by means of inspiration. As such, nothing can prevent the community from attaining the truth. It is disputed whether an evidence is required to attain the truth after *Ijmāʿ* has taken place.

2. It is already established that the Prophet cannot be erroneous in his opinion, and this is also true of the consensus of the whole community. Now suppose the Prophet gives an opinion or makes a decision without any evidence, that would be surely right because it is impossible, of necessity, that he falls into an error. Besides, the Prophet according to verses 53:3-4 cannot give an opinion or make a decision without an authority. But the case of the agreement of

[7] Al-Baṣri, *op. cit.*, II, 520-21; Al-Āmidī, *op. cit.*, 1, 375-77.

the community is different from that of the Prophet. The religious sanction of *Ijmāʿ* shows that their total agreement is infallible. It nowhere shows that the community will always agree on a decision on the basis of some authority. These are two different cases which have been clubbed together in the agreement. One does not actually apply to the other.

3. The superiority of the collective opinion over the individual opinion may be considered from two angles: first, the agreement of the whole body is an authority over against the opinion of each and every individual; second, the individual opinion is considered in *Ijmāʿ* on condition that the opinions of the remaining individuals are combined with it. The individual opinion has no value in *Ijmāʿ* if the opinions of others are not added to it. Thus, the total agreement is an entity by itself entirely different from an individual opinion. The total agreement is valid unconditionally while the individual opinion is valid conditionally.

4. An opinion on a religious question not supported by any evidence may be erroneous before *Ijmāʿ* is reached thereon. But when *Ijmāʿ* takes place, there is no question of error.

5. It is correct to say that a rule of law which is not supported by any evidence cannot be attributed to the lawgiver. But the attribution to the lawgiver can be interpreted in a three-fold way: first, there is no legal proof (*Dalīl Sharʿī*) to show that the point in question has been ascribed to the lawgiver; second, it is not known for certain that the point in question is correct, agreeing with the prescription of the lawgiver; third, there might be some other condition which it does not fulfill. In the first case, it is admitted that the point in question may be wrong if it is based on individual opinion, but not wrong in case it is supported by *Ijmāʿ*. This is the point in dispute. In the second case, the claim of its fallibility is disputable. In the third

case, the details of the condition which it does not fulfill should be supplied and explained.

6. The condition of *Ijtihād* is necessary for *Ijmāʿ* in either of the following two cases: either there exists "no state of agreement (*lā ḥālat al-Ijmāʿ*)" or there does exist the "state of agreement (*ḥālat al-Ijmāʿ*)." In the former case, it is admitted that the evidence is necessary; but in the latter, the point is already in dispute. Furthermore, when the exponents of the theory of evidence themselves assert that *Ijmāʿ* is all-correct and infallible even if it is not based on any authority, how then is the condition of *Ijtihād* necessary in the present case?[8]

The opponents of the theory of evidence contend in a twofold way, theoretically and practically. It is argued theoretically that *Ijmāʿ* in itself is an authority. If an evidence is required for its validity, the real authority will be the evidence, and *Ijmāʿ* will be meaningless. As for practice, it is contended that *Ijmāʿ* was actually reached in the past in a number of cases without any evidence. It took place, for example, on the charges for hot bath, on installation of the huge water pitchers at the roadside, on the rates of wages of barbers, and the levying of tax on cultivated land (*Kharāj*).

To their theoretical contention, it is replied that *Ijmāʿ* has a number of advantages independently. As it is used as a source of law, there is no need of a supporting evidence. Opposition to *Ijmāʿ* is unlawful, but opposition to an individual opinion is permissible. Finally, the fact cannot be gainsaid that the Prophet always made decisions on the basis of some authority, i.e. revelation.

As for the question on which *Ijmāʿ* was reached in the past, it is said to reply that this claim is not correct. It is inconceivable that *Ijmāʿ* might have taken place without any evidence. At most, it can be said

---

[8] Al-Āmidī, *op. cit.*, I, 375-77.

that the evidence was not reported in the cases referred to by the opponents, as *Ijmā‘* was considered sufficient a sign for the existence of evidence.[9]

Summing up the discussion Al-Āmidī observes that all the arguments, for and against, the theory of evidence, are weak. The contending groups can hardly refute each other. The decisive opinion may be that if *Ijmā‘* is reached on a certain question without a supporting evidence, that *Ijmā‘* will be considered right because the community cannot agree on an error. Now the question remains whether in the presence of evidence, *Ijmā‘* can be conceived of or not. To this Al-Āmidī does not give any answer because the arguments, he says, of the contending groups are all weak.[10] He himself holds the opinion that what is disputed is the permissibility (*Jawāz*) of *Ijmā‘* without evidence and not its actual occurrence (*Wuqū‘*) in practice.[11] This has been challenged by some scholars, as we shall see in the course of discussion.

Abu'l-Husayn al-Baṣrī supports the majority view that *Ijmā‘* is not valid without an evidence. It takes place on the basis of some evidence, decisive (*Dalālah*) or speculative (*Amarah*). The community never agrees without some basis (*'abathan*). Discussing the arguments of the contending groups he concludes that evidence is necessary for *Ijmā‘*. He does not accept *Ijmā‘* reached in the past on a number of questions cited by the opponents. He replies that there must have been some kind of evidence, though not transmitted. The practice of manufacturing things on order (*Istithnā'*), and sale transaction by mutual tacit consent (*Bay' al-Murādāt*) were common in the days of the Prophet, and no one objected to them. The sale transaction by tacit consent became customary in the wake of

---

[9] *Ibid.*, pp. 377-78.
[10] *Ibid.*
[11] *Ibid.*, 1, 375.

continuous practice and the procedure of give-and-take tacitly was taken to mean mutual consent by verbal expression. Similar was the case of the charges of hot bath (*Ujrat al-Ḥammām*). As regards apportioning the lands of enemy territory, it should be noted that this question depends on the discretion of the ruler. He has full liberty to distribute or retain them as the situation demands. The Prophet did not apportion the houses of Mecca after its capture, nor did he distribute the wells and other sources of water belonging to Hawāzin. As to the levying of zakat on horses, it is important to note that *Ijmāʿ* was never reached on this question. Those who consider it obligatory have no evidence to show that the Prophet levied zakat on horses when they increased in number. Levying zakat on horses, in the absence of any evidence, is tantamount to repealing the *Shari'ah*, and that must be criticized.[12]

Al-Ṣayrafi (d. 330 A.H.) criticizes al-Amidīs view that what is disputed is the permissibility of *Ijmāʿ* without evidence and not its actual occurrence. According to him, the matter is exactly reverse. In fact, the occurrence of *Ijmāʿ* practically without evidence is disputed. That is why *Ijmāʿ* by secret or tacit understanding (*Tawātu*) can hardly take place. The Companions never agreed on such matters; rather they expressly discussed moot questions among themselves. Their polemic on such questions sometimes resulted in invoking the curse of God on the wrongdoer. This shows that *Ijmāʿ* takes place practically only if it is supported by evidence.[13]

Arguing in favour of the theory of evidence Ibn Humam (d. 861 A.H.) remarks that in case there is no evidence, all baseless (Abāṭīl)) questions would be considered right (*Sawāb*) in Islam through *Ijmāʿ*. Moreover, in that case, the community might agree on an error because *Ijmāʿ* is the opinion of the whole body and the opinion of the

---

[12] Al-Baṣri, *op. cit.*, II, 520-22.
[13] al-Shawkānī, *Irshād al-Fuhūl*, Cairo, 1347 A.H., p. 70.

whole body without evidence is unlawful (*Muharram*). Besides, the agreement of all people without any motive (*Dā'in*) is usually impossible, since it is not possible that all people agree on taking the same kind of food without any cause. Here one might say that they might agree on it by inspiration from God. Divine inspiration entails necessary knowledge (*Darūri*) which is considered correct by general consensus. To this he replies that this proposition is a mere conjecture; this does not actually happen. The divine injunctions are not established by rational proofs (*'Aqliyyah*); instead, they are based on oral proofs (*bil-Sam'*). If a person receives inspiration from God on a certain problem, that will not be considered an authority. Divine inspiration is an authority only from a prophet. Hence an evidence is required for the establishment of *Ijmā'* by all means.[14] According to al-Mawardī and al-Rūyani, the dispute over the theory of evidence of *Ijmā'* has resulted from the question of whether divine inspiration (*Ilhām*) is a valid authority.[15]

Both the exponents and the opponents of theory of evidence stipulate the existence of a motive (*dā'in*) for the establishment of *Ijmā'*. But they differ on the nature of motive. According to the former, the external evidence, whether decisive (*Dalālah*) or speculative (*Amārah*), constitutes the motive. In the opinion of the latter, the motive comes from within. This may be something intuitional, inspiration, immediate divine help (*Tawfīq*) and fortune (*Bakhī*). People may agree on a point by intuition or inspiration from God without any reasoning on the basis of evidence. Hence, according to the latter group, external evidence is not a necessary condition of *Ijmā'*.[16]

---

[14] Ibn Humam, *op. cit.*, p. 411.

[15] al-Shawkānī, *op. cit.*, p. 70.

[16] Al-Qaraft, *Sharḥ Tanqīḥ al-Fuṣūl*, Cairo, 1306 A.H., pp. 147-48; al-Isnawi, *Nihdyat al-Sūl*, Cairo, n.d. II, 260.

If a rule of law is based on a decisive evidence (*Dalālah*), the exponents of evidence agree that an evidence is necessary for the establishment of *Ijmāʿ* on such a rule. But there is a difference of opinion among them if the evidence is speculative (*Amārah*). One point of view says that *Ijmāʿ* on such a rule is absolutely valid and that it is also valid on a rule based on analogical deduction. It matters little whether the evidence is patent (*Jaliyyah*) or latent (*Khafiyyah*). This view is held by the majority of the scholars. Another view is that *Ijmāʿ* on a rule based on a speculative evidence (*Amārah*) is not valid. This is held by the Zahiris and Muhammad b. Jarir al-Tabari. The Zahiris deny this kind of *Ijmāʿ* because they reject the analogy. Al-Tabarī disallows it, for *Ijmāʿ* is decisive while the analogy is speculative. There will be a contradiction if both are combined. A third viewpoint is that such an *Ijmāʿ* is conditionally valid. If the speculative evidence (*Amārah*) is patent (*Jaliyyah*), the *Ijmāʿ* is valid; but it is invalid if the evidence is latent (*Khafiyyah*). This is held by a group of Shāfiʿī scholars. A fourth opinion says that *Ijmāʿ* is valid only on rules based on speculative evidence (*Amārah*), but not valid on points supported by decisive evidence (*Dalālah*) because the evidence in such cases is self-sufficient. It does not require any endorsement by *Ijmāʿ*.[17]

Al-Bazdawī also thinks there is no need of *Ijmāʿ* for a point supported by a decisive evidence *Qaṭʿī* derived from the Qurʾān or the Sunnah. He contends that the certainty of a decision taken on the basis of *Ijmāʿ* is not provided by the evidence but by the *Ijmāʿ* per se. *Ijmāʿ* is a privilege of the community gifted from God (*karāmah*); it perpetuates the supporting evidence (*Idāmah liʾl-Ḥujjah*); it protects the community from error and causes their stability on the right path (*Ṣiyānah wa Taqrīr Lahum ʾalaʾl-Maḥajjah*). If there is an evidence which entails certain knowledge in addition to *Ijmāʿ*, the *Ijmāʿ* will

[17] Al-Shawkānī, *op. cit.*, pp. 70-71.

become redundant (*Laghw*). Hence *Ijmāʿ* is not needed for such cases.[18] From this statement of Al-Bazdawī it seems that he is denying the validity of *Ijmāʿ* on questions based on decisive evidence. But this is not fact, as his commentators think. He might have refuted the point of view held by the Zähiris and al-Tabarī that *Ijmāʿ* is valid only in the case of decisive evidence. Explaining this point al-Taftazānī says that from such statements (as of al-Bazdawī) one should not jump to the conclusion that *Ijmāʿ* is not permissible on questions based on decisive evidence. In the presence of a decisive evidence the *Ijmāʿ*, of course, becomes redundant in the sense that it does not originally establish the rule, but only confirms it. Confirming a rule is not as primary an object as establishing it. *Ijmāʿ* of course establishes the certainty of a rule in the case of speculative evidence such as analogy or solitary tradition. But in the case of decisive evidence, it remains only confirmatory just like many similar texts (*Nuṣūṣ*) about a single rule. Here *Ijmāʿ* is not redundant in the sense that it has no utility and hence not permissible. Concluding, al-Taftāzānī observes that there is no sense in disputing over the permissibility of *Ijmāʿ* on a rule based on decisive evidence. If by it the opponents mean that there may be a rule which is already established by decisive evidence, but the jurists may not agree on it, this is obviously absurd because there is no reason for disagreement in the presence of a decisive evidence. If by it is meant that the term *Ijmāʿ* would not apply to it, that is also untenable, since the definition of *Ijmāʿ* does apply to such an agreement. If they mean that *Ijmāʿ* does not establish the rule already established by a decisive evidence, that may be correct. Nonetheless, there is no reason for arguing about it, for what is already established cannot be established again.[19]

---

[18] Al-Bazdawī, *Uṣūl al-Bazdawī*, Karachi, 1966, p. 247.
[19] Al-Taftāzāni, *Sharḥ al-Talwīḥ Wal-Tawḍīḥ*, Cairo, 1957, II, 51-52.

Al-Bazdawī's commentator ʿAbd al-Aziz al-Bukhari says that his (al-Bazdawī's) statement apparently shows that he denies the validity of *Ijmāʿ* in the case of decisive evidence. But this is not fact. When he allows *Ijmāʿ* on questions based on speculative evidence, he should a fortiori allow it on questions supported by decisive evidence. Al-Bukhārī furnishes the same explanation for the redundance of *Ijmāʿ* in the case of decisive evidence as provided by al-Taftāzānī.[20]

Al-Baṣrī supports the view that *Ijmāʿ* on a rule based on speculative evidence (*Amārah*) is valid. He contends that speculative evidence is a means to derive a rule like a decisive evidence (*Dalālah*). There is nothing which prevents the establishment of *Ijmāʿ* on a question supported by speculative evidence. As agreement on decisive evidence, whether patent or assumed, is possible, likewise, it is equally possible on speculative evidence. He then describes the misgivings of the opponents. The opponents contend that speculative evidence (*Amārah*) being assumed or latent (*Khafiyyah*) cannot move the whole community to agree unanimously on a certain point. Besides, the speculative evidences may be heterogeneous (*Mutaghayyirah*). One may argue on the basis of an evidence which may differ from the one adduced by the other. Hence such a single doubtful evidence cannot be a motive for the agreement of all the people on a moot question.

If *Ijmāʿ* takes place on questions based on such weak evidence, that would correspond to the agreement of all people on eating the same kind of food at the same time or telling a lie about a same thing things which are obviously impossible. The agreement on speculative evidence differs from the agreement on a decisive (*Dalālah*) or resembling (*shabah*) evidence. In the former case (i.e. *Dalālah*) the evidences are obvious (*Ẓāhirah*). There is no doubt about them. In the latter case, the resemblances are determined by the

---

[20] ʿAbd al-Aziz al-Bukhari, *Kashf al-Asrār*. Istanbul, 1307 A.H., III, 984-85.

value judgement of the proofs (*taqdir al-Adillah*). Hence, they carry more weight than speculative evidence. The case of *Ijmāʿ* on a question based on a speculative evidence also differs from the case of the gathering of a large number of people at one place on the occasion of Id, because the motive for this gathering is manifest to them.

Further, there are persons in the community who believe in the falsity of a rule based on a speculative evidence (*Amarah*). This prevents them from deciding a case on this basis. There is no other motive which moves them to accept this rule. This would constitute a preventive from the agreement of the community on that rule.

Al-Baṣrī answers to their objections. This is a mere claim, he asserts, that the community with its large number and variety of ends and desires cannot agree on a rule based on speculative evidence. This certainly has no proof. It is well-nigh possible that people may agree on a point on account of one or many evidences (*Amārāt*), in spite of their huge number and variety of ends. This is because it is already accepted by general consensus that the community should have a resort in reasoning to some kind of speculative evidence (*amarah*). When such an evidence manifests itself clearly to all people, it would naturally be attributed to the whole body. Hence the disciples of Abū Hanifah, despite the largeness of their group, agreed on most of the problems. A large number of people agree on moving to the place of ʿEid prayer because previously they had a belief in doing so.

The present case differs from their agreement on telling a lie about a particular thing because there is no such motive. The same thing cannot occur to all of them at the same time except that they contact each other by some kind of communication. But there is no need of contacting each other in deriving a rule on the basis of speculative evidence. This is because speculative evidences are generally known to the scholars who do not require any contact with each other.

As regards the agreement of people on taking the same kind of food, it should be noted that this is subject to the equality of their appetites and of their possibility of satisfying them. It is already known that people vary in their appetites and possibility of satisfying them. Some like a thing which is disliked by others; some have an appetite which is stronger than that of others. It is possible that two persons may like a thing together, but one of them may not obtain it, or obtain it with great difficulty, but there may be no difficulty for the other to get it. For these reasons, all people cannot agree on taking the same kind of food at the same time.

As for the belief in the falsity of a decision based on speculative evidence, al-Baṣrī replies that the difference of opinion on this question appeared in later generations. The Companions agreed on the validity of *Ijtihād*. Hence this objection does not apply to their generation. Moreover, a person may possibly have a belief in the falsity of a rule based on speculative evidence, still he may follow it regarding the evidence as decisive. This may serve as a motive (*dain*) for others to agree on the rule. Further, a man may follow such a rule, despite his belief that it is corrupt because he may not find any other evidence except this single one. The contradiction between beliefs and acts of some persons in the community is obviously possible.[21]

Al-Sarakhsi maintains that *Ijmāʿ* is permissible on all sorts of questions, whether the evidence is decisive or speculative. He illustrates it by citing examples of *Ijmāʿ* on both categories. There is an *Ijmāʿ* on the prohibition of marrying a woman and her daughter together a rule derived from the clear verses of the Qur'ān.

---

[21] Al-Baṣri, *op. cit.*, II, 524-27.

Similarly, there exists an *Ijmāʿ* on the rule that a full bloodwit shall be paid if both hands are cut off; but half the bloodwit shall be paid in case one hand is amputated. The rule that the sale of food grains is invalid before taking possession by the purchaser has been approved by *Ijmāʿ*. These rules have been derived from the Sunnah. Questions based on individual opinion (*Raʾy*) have also been sanctioned by *Ijmāʿ*. Levying *Kharāj* on agricultural lands of Iraq (*sawad*) is a question of *Ijtihād* and the rule of law was derived by ʿUmar from the Qurʾān. He also derived the religious sanction of Abū Bakr's caliphate, when people quarrelled about it, on the basis of an analogy between his leadership in prayer in the lifetime of the Prophet and the leadership in worldly affairs. These rules were derived from the Qurʾān and the Sunnah by individual interpretation. Consequently, *Ijmāʿ* was reached on them. The time limit for an impotent husband approved by *Ijmāʿ* was originally determined on the basis of *Raʾy*. The *Ḥadd* punishment of eighty lashes for drinking has also been determined, according to the prevalent view, by individual opinion. But al-Sarakhsi rejects this viewpoint. He believes that it was determined on the basis of the Sunnah. It is already established, he contends, that the Prophet ordained to strike the drunkard in his day with sticks and shoes. The Companions and the early jurists then fixed the limit of punishment for drinking by investigating the punishments inflicted by the Prophet in such cases. It is reported that the persons present at the moment of punishing the drunkard during the time of the Prophet were forty. Each of them struck him with both of his shoes. The early jurists who fixed the limit of punishment took them as eighty strokes of shoes and consequently converted them into eighty flogs by drawing an analogy with the punishment of slandering (*Qadhf*) prescribed in the Qurʾān. Thus, the punishment of drinking is based on the clear prescription of the Prophet and not on personal opinion.[22]

The opponents of the theory of evidence differ among themselves on the fact whether or not an *Ijmāʿ* which has no supporting evidence is an authority. The majority of scholars take it as an authority while others reject its authority. There is also a difference of opinion on the question of whether it is necessary for a jurist to search for the evidence if the *Ijmāʿ* is devoid of it. It is not necessary in the opinion of Abū Ishaq. If later on an evidence comes to light or is reported by someone, that would be taken as one out of many others, and not the only evidence. Abu'l-Hasan al-Suhayli observes that if *Ijmāʿ* is established on a certain point, but it is not known whether the evidence is based on the Qur'ān or analogy, the *Ijmāʿ* should be followed by all means. The reason is that *Ijmāʿ* is never reached without an evidence, and the acquaintance with it is not necessary.[23]

There is an acute controversy among the classical jurists over the validity of *Ijmāʿ* on questions based on analogy (*Qiyās*) and individual interpretation (*Ijtihād*). As stated earlier, the Shah, Dawud al-Zahiri, and Ibn Jarir al-Tabarī disallow it. The preferable opinion, according to Al-Āmidī, is that *Ijmāʿ* is valid on questions based on *Ijtihād* and analogical deductions. It is permissible rationally and also took place practically in the past. The exponents argue as follows:

Rationally speaking, a large number of people may agree, in "practical life, on baseless questions and rulings not supported by positive or speculative evidence. *Ijmāʿ* therefore must take place for

---

[22] Al-Sarakhsi, *Uṣūl al-Sarakhsī*, Cairo, 1372 A.H., I, 301-302. Al-Sarakhsi's contention seems to be untenable. The point in question clearly involves the exercise of opinion and analogy by the early jurists. The Prophet prescribed only forty and not eight flogs for drinking. Hence one can hardly agree with him on the fact that the punishment for drinking is based on the *Sunnah* and not on *Ra'y*.
[23] Al-Shawkāni, *op. cit.*, p. 71.

stronger reason on obvious speculative questions. This is not denied by reason.

Historically, the Companions agreed on the caliphate of Abū Bakr on the basis of individual interpretation and personal opinion. The well-known remark made on this occasion is as follows: "The Prophet was satisfied with him for our religion; should we not be satisfied with him for our worldly affairs?" The Prophet selected him as a leader in prayer in the mosque in his own place. The Companions elected him as a caliph (a political leader) by drawing an analogy with his selection by the Prophet as a leader in prayer (religious affairs). Besides, the Companions exercised *Ijtihād* in Fighting with the tribes who refused to pay *Zakāt*, and finally agreed on the decision of Abū Bakr. On this occasion, Abū Bakr reportedly contended that he would not split up the injunctions which God combined together, i.e. prayer and zakat. They also agreed on the unlawfulness of the fat of pig by drawing an analogy with its meat. Similarly, they agreed on disusing the oil of sesame (*Shirāj*) and liquid juice of fresh ripe dates (*al-Dibs al-Sayyāl*) if a mouse falls in them and dies therein. They derived this rule on the basis of analogy with the accepted rule of disusing the ordinary oil when a mouse falls in it. The *Ḥadd* punishment for drinking was also determined on the basis of analogy. Moreover, the compensation for hunting a prey, the amount of fine in case one commits a sin during the hajj, the amount of subsidy to near relatives, and the criterion of reliability of religious leaders (*A'immah*) and judges (*Quḍāt*), were determined by analogy and individual judgement. These questions were later on approved by *Ijmā'*.[24]

[24] Al-Āmidī, *op. cit.*, I, 379-80.

The opponents express their misgivings about the validity of *Ijmāʿ* on rules based on analogical deduction. Al-Āmidī and others have replied to their doubts. We summarize below their deliberation:

Q. The validity of *Qiyās* (analogy) was constantly denied by a group of scholars in every generation in the past. Hence no *Ijmāʿ* can be valid on analogical deduction.

A. It cannot be accepted that there was a disagreement on the validity of *Qiyās* in the early period of Islam. In fact, the disagreement on this question appeared in the later generations. By denying the validity of *Qiyās* they aimed at denying the validity of *Ijmāʿ* on analogical deduction after disagreement on it. The *Ijmāʿ* on analogical deduction corresponds to the *Ijmāʿ* on solitary traditions which has been generally recognized by the scholars, despite their difference of opinion about the reliability of the solitary traditions themselves. Besides, if the opponents themselves accept the validity of *Ijmāʿ* on analogical deduction, this would contradict their view about solitary traditions.

Q. Analogy is a speculative matter. The intellectual faculties of people vary from person to person in making acquaintance with it. And this usually makes it impossible for them to agree on the establishment of a rule.

A. If the deriving of a rule by means of analogy becomes clear to all, and there is no inkling of partiality (*Mayl*) and evil desire (*Hawā*) in exercising it, the intellectuals may agree on it, and this may be a motive to establish a rule on its basis. Although it is difficult for them to agree on the rule established on the basis of analogy at a definite period of time because of their diverse understandings and approach with respect to thinking (*Naẓar*) and interpretation (*Ijtihād*), yet it would not be difficult for them to agree on it during a long period of time (*Azminah Mutatāwilah*). This corresponds to their agreement on adhering to a solitary tradition, in spite of the fact that its reliability is doubtful for various reasons.

Q. *Ijmāʿ* is a decisive and definite authority. Those who reject it are condemned as impious and heretics. But rules established by analogy and individual interpretation are doubtful an antithesis of *Ijmāʿ*. How can the two be combined?

A. This can be replied in a twofold way. In the first place, when the community has already accepted by general consensus the principle of establishing a rule on the basis of analogy, their consensus on the validity of analogy outstrips their consensus on a certain rule derived by exercising analogy. This takes out the rule from being doubtful and speculative. Thus *Ijmāʿ*, which is a decisive authority, is attributed to a decisive authority and not to a speculative one. There is no contradiction between the two. Secondly, the opponents themselves accept the validity of *Ijmāʿ* on a solitary tradition. But the former is decisive while the latter is speculative. Their answer to this question is also an answer to their misgiving about *Ijmāʿ* on analogical deduction.

Q. *Ijmāʿ* is an independent and infallible source of law, while analogy is an auxiliary and fallible source. An independent and infallible source cannot be supported by a subsidiary and fallible one.

A. Analogy which is a supporting evidence to *Ijmāʿ* is not subservient to *Ijmāʿ* but to the Qurʾān and Sunnah. Hence, this does not constitute the case of supporting an independent source, i.e. *Ijmāʿ* supported by its derivative (*Farʿiyyah*).

Q. It is already established by *Ijmāʿ* that a jurist can differ with another jurist on a legal question. If *Ijmāʿ* is reached on a rule derived on the basis of analogy or individual interpretaion, the liberty of disagreement allowed by *Ijmāʿ* will be arrested. This is because disagreement is not allowed after *Ijmāʿ* has been established on a certain point. This is a sheer contradiction.

A. *Ijmā* allows to differ with the individual interpretation of the jurists, say of one or two persons, but never allows to differ with the interpretation or opinion of the community at large. Disagreement is allowed so long as *Ijmāʿ* does not take place on a question.

The opponent's contention that the instances cited from history were based on textual evidence is not correct. In some cases, there might exist textual evidence; but there are many cases where no textual evidence is found. Rather, in such cases, it has been expressly stated that they were settled by the exercise of analogy between parallel cases. It is evident that if there had existed a clear textual evidence, no one would have resorted to analogy, thus setting aside a clear evidence.[25]

Concluding, Al-Āmidī observes that it is finally established that *Ijmāʿ* is allowed on points based on analogy or other speculative evidence. If a speculative evidence on a certain question comes to light and the community decides the case accordingly, and it is also proved that there exists only one single evidence in the case, still, that evidence cannot be accepted as the only valid evidence because of the possibility of some other evidence, too. But Abū ʿAbd Allāh al-Baṣrī differs with him on this theory.[26]

In the preceding paragraphs, we have analyzed the arguments, for and against, the supporting evidence of *Ijmāʿ*. We think *Ijmāʿ* does not take place by divine inspiration. It must be supported by some kind of evidence, decisive or speculative. In case the evidence is explicit and decisive, derived directly from the Qurʾān or Sunnah, there is no need for *Ijmāʿ* for such a question. In case the evidence is

---

[25] Al-Āmidī, *op. cit.*, I, 382-84; al-Baṣri, *op. cit.*, II, 522-31.

[26] Al-Āmidī, *op. cit.*, I, 384.

doubtful, it certainly requires the approval of *Ijmāʿ*. However, the point of view that *Ijmāʿ* requires no evidence is untenable.

Chapter X: The Condition of Time in *Ijmāʿ*

In the previous chapter, we have noted that questions based on personal opinion and individual interpretation require their confirmation by *Ijmāʿ* for the sake of certainty. Decisive questions based on clear textual evidence are already certain. If *Ijmāʿ* is at all reached on them, their certainty originally comes not from *Ijmāʿ* but from the evidence. From this, it follows that the questions mostly dealt with in *Ijmāʿ* are speculative. As such, there is a possibility, even after the unanimous consensus on such questions, of changing the opinion by a scholar who subscribed to the establishment of *Ijmāʿ*. Suppose a scholar finds a fresh evidence on a certain question after its settlement by the total agreement of the scholars, and he withdraws his opinion, naturally, the question arises whether such an agreement on that point would be called an *Ijmāʿ* and whether it would continue to be operative even after disagreement. Or, thinking over a point upon which a total agreement has been reached is finally closed. That is to say, the difference of opinion is allowed before the total agreement is reached and not after it. This gave rise to the question of time lag in *Ijmāʿ* after total agreement. The majority of scholars hold that *Ijmāʿ* is final and operative as soon as the community at large agrees on a certain point. No change of mind is allowed after universal consensus. Some are of the view that lapse of time (*Inqirāḍ al-ʾAṣr*), i.e. death of all scholars who participated in *Ijmāʿ*, is a necessary condition for the validity of *Ijmāʿ*. Others maintain that lapse of time is necessary for speculative questions and not for decisive ones. There are some other minor differences that we shall discuss in due course.

Let us start with the majority view that lapse of time is not necessary for the validity of *Ijmāʿ*. The moment total agreement of the scholars or the total agreement of the community is reached, *Ijmāʿ* becomes final. This view is said to have been held by the majority of the followers of al-Shāfiʿī, Abū Hanifah, and by most of the Ashāʿirah and Muʿtazilah. We analyse their arguments as follows:

First, it is contended that if the validity of *Ijmāʿ* is conditioned by the lapse of time, *Ijmāʿ* would not remain an authority by itself, but lapse of time would be an authority. Secondly, if *Ijmāʿ* is conditioned by the lapse of time, *Ijmāʿ* would never take place. This is because in the generation of the Companions the Successors who are competent for *Ijtihād* may differ with the Companions on a point on which *Ijmāʿ* was reached by them. And it is necessary for the establishment of *Ijmāʿ* that the Successors who are competent should agree with the Companions on the point in dispute. Similarly, in the generation of the Successors if *Ijmāʿ* is arrived at on a certain point, the scholars of the next generation, i.e. the followers of the Successors, may disagree with the Successors on the point decided by *Ijmāʿ* in their generation. Thus, the scholars of one generation would differ with the scholars of another generation by interpenetration of generations. And this process would go on ad infinitum. As such, the establishment of *Ijmāʿ* would be impossible in any generation. Thirdly, *Ijmāʿ* is an authority like the Naṣṣ (text) of the Qurʾān and the Sunnah. The rule established by *Ijmāʿ* is similar to the rule of law established by textual evidence. There is avowedly no condition of time for a textual evidence. Similarly, there should be no condition for *Ijmāʿ*, too. Fourthly, the Qurʾānic verses and the traditions of the Prophet which justify the authority of *Ijmāʿ* do not stipulate any condition of time for its validty. Fifthly, Successors, like Saʿid b. al-Musiyyb, Ibrahim al-Nakhaʿi, and al-Baṣri used to give their opinion on legal issues, and occasionally differed with the Companions, If the condition of the lapse of time were necessary, the *Ijmāʿ* of the Companions would never be reached on any point. Furthermore, in the later days of the Companions when Anas b. Mālik was alive, the Successors used to argue from the consensus of the Companions. The validity of their reasoning on the basis of *Ijmāʿ* was not conditioned by the death of the surviving Companions towards the end of their generation. This clearly shows that lapse of time was not a necessary condition for *Ijmā'* in the day of the Successors. Sixthly, what actually constitutes the authority is the universal agreement and not the death of the scholars or the extinction of generation. The moment the scholars agree, their agreement emerges as an authority long before their death. Their death would no more augment the authority of *Ijmā'*. Seventhly, suppose it is established by universal consensus that *Ijmā'* is valid if the whole generation passes way, then the authority lies either in the total agreement or in the lapse of time or in both. The second alternative is not permissible, otherwise lapse of time will be an authority instead of the agreement. And this is impossible. The third is also not possible, otherwise their death will be a cause for making their opinions an authority. But death, it is remarkable, is not a necessary condition of the authority of the Prophet's opinion, how can it be a condition for *Ijmā'*? In view of these arguments lapse of time is not a necessary condition for *Ijmā'*. Difference of opinion on a point at issue is allowed during the course of discussion which may extend to any length of time. As soon as the scholars in a particular generation agree universally, which may be in a moment or in a full generation, *Ijmā'* will be final, and no scholar is allowed to change his mind henceforth. The lapse of time, according to some, means the time involved in thinking, discussing, and studying the problem, and according to others, the lapse of the whole generation or death of all the scholars present at the time of the occurrence.[1] Further, silence over a point at issue will not be taken as consent during the course of discussion. But when the discussion is finished, and the matter is finally settled, silence then will be considered consent. No

[1] Al-Jaṣṣāṣ, *Kitāb Uṣūl al-Fiqh*, Ms. No. 229-Uṣūl, Dār al-Kutub al-Miṣriyyah; fos. 227a-228b; al-Sarakhsi, *Uṣūl al-Sarakhsī*. Cairo, 1372 A.H., 1, 316-17; Al-Ghazālī al-Mustasfa, Cairo, 1937, 1, 122; Al-Āmidī, *al-Ihkām fi Uṣūl al-Ahkām*, 1914, 1, 366-68.

fresh opinion is worth consideration after the total agreement has been reached.[2]

Another point of view says that lapse of time is a necessary condition for the validity of *Ijmāʿ*. So long as any single scholar of the participants in *Ijmāʿ* is alive, *Ijmāʿ* will not be materialized. During the lifetime of the scholars who contributed to the *Ijmāʿ* on a certain point, there is always a comprehension that any of them may change his mind. *Ijmāʿ* materializes only after the death of all the scholars, or after the extinction of the whole generation if the masses are involved in it. Ahmad b. Hanbal (d. 241 A.H.), Abū Bakr b. Fawrak (d. 406 A.H.) and Sulaym al-Razī (d. 447 A.H.) are said to have held this view. This is also attributed to al-Shāfiʿī.[3] The condition of lapse of time has been imposed, according to Ibn Hanbal and his followers, with a view that the scholars may have a margin to withdraw their opinion after agreement. It does not aim at including the scholars of the following generation in the *Ijmāʿ* of the previous generation. If the scholars of a generation agree on a certain point, and they pass away with no change of mind, *Ijmāʿ* would then be final, though their agreement is controverted by the scholars of the following generation who live in their own time by the interpenetration of the generations. Another advantage of this condition is that a dissenter may not be acquainted with the establishment of *Ijmāʿ*. This is because so long as disagreement exists it cannot be finally decided that *Ijmāʿ* has taken place. Mere agreement of the scholars does not constitute *Ijmāʿ*. In fact, it remains suspended until the extinction of their generation. When all of them pass away, the disagreement of the next generation will not be taken into consideration. Rather the opinion of a dissenter will now be regarded as a violation of *Ijmāʿ* after the lapse of the

---

[2] Al-Sarakhsi, *op. cit.*, I, 306; Ṣadr al-Sharīʿah, *al-Tawḍīḥ*, Cairo, 1975, II, 42.

[3] Al-Āmidī, *op. cit.*, 1, 366; Tāj al-Dīn al-Subkī, *Jamʿ al-Jawāmiʿ*, Cairo, 1297 A.H. II, 160; ʿAbd al-ʿAzīz al-Bukhārī, *Kashf al-Asrār*, Istanbul, 1907, III, 963.

generation. But this theory, it should be noted, seems to conflict with the theory of total agreement. One cannot conceive of *Ijmāʿ*, even after a lapse of time, in the presence of dissenting minority. How can the disagreement which is considered at the time of *Ijmāʿ* be ignored after the death of the people of *Ijmāʿ*? Some hold that the purpose of this condition is to allow the scholars to withdraw their opinion before the extinction of their generation, and to include in the *Ijmāʿ* the scholars of the following generation which is emerging. But this does not permit the inclusion of the scholars of the third generation; otherwise, *Ijmāʿ* will never be established.[4]

The exponents of the theory of lapse of time substantiate their point of view on the basis of the Qurʾān, the practice of the early Muslims, and reason. Adducing the Qurʾānic verse 2:143 they contend that the agreement of an existing generation is an authority over the subsequent generation because the former are at liberty to withdraw their opinion during their lifetime. Those who maintain that the scholars of an existing generation have no choice to withdraw their opinion after the establishment of *Ijmāʿ*, tend to make their *Ijmāʿ* an authority over themselves, (i.e. the scholars of the same generation), and not over others. The Qurʾān, on the contrary, makes it binding on the subsequent generation, and not on themselves. Further, there is an evidence which shows that the Companions disagreed after their complete agreement on a given question. On the question of the sale of salve mother, ʿAlī is reported to have disagreed with ʿUmar later on, although initially he agreed with him. Abidah al-Salmani (d. 72 A.H.), an eminent Successor, reportedly remarked about his disagreement, "Your agreement with he community (*Jamāʿah*) is dearer to us than your personal opinion alone." This shows that *Ijmāʿ* of the Companions was reached on ʿUmar's opinion, but ʾAlf withdrew his opinion

[4] ʿAbd al-ʿAzīz al-Bukhārī, *op. cit.* III, 963.

subsequently. Again, ʿUmar opposed the agreed practice of equal distribution of booty prevalent during the caliphate of Abū Bakr. Besides, he reportedly fixed eighty lashes as *Ḥadd* punishment for drinking instead of the forty lashes practiced during the time of Abū Bakr. All these instances prove that lapse of time is an essential condition for the validity of *Ijmāʿ*. If this condition is waived, there is no possibility of establishing an *Ijmāʿ* because scholars can withdraw their opinion at any moment after the agreement has been reached.[5]

The condition of lapse of time is also substantiated rationally. It is argued that *Ijmāʿ* is sometimes reached on a point disputed among the scholars for their diverse interpretations. Scholars are free to change their opinion after their agreement. If this liberty is curtailed, the scholars will not put forward their opinions. This would ultimately arrest freedom of thinking in law. Moreover, an opinion becomes mature and crystallized after deep and repeated consideration for which sufficient time is required. This is also supported by the Qurʾānic verse 11:27 which condemns immature judgment. Secondly, if the disagreement of a jurist is not taken into consideration during his lifetime when *Ijmāʿ* is reached, his opinion will be nullified after his death. This is because after his death the scholars who survive him will give their opinion. His opinion will thus be neglected. This contradicts the theory of total *Ijmāʿ*. Thirdly, the agreement of the community is not superior to the opinion of the Prophet. His opinion becomes final after his death (probably because he changes it in his lifetime with the change of conditions or by the revelation). Fourthly, the scholars who agreed on a certain point might recollect any tradition of the Prophet which ran counter to their *Ijmāʿ*. Now if they withdraw their opinion, the previous *Ijmāʿ* will be considered erroneous. In case they do not

---

[5] Al-Āmidī, *op. cit.* I, 370-71.

change their point of view, this will be taken as their insistence on error. Lapse of time, therefore, is the only way out of this impasse.[6]

Al-Āmidī refutes these arguments severally as follows:

It is only by implication that verse 2:143 indicates that the agreement of the existing generation is an authority over themselves. But this cannot be proved on the basis of the verse in question, Moreover, the existing generation in more liable to apply their agreement to the themselves than to others. The Qur'ān no doubt indicates that this community will be called to bear witness to other communities. The community is thus particularized for this purpose. But according to the principle of particularization, the inferior is included in the superior. Therefore, the bearing of witness would logically apply to the existing generation before it applies to the subsequent one. As such, the agreement of the existing generation of the community will be binding on themselves. Furthermore, the acknowledgement of a person is at times accepted in his own favour, though his witness to others is rejected. Above all, this community will bear witness to other communities on the day of judgment after getting information from the prophets of respective communities. Therefore, the verse in question constitutes no evidence for the theory of lapse of time.

As regards the historical evidence adduced in support of lapse of time it should be noted that by his statement Ali did not mean the agreement of the whole community. Had it been so, he would have said, 'My opinion and the opinion of the community coincided', instead of saying, 'My opinion and the opinion of ʿUmar coincided.' Moreover, Jabir b. ʿAbd Allah is reported to have held the opinion during the caliphate of ʿUmar that the sale of slave-mother was permissible. This shows that there was disagreement on this

---

[6] *Ibid.*, pp. 370-71.

question during the caliphate of ʿUmar, and unanimous agreement was not reached on it. Also, the remarks of al-Salman do not prove the theory of lapse of time. This is because by these remarks he might have meant that his (ʿAlī's) opinion during the period when the community was characterized by unity, integrity, and obedience to the ruler was dearer to him than his opinion during the period when perversion and dissension prevailed. By this, he might have intended to save ʿAlī from any possible accusation of disobedience to Abū Bakr and ʿUmar. This is on the supposition that All changed his opinion after the establishment of *Ijmāʿ* on the prohibition of the sale of slave-mother. But this is already disputed. Besides, ʿAlī might have believed in the theory of lapse of time in *Ijmāʿ*.

As for the deviation of Umar from the established practice of equal distribution of booty during the caliphate of Abū Bakr, it is not correct to say that Umar changed his opinion after *Ijmāʿ* was reached on the point in question. Actually, he differed with Abū Bakr on this question from the very beginning during the latter's regime. Addressing Abū Bakr he is said to have remarked: 'Do you make a person who strives in the way of God by his life and property equal to a person who enters the fold of Islam unwillingly." Abū Bakr is reported to have replied: "They worked for God, and their reward lies on Him in the next world. But in this world, everyone should be provided according to his needs". There is no evidence to show that ʿUmar had withdrawn his opinion and finally agreed with Abū Bakr. He apportioned the spoils of war among the people on the basis of merit according to their work and service to Islam and not equally as Abū Bakr had done. He persistently followed his point of view because he held it originally during the caliphate of Abū Bakr.

As regards their contention that ʿUmar prescribed eighty lashes as punishment for drinking, it may be noted that in this case, he violated the *Ijmāʿ* by silence, as he was one of those who kept silent on this question during the caliphate of Abū Bakr. And lapse of time is permissible in tacit *Ijmāʿ*.

The rational arguments advanced by them are not sound. In the first place, change of opinion is permissible in case a total agreement is not reached on a certain rule and that is still speculative. A speculative rule can be changed by another speculative rule. But when a rule becomes decisive and definite by the establishment of *Ijmāʿ*, no one is allowed to change his opinion and dissent from the unanimous agreement. It should be noted that a definite point cannot be changed by a speculative point. Change of mind, therefore, is allowed only prior to the establishment of unanimous agreement.

Secondly, there is a difference of opinion amongst the jurists on the question of the establishment of *Ijmāʿ* after the death of a dissenting scholar. Some are of the view that *Ijmāʿ* is valid after the death of a dissenter; others maintain that *Ijmāʿ* cannot be reached after the death of a dissenter because his opinion will be taken into consideration in *Ijmāʿ* And after his death, there is no possibility of his agreement with other scholars. The rest of the scholars who survived him do not constitute the totality of the community with respect to the question in dispute. Besides, the opinion of the scholar who passes away is not nullified after his death. It is as standing as it was during his lifetime.

Thirdly, the opinion of the Prophet is not established finally before his death because there is a possibility of its abrogation by fresh revelation during his lifetime. But it should be noted that the abrogation of a rule of law revealed to the Prophet is brought about by divine revelation which is decisive. A decisive rule no doubt can be repealed by another decisive rule. But *Ijmāʿ* which is decisive cannot be changed by an individual opinion which is speculative.

Fourthly, the presumption that a scholar might recollect a tradition of the Prophet that escaped his notice at the time of agreement is baseless. God protects the community from reaching an agreement against the Prophetic tradition. If unanimous agreement takes place on a certain question, one should rest assured that there would be no contradictory tradition from the Prophet on the question already agreed upon, or God would protect the narrator of the tradition from forgetfulness at the time of the establishment of agreement. Therefore, the question of making a decision against *Ijmāʿ* on the basis of a contradictory tradition does not arise.[7]

Al-Āmidī himself is of the view that lapse of time is not a necessary condition for the validity of *Ijmāʿ* if the unanimous agreement of scholars takes place expressly by word or deed or by both in their generation. These scholars constitute the totality of the community in their generation with respect to the point on which *Ijmāʿ* was reached. Their agreement is infallible in their day. No lapse of time is necessary for its validity. But a lapse of time is necessary if *Ijmāʿ* is established by silence. This is because sufficient time is required for the scholars who kept silent over a disputed point for consideration. Silence over a question does not necessarily indicate the assent or dissent of the scholars. Hence the death of scholars is necessary in tacit *Ijmāʿ*. Al-Āmidī describes this as the preferable and generally accepted opinion.[8]

We find a full-dress discussion of this problem in ʿAbd al-Mālik al-Juwayni (d. 478 A.H.). He analyses the arguments in favour of lapse of time and generation and refutes them. He, then, presents his own point of view. The argument for lapse of generation is summed up as follows: *Ijmāʿ* is not considered valid so long as a single scholar out of those who contributed to *Ijmāʿ* survives. But it is not necessary

---

[7] *Ibid.*, pp. 371-74; al-Ghazālī *op. cit.*, 1, 122-23.
[8] Al-Āmidī, *op. cit.*, pp. 1, 366, 369.

that the scholars of the subsequent generation who join the previous generation should pass away. If the extinction of these fresh scholars too is stipulated, the idea of lapse of generation becomes absurd. Lapse of time and generation is essential to *Ijmāʿ* so that the scholars of the existing generation may not withdraw their opinion and thus *Ijmāʿ* is completely established. If the condition of lapse of generation is fulfilled, the *Ijmāʿ* is complete. Suppose the scholars of a generation are agreed on a question, and a roof falls on them shortly after their agreement, or all of them die of some epidemic, *Ijmāʿ* would be considered to be finally established because of the fulfillment of the condition of lapse of generation.

Al-Juwaynī partly differs from the jurists on this point. He thinks lapse of time or generation is not essential to the validity of *Ijmāʿ* in all circumstances. He divides *Ijmāʿ* into definite (*Maqti*) and speculative (maznūn). Dennite *Ijmāʿ* is based on a clear evidence. Sometimes the evidence is not clear but the scholars confirm it by their agreement. This makes an *Ijmāʿ* definite. A lapse of time or generation is not required for the validity of this type of *Ijmāʿ*. Here evidence carries more weight than agreement. Suppose the *Ijmāʿ* in a certain case is definite, but the evidence is not known, it would be considered that the scholars who agreed must have had some evidence which was not known to the subsequent generation. Besides, it is unusual that scholars agree on a point without an evidence. Hence lapse of time is not an essential condition for definite *Ijmāʿ*. As regards speculative *Ijmāʿ*, lapse of time is indispensable for its validity. If the scholars agree on a disputed point, and they consider it uncertain for want of evidence, their agreement is not valid unless sufficient time passes away. A lapse of time is necessary for this kind of *Ijmāʿ* for the sake of deep thinking and mature judgment. Hence it is not correct to say that *Ijmāʿ* is established if the scholars die shortly after their agreement. How can *Ijmāʿ* be valid when the scholars could not find considerable time for consideration? It is important to note that several aspects of a point on which *Ijmāʿ* was established remain hidden. If sufficient time is not allowed to think over it. various aspects of it would not come to light. In fact, the lapse of time redeems the lack of evidence for the point agreed upon.[9] Further, al-Juwayni maintains that it is not necessary for the validity of *Ijmāʿ* that all the scholars of a generation should die. Such a condition is meaningless. Only a lapse of time sufficient for consideration would serve the purpose.[10] The lapse of the whole generation is stipulated so that the scholars of that generation who participated in *Ijmāʿ* may withdraw their opinion. If they do not change their mind and pass away, *Ijmāʿ* would be finally established. But al-Juwayni does not agree with this view because there is every possibility that some scholars may withdraw his opinion in the long duration closing with the extinction of the whole generation. *Ijmāʿ* would thus never take place on any question. Therefore, he holds the opinion that it is worthwhile to allow sufficient margin for consideration even after the establishment of total agreement, but not necessarily the death of scholars.

Another point of view is that lapse of time is a necessary condition for the *Ijmāʿ* by silence. Al-Juwayni does not agree with this view. He thinks silence over a speculative point cannot be taken as *Ijmāʿ*, because whenever the scholars express their consent, *Ijmāʿ* would be uncertain if they have no definite evidence. Hence tacit or explicit evidence has no relevance to the lapse of time. What is important is that a question on which *Ijmāʿ* is reached must be speculative, having no decisive evidence. In such cases, lapse of time

---

[9] ʿAbd al-Malik al-Juwaynī, *Al-Burhān fī Uṣūl al-Fiqh*, Ms. No. 714-Uṣūl, Dār al-Kutub al-Miṣriyyah, fos. 195-96.
[10] *Ibid.*, fos. 196-97.

is, of course, an indispensable condition. Questions supported by a decisive evidence do not require a lapse of time for *Ijmāʿ*.[11]

Arguing in favour of unconditional *Ijmāʿ*, al-Bukhari, the commentator of Al-Bazdawī, remarks that the authority which justifies *Ijmāʿ* imposes no such condition as that of lapse of time for its validity. Moreover, the imposition of a condition not originally required by the sanctioning authority amounts to abrogating *Ijmāʿ*. Besides, it is already established that truth does not go beyond *Ijmāʿ*. The infallibility of *Ijmāʿ* is in fact a grace from God and it is not based on rational grounds. Had it been grounded in reason, it would not have been confined to this community alone. As such, truth is proved by *Ijmāʿ* per se without lapse of time. This is because if truth depends on the lapse of time, the community may possibly agree on an error by its unanimous agreement on a certain point before the lapse of time. But this is impossible as already proved. The contention of the opponents that no question is settled before the lapse of time is baseless. It should be noted that the time of consideration is already provided before their unanimous agreement. *Ijmāʿ* takes place when the community definitely agrees on a certain point and then the scholars express clearly that they believe in the point already settled by the consensus of the community. Hence there is no need of the condition of lapse of time.

Al-Bukhari expounds the orthodox view about the lapse of time as presented by Al-Bazdawī. When it is accepted, he says, that the truth is established by agreement per se with no condition of time, then no scholar would be allowed to withdraw his opinion after the agreement of the community. He then refers to al-Shaft who holds that a scholar can withdraw his opinion after unanimous agreement of the community. *Ijmāʿ* is not valid, al-Shafiʿi argues, if the total agreement is not found in the beginning just before its

---

[11] *Ibid.*

establishment. Similarly, it is not valid if total agreement is not found in the sequel when *Ijmāʿ* is in operation (*Fī Ḥāl al-Baqāʾ*). Total agreement is a necessary condition in the beginning and during the period of its continuity. This is possible only when all the scholars pass away. *Ijmāʿ* stands on the charismatic character of the community. In case a certain scholar changes his mind after the total agreement of scholars, the community would lose its charismatic character and would not be entitled to the grace of God. Hence *Ijmāʿ* would not be an authority before the lapse of generation. But it would be settled after the death of the scholars. This shows that *Ijmāʿ* takes place after the agreement of the community, but it operates and becomes an authority after the lapse of generation.

To these arguments, al-Bukhārī replies that no scholar is allowed to dissent from the unanimous agreement. The moment the community agrees on a certain point, it is as certain, settled, and final, as it becomes so after the lapse of generation. The agreement of scholars shows that truth lies therein, and it operates as a decisive authority. Disagreement after its establishment amounts to the violation of a decisive authority like the Qurʾān and Sunnah. The disagreement before *Ijmāʿ* does not correspond to the disagreement after *Ijmāʿ* which renders it invalid. Before the establishment of *Ijmāʿ* every scholar is allowed to follow his opinion, because the truth may lie in any opinion in the absence of *Ijmāʿ*. On the contrary disagreement after *Ijmāʿ* is the violation of *Ijmāʿ*. Such a disagreement shall be neglected. whether the generation lapses or not.[12]

There are some details about the theory of lapse of time. By this the advocates of this theory mean either (1) lapse of the whole generation, or (2) majority of the scholars, or (3) major part of a

---

[12] ʿAbd al-ʿAzīz al-Bukhārī, *op. cit.*, III, 964-65.

generation in general, or (4) all the scholars of a generation. In the first case, both the masses and scholars are taken into consideration; in the second case neither the masses nor the scholars exclusively, but both in part; in the third case only the masses; and in the fourth case only the scholars. Those who believe in one category do not believe in the other.[13]

A group of scholars holds the opinion that the condition of lapse of time is necessary for those questions which require time lag, such as homicide and marriage, because they are settled after deep consideration. They cannot be compensated after a decision has been taken and enforced. Another view says that lapse of time is necessary in case the majority of the participants in *Ijmāʿ* survives. But if the minority survives, *Ijmāʿ* will be established in their lifetime before the lapse of the whole generation. According to this view, *Ijmāʿ* takes place if the majority of the scholars passes away.[14] A third view says that questions not involving destruction (*Itlāf*) and deliberate annihilation (*Istihlāk*) do not require lapse of time. This is the opinion of al-Mawardi. A fourth view says that lapse of time is necessary in the case of the *Ijmāʿ* of the Companions, and not in the case of others. This is held by al-Tabarī.[15]

Abū Ali al-Jubbāʿi, an eminent Muʿtazilī thinker and an advocate of this theory, contends that lapse of generation is a means to acquire the knowledge of *Ijmāʿ*. An opinion spreads widely among the people during an extensive period of time when the whole generation passes away. If there is a person who dissents from the view agreed upon by the scholars can express his opinion before his death. Al-Baṣri refutes this line of argument. He remarks that either lapse of generation is the only means to acquire the knowledge of *Ijmāʿ* or

---

[13] Tāj al-Dīn al-Subkī, *op. cit.*, II, 160-161.

[14] *Ibid.*, p. 161. Al-Ghazālī describes this view as arbitrary having no proof in its support. Al-Ghazālī, *op. cit.*, 1, 122.

[15] ʿAlī ʿAbd al-Rāziq, al-*Ijmāʿ fil-Shariʿah al-Islamiyyah*, Cairo, 1947, p. 85.

there are other means, too. The former is not correct because one can get information about *Ijmāʿ* cither by hearing directly from each and every scholar or by asking some of them directly and getting information indirectly about others. The latter is also not sound because the spreading of an opinion widely among the people, of course, depends on a long period of time, but not indeed on the lapse of the whole generation. If it depends on the annihilation of a generation, people may differ among themselves on this point as they differ on the question of *Ijmāʿ* by silence.[16]

In the preceding paragraphs, we have noted the difference of opinion on the theory of lapse of time. We have seen that the majority of the scholars allow disagreement prior to the establishment of *Ijmāʿ* and not after it. According to the orthodox view, *Ijmāʿ* takes place as soon as total agreement is found. Others impose the time-condition to allow the scholars to rethink the point agreed upon. We are of the view that both groups have gone to extremes. It is not correct to say that thinking over a problem after the establishment of *Ijmāʿ* is not allowed. And the proposition that *Ijmāʿ* is finally settled after the lapse of the whole generation is also not sound. The middle way would be that a time lag is of course necessary after the establishment of *Ijmāʿ*. For this purpose, a time limit is to be defined after which no one should be allowed to differ. But since *Ijmāʿ* is an informal phenomenon, having no organized machinery, it seems to be difficult to observe such formalities.

---

[16] Abūl-Ḥusayn al-Baṣrī, *Kitāb al-Muʿtamad*, Damuscus, 1964, II, 538.

Chapter XI: The Value of *Ijmā*ʿ and Its Abrogation

In the previous chapter, we have shown that *Ijmā*ʿ is an autonomous authority, though it requires a supporting evidence from the Qurʾān or the Sunnah. The classical theory indicates that *Ijmā*ʿ is always based on an evidence, whether known or unknown. It never lacks it. There is prima facie a contradiction between the statements that *Ijmā*ʿ is an independent authority, and that it requires a supporting evidence. Either *Ijmā*ʿ or the evidence on which is stands is an independent authority, not both at the same time. The question has been dealt with in greater detail by the classical jurists as we have shown in Chapter IX. This gave rise to a controversy over determining the value of *Ijmā*ʿ whether it is a decisive (*Qaṭʾī*) authority or a speculative (*zanni*) one, and that in case it is a decisive authority, whether or not it can abrogate a rule and be abrogated. There is again, like many other problems, a difference of opinion among the scholars on these questions, as we shall see in the following paragraphs.

I

As *Ijmā*ʿ derives its sanction from the Qurʾān and the Sunnah, it is generally considered to be a decisive (*Qaṭʾī*) authority. Explaining its value Al-Bazdawī remarks that *Ijmā*ʿ establishes a rule of law with certainty. In other words, a speculative rule or a moot point becomes definite and certain by means of the approval of *Ijmā*ʿ. There remains no room for doubt, debate, and disagreement when it is confirmed by it. The dissenting opinion is then neglected. Hence Muslims recognized it as a decisive authority (*Ḥujjah Maqṭūʾ Bihā*).

Jurists, like al-Ṣayrafi, Ibn Barhān, al-Dabūsī, and al-Sarakhsi, hold the same view.[1]

Generally speaking, *Ijmā*ʿ necessitates action and certain knowledge. It stands parallel to a Qurʾānic verse or *Mutawātir* tradition in respect of certainty. The various categories of *Ijmā*ʿ have been determined on the basis of its transmission. The most effective of them is the *Ijmā*ʿ of the Companions transmitted by themselves by verbal expression. It corresponds to a Qurʾānic verse and a *Mutawātir* tradition. This is a decisive *Ijmā*ʿ in its true sense. The second category is the *Ijmā*ʿ of the Companions transmitted in part by verbal expression and in part by silence, i.e. some Companions expressed their consent verbally and others kept silent. This is below the first category. The third category is the *Ijmā*ʿ of the Successors on questions not disputed among the Companions. This is like a *Mashhūr* tradition. The last category is the *Ijmā*ʿ of subsequent generations on questions already disputed among the previous generations. This is like a solitary tradition which entails action and not certain knowledge. It is, however, superior to a rule derived on the basis of analogy. The first category of *Ijmā*ʿ entails both certain knowledge and action. Others entail only action. Another point of view is that all forms of *Ijmā*ʿ entail action and not certain knowledge. The first category of *Ijmā*ʿ is illustrated by the agreement of the Companions on essentials of Islam, such as belief in the Qurʾān being the word of God, and in the obligatory prayers, etc. The example of other forms of *Ijmā*ʿ is found in the following statement of ʿAbidah al-Salmānī, (d. 72 A.H.), "The Companions of the Prophet never agreed on any question as they agreed on offering four *Rakʿāt* of supererogatory prayer regularly before noon prayer, on saying dawn prayer in congregation in the light of dawn, on

---

[1] Al-Bazdawī, *Uṣūl al-Bazdawī*, Karachi, 1966, p. 245; ʿAbd al-ʿAzīz al-Bukhārī, *Kashfal-Asrar*, Istanbul, 1307 A.H., III, 971., al-Shawkānī, *Irshād al-Fuhūl*, Cairo, 1347 A.H. p. 70; Muhammad al-Khudari, *Uṣūl al-Fiqh*, Cairo, 1938, p. 279.

unlawfulness of marrying wife's sister during her (wife's) waiting period, and on paying the dower after consummation of marriage." Ibn Masʿūd, in one of his statements, refers to the *Ijmāʿ* of the Companions on pronouncing four Takbīrāt (i.e. Allah is most great) in a funeral prayer.[2]

Some jurists have exaggerated the value of *Ijmāʿ* so much so that they consider it prior to the Qurʾān and Sunnah. In favour of this view, it is argued that both the Qurʾān and Sunnah are liable to abrogation and interpretation. But *Ijmāʿ* is infallible and decisive. There is no room for doubt if a rule is supported by *Ijmāʿ*. It is also prior to *Qiyās* (analogy) because the latter is sometimes liable to fallacy. It is worthy of remark that the *Ijmāʿ* which is considered prior to the Qurʾān and Sunnah is the kind which is decisive (*Qatʾi*), verbal (*Lafzi*), visible or tangible (*Mushāhad*), or reported by *Tawātur*. As regards speculative *Ijmāʿ*, the Qurʾān and Sunnah are prior to it.[3] Supporting this viewpoint al-Isfahanī remarks that *Ijmāʿ* is superior to all sources of law (*Adillah*) and no authority can be basically compared with it. He ascribes this view to a large number of scholars.[4]

Another group of scholars, including al-Rāzi and Al-Āmidī, maintain that *Ijmāʿ* is a speculative (*Zanni*) authority, and not decisive, as generally understood. Their contention is, as discussed in previous chapters, that *Ijmāʿ* is established on questions based on analogy or solitary traditions which entail uncertainty. A third view is that if *Ijmāʿ* is established by unanimous agreement of competent scholars, it is decisive. In case it is preceded by disagreement, such as *Ijmāʿ* by

---

[2] Al-Bazdawī, *op. cit.*, pp. 245-247; al-Sarakhsi, *Uṣūl al-Sarakhsī*, Cairo, 1372 A.H., 1, 302-3, 318-19; al-Shawkānī, *op. cit.*, p. 70; Ibn al-Malak, *Sharḥ al-Manār*, Istanbul, 1306 A.H., pp. 258-59.

[3] Al-Qarafi, *Sharh Tanqih al-Fuṣul*, Cairo, 1306 A.H., pp. 146-47.

[4] Al-Shawkāni, *op. cit.*, p. 70.

silence, or the dissenters are in a minority, it is then speculative (probable).[5]

If the *Ijmāʿ* on a certain point is found contradictory to a clear text, the text would be taken as abrogated or interpreted, because a decisive *Ijmāʿ* is not liable to abrogation or interpretation. The *Ijmāʿ* of the Companions shall be preferred to that of the Successors, because the former are superior to the latter. The universal *Ijmāʿ* takes precedence over the *Ijmāʿ* which runs counter to universality. The *Ijmāʿ* reached in a generation which totally passed away, and the one not proceeded by disagreement, are prior to other forms of *Ijmāʿ*.[6]

II

The *Ijmāʿ* transmitted by a solitary report is speculative (zanal or probable). There is a controversy over the validity of such an *Ijmāʿ*. It is allowed by the Hanablis and a group of the Shāfiʿīand Hanafl jurists. Some of the Hanafīs and Shafit's like al-Ghazāli reject such a form of *Ijmāʿ*. There is, however, a general agreement on the fact that what is established by an isolated report is speculative (probable) in respect of transmission (*Sanad*), but it may be decisive in respect of its text.

The supporters of this view argue from the tradition of the Prophet which says: "We decide on the basis of what is obvious (*al-Zahir*), and God has control over secrets." The definite particle prefixed to the *Zahir* (obvious) denotes generality of meaning which covers the *Ijmāʿ* transmitted by a solitary report. This sort of *Ijmāʿ* is probably and obviously valid. Further, this can also be established analogically. A solitary report about the existence of *Ijmāʿ* on a

---

[5] *Ibid.*
[6] ʿAlī ʿAbd al-Rāziq, *al-Ijmāʿ fil-Sharīʿah al-Islāmiyyah*, Cairo, 1947, pp. 96-97.

certain question entails probability. It is an authority equally valid like a solitary tradition of the Prophet which also entails probability.

The opponents contend that *Ijmāʿ*, like analogy and solitary tradition, is a recognized principle of jurisprudence. But neither any positive consensus nor any definite textual evidence from the Qurʾān of the Sunnah shows that such a type of *Ijmāʿ* is an authority. Other additional obvious evidences (*Zawāhir*) cannot be employed in fundamentals (Uṣūl). though they may be used in subsidiary cases (*fur*). That such a kind of Ijmāʿ is an authority or not in fact depends on its value. Those who regard *Ijmāʿ* as a decisive authority believe that a solitary report cannot be useful in transmitting *Ijmāʿ*. But those who regard it as a speculative authority believe that the *Ijmāʿ* transmitted by the solitary report is a valid authority.[7]

Some Shāfiʿī jurists raise the objection that the *Ijmāʿ* transmitted through an isolated report cannot entail action because the former is a decisive authority while the latter is a probable and speculative authority. To this, it is replied that a decisive *Ijmāʿ* is not established by a solitary report. The *Ijmāʿ* established on its basis is probable and speculative.[8]

III

Rejection of *Ijmāʿ* amounts to heresy because it is a decisive authority like the Qurʾān and the Sunnah. The denial of this doctrine, says al-Bazdawī, in principle (*Fil-Aṣl*), i.e. as a source of law and an autonomous valid authority, is disbelief.[9] But there is a difference of opinion on the rejection of *Ijmāʿ* established on a particular question based on speculative evidence. There is a general agreement of the jurists on the point that rejection of

---

[7] Al-Āmidī, *al-Ihkam fi Uṣūl al-Ahkām*, Cairo, 1914, I, 404-405.
[8] Ibn al-Malak, *op. cit.*, p. 257.
[9] Al-Bazdawī, *op. cit.*, p. 245.

speculative (*zanni*) *Ijmāʿ*, such as *Ijmāʿ* by silence, or the one transmitted through a solitary report, is not disbelief. Besides, some Muʿtazili scholars do not regard the rejection of even decisive (*Qaṭʿī*) *Ijmāʿ*, such as the *Ijmāʿ* of the Companions, as disbelief. The reason is that *Ijmāʿ* in their opinion is a speculative and uncertain (*zanni*) authority. The majority of the jurists maintain that rejection of the *Ijmāʿ*, which involves questions that are known both to the masses and to the scholars, is disbelief. The following may be mentioned as an example: the number of obligatory prayers, the number of their *Rakʿāt*, the hajj pilgrimage fasting during Ramadan, unlawfulness of adultery, drinking, theft, and usury. But the rejection of the *Ijmāʿ*, which involves questions exclusively known to the scholars, is not disbelief. Some of them are: unlawfulness of the combination of a woman and her aunt in marriage, invalidity of hajj by having sexual intercourse before staying at ʿArafat, giving one-sixth of the property to the grandmother of the deceased, excluding uterine brother from inheritance in the presence of grandfather, and excluding a person who killed his relative from inheritance. A man who rejects *Ijmāʿ* on such questions is not a disbeliever, but will be considered a heretic. Likewise, a person who interprets a religious question which is open to interpretation (*Ijtihād*) will not be called a disbeliever.[10] Rejection of *Ijmāʿ* on questions not related to religion, such as the existence of Baghdad, is not disbelief.[11]

The various points of view on this question are summed up as follows:-

1. Rejection of speculative (*Maẓnūn*) *Ijmāʿ* is not disbelief. This view is unanimously held by the scholars.

---

[10] ʿAbd al-ʿAzīz al-Bukhārī, *op. cit.*, III, 381-82; Al-Āmidī, *op. cit.*, I, 405.

[11] Al-Maḥallī, *Sharḥ Jamʿ al-Jawāmiʿ*, Cairo, 1297 A.H., II, 172.

2. Rejection of decisive *Ijmāʿ* is disbelief according to one point of view.

3. It is not disbelief according to another point of view.

4. Rejection of *Ijmāʿ* on essentials of Islam known to all of necessity is disbelief. This opinion is unanimously held by the scholars.

5. Rejection of *Ijmāʿ* on points of detail or on questions other than fundamentals of Islam is disputed. It is disbelief according to some, and not disbelief according to others. The correct view is that such a type of *Ijmāʿ* is not disbelief.[12]

Al-Juwaynī and al-Ghazālī vehemently criticize the orthodox view about the rejection of *Ijmāʿ*. They are of the opinion that one should be very scrupulous in excommunicating a Muslim because the matter is not so easy as generally understood.[13] Further, al-Ghazali observes that violation of a rule of law based on *Ijmāʿ* is not disbelief, for there is a great deal of controversy over the doctrine of *Ijmāʿ* among Muslims. When the jurists excommunicate a Muslim who violates *Ijmāʿ*, by this they mean the *Ijmāʿ* supported by an indubitable authority (*Mā Maqtūʾ Bih*) which may be a Qurʾānic text or *Mutawātir* tradition (a tradition which has been transmitted constantly by a large number of people).[14]

IV

We may now discuss the problem of the abrogation of *Ijmāʿ*. According to the classical theory, any rule established by *Ijmāʿ*, can neither be abrogated by the Qurʾānic injunction, or the Sunnah, or

---

[12] Al-Qadi ʿAbdu al-Din al-Iji, *Sharḥ Mukhtaṣar al-Muntahā*, Cairo, 1307, A.H., p. 144.

[13] ʿAbd al-Malik al-Juwaynī, *al-Burhan*, Ms. 714. Uṣūl Dār al-Kutub al-Miṣriyyah, fo. 205; Al-Ghazālī, *al-Tafriqah bayn al-Islām Wal-Zandaqah* (in Majmuʿah al-Rasaʾil), Bombay n.d., 4, 8, 12-14.

[14] Al-Ghazālī, *al-Mankhūl,* Damuscus, Dar al-Fikr, n.d. p. 309.

subsequent *Ijmā'*, nor can it abrogate any rule based on them.[15] In opposition to the orthodox view, Al-Bazdawī maintains that a previous *Ijmā'* can be abrogated by a subsequent *Ijmā'* in the same or next generation.[16] We analyze presently the arguments in favour of the orthodox viewpoint.

In his *Al-Risālah*, al-Shāfi'ī has discussed the question of abrogation in greater detail. According to him over against the classical theory, a Qur'ānic rule can be abrogated only by another Qur'ānic rule, and the Sunnah by the Sunnah, and not the Qur'ān by the Sunnah and vice versa. But he does not talk of the abrogation of *Ijmā'*. The chapter captioned, "The abrogating and the abrogated (prescripts) which are indicated by the Sunnah and *Ijmā'*, implies that *Ijmā'*, in his opinion, indicates the rules abrogated by the Qur'ān or the Sunnah. *Ijmā'* does not abrogate a previous *Ijmā'*. Al-Shāfi'ī, however, is not clear on this point.[17] This shows that the notion of the abrogation of *Ijmā'* might have emerged in the post-Shāfi'ī period when the principles of law were formulated and finalized.

We may take up the theory that *Ijmā'* cannot be abrogated by the Qur'ān, the Sunnah, or *Ijmā'*. The argument is that the *Ijmā'* reached on a certain question after the lifetime of the Prophet will be abrogated by the explicit text (Naṣṣ) of the Qur'ān, Sunnah, *Ijmā'*, or *Qiyās*. If it is repealed by the text of the Qur'ān or the Sunnah, that must have existed during the time of the Prophet preceding the establishment of *Ijmā'*. And it is impossible that a explicit revealed text may come into being after the death of the Prophet. It is an established fact that the explicit revealed text (Naṣṣ) precedes *Ijmā'*. Now if *Ijmā'* runs contrary to the revealed text, such an *Ijmā'* would be erroneous. But *Ijmā'* of the community can never be erroneous.

---

[15] Al-Qarafi, *op. cit.*, p. 137.
[16] Al-Bazdawī, *op. cit.*, p. 247.
[17] Al-Shāfi'ī, *al-Risālah*, Cairo, 1321 A.H., pp. 16-21.

Hence it cannot be abrogated by the Qur'ān or the Sunnah. Similarly, it cannot be repealed by a subsequent *Ijmā'* because the latter is either based on an evidence contrary to the evidence of the former or it has no evidence. If the subsequent *Ijmā'* is not based on an evidence it would be erroneous. But that is impossible. If it is based on some evidence, that evidence would either be a text of the Qur'ān or the Summah, or it would be an analogy. The evidence cannot be a text of the Qur'ān or the Sunnah because it precedes *Ijmā'*. Now if *Ijmā'* contradicts the text, it is impossible. The evidence cannot be an analogy because it requires an original basis. The original basis would again be a clear injunction from the Qur'ān or the Sunnah or that would be an *Ijmā'* or *Qiyās* (analogy). In the case of *Ijmā'*, it again requires a supporting evidence from the Qur'ān or the Sunnah or analogical extension. In both cases, an original basis is again required, and the reasoning goes on ad infinitum. This constitutes a vicious circle. Hence the abrogation of *Ijmā'* by any other authority is not allowed.[18]

Conversely, *Ijmā'* cannot abrogate any rule of law based on the Qur'ān, Sunnah, *Ijmā'*, or *Qiyās*. It is contended that no one knows how long a divine injunction will remain good (valid) and when it will become evil (invalid) for the Muslims. The period of time of the validity and invalidity of the divine prescription is known to God alone. Hence the injunctions enunciated in the Qur'ān or the rules ordained by the Prophet could be repealed in his lifetime, and not by *Ijmā'* after him. This view is agreed upon by the scholars in general. Further, no rule of law can be repealed by *Ijmā'* during the time of the Prophet, for the *Ijmā'* established in his time must have

[18] Al-Āmidī, *op. cit.*, III, 226-29; al-Baṣri, *Kitāb al-Mu'tamad*, Damuscus, 1964, 1, 432-34.

his approval. If he abrogates a rule expressly, his statement will count and not the *Ijmāʿ*. Hence *Ijmāʿ* in his time carries no value.[19]

Al-Āmidī defends the orthodox view in a more logical way. He argues that a rule repealed by *Ijmāʿ* would be based either on an explicit text (Naṣṣ) or *Ijmāʿ* or *Qiyās*. The annulment of a rule based on a text by *Ijmāʿ* is impossible. The reason is that *Ijmāʿ* must be supported by an evidence. In case it is not supported by an evidence, it is erroneous. If it has an evidence, that evidence must be either a text (Naṣṣ) or *Qiyās*. If it is a text, the rule is actually repealed by that text and not by *Ijmāʿ*. Suppose that *Ijmāʿ* at all repeals a rule it repeals in the sense that it shows the rule which actually abrogates. If *Ijmāʿ* repeals a rule based on a previous *Ijmāʿ*, the subsequent *Ijmāʿ* is valid, for contradiction between the two cases of *Ijmāʿ* on the same question is not allowed. If the rule is based on *Qiyās*, then it would be seen whether the *Qiyās* is valid or invalid. In case the *Qiyās* is valid, *Ijmāʿ* contradicts it. If the *Ijmāʿ* is not supported by any evidence, the *Ijmāʿ* is erroneous and *Qiyās* is valid. If the *Ijmāʿ* is supported by an evidence, the evidence would be either a text (Naṣṣ) or *Qiyās*. If it is a text, the rule is actually repealed by the text and not by *Ijmāʿ*. If the evidence is based on *Qiyās*, this *Qiyās* would be either superior or inferior or equal to the former *Qiyās*. If it is superior or equal, the former *Qiyās* on which the rule is based does not establish the rule perfectly, because a rule established by *Qiyās* should be superior to all possible cases. If the fomer *Qiyās* is superior, it means that the *Qiyās* on which, *Ijmāʿ* was reached was erroneous. But this is impossible. Hence *Ijmāʿ* cannot be an abrogative.[20]

Isa b. Aban (d. 221 A.H.) and some Muʿtazilī thinkers oppose the classical view. They contend that the orthodox theory conflicts with the historical evidence and reason. As regards history, Ibn ʿAbbas

---

[19] Al-Sarakhsi, *op. cit.*, II, 66-67.
[20] Al-Āmidī, *op. cit.*, 111, 229-30.

reportedly asked ʿUthman, "In the presence of two brothers how did you reduce mother's share from 1/3 to 1/6 in the law of succession, whereas the Qurʾān says: If he has brothers, to his mother a sixth?" (4:11) Grammatically, two brothers cannot be called brothers (in plural) as the Qurʾān prescribes". Uthman replied, "Your community reduced her share, O boy! I cannot violate a rule established before me, and practised by the people continuously." This clearly shows that a rule based on the Qurʾān can be repealed by *Ijmāʿ*.

This also can be justified on the basis of reason. *Ijmāʿ*, being a decisive source of law, entails certain knowledge like the Qurʾān and the Sunnah. It should, therefore, be allowed to repeal a rule of law like other decisive sources. Besides, *Ijmāʿ* is superior in authority to a well-known tradition. When the inferior can abrogate a rule, the superior a fortiori should do so.

Replying to the aforesaid contentions Al-Āmidī remarks that the instance quoted from history is not correct. The argument could be valid if the prescription of the Qurʾān, i.e. 1/3 share, were abrogated. But this is not so. In fact, the question is disputed. Further, there is also a difference of opinion among the scholars whether plural applies to two or more than two in number, Zayd b. Thabit is said to have held the view that 'the two brothers' occurring in the verse in question are identical to 'brothers' (in plural), and that the minimum number required for plural is two.

As for their rational argument, Al-Āmidī replies that it is correct to say that *Ijmāʿ* has been given a position on a par with the text of the Qurʾān and the Sunnah. But this is true in general. In some exceptional and particular cases, like the question of abrogation,

Ijmā' cannot be placed on an equal footing with the Qur'ān and the Sunnah.[21]

In opposition to the classical theory of abrogation of *Ijmā'*, Al-Bazdawī thinks a rule established by a previous *Ijmā'* can be repealed by a subsequent *Ijmā'* of the same form in the same generation or in two different generations.[22] Explaining his viewpoint al-Bukhari says that a decisive *Ijmā'* can be repealed by a decisive *Ijmā'* and not by speculative one. A speculative *Ijmā'* can be abrogated by a decisive as well as a speculative *Ijmā'* because the former is inferior to the latter. If the Companions agree on a certain question at a certain time, it is permissible that they may change their previous agreement, and establish a fresh agreement on the same question after lapse of time. The subsequent *Ijmā'* will abrogate the previous one. This is because the *Ijmā'* of the Companions, whenever it may take place, carries the same value and importance. All cases of the *Ijmā'* of the Companions resemble each other in value and form. But the *Ijmā'* of the Companions cannot be abrogated by the *Ijmā'* of the Successors because the latter are inferior to the former. The *Ijmā'* of the Successors can be repealed by their own *Ijmā'* subsequently because they are all equal in status. The abrogation of *Ijmā'* by a subsequent *Ijmā'* is lawful because it is possible that the term prescribed for a rule established by *Ijmā'* may lapse, and this lapse of term is discovered by the jurists by their agreement contrary to their previous agreement. This is just like the replacement of a text (Naṣṣ) by another text (Naṣṣ), indicating that the term of the previous rule of law has come to an end. Further, previous *Ijmā'* might have taken place in a given situation. Therefore, it may change with the change of the situation.

---

[21] Al-Āmidī, *op. cit.*, II, 328-29, III, 229-31; al-Sarakhsi, *op. cit.*, II, 66.

[22] Al-Bazdawī, *op. cit.*, p. 247.

He refutes the classical theory that the abrogation of *Ijmāʿ* is not possible after the death of the Prophet owing to the close of the revelation. The injunctions, he says, are of two kinds. Some are based on revelation, others on individual interpretation and agreement. The injunctions based on revelation and explicit pronouncements of the Prophet cannot indubitably be repealed after the close of the revelation. But the injunctions established by the individual interpretation and consensus of opinion can be repealed after his death because the time of establishing *Ijmāʿ* has not elapsed. It still survives and continues, and *Ijmāʿ* may take place at any time. The scholars of a subsequent generation might argue, with the help of God, in all probability, on the basis of a better authority than the scholars of the previous one. This *Ijmāʿ* may run contrary to the previous *Ijmāʿ*. The subsequent *Ijmāʿ* on the same question will indeed serve as an indication of the expiry of the term of the previous rule based on *Ijmāʿ*. One might ask, "How is it permissible to determine by the individual opinion the expiry of the term of a rule established by *Ijmāʿ*? The expiry of the term of a rule cannot be determined by the individual opinion." To this, it is answered that the argument does not suggest that the expiry of the term of a rule of law is determined by the individual opinion. In fact, it says that when the term of a rule of law expires by the lapse of interest and expediency (*Maṣlahah*) involved in that rule, God helps the scholars of the following generation to agree on a rule of law contrary to the previous one. Their agreement on a contrary rule of law shows that the rule has changed with the change of expediency and public interest and that the term of the previous rule of law has come to an end, though the scholars may not realize the change of expediency and of the term at the time of their agreement.[23]

---

[23] ʿAbd al-ʿAzīz al-Bukhārī, *op. cit.*, III, 896, 970, 982.

Rules bearing eternal value, i.e. which do not change with the change of time and space, are not liable to abrogation. They are, for example, faith in God, obedience to the parents, truth in speech, the unlawfulness of disbelief, of doing harm to the parents, and telling a lie. Rules whose eternity has been expressly indicated in the text itself are also not subject to annulment. Al-Māwardi, Shurayh b. Abd al-Karim al-Rūyānī (d. 505 A.H.) are of the view that such rules may be abrogated and may not be abrogated. They may not be abrogated because the text expressly indicates their eternity. They may be abrogated because the word 'eternity' might stand for a long duration of time by way of emphasis and not for infinite time in its true sense. Permissibility of abrogation in such cases has been taken as a sound and accepted view, and attributed to a large number of scholars. Some jurists are of opinion that traditions (*Akhbār*) are not liable to abrogation because nothing can happen contrary to the pronouncements of the Prophet. Finally, those who believe that acts are good and bad by divine declaration hold the view that all kinds of rules, whether of permanent or ephemeral nature, are liable to annulment. But those who determine the quality of acts by reason draw a distinction between eternal and changing rules for applying the principle of abrogation.[24]

V

We may now discuss the problem of the compound *Ijmāʿ* (al-Ijmāʿ al-Murakkab). According to the classical theory, if the scholars agree on two different opinions about a disputed point, this agreement would be taken as *Ijmāʿ*. This kind of *Ijmāʿ* is technically known as compound agreement (*al-Ijmāʿ al-Murakkab*). The scholars of the

---

[24] Al-Shawkāni, *op. cit.*, p. 163; al-Baṣri, *op. cit.*, 1, 401-6, 413-15; al-Khudari, *op. cit.*, p. 252.

next generation are not allowed to agree on a third opinion which nullifies the two agreed opinions of the past generation. The next generation should follow either of these two opinions already agreed upon by the previous generation. Let us illustrate this point by giving examples. A person buys a slave girl and finds a defect in her after he had intercourse with her. There are two points of view regarding her return to the seller. According to one, the buyer cannot return her to the seller in any case. The other says that he can return her after the payment of indemnity (*'Uqr*). Now if the scholars in the following generation agree on a third point of view that the purchaser can return her without payment of indemnity (*'Uqr*), this sort of agreement would not be valid. Take another example. There is a difference of opinion on the question of giving share to the grandfather and the brothers of a deceased. Some jurists hold that all the property will go to the grandfather, and the brothers will have no share. Another group holds the view that both will have a share in the property. These are two agreed opinions. The third opinion would be that the brothers should take all the property, while the grandfather will have no share. Agreement on such an opinion is not valid. Let us consider a third example. Opinion is divided on the question of having intention in different kinds of ritual purity. According to one point of view, intention is necessary in all kinds of ritual purity. According to another, it is necessary in some kinds and not necessary in others. The third opinion would be that intention is not necessary in any kind of ritual purity. Agreement on this opinion is not valid. The reason for the invalidity of agreement on the third opinion in the aforesaid cases is that it nullifies the agreement of the previous generation.[25] Further, it is argued in support of the orthodox view that agreement on the third opinion against the agreement on two opinions in the past generation presupposes that the community previously agreed

[25] Al-Āmidī, *op. cit.*, I, 38,

on an error. But it has been established on the basis of traditions that the Muslim community cannot agree on an error. It is objected to this argument that the fresh opinion might be based on a different evidence stronger and sounder than the previous one. To this, it is answered that knowledge of all sorts of evidence is not necessary for attaining the truth. Even a single evidence is sufficient for ascertaining the truth. There is, of course, no harm if one has a fresh opinion on the basis of different evidence in one's individual capacity. But if the community agrees on this opinion, thereby infringing the agreement held in the past generation, then error would be attributed to the previous *Ijmāʿ* of the community. But this cannot be allowed because *Ijmāʿ* of every generation is infallible.[26]

The agreement on the third opinion in the following generation is allowed provided it is not contrary to the previous *Ijmāʿ*. It should partially agree with the *Ijmāʿ* of the previous generation. This can be illustrated by the example of intention in ritual purity. If the scholars in a generation agree that intention is necessary in some kinds of ritual purity and not necessary in others, this sort of *Ijmāʿ* will be all right. The reason is that this does not nullify the former *Ijmāʿ*, rather it partially agrees with it.[27] Slaughter of an animal by a Muslim is another illustration. Some jurists hold that if a Muslim slaughters an animal, and does not utter the name of Allah intentionally or inadvertently, eating the flesh of this animal is lawful. Others hold that it is unlawful to eat the flesh of such an animal. *Ijmāʿ* was held on both these views. Now if the scholars in a generation agree on the view that it is lawful to eat the flesh of an animal if a Muslim forgets to utter the name of Allah at the time of

[26] Al-Ghazālī, *al-Mustasfā*, Cairo, 1937, 1, 124.
[27] Al-Āmidī, *op. cit.*, 1, 386-87.

slaughter, but unlawful if he does so intentionally. Such an *Ijmāʿ* is valid because it does not nullify the previous *Ijmāʿ*.[28]

There is also an important point relating to the problem discussed above. If a legal issue remained disputed in a particular generation. can the scholars of the following generation adopt any of the divergent views about that issue by their total agreement, and reject the rest of them? There is a difference of opinion on this point. Abū Bakr al-Ṣayrafi, Ahmad b. Hanbal, Al-Ashʿarī al-juwayni, and al-Ghazali are said to have held the view that this sort of *Ijmāʿ* is invalid. Those who reject this kind of *Ijmāʿ* contend that difference of opinion on a legal point means that agreement was held on divergent views and that truth lies within the different views agreed upon by the previous generation. The following generation, therefore. may adopt any of them, but not reject others. Agreement on a particular view and rejection of the rest in a subsequent generation would entail that the community agreed on an error in the previous generation. But this is not correct in principle because the Muslim community. according to the classical theory, cannot agree on an error. Further, although the scholars of the previous generation are gone, their points of view still survive. How can *Ijmāʿ* take place in the presence of difference of opinion of the scholars of the previous generation? Had the scholars of the past generation been alive, no *išmā* could have been valid without their consent. Therefore, agreement on the issue disputed in the previous generation is not permissible. The opponents argue that *Ijmāʿ* of the existing generation is an authority by itself. The arguments of the scholars of the past or future generation are not taken into consideration for the validity of *Ijmāʿ*. Suppose a disputed legal issue is brought to the Prophet who gives his final decision. This verdict would be an authority henceforth, and the diverging opinions about

---

[28] Al-Isnawi, *Nihāyat al-Sūl*, Cairo, n.d., II, 247.

that issue before this verdict would not be deemed erroneous. For instance, people living at Quba during the time of the Prophet continued to say their prayers facing Jerusalem, and they did not know that the commandment to face the Kaʿbah was already revealed. They followed this commandment when they were informed, and their prayers during this period were declared valid by the Prophet. Similarly, the agreement of the scholars on different views about an issue in the previous generation would not be taken into consideration if the Muslims in a subsequent generation agree on any of their opinions, and reject the rest.[29]

The question of the sale of a slave-mother (*Umm al-Walad*) is an important illustration of the problem under discussion. This issue remained disputed among the Companions. Umar, the second Caliph, is reported to have imposed a ban on the sale of the slave women who had children. ʿAlī is said to have disagreed with him and held the view that they could be sold. The Successors are reported to have agreed after the generation of the Companions on ʿUmar's opinion, i.e. the slave-mothers should not be sold after their master's death. Al-Shaybāni, the well-known Hanafi jurist, recognized the consensus of the Successors on the point at issue, and is reported to have considered as invalid the judgement for their sale if given by any judge. In this connection, he is said to have laid down a principle which says: If there is a legal question on which the Companions of the Prophet differed with one another and the Successors after them adopted any of their opinions by unanimous consensus, and rejected the rest, and no one followed those rejected opinions until today, such rejected opinion should not be followed. If a ruler comes and follows any of the rejected opinions against *Ijmāʿ* and gives legal judgement on the basis of that opinion, the judge appointed by the government should not allow

[29] Al-Sarakhsi, *op. cit.*, I, 318-21; Al-Āmidī, *op. cit.*, I, 394-95.

him to follow the rejected opinion about that legal question. He should, instead, refute him, and give himself a fresh legal judgement in consonance with the consensus of the Muslims."[30]

It is remarkable that Abū Hanifah and Abū Yūsuf are said to have differed with al-Shaybanī. The sale of slave mothers, according to them, is valid because it is doubtful, in their opinion, whether any such *Ijmā*ʿ ever took place on the point at issue after the generation of the Companions.[31]

Abū Bakr al-Jaṣṣāṣ has cited a host of examples where Companions differed among themselves during their generation, and Successors after them agreed on one of their diverse views during subsequent generation. Therefore, no difference of opinion, according to him, is allowed for such points. Besides, he does not allow differences of opinion on a rule agreed upon by the four recognized Sunni schools of law on a certain point. We give one example out of many cases. The Companions differed on the question of waiting period (*ʾIddah*) of a pregnant widow. Umar and Ibn Masʿūd are said have held that she must wait till the birth of her child. ʿAlī and Ibn ʿAbbās are reported to have held the view that she must wait for the period which is longer of the two, i.e. four months and ten days or the period lasting till the birth of her child. Both the groups adduced their arguments in support of their points of view. Subsequently, it was agreed by the Successors and the later jurists of the four established Sunni schools that the birth of her child is the end of her waiting period. It is objected to this sort of *ijmā*ʾ that truth is confined to all the diverse opinions of the Companions and not to a

---

[30] Al-Jaṣṣāṣ, *Kitāb Uṣūl al-Fiqh*, Ms. 229-usūl, Dār al-Kutub al-Miṣriyyah, fo. 232. It should be noted that ʿUmar might have prohibited the sale of slave-mothers on the basis of the traditions of the Prophet which do not allow such a transaction. Al-Bayhaqi, *al-Suman al-Kubra*, Hyderabad, Deccan, 1355 A.H., X, 344-48.

[31] Al-Sarakhsi, *op. cit.*, 1, 319-20; ʿAbd al-ʿAzīz al-Bukhārī, *op. cit.*, III, 968; al-Jaṣṣāṣ, *op. cit.*, fo. 232.

particular opinion agreed upon by the subsequent generation. When the Companions themselves allowed difference of opinion on a certain issue, it is not reasonable to impose a particular point of view on the community through *Ijmāʿ*. To this, al-Jaṣṣaṣ replies that *Ijmāʿ* is an authority parallel to the Qur'ān and the Sunnah. Reasoning and difference of opinion are allowed when textual evidence (Naṣṣ) and *Ijmāʿ* are not found about an issue. But no reasoning is allowed when one finds textual evidence or *Ijmāʿ* on a particular point. He illustrates his standpoint by citing the examples of the Companions who withdrew their decisions based on personal opinion after their acquaintance with the textual evidence.[32] This sort of thinking in the sphere of law in the medieval period reinforced the doctrine of *Taqlīd* (conformity). One is hard put to trace the agreement of the Successors and of the later jurists on disputed questions. If the classical jurists supposedly formed a unanimous opinion about a question, it does not follow that their agreement disallowed further thinking and interpretation. The following generations may find out a better evidence and reach an agreement sounder and stronger than the previous one. Human reason is developing with the march of time. There seems no reason to put a stop to further thinking and reviewing the problems answered in the past.

---

[32] Al-Jaṣṣāṣ, *op. cit.*, fos. 233a-234a.

Chapter XII: Divergence In the Theory of *Ijmāʿ*

I

As we noticed earlier, the doctrine of *Ijmāʿ* was recognized in Islamic legal theory on practical grounds. It started primarily with the aim of integrating the community. Hence divergence was inevitable in its theory. But the theory was not recognized by the community universally. Opinion was divided into three groups, viz. (a) those who believed in the orthodox theory of *Ijmāʿ*; (b) those who rejected it outright; and (c) those who adopted a middle course, believing in it in part and rejecting it in part. In previous chapters, we dilated mainly on the arguments of the first group, i.e. the exponents of *Ijmāʿ*. We, of course, discussed doubts, objections, and questions raised by the opponents in the course of analysis of the orthodox viewpoint. Here we shall analyze the arguments of the last two groups, along with the views of some eminent legal thinkers, like al-Nazzām, Ibn Hanbal, Ibn Hazm, Najm al-Din *al-Ṭūsī*, Ibn Taymiyah, and al-Shawkānī.

The arguments, for and against *Ijmāʿ*, have been analyzed in Chapter III. The moderate group holds diverse opinions about *Ijmāʿ*. Some of them validate the *Ijmāʿ* of the members of the Prophet's family, and some accept it only in rituals and not in social dealings. In previous chapters, we have partly discussed the views of this group such as the *Ijmāʿ* of the people of Medina, and *Ijmāʿ* of the Companions. The rest will be analyzed later.

It is worthwhile to mention the important points of difference in the theory of *Ijmāʿ*. Ibn Hazm has summed up such points, as enumerated below:

1. Only the agreement of the Companions is valid; the agreement of the later generations is not worth consideration.

2. The agreement of Muslims in every generation is valid.

3. The Muslims of the later generations are not allowed to violate the agreement reached by the Muslims in the early centuries of Islam.

4. *Ijmāʿ* is valid on the condition that nobody opposes it in the generation in which it is reached. In case anyone dissents, there would be no *Ijmāʿ*.

5. If the scholars of a generation differ on a question, agreement on its being disputed is established.

6. If the Muslims of a generation differ on a question, and the Muslims of the subsequent generations adopt any of these divergent opinions, their agreement would be valid.

7. *Ijmāʿ* is valid on a question about which disagreement is not known.

8. According to another point of view, such an *Ijmāʿ* is not valid. There must exist explicit reports about the agreement on that question in previous generations.

9. If the majority of the scholars agree on an opinion, while the minority differs with them, *Ijmāʿ* is not valid.

10. According to al-Tabari, if only one scholar differs, *Ijmāʾ* is valid.

11. Another opinion says that the majority opinion constitutes *Ijmāʿ*.

12. If a single scholar who is competent for *Ijmāʿ* opposes the agreement, then *Ijmāʿ* is not valid.

13. According to Mālik and his followers, the agreement of the scholars of Medina constitutes *Ijmāʿ*.

14. According to another point of view, the *Ijmāʿ* of the people of Medina is valid on points based on traditions, and not on analogical deduction.

15. According to a group of jurists, the agreement of the scholars of Kufa and Baṣra constitutes *Ijmāʿ*.

16. If the opinion of a Companion of the Prophet about a certain point is reported and no difference of opinion about that point is known, that opinion of the Companion would be considered *Ijmāʿ*.

17. *Ijmāʿ* is valid on condition that the opinion of scholars about a given problem spreads widely among the community, and no difference of opinion is known, in case the opinion is not diffused widely, *Ijmāʿ* is not valid.

18. Tacit agreement (*Ijmāʿ Sukūtī*) is valid according to a group of jurists, and invalid according to another. Others have imposed certain conditions for its validity.[1]

19. Al-Nazzām is said to have rejected *Ijmāʿ* outright.

20. The Kharijīs are also reported to have rejected *Ijmāʿ*.

21. The Shīʿah validate the *Ijmāʿ* of the members of the Prophet's family.

22. *Ijmāʿ* is valid on the points based on traditions and not on the points based on analogical deduction.

23. *Ijmāʿ* is valid only on *Mutawātir* (transmitted constantly by a large number of people) and not on solitary traditions.

24. *Ijmāʿ* is an opinion which reveals truth. It is immaterial whether the opinion is held by a single scholar or by more.

---

[1] Ibn Hazm, *Al-Iḥkām fī Uṣūl al-Aḥkām*, Cairo, 1347 A.H., IV, 128.

25. *Ijmā'* is valid provided it is supported by an evidence.[2]

II

Since the Khawārij are the earliest sect in Islam, we started our study with them. The Khawārij are reported to have rejected the doctrine of *Ijmā'*.[3] There seems no reason to doubt the reports about their rejection of this doctrine. The first problem on which we find their departure from *Ijmā'* is the question of levying tax on agricultural lands of Arabia. According to the established practice in the early days of Islam, no Kharāj was levied on the agricultural lands of Arabia. Only 'Ushr (1/10) could be levied on them. But *Kharāj* was levied on the lands outside Arabia. Thus, a distinction was drawn between the agricultural lands of Arabia and those lying outside it. The Khawārij did not recognize this distinction. They maintained that the agricultural lands of Arabia were as equally liable to *Kharāj* as the non-Arabian lands. Abū Yūsuf criticizes their stand for opposing the agreement of the Companions and the opinion of 'Umar and 'Alī on this question. He thinks the agreed practice of the early Muslims and the agreement of the Companions carried more weight than the individual opinion of the Khawārij.[4]

The Khawārij emerged as an opposition group out of political upheaval in the early decades of Islam. With the establishment of orthodoxy in the course of time, they founded their own school of thought. They differed from orthodoxy on law, dogma, and rituals. Their disagreement started from the question of arbitration (Taḥkīm). They rejected arbitration because they stressed the

---

[2] Al-Āmidī, *Al-Ihkām fi Usūl al-Ahkam*, Cairo, 1914, I, 286, 380, 381, 404, 405; al-Shawkāni, Irshād al-Fuhūl, Cairo, 1347 A.H., pp. 70, 79-80.
[3] Al-Āmidī, *op. cit.*, I, 286; al-Baghdadi, Kitāb Usūl al-Din, Stanbul 1928, p. 19; al-Shawkānī, *op. cit.*, p. 65.
[4] Abū Yūsuf, *Kitāb al-Kharāj*, Cairo, 1302 A.H., p. 33.

authority of the whole community. Since arbitration divided the community into two groups with two leaders, they vehemently opposed this doctrine. We are told that the Khawārij had not earlier believed in electing a caliph and establishing a state. They believed that Muslims should regulate their affairs of life in accordance with the injunctions of the Qur'ān. But later on, they changed their opinion and elected 'Abd Allah b. Wahb al-Rasibi (d. 38 A.H.) as their leader.[5] But al-Najadāt, a well-known Khārijī sect, continued to hold the same view. According to them, the Muslim community does not require any *Imām* (leader); people should settle their affairs in the light of the teachings of the Qur'ān.[6] It appears that their disagreement with the moderate group was a reaction to the severe criticism directed against them. Primarily, they believed in the authority of the whole community - a belief consequently held by orthodoxy in the form of *Ijmā'*. The concept of *Ijmā'* started with the idea of the infallibility of the community.[7] This authority of the community then shifted to the body of *'Ulamā'*. The Khawārij in a way were actually the pioneers to invoke the concept of the infallibility of the community, i.e. *Ijmā'*.

The Khawārij differed with orthodoxy not only on points of detail, but also on essentials. The only authority in their opinion was the Qur'ān. According to them, the Sunnah and *Ijmā'* were not independent authorities. Hence, the majority of them rejected the doctrine of stoning an adulterer and wiping the shoes in ablution, because these doctrines were not based on the Qur'ān. They amputate the hand of a thief for stealing anything. big or small. There is no consideration of the value of a thing because the Qur'ān

[5] Ibu Abil-Hadid, *Sharh Nahj al-Balaghah*; Cairo, a.d. I, 215.

[6] Al-Nawbakhti, *Kitāb Firaq al-Shī'ah*, Istanbul, 1931, p. 10; Al-Ash'arī, *Magālat al-Islamiyyin*, Cairo, 1950, 1, 190.

[7] Ahmad Hasan, The Concept of Infallibility in Islam, Islamic Studies, March, 1972, pp. 2-3.

does not mention it.[8] Al-Najadāt reportedly abrogated the punishment of drinking as enunciated by the Prophet. Al-Maymūnīyah allowed a person to marry the daughters of his daughter against the *Ijmā'* of the community, and they also denied Sūrat Yūsuf being a part of the Qur'ān.[9] They believed in the createdness of the Qur'ān,[10] and maintained that their opponents and those who commit grave sin are unbelievers.[11] They excommunicated 'Alī, 'Uthman, and other Companions who were involved in the civil war.[12] They believed, against the unanimous *Ijmā'* of the Muslims, that prophets could commit major or minor sins. They formulated the laws of rituals of their own. They maintained that ablution becomes void by telling a lie, backbiting, abusing, committing calumny, and by bearing similar immoral qualities. For their divergence from the four orthodox schools of law they are known as Khawāmis (a fifth school) in history.[13] It appears that Khārijism emerged as a separate school of thought during the caliphate of 'Alī because in a speech he criticized them for their divergence from the established practice of the Muslims.[14]

III

Among the Mu'tazilah al-Nazzām (d. 231 A.H.), Ja'far b. Harb (d. 236 A.H.) and Ja'far b. Mubashshir (d. 234 A.H.) are said to have rejected the doctrine of *Ijmā'*. Al-Nazzam is reported to have rejected *Ijmā'*

---

[8] Al-Baghdadi, *op. cit.*, p. 19.
[9] *Ibid.*, pp. 332-33; Al-Ash'arī, *op. cit.*, I, 166.
[10] Al-Ash'arī, 1, 174.
[11] Al-Baghdadi, *op. cit.*, pp. 332-33; idem, *al-Farq bayn al-Firaq*, Cairo, 1948, p. 70.
[12] Al-Khayyat, *Kitāb al-Intiṣār*, Cairo, 1952, p. 140.
[13] Ignaz Goldziber, *Le Dogme et la Loi de l'Islam*, Paris, 1958, pp. 161, 163; Atfish, Muhammad b. Yūsuf, *Shamil al-Asi Wal-Far'*, Cairo, 1332 A.H., I, 211, 233 passim.
[14] Ibn Abil-Hadid, *op. cit.*, II, 306-8.

for the first time.[15] There appears contradiction in the reports about al-Nazzām's view on *Ijmāʿ*. Some state that he rejected this doctrine outright, while others tell us that he recognized this doctrine but interpreted it in a different way. Accordingly, he believed that the whole Muslim community could agree on an error. [16] The authority, in his opinion, rests with the imam (spiritual leader)[17] and not with the agreement of the community. Al-Nazzām reportedly defined *Ijmāʿ* as an opinion which is considered to be an authority even if it is held by a single person.[18] Commenting on this definition al-Ghazali observes that it goes against the rules of etymology and common usage. He, however, defends him by saying that it is established by reports based on *Tawātur* that he considered opposition to *Ijmāʿ* unlawful.[19] Al-Āmidī's observation about al-Nazzam's definition shows that he recognized this doctrine as an authority. He remarks that al-Nazzām, in this definition, partly agrees and partly disagrees with this doctrine. He rejects the idea of the agreement of the people in authority (*Ahl Al-Hall wal-ʾAqd*) on the one hand, and accepts, on the other hand, the general opinion of the *ʿUlema* that opposing the doctrine of *Ijmāʿ* is unlawful. What is objectionable in his definition is that he applies the term *Ijmāʿ* to a single opinion. This sort of usage goes against the rules of etymology, and here it becomes more serious because in jurisprudence principles are derived simply from words.[20]

It appears that there is some misunderstanding about al-Nazzām's view on *Ijmāʿ*. Since he disagrees with orthodoxy in respect of a large

---

[15] Ibn Qutaybah, *Taʾwīl Mukhtalif al-Ḥadīth*, Cairo, 1326 A.H., pp. 21-22; al-Khayyat, *op. cit.*, p. 51; al-Tūsi, *"Uddat al-Uṣūl*, Bombay, 1312 A.H., II, 64; al-Baṣri *op. cit.*, II, 458.

[16] Ibn Qutaybah, *op. cit.*, pp. 21-22; al-Baghdadi, *Kitāb Uṣūl al-Dīn*, *op. cit.*, p. 20.

[17] Al-Shahrastāni, *Kitāb Milal wal-Nihal*, Cairo, 1910, II, 82.

[18] Al-Ghazālī, *al-Mustasfā*, Cairo, 1973, I, 110.

[19] *Ibid.*

[20] Al-Āmidī, *op. cit.*, I, 280-81.

number of doctrines, he is considered to be the opponent of *Ijmā*ʿ He rejected, for instance, the validity of divorce by making a sign. He also reportedly held that ablution does not become void by sleep.[21] He is said to have maintained that a solitary report entails certain knowledge provided it is combined with indications confirming the report. And the report of a huge body fails to entail certain knowledge if not confirmed by indications.[22] He asserted that the teachings of the *Shariʿah* should be definite. This is possible only when they are borne out by the letter of the text (Naṣṣ) or by the opinion of the imam. Hence, he is said to have believed in the authority of the imam. Again, he reportedly rejected the *Ijmā*ʿ based on a personal opinion or on analogical reasoning. It seems that such views might have naturally provoked hostile feelings against him. But al-Khayyat refutes the charges levelled against him about *Ijmā*ʿ. The works of al-Nazzām, he says, belie the views ascribed to him by his opponents. He also remarks that al-Jāḥiẓ might have been mistaken in communicating his point of view about various doctrines.[23]

Al-Nawbakhti (d. 310 A.H.) reports that al-Nazzam believed in the caliphate of Abi Bakr and validated it on the basis of *Ijmā*ʿ. He gives his reasoning to substantiate the caliphate of Abū Bakr as follows. The caliphate of Abū Bakr was valid on two grounds, namely on the basis of reason and of tradition. Rationally speaking, a person subdues himself to another person for one of three reasons: either he belongs to a powerful clan which supports him in case he enslaves others, or he is so well off that people obey him for his opulence, or he has superiority over people in respect of religion. Abū Bakr belonged neither to a powerful clan, nor was he a rich man. Therefore, he was elected as a caliph only by virtue of his

---

[21] Ibn Qutaybah, *op. cit.*, pp. 22-24.
[22] ʿAbd al-Jabbar, *al-Mughnī*, Cairo, 1965, XV, 392; al-Baṣri, *op. cit.*, II, 567.
[23] Al-Khayyat, *op. cit.*, p. 51.

religious supremacy. As regards traditional grounds, the multitude of reports state that the people had agreed on his caliphate and gave their consent unanimously. Hence Abū Bakr's caliphate is valid on the basis of *Ijmāʿ*. As for the legitimacy of *Ijmāʿ*, the Prophet is reported to have said, "God will not let my community agree on an error." Now if the agreement of the Muslims on his caliphate is erroneous, it follows that all prayers and other obligatory duties which are based on *Ijmāʿ* would become corrupt, and this would falsify the Qurʾān because it is also based on *Ijmāʿ*.[24] If this reasoning on the basis of *Ijmāʿ* attributed to al-Nazzām is correct, the reports about his objection to *Ijmāʿ* are not genuine.

Abū Rīdak attempts to defend al-Nazzām in a twofold way. First, he asserts that al-Nazzam had not rejected *Ijmāʿ* in principle, as is evident from the statements of al-Ashʿarī, al-Khayyat, and al-Nawbakhti. Second, he thinks the assumption of the rejection of *Ijmāʿ* by him arose from his laying emphasis on the certainty of the teachings of the *Shariʿah*. He opposed the orthodox practice to validate the rules based on personal opinion, analogical reasoning, and *Ijmāʿ* none of which constitutes a final authority. Hence, he criticized those Companions of the Prophet who pronounced verdicts in legal matters on the basis of personal opinion. On the contrary, he asserted that the injunctions of the *Shariʾah* should be based on the text. Moreover, he believed that it was difficult, rather impossible, that people unanimously agree on a single opinion. Concluding, Abū Ridah remarks that al-Nazzām might have doubted the doctrine of *Ijmāʿ* due to its theoretical complications, and for his belief that the rules of the *Shariʿah* should stand on a surer footing.[25] Al-Subki and some other scholars are of the view that al-Nazzām

---

[24] *Op. cit.*, pp. 10-11.

[25] M. Abū Ridah, *Ibrahim b. Sayyār al-Nazzām*, Cairo, 1964, pp. 23-24; cf. Marie Bernand, L'Igma' chez Abd al-Gabbar et l'objection d'An-Nazzam, Stvdia Islamica, XXX, 34-46.

himself believed in the possibility of *Ijmāʿ*. It is some of his disciples who rejected it. Their opinion might have been attributed to al-Naẓẓām.[26] It is worthy of note that the Muʿtazilah in general believed in the established practice and agreed traditions in the early centuries of Islam. It seems, therefore, quite certain that al-Naẓẓām must have recognized *Ijmāʿ* in principle. He might have criticized its theory as developed by orthodoxy.

IV

Let us now discuss the Muʿtazili viewpoint of *Ijmāʿ*. While writing on Muʿtazilah one faces the difficulty that their own extant works are rare. Therefore, one has to depend mostly on the works of their opponents. We have shown previously that at the early stage of the development of legal doctrine, especially in the pre-Shāfiʿī period, established practice and well-known traditions stood par excellence. Hence, the early schools of law followed the agreed practice and neglected the isolated traditions. We illustrate their views presently by giving examples.

Al-Shāfiʿī criticizes the *Ijmāʿ* of the scholars and asks his opponent (probably a Muʿtazili) to elaborate on this conception. Replying to him he observes: "This is the agreement (*Ijmāʿ*) of the scholars only. for they are the people who alone can know and agree on it. Thus, when they agree, this becomes an authority over those who do not know (i.e. for laymen); but if they do not agree, their opinions are no authority over anyone, and such matters must be referred back to a fresh *Qiyās* (analogical reasoning) on the basis of the previous agreement.... It matters little whether their agreement is based on tradition reported by them or without a tradition. And even when they disagree, it is immaterial whether there exists a tradition reported by them which agrees with what some of them held or not.

---

[26] ʿAli, ʿAbd al-Razīq, *al-Ijmāʿ fil-Shariʿah al-Islāmiyah*, Cairo, 1947, pp. 10-12.

For I do not recognize any traditions (*Ahadīth*) expect those which are agreed upon." To this, al-Shāfiʿī replies:" This is the refutation of traditions and justification of agreement (*Ijmāʿ*) because you believe that their agreement is authoritative and disagreement is no authority. It is immaterial (for you) whether there exists a verbal report or not."[27] From this it is evident that the Muʿtazilah in the early centuries were the exponents of *Ijmāʿ*.

Our presumption is further corroborated by the definition of *Ijmāʿ* enunciated by al-Jahiz (d. 255 A.H.). He gives this definition in the course of his criticism on the Shīʿah. The Shīʿah justify the caliphate of ʿAlī and his progeny on the basis of the Qurʾānic verse 4:58 applying the phrase *Aulī al-Amr* (men in authority) to them. Commenting on their interpretation al-Jahiz remarks that if their interpretation is supported by a tradition transmitted by reliable traditionists (*Aṣḥāb al-Akhbār*), then, of course, it is binding. But it is remarkable that all traditions are not binding. Some are solitary, and others are well known. The authentic tradition is one which is transmitted in a way that there should be no possibility of connection and meeting of the reporters together to agree on it. This sort of tradition is called *Ijmāʿ*. In case these two conditions are not fulfilled, then a tradition is not called *Ijmāʿ* even if the narrators are trustworthy. *Ijmāʿ* denotes (the agreement of) a number of persons about whom it is known that none of them met each other, nor communicated with each other, nor agreed on a fabricated tradition. Further, they transmitted the tradition in their varying circumstances. Besides, the hearer of the tradition must realize that they transmitted the traditions from the narrators like them and in like circumstances.[28] By this definition of *Ijmāʿ al-Jahiṣ* probably means transmission of a tradition by *Tawātur* (constant

[27] Al-Shāfiʿī, *Jimaʿ al-ʿIlm*, ed. Shakir, Cairo, 1940, pp. 52-53,
[28] *Al-Jahiz, al-ʿUthmāniyyah*, Cairo, 1955, pp. 115-16; Charles Pellat, *The Life and Works of Jahiz*, (Eng. tr. D.M. Hawke), London, 1969, p. 76.

transmission of a report by a large number of narrators). The term *Tawātur* might have gained currency in his time. The definition of *Ijmā'* put forward by him is different from the one furnished by the jurists in later ages. Al-Jahiz imposes a condition that the reporters should not meet, while the classical definition of *Ijmā'* says that the people eligible for *Ijmā'* should agree on a point by meeting or by silent consent. Further, he believes that the agreement of the people en masse on truth is well-nigh impossible. Hence disagreement of one or two persons about the point agreed upon is negligible.[29] This shows that al-Jahiz considers the majority opinion *Ijmā'* of the community.

With the popularization of traditions (*Ḥadīth*) towards the end of the second century of the Hijrah there arose a conflict between the agreed practice and the isolated traditions. The Mu'tazilah objected to the traditions which ran counter to the Qur'ānic teaching and the generally recognized practice. On the basis of this criterion, they frequently charged orthodoxy with accepting solitary traditions and deviating from the established practice of the community, i.e. *Ijmā'*.[30] This shows the paramount role of *Ijmā'* which it played in the formulation of law and dogma in Islam. In view of the supreme importance of this doctrine, Ibn Qutaybah, in his answer to the criticism of the Mu'tazilah, defends *Ijmā'* instead of solitary traditions. He remarks: "We believe that truth is established on the basis of *Ijmā'* more than on the basis of tradition (*riwāyah*). This is because *Ḥadīth* is subject to oblivion, interpretation, abrogation and the qualities of reporters. *Ḥadīth* sometimes states contradictory rules which are correct in different contexts. For instance, it is disputed whether one should pronounce one salutation or two at the end of the prayer. Both views are supported by traditions. The

---

[29] *Ibid.*, pp. 194-95.
[30] Ibn Qutaybah, *op. cit.*, 284-85.

Prophet sometimes commanded a person to do a certain work in a certain way, and subsequently, he commanded another person to do the same work in a different way, which was not known to the previous person. This latter command contradicts his former command. Now the same person, because of his ignorance, narrates his earlier command and not his subsequent command. But *Ijmāʿ* is immune to all these suspicions. This is why Mālik sometimes reports a tradition from the Prophet in al-Muwattā, and then says: "The practice in our town is so-and-so which contravenes the traditions." This he did because his town (Medina) was the home of the Prophet. If anything was in practice in his day, it continued to have been practised in subsequent generations. It is unthinkable that all later generations deviated from the practice prevalent in his town during his lifetime. This is because the practice of a generation carries more weight than a solitary tradition. Even traditions with perfect chains were not sometimes literally followed by the community. For instance, a tradition says that the Prophet combined noon and afternoon prayers, and sunset and night prayers in Medina in the time of peace without facing any terror. But the jurists are unanimously agreed that this tradition should not be followed literally. According to them, this is either abrogated or the Prophet had done so under a pressing necessity, i.c. due to rain or some other reason."[31] Ibn Qutaybah gives numerous examples of such traditions as were neglected because of their conflict with the established practice.[32]

This state of affairs continued in the formative phase of Islam. With the end of this period, the stray opinions against orthodoxy were considered opposed to *Ijmāʿ*. We stated in Chapter I that *Ijmāʿ* and orthodoxy became identical and the law and dogma were

---

[31] *Ibid.*, pp. 331-32.
[32] *Ibid.*, pp. 332-33.

standardized on the basis of *Ḥadīth*. This was done mainly through the efforts of al-Shāfiʿī and the traditionists. The traditions at this stage were universally recognized as a valid source of knowledge in Islam. Now the Muʿtazilah who were exponents of the established practice and well-known traditions, i.e. *Ijmāʿ*, were henceforth accused of deviation from *Ijmāʿ*, because solitary traditions which were opposed by the Muʿtazilah were recognized by *Ijmāʿ*. They were first criticized for holding the belief that a believer who commits a major sin is neither a believer nor an unbeliever. At the time when they pronounced this belief, there were three opinions prevalent among the community about this question. The Khawārij regarded such a person as an unbeliever. The Murjiʿah considered him a believer. Al-Hasan al-Baṣrī held him to be a hypocrite. We are told that the truth about his question was confined only to these three viewpoints. In other words, the community recognized these three opinions as the agreed belief of Muslims. Since the Muʿtazilah held a view which conflicted with the agreed belief, they were considered to have opposed the *Ijmāʿ* on this question. Al-Khayyat refutes the opinions prevalent about this question in his day and seeks to establish the Muʿtazilī viewpoint on the basis of the Qurʾān.[33]

There is another line of argument which seeks to prove that the Muʿtazilah were the opponents of *Ijmāʿ*. It is contended that, in the early days of Islam, a believer who committed a major sin was regarded as impious (*fāsiq*) by unanimous consensus. The Khawārij called him an unbeliever and impious; the Murjiʿah a believer and impious; the Shrah an ungrateful impious; and al-Hasan al-Baṣrī considered him a hypocrite and impious. All the sects thus agreed on calling him an impious (fāsiq). Since the Muʿtazilah opposed *Ijmāʿ* on this question, they earned the name 'Muʿtazilah' (seceders). ʿAmr b. ʿUbayd (d. 142 A.H.), a well-known Muʿtazili thinker, is said to have

[33] Al-Khayyāt, *op. cit.*, pp. 164-65.

withdrawn his belief about this question and accepted the one held by orthodoxy. Refuting the charge against the Muʿtazilah Ibn al-Murtada (d. 840 A.H.) observes that they had not diverged from *Ijmāʿ*, but they followed the practice agreed upon in the early days of Islam. In fact, they rejected the accretions which had crept into the established practice.[34] This corroborates the proposition that the Muʿtazilah believed in the doctrine of *Ijmāʿ*; they actually rejected the theory of *Ijmāʿ* as developed in the later centuries of Islam. Hence, al-Khayyat defends the Muʿtazilah against the charge of the rejection of *Ijmāʿ*.[35] The fact is also borne out by the Muʿtazili works on *Uṣūl al-Fiqh* such as al-Baṣri's Kitāb al-Muʿtamad and ʿAbd al-Jabbar's al-Mughnī.

V

The Shah, too, are reported by the Sunni jurists to have rejected the doctrine of *Ijmāʿ*.[36] Such reports, in fact, make an over-statement about their views on *Ijmāʿ*. We shall see presently that they do not reject the doctrine in principle, but interpret it in a different manner. Of course, we notice in the early Shīʿī writings the condemnation of personal opinion and analogical deduction frequently exercised by the Sunnis in their legal reasoning. But this was a general phenomenon in the post-Shāfiʿī period under the dominance of the traditions. Abū ʿAbd Allah Jaʿfar al-Ṣadiq (d. 148 A.H.), in his epistle addressed to the Shīʿah, severely criticizes the exercise of *Raʾy* and *Qiyās* and having recourse to *Ijmāʿ* in reasoning after the death of the Prophet. He condemns these principles on the basis of the Qurʾān and reason. He lays emphasis on unquestioning

---

[34] Ibn al-Murtada, *Ṭabaqāt al-Muʿtazilah*, Beirut, 1961, pp. 5, 38-40.

[35] Al-Khayyat, *op. cit.*, 51, 89, 94, 159-65.

[36] Al-Āmidī, *op. cit.*, I, 286; al-Shawkānī, *op. cit.*, pp. 63-64.
Almost all the Sunni works on *Uṣūl* attribute the rejection of *Ijmāʿ* to the Shīʿah. All that is affirmed by them is that they believe in the agreement of the members of the Prophet's family.

obedience to the infallible *Imām*.[37] Loyalty to the Imam is one of the fundamental doctrines of Shīʿism. The Sunnis formulated the principle of *Ijmāʿ* as a check against the fallibility of analogical reasoning. This principle, in the long run, became a supreme authority in all religious matters. The Shīʿah, on the contrary, took their imam as a final authority. Hence there is no question of recognizing *Ijmāʿ* as an authority by them. Yet it seems that they recognized this doctrine with a different interpretation probably under the influence of the Sunnis or as a compromise with them. That is why we find that some early authorities, like ʿAlī al-Rida (d. 203 A.H.), are reported to have recognized *Ijmāʿ* as an authority.[38] Al-Rawandi (d. 298 A.H.) regards *Ijmāʿ* as one of the sources of law, and frequently refers to it.[39]

The Shīʿī sources of the later period discuss the principle of *Ijmāʿ* in greater detail. Once *Ijmāʿ* was recognized in principle by them, the later Shīʿī jurists theorized it like the Sunnis. Really speaking, *Ijmāʿ* in Shīʿism is not an authority *pre se*; the actual authority lies with the person of the infallible imam. The function of *Ijmāʿ* in the Shīʿī legal theory is to unveil the opinion of the imam which is always included in the agreement of the entire Shīʿah community. In other words, the opinion of the imam cannot be known directly, especially when he is hidden, without the agreement of the Shīʿah scholars of the community. The agreement of the Shīʿah community is identified with the opinion of the imam. Here lies the significance of *Ijmāʿ* according to the Shīʿah. *Ijmāʿ*, in fact, is an instrument or a channel to reach the original authority. Thus, *Ijmāʿ* is a subservient authority and not an original one in their legal system.

---

[37] Al-Kulini, *al-Rawdah min al-Kafi*, Tehran, 1377 A.H., VIII, 5-8, 10, 13, 35.
[38] Al-Kulini, *al-Uṣūl min al-Kāfī*, Tehran, 1382 A.H., I, 169.
[39] Al-Khayyat, *op. cit.*, p. 131.

Explaining the doctrine of *Ijmā'* Abū Ja'far al-Tūsī (d. 460 A.H.) remarks: "We believe that the community cannot agree on an error, and what is agreed upon is right and authoritative. According to our belief, no generation is devoid of the existence of the imam, the custodian of the law. His opinion is authoritative. It is equally obligatory to refer to him as to refer to the Prophet... When this is established, the agreement of the community becomes authoritative because it includes the opinion of the infallible *Imām*.... But one might ask: When the imam and not *Ijmā'* has the authority, why do you mention it? Of course, the fact is what the question says. Nevertheless, the utility of *Ijmā'* is obvious. Sometimes the opinion of the imam about a given point is not known. On such occasions the necessity of *Ijmā'* arises, because the opinion of the *Imām* is incorporated in the agreement of the community. But in case the opinion of the *Imām* is definitely known, his opinion alone is the authority, and we shall neglect all other considerations."[40] It is clear from al-Tūsī's statement that *Ijmā'*, according to the Shī'ah, is an indirect authority. Although al-Tūsī himself justifies *Ijmā'* on rational grounds, he refutes the theory of *Ijmā'* as elaborated by the Sunnis. Since *Ijmā'*, according to the Sunnis, does not incorporate the opinion of the *Imām*, it has no value in the eyes of the Shiah. Hence, al-Tūsī and other Shī'ah jurists criticize the Sunnī's contention to substantiate *Ijmā'* on traditional grounds. They refute the interpretation of the Qur'ānic verses and the traditions adduced by the Sunnis in support of *Ijmā'*. But it is interesting to note that they too cite similar verses and traditions to justify the authority of the infallible *Imām*.[41]

We may now discuss some important points relating to the Shī'ī theory of *Ijmā'*. According to them, the definition goes; "Agreement of a body of the Shī'ah scholars which signifies, directly or indirectly

---

[40] Al-Tusi, *op. cit.*, II, 64; Abul-Qasim al-Qummi, *Kitāb Qawanin al-Usūl*, Tehran, 1304 A.H., p. 177.

[41] *Ibid.*, pp. II, 65-75.

by some other indications, the consent of the infallible imam on a rule of law which reveals his opinion."[42] *Ijmāʿ* is the agreement sometimes of all the Shīʿah community, and sometimes of a body of the scholars. In case some scholars give their legal opinion on a given point and it is not opposed after it spreads widely among the community, but it does not disclose the opinion of the imam positively, such a tacit agreement is not valid.[43] The tacit agreement in the Shīʿī legal theory is considered neither *Ijmāʿ* nor authority.[44] If the Shīʿah scholars differ on a given point, the opinion which clearly conforms to the teachings of the Qurʾān and the Sunnah shall be accepted. If two groups of scholars differ on a question, the opinion of the scholars whose person and genealogy are known shall not be accepted. The reason is that the imam is not included among them. In case the person and genealogy of both groups are not known, the opinion of either of the two groups can be accepted. In such a case, one opinion cannot be preferred to the other, because it is supposed that truth lies in either of the two.[45] The Shīʿah, too, believe in the simple and compound *Ijmāʿ*. They do not allow deviation from the compound *Ijmāʿ*. If the consensus was established in the past on three opinions about a point, any of them shall be followed, and no fresh opinion can be introduced.[46]

Ijmāʿ, according to the Shīʿah, is substantiated on four grounds, namely inclusion of the imam (*Dukhūl*) in the Shīʿah community when they agree, kindness (*Lutf*), intuition (Ḥads) and meeting the imam directly when he is hidden (*Tasharruf*). We elaborate these points presently. The inclusion of the imam in the Shīʿah community, in the case of their unanimous agreement, is a basic

---

[42] Al-Qummi, *op. cit.*, p. 172.
[43] *Ibid.*, p. 179.
[44] Muhammad Brūjirdi, *Mukhtalif al-Uṣūl*, Tehran, 1341 A.H., pp. 137-138.
[45] Al-Tūsi, *op. cit.*, II, 76-78.
[46] Al-Qummi, *op. cit.*, p. 181; Muahmmad Brūjirdi, *op. cit.*, p. 133.

conception on which the Shīʿī theory of *Ijmāʿ* stands. If the Shiah community at large or the scholars alone agree on a certain point, their agreement implies that this is the opinion of their imam which is always incorporated in the consensus of the community. But it is remarkable that in the case of *Ijmāʿ*, the person of imam is not individually known. If his person is known, this is called a khabar (direct report from him), and not an *Ijmāʿ*. The agreement of the Shīʿah community is identified with the opinion of the infallible imam on presumption that the imam is always hidden in the community. The principle of *Lutf* (kindness) was devised by al-Tūsī to justify *Ijmāʿ*. It means that God sends prophets and appoints imams out of kindness for the guidance of people. Now if people go astray by their agreement on an error, it is obligatory on God, as His attribute of kindness requires, to reveal the truth in order to save them from falling into error. In such a situation the infallible imam is duty-bound to come out of his hiddenness and point out the truth to the people. If the imam does not come out in person to tell the truth, it would be supposed that the agreement of the community conforms to the will of the imam; otherwise, it follows that God is not kind to His servants. *Ijmāʿ* is thus justified on the basis of the principle of *Lutf*. This principle is recognized by the early Shīʿah jurists, but doubted by their successors.

Ḥads (intuition) is a sort of a priori knowledge. It means that one feels definitely sure by intuition that the knowledge one acquires comes directly from the imam. As the disciples of a teacher who strictly follow him and never disobey him agree on a certain point, their agreement shows that this must be the opinion of their teacher. Similarly, if the scholars, who strictly follow the *Shariʿah* and never do anything against its dictates, agree on a point, one can logically conclude that their agreement definitely points to the will of the imam. The *Ijmāʿ* on the basis of Ḥads (intuition) in justifiable provided there exists no other evidence from the Qurʾān or the

Sunnah, and it is not supported by the principles of *Lutf* (kindness), *Tasharruf* (meeting the *Imām* directly) or *Dukhūl* (inclusion of the imam). Further, the opinion of the imam is known in a majority of cases by intuition. Therefore, the principle of Ḥads is the last resort to substantiate *Ijmāʿ*.

Lastly the doctrine of *Ijmāʿ* is established on the ground of *tasharruf* (to have the honour of meeting the imam directly). It means that sometimes a scholar has an occasion to see the *imām* durnig his hiddenness and asks him about his opinion on the disputed point. The knowledge acquired from the imam in this way is certain. Al-Muqaddas al-Ardabīlī (d. 993 A.H.) and others are reported to have had a chance to see the imam directly. The *Ijmāʿ* reached on such a definite report from the imam is undoubtedly valid. But this happens in rare cases. and cannot, therefore, be generalized.[47]

The doctrine of *Ijmāʿ* was theorized widely by the Shīʿah. But, according to them, to put this theory into practice in modern times is hardly possible. Hence, they depend on the points already agreed upon by their scholars in the presence of the imam or during the period immediately following his hiddenness. It is argued that in modern times there is no way of realizing the opinion of the imam which is included in the agreement of the unknown scholars. But such scholars do not exist in the present day. Therefore, practically no *Ijmāʿ* is possible. As regards the reports about *Ijmāʿ* on legal questions during the period beginning from al-Tūsī (d. 460 A.H.) till the present day cannot be called a real *Ijmāʿ* because they are not based on *Mutawātir* traditions. They are at most well-known traditions attributed to the imam and not *Ijmāʿ*. The agreement reached during the generation of the Companions can be easily known, because they were small in number, and one could realize

---

[47] Muhammad al-Mahdi al-Husayni, *al-Wuṣūl ilä Kifayat al-Uṣūl*, Najaf, n.d., III, 272-74, 282-87.

them in toto.[48] The theory of *Ijmāʿ* as developed by the Sunnis and the Shīʿah casts doubts on the validity of *Ijmāʿ* established in the later generations. But the *Ijmāʿ* reached in the generation of the Companions is universally recognized. It appears that *Ijmāʿ* became retrospective in the phase when it was theorized. The practice of the first four Caliphs was considered ideal by the Muslims in the early period. The idea of the ideal practice might have been converted into the notion of the *Ijmāʿ* of the Companions at a later date. The Muslims in the later centuries validated also the *Ijmāʿ* of the Successors. The first three generations were consequently considered sacrosanct according to a well-known tradition of the Prophet. The doctrine of *Ijmāʿ*, of course, continued theoretically in the medieval times, but it was questioned both by the Sunnis and by the Shīʿah. In the present study, we have noted that the prospective aspect of *Ijmāʿ* was not much emphasized by the medieval jurists. Practically the whole body of law and dogma both in Sunnism and in Shīʿism stands on the agreement of the Companions, or on the opinions of the imam, the so-called *Ijmāʿ* of the Shīʿah, respectively.

VI

Let us now discuss the views of the moderate group which partly believes in *Ijmāʿ*. We start with Ahmad b. Hanbal. Unfortunately the extant works of Ahmad b. Hanbal do not tell us much about his point of view on *Ijmāʿ*. For this, we have to depend on others. Numerous statements attributed to him tend to show that he did not recognize *Ijmāʿ* as an authority. It appears that being a disciple of al-Shāfiʿī he might have doubted the authority of the *Ijmāʿ* of the scholars. On the contrary, there are reports which indicate that he believed in the *Ijmāʿ* of the Companions alone. The statements ascribed to him are as follows: (a) He who claims *Ijmāʿ* on a certain point is a liar. There might have been disagreement on that point. One should, instead,

[48] Hasan b. Zayn al-Din al-Shahid al-Thani, *Maʿalim al-Uṣūl*, Tehran, 1379 A.H., p. 316.

say: 'I am not sure that people have disagreed on this point', or 'their disagreement has not been reported to me; (b) How do the people make a statement about *Ijmāʿ* simply by hearing the people say: 'There is an agreement on a certain point.' Instead, they should say: 'We are unaware of the disagreement'. (c) To lay a claim about the agreement on a certain point is falsehood, particularly when one is not sure about it. One should better say: 'I am not aware of the disagreement which has not been reported.'[49] These statements, though diverse in expression, contain a common theme, namely one should not lay a false claim about *Ijmāʿ* on a certain point, especially when nothing definite is known about it. This is to a large extent true because the claim of *Ijmāʿ* on a certain point is usually based on reports. Ibn Hanbal is, therefore, very careful in this respect. Ignorance of disagreement, in his opinion, is not essentially a proof of agreement. This is, in fact, a problem of the validity of express and tacit *Ijmāʿ*. The *Ijmāʿ* claimed by the jurists in the past is usually a tacit agreement of the community. Al-Shāfiʿī totally rejected the theory of tacit *Ijmāʿ*.[50] Ibn Hanbal presumably doubted the doctrine of *Ijmāʿ* on the same grounds.

In support of his point of view, Ibn Hanbal is reported to have argued that one cannot possess the knowledge of *Ijmāʿ* of the scholars unless one meets each and every scholar and witnesses his actions. And this is naturally not possible because scholars live in different places remote from each other. Suppose one succeeds in meeting all the scholars individually, and one witnesses their actions and understands their opinion, even this does not indicate that one has ascertained the real point of view of each scholar. This is because a scholar might have spoken or acted against his belief under some necessity. Again if one knows the opinion of a scholar

---

[49] Ibn Qayyim, *Iʿlām al-Muwaqqiʿin*, Delhi, n.d., I, 238.
[50] *Jimaʿ al-ʿIlm*, Cairo, 1940, p. 67; idem, *Ikhtilāf al-Ḥadīth* (on the margin of K. al-umm) p. 143.

with certainty, there is still a possibility that he may change his point of view before it is reported to the people. Hence one cannot claim that scholars have agreed on a certain point.[51] From such an argument we discern that Ibn Hanbal doubted the validity of the *Ijmāʿ* of the scholars and not the *Ijmāʿ* of the community at large.

Ibn Taymiyah tells us that Ibn Hanbal recognized the authority of the *Ijmāʿ* of the Companions. His contention is as follows: There is no question on which the Companions had not given their opinion. With the territorial expansion and the spread of Islam, they were confronted with a number of complex problems. But they sought their solution on the basis of the Qurʾān and the Sunnah. Some of them exercised their personal opinion in deciding legal questions, but not very frequently. In their own day the Companions in general did not argue on the basis of *Ijmāʿ*. The reason is that the Companions themselves were the people of *Ijmāʿ* (*Ahl al-Ijmāʿ*). Further, there existed no idea of *Ijmāʿ* in their generation. In the generation of the Successors, ʿUmar, the second Caliph, is reported to have issued an edict to Shurayh: "Decide cases on the basis of the Qurʾān; if you do not find the answer there, consult the Sunnah of the Prophet. In case the Sunnah, too, is silent, decide on the basis of the practice and precedent of the 'pious ancestors (al-Salaf al-Ṣāliḥ)', or, as another version says, "on the basis of the agreement of the people." Ibn Masʿūd reportedly said, "Consult primarily the Qurʾān, then the Sunnah, and finally *Ijmāʿ*." When Ibn Hanbal talks about *Ijmāʿ* in every generation, he actually means the *Ijmāʿ* of the Successors. It is, however clear that he rejects the verbal *Ijmāʿ* claimed by the jurists. Justifying the rejection of such a type of *Ijmāʿ* by Ibn Hanbal, Ibn Taymiyah observes that the jurist-theologians, like al-Marisi and al-Aṣamm, claim *Ijmāʿ* on a number of questions, but they are acquainted with the opinions of Mālik and Abū Hanifah,

[51] Al-Āmidī, *op. cit.*, I, 282-85.

and not with the opinions of the Companions and Successors. Many a jurist, like Mālik, al-Shaybāni, al-Shāfiʿī, and Abū ʿUbayd, claimed the establishment of *Ijmāʿ* on various questions. These questions were, in fact, disputed but the jurists were not familiar with the disagreement.[52]

Al-Baqillani (d. 403 A.H.) is of the view that Ibn Hanbal might have doubted the reports of *Ijmāʿ* out of piety (war'). It is well-nigh possible that there might be disagreement on a certain question, but not reported to the people. Or he might have made such a statement about a person who was ignorant of the disagreement of the early jurists. It seems however, correct, he believes, that Ibn Hanbal did not reject the validity of *Ijmāʿ* as he refers to the *Ijmāʿ* of ʿUmar, ʿAlī, Ibn Masʿūd, and Ibn ʿAbbās on the question of pronouncing takbīr, a specified supplication after prayers in the month of Dhuʾl-Hijjah.[53]

The statement about the rejection of *Ijmāʿ* ascribed to Ibn Hanbal was cited by Ibn Hazm (d. 456 A.H.) for the first time.[54] It was adopted by the later scholars who quoted it continuously. Ibn Hajib and some other scholars have expressed their surprise on its ascription to him.[55] The interpretation of this statement in favour of *Ijmāʿ* by many scholars implies that they were not convinced of its genuineness. But the scholars who deny the classical theory of *Ijmāʿ*, like Ibn Hazm and al-Shawkānī, are glad to find support of their views in this statement of Ibn Hanbal and admire him profusely for making such a true and pithy remark about *Ijmāʿ*.[56]

VII

---

[52] Ibn Taymiyah, *Maʿārij al-Wuṣūl*, Cairo, 1964, p. 316; idem, *Maʿārij al-Wuṣūl* included in *Majmūʿah al-Rasāʾil al-Kubrā*, Cairo, 1323 A.H., pp. 215-16.
[53] *Ibid.*
[54] Ibn Hazm, *al-Ihkam fi Uṣūl al-Ahkam*, Cairo, 1347 A.H., IV, 188.
[55] ʿAlī ʿAbd al-Rāziq, *op. cit.*, pp. 16-17.
[56] Ibn Hazm, *op. cit.*, p. 188; al-Shawkāni, *Irshād al-Fuhūl*, Cairo, 1347 A.H., p. 64.

Ibn Hazm has his own point of view about *Ijmāʿ*. He believes in the *Ijmāʿ* of the Companions with respect to those questions that are based on the text of the Qurʾān and the Sunnah. He remarks that one who follows the rules established explicitly by these two sources definitely follows *Ijmāʿ*. Whoever violates the clear prescriptions of these sources does not follow *Ijmāʿ*. By adherence to the community, he means adherence to the Companions, Successors, and the later scholars in those points supported by the text. He does not believe in the allegiance to a person but to the text. He vehemently condemns allegiance to a person other than the Prophet. In his opinion, a person who follows anyone other than the Prophet, follows neither the Sunnah (practice) nor the *Jamāʿah* (community). Being a literalist and a staunch upholder of *Ḥadīth*, he calls himself and his school 'followers of the Sunnah, *Jamāʿah*, and *Ijmāʿ*".[57]

He opposes the classical theory of *Ijmāʿ* in a twofold way. First, he refutes the presumption that *Ijmāʿ* is valid on questions that are not based on the text (Naṣṣ). On the contrary, he believes that the conception of *Ijmāʿ* is not possible without the support of the text. Therefore, he rejects the validity of *Ijmāʿ* on points based on personal opinion or analogical reasoning. Secondly, he thinks that the *Ijmāʿ* on a large number of legal questions generally claimed by the scholars is not correct. Some of them are definitely disputed, and others are open to suspicion. He remarks that the agreement of the people on point for which no text is found is absurd. The reason is that everything in religion is governed by the clear prescriptions of the Qurʾān and the Sunnah. In *Ijmāʿ*, as it stands, there is a possibility that people may have agreed on a rule which contradicts the relevant express rule mentioned in the text not known to them. If they do so, this is pure blasphemy. As regards the second point, he contends that the scholars in the past had agreed on some rules

[57] Ibn Hazm, *op. cit.*, p. 128.

clearly mentioned in the Qur'ān and the Sunnah, and they also disagreed on a number of questions. In cases where their disagreement is not reported, one cannot claim definitely their agreement on them. Hence *Ijmā'* in such cases is doubtful.[58]

Justifying *Ijmā'* he adduces a number of traditions of the Prophet which emphasize the solidarity of the community. He thinks the tradition 'my community will not agree on an error is sound with respect to its meaning, as supported by other traditions; it is not sound in its reported version and the chain of narrators. The tradition, however, like many others, supports the conception of *Ijmā'*.[59] He also substantiates it on the basis of the Qur'ānic verse 4:115. But he construes the believers' way as 'adherence to the Qur'ān and the established Sunnah of the Prophet.' Any rule formulated afresh, not based on the text, is not the way of the believers. It is, in fact, a way of disbelief. He also cites verse 24:51 to support this viewpoint.[60]

He interprets the term *Aulī al-Amr* (men in authority), which occurs in verses 4:59, 83, as the rulers (*umara*) and the scholars (*'Ulamā'*). He, however, presumes that God commanded Muslims to obey them in matters not clearly mentioned by Him in the Qur'ān, or by the Prophet in *Ḥadīth*. He criticizes those who argue from these two verses in favour of the exercise of *Ra'y* (personal opinion) and *Qiyās* (analogical reasoning).[61]

As we stated earlier, he is opposed to the personal allegiance. He proves by citing verse 7:3 that Muslims are required to follow only what has been revealed. According to him, *Ijmā'* on questions not conforming to the text is false. The religion became perfect, as verse

---

[58] *Ibid*. pp. 131-141.
[59] *Ibid*. pp. 130-131.
[60] *Ibid*., pp. 131-132.
[61] *Ibid*., pp. 132-135.

5:3 shows, in the day of the Prophet; hence the community cannot agree upon a question not mentioned in the Qur'ān and the Sunnah.[62]

He rejects the *Ijmāʿ* of the scholars established after the generation of the Companions. The gathering of all the scholars, he contends, who are scattered in different parts of the world, is impossible. Further, people cannot agree on a single opinion owing to their diversity of opinion, nature, and design. Hence no *Ijmāʿ* is valid on questions not supported by the text.[63] If *Ijmāʿ* is supposed to have been established on questions not supported by the text after the death of the Prophet, there would be four considerations: (a) Either the scholars agreed on the prohibition of a thing not prohibited by the Prophet; (b) or on the lawfulness of a thing forbidden by him; (c) or on making a thing obligatory not made obligatory by him; (d) or upon deletion of an obligatory duty made obligatory by him. Such a type of *Ijmāʿ* amounts to disbelief and to changing the religion of Islam. Allowing such considerations is nothing short of falsifying the essentials of religion.[64] From all this discussion he draws the conclusion that (a) *Ijmāʿ* will be established on questions not supported by the text in a way as pretended by the jurists, i.e. doubtful *Ijmāʿ*; (b) or it will be established in contradiction to the text, not abrogated, particularized, or rejected by the Prophet in his lifetime; (c) or it will take place on questions supported by the textual evidence. He has already refuted (a) and (b) and established (c). According to him, adherence to the text is an obligatory duty, and agreement or disagreement does not count in the presence of the text. Truth shall remain truth, though people may disagree; falsehood shall continue falsehood, though people agree on it, and however large the number of its upholders may be. If the infallibility

[62] *Ibid.*, pp. 136-137.
[63] *Ibid.*, pp. 137-139.
[64] *Ibid.*, pp. 139-140.

of *Ijmāʿ* had not been established by a tradition of the Prophet, the community could have agreed on falsehood. All that is required from the Muslims is to follow the injunctions contained in the Qurʾān and the Sunnah of the Prophet. The religion is nothing but the contents of both these sources. In view of this position, there is no sense in seeking agreement or disagreement on a certain question.[65]

Elucidating his standpoint about *Ijmāʿ* he remarks that both agreement and disagreement are in existence, but God does not require the Muslims to be acquainted with either of them. All that He requires is adherence to the Qurʾān and the traditions of the Prophet transmitted by reliable persons. The prescriptions contained in these sources have been communicated to the community in a threefold way: (a) questions communicated by the whole community from generation to generation, such as faith, prayer, fasting, etc. This is the *Ijmāʿ* in its true sense. Questions falling under this category are all unanimously agreed upon by the community; (b) questions transmitted by a large number of people to a large number of people since the time of the Prophet. Some of these questions are agreed upon and others are disputed, such as the question of leading the prayer by the Prophet in sitting condition while the people were standing, or the question of allotting the lands of Khyber to the Jews by the Prophet on condition of giving half of its produce to the Muslims; (c) questions reported by reliable person to reliable persons since the time of the Prophet. Some of them are agreed upon and some are disputed. These are the only three types of *Ijmāʿ*. The claim of any other type is untenable.[66]

We stated previously that Ibn Hazm believed in the *Ijmāʿ* of the Companions. He refers to Abū Sulaymān, an eminent scholar of his

---

[65] *Ibid.*, pp. 140-141.
[66] *Ibid.*, pp. 141-42.

school, who puts forward the following arguments to justify the *Ijmāʿ* of the Companions. (1) The Companions received direct information from the Prophet (*Tawqīf*) about the questions agreed upon in his day. And it is a fact that *Ijmāʿ* is valid on those questions that are known through direct information from the Prophet. (2) The Companions were believers in totality, i.e. they constituted the entire community. There was no other believer except them on the day of the Prophet. Those bearing such qualities must be competent to constitute *Ijmāʿ* in its real sense. Such a kind of *Ijmāʿ* will be of decisive nature. (3) The believers of the later generations constituted a part of the community and not the entire community. And the agreement of a part of the community constitutes no *Ijmāʿ*.

(4) In theti me of the Prophet, the Companions were limited in number. One could count them easily and their point of view could be known. But this is not true of the Muslims of the later generations.[67] Even here he differs with the classical jurists. *Ijmāʿ* of the Companions, according to him, means 'strict adherence to the explicit texts (*Nuṣūṣ*). He expresses the opinion that the individual opinion of a Companion should be followed provided it is confirmed by the text of the Qurʾān or the Sunnah. *Ijmāʿ* stands for adherence to the texts. He justifies his viewpoint by quoting, in part, the speech of ʿUmar which he made on the occasion of Abū Bakr's election. It says: "Yesterday I made a speech before you, but it does not hold good now. I could not find its ratification from the text of the Qurʾān or from the practice of the Prophet. Would that the Prophet had been alive, and directed us in these matters. God chose for His Prophet what is with you, i.e. the Qurʾān. This is the Book by which He guided His Prophet. Therefore, follow it strictly, and you will be guided as the Prophet was guided by God through this Book." From this Ibn Hazm infers that the 'personal opinion', though it is

---

[67] *Ibid.*, pp. 147-149.

exercised by the Companions, has no value in legal theory if it is not supported by the text of the Qur'ān and the Sunnah.[68] We dilated earlier on these arguments and their refutation by orthodoxy.

Ibn Hazm in fact believes in the indubitable consensus (al-*Ijmā' al-Mutayaqqan*) which he divides into two categories: first, the *Ijmā'* which is not doubted by any Muslim, such as confession of faith, five daily prayers, fasting in the month of Ramadan, prohibition of eating the meat of animals not slaughtered according to the established method, blood, swine and others. He thinks a Muslim who does not believe in this category of *Ijmā'* is not a true Muslim; second, the *Ijmā'* is universally known to the Companions. The Prophet, for instance, concluded a contract with the Jews that they would, give half of the produce of the lands of Khyber to the Muslims, and vacate the territory when required. This contract of the Prophet was widely known to the Companions in the whole Arabian peninsula. But this kind of *Ijmā'*, he says, is disputed among the scholars.[69]

At another place, he divides *Ijmā'* into binding (*lāzim*) and sufficient (*jāzi*). The former applies to the points recognized by the unanimous consensus of the community as obligatory or forbidden or indifferent. The latter embraces the rules of law on which the scholars agree that if a person follows them, he will be considered as having performed his duty. Between these two categories lie a large number of points that are disputed among scholars. But according to Ibn Hazm, the truth lies only in one single point of view.[70]

To ascertain the fact that there is no disagreement of any scholar in *Ijmā'*, it should be scrutinized like the scrutiny of traditions.

[68] *Ibid.*, pp. 150-151.
[69] *Ibid.*, pp. 149-150.
[70] Ibn Hazm, *Marātib al-Ijma*, Cairo, 1357 A.H., pp. 8-9.

Traditions are recognized as genuine and reliable when there remains no room for doubt after their examination. Similarly, the *Ijmāʿ* on a certain question should be known to all people, as it is known that the Muslims came out from Hijāz and the Yemen, and conquered Irāq, Egypt, and Syria, and that the Umayyads and ʿAbbāsids ruled for a long time, and that the battle of Ṣiffīn and Harrah took place. All such events are known to all and sundry with certainty and of necessity.[71]

Ibn Hazm refutes all those points of view about *Ijmāʿ* listed in the beginning of this chapter except the *Ijmāʿ* of the Companions. He also vehemently criticizes the viewpoint that during the time of the Companions *Ijmāʿ* took place on questions based on personal opinion and analogical reasoning in conflict with the practice of the Prophet. He selects, as an illustration, the questions of the prohibition of the sale of slave-mother, determining eighty lashes as the punishment for drinking, and reading the Qurʾān in one dialect against the practice of reading it in seven dialects (*Al-Ahruf Al-Sabʾah*) prevalent in the day of the Prophet. He expatiates on these questions and refutes the opposite viewpoints with full vigour.[72] He also differs from orthodoxy on the view that *Ijmāʿ* has been established on the prohibition of revolt and resistance against tyrant and oppressive rulers. He cites a number of instances from history where the notable Companions and the Successors revolted against the tyrants in their day. By these historical facts, he seeks to prove that resistance against tyrannical rulers is permissible.[73]

Over against the practice of writing works on disagreement of the artists he produced a work entitled *Marātib al-Ijmāʿ* (degrees of consensus), listing legal questions relating to all subjects that are

---

[71] *Ibid.*, p. 112.
[72] Ibn Hazm, *al-Iḥkām fī Uṣūl al-Aḥkām*, *op. cit.*, IV, 156-72.
[73] Ibn Hazm, *Marātib al-Ijmāʿ*, *op. cit.*, pp. 177-178.

agreed upon by the jurists, and no disagreement is reported about them.

In short, Ibn Hazm narrowed down the scope of *Ijmāʿ* in a twofold way, namely by limiting it to the generation of the Companions, and by confining it to the questions based on the text.

VIII

Najm al-Din *al-Ṭūsī* (d. 716 A.H.), a Hanball jurist of Spain, raised serious objections to the classical theory of *Ijmāʿ*. His criticism of its justification on the basis of the Qurʾān is almost identical with the one made by many other opponents of *Ijmāʿ*. His emphasis centres on expediency and public interest (*maslahah*) which he considers a source of law prior to the Qurʾān and the Sunnah. He derived this principle from the legal maxim (there shall be) no damage and mutual infliction of damage' (*Lā Darara Wa Lā Dirāra*) mentioned in a tradition of the Prophet.[74] Elucidating the meaning of this tradition he dwelt on the principle of public interest and attached supreme importance to it in the Islamic legal theory. He concludes his criticism on *Ijmāʿ* with the following remarks:

"By all this criticism we do not aim at degrading *Ijmāʿ* and its total condemnation. But we regard it as valid in rituals (*ʾibādāt*) and in matters prescribed definitely in the *Shariʾah*. Our chief purpose is to show that the consideration of public interest (*maslahah*), a principle derived from the Prophet's tradition 'there shall be no damage and no mutual infliction of damage' is stronger than *Ijmāʿ*, and its authority is more potent than the authority of the latter. This is evident from our discussion and criticism of the arguments of *Ijmāʿ*."[75]

---

[74] Schacht, Joseph, *The Origins of Muhammadan Jurisprudence*, Oxford, 1950, p. 183.
[75] *Al-Tūsi*, Najm al-Din, *Sharh al-Arbaʿin lil-Nawawi*, quoted in Mustafa Zayd, *al-Maslahah fil-Tashriʿ al-Islāmi wa Najm al-Din al-Tūfi*, Cairo, 1964, p. 217, 218-225.

It is clear that *al-Ṭūsī* confines *Ijmāʿ* to rituals (*'ibādāt*) and excludes social dealings (*Muʾamalāt*) and customary affairs (*'adat*) from its scope. In the latter category he prefers public interest to *Ijmāʿ*. For this, he gives the reason that consideration of public interest in social dealings is the principal aim of the *Shariʿah*. But rituals are the right of the *Shariʾah* alone. The manner of their performance can be known only through the text or *Ijmāʿ*.[76]

To prove the priority of public interest he contends that it is the pivotal point in the multitude of ends which the lawgiver had in view Hence it is the strongest proof. The lawgiver always kept the public interest in view in all his proofs. All the Qurʾānic verses involve public interest The Sunnah, being an explanation and commentary of the Qurʾān, follows it. As regards *Ijmāʿ*, almost all the scholars substantiate its authority on the basis of the principle 'to acquire what is good and to remove what evil'. Reason also supports the supremacy of public interest in law Every sensible person believes that the ultimate goal of the law relating to social dealings and customs in all legal systems is to provide for the people what is good and beneficial for them. Islamic *Shariʿah*, being characterized by equity and justice, is superior to all other legal systems. Hence it gives vital importance to public interest in all its commandments.[77]

Al-Tūsi presents the following reasons for priority of public interest over the text:

1. The texts (*nuṣūṣ*) contradict each other for their diversity; they generate in law disagreement which is condemned by the *Shariʾah* itself.

---

[76] *Ibid.*, p. 213, also p. 149.
[77] *Ibid.*, pp. 143, 212-13.

2. Consideration of public interest in legal matters is a point unanimously agreed upon by the scholars. It is rather a cause for agreement required by the *Sharīʿah.*

3. A number of illustrations can be produced from the Sunnah (i.e. *Ḥadīth*) where the text conflicts with public interest.[78]

He divides the text (Naṣṣ) into four kinds and proves that all types of texts are doubtful. No text is definite. *Ijmāʿ* can neither be proved by *Ijmāʿ* because it would be a reasoning by vicious circle, nor can it be justified by a text for its doubtfulness. Hence there is no alternative but to have a resort to public interest.[79] Public interest, in his opinion, is a stronger proof than *Ijmāʿ*. And this indicates that public interest is the strongest of all proofs of the *Sharīʾah.*[80]

It is, of course, true to say, as *al-Ṭūsī* conceives, that the primary goal of all prescriptions of the *Sharīʿah* is public interest, i.e. to provide what is good and beneficial and to remove what is bad and harmful. This is a general principle which applies to all injunctions. But however great importance we may attach to public interest, it would be fallacious to call it a primary source of law. Public interest, equity, and good conscience, and similar other considerations may constitute a ratio or motive for legislating fresh rules of law, but never a source of law. Al-Tūff undoubtedly presented a valuable principle for legislation in changing conditions, but his extreme viewpoint and exaggerated exposition of this principle provoked orthodoxy. His point of view has been severely criticized by a number of scholars of modern times.[81]

---

[78] *Ibid.*, p. 145.
[79] *Ibid.*, pp. 123-124.
[80] *Ibid.*, p. 210; cf. S. Mahmassani, *Falsafat al-Tashri fil-Islām*, Eng. tr. by Farhat J. Ziadeh, Leiden, 1961, pp. 116-117.
[81] Mustafa Zayd, *op. cit.*, pp. 150-51, 164-65; al-Buwati; *Dawābit al-Maslahah*, *Damuscus*: al-Maktabah al-Umawiyah, 1967, pp. 202-15.

Al-Qadi ʿAbd al-Jabbar (d. 415 A.H.), a renowned Muʿtazili jurist and theologian, discusses the doctrine of *Ijmāʿ* at a greater length.[82] He defends the classical theory, though differs with it in many points, on traditional grounds. In his study of *Ijmāʿ* we find some original ideas and fresh interpretations of its definition which distinguish him from others. Here it is not possible to discuss his viewpoint in detail; we shall confine ourselves to describe his definition of *Ijmāʿ* and some of his answers furnished by him to the objections raised by the opponents.

Discussing the concept of *Ijmāʿ* he remarks that it is not correct to establish its authority unless one has the knowledge of its concept and is acquainted with its real position. Explaining its definition and infallibility he remarks: In *Ijmāʿ* people cooperate with each other on a point which is considered the object of their agreement. As such, a point can be described as *Ijmāʿ* at the moment when the agreement of people takes place intentionally from them. This is because the agreement reached in forgetfulness is not valid, nor is the one arrived at under duress. It makes no difference if their agreement is reached at one time or at various times, for there is no difference if it takes place on various actions: on actions relating to heart, or relating to limbs, or on others. In all these cases the situation remains the same, i.e. that it constitutes an *Ijmāʿ*. Viewed from an etymological standpoint, *Ijmāʿ* does not signify the truth or falsehood of a thing. The agreement of people is just like an action of the individual or like a solitary report with respect to the fact that they do not indicate the truth by themselves. This in fact depends on proof or indication (*Dalālah*). *Ijmāʿ* does not indicate truth unless

---

[82] ʿAbd al-Jabbar, *op. cit.*, XVII, 153-245. A full-dress study of his point of view about *Ijmāʿ* will be found in Marie Bernand, *loc cit.*, pp. 26-38.

there exists some proof.[83] The following conclusions can be drawn from the preceding statement:

1. *Ijmāʿ* is a common denominator of diverse opinions that comes out after mutual consultation.

2. It is a deliberate agreement of people.

3. It is not an authority by itself in its literal sense.

4. It is an authority by proof.

He thinks the proofs of the infallibility of *Ijmāʿ* by consensus and reason are weak. The argument for justifying *Ijmāʿ* on the basis of another *Ijmāʿ* is circular and self-contradictory. As for its legitimacy by reason, he maintains that there is no indication that a special body of people is more infallible in their actions and sayings than any individual. Furthermore, *Ijmāʿ* cannot be proved rationally from the need of mankind. The contention that it fills the gap of revelation and protects them from falling into error after the close of revelation is untenable. The proofs of scripture or of reason are sufficient to fulfill this need whether the people are agreed or not. Muslims can manage their affairs with their scripture alone as the religious communities did in the past. He believes that *Ijmāʿ* can be justified only on the basis of the Qurʾān and the Sunnah.[84]

A general objection raised by the opponents of *Ijmāʿ* is that a group is composed of the individuals who are liable to commit an error in their decisions, why is it not allowed in the case of a group? This question has been answered in different ways, as we already noted in previous chapters. ʿAbd al-Jabbar has his own reply. He says that drawing an analogy between the actions of the individuals and those

---

[83] *Ibid.*, p. 153; Marie Bernand, loc cit., pp. 28-30.

[84] Abd al-Jabbar, *al-Mughnī*, XVII, 160, 186, 199, 200; cf., Hourani, George F. *The Ethics of ʿAbd al-Jabbar*, Oxford, 1971, pp. 138-39.

of a group declared infallible by the Prophet is a fallacy. The actions of the individual are subject to error because no authority declares him infallible. This is just like the actions of the Prophet which have been declared infallible. Hence it does not follow from the infallibility of the actions of a group that the actions of individuals would necessarily be infallible. In the case of *Ijmāʿ* the reasoning that if a quality is borne by individuals, that would be borne by the whole, does not hold good.[85]

X

Ibn Taymiyah (d. 728 A.H.), though a follower of Ibn Hanbal, is an original thinker. He differs from him on a number of problems. He is out and out a traditionist, laying tremendous stress on the adherence to *Ḥadīth*. He is, however, not an extreme literalist like Ibn Hazm. His writings present a subtle combination of tradition and reason. One finds great emphasis on adherence to the text (Naṣṣ) in his reasoning. He believes that the Qurʾān and the Sunnah are self-contained authorities, sufficient to settle all religious matters. The *Ijmāʿ* of the community in his opinion is in itself a truth; but it does not lie outside these sources.

Like many other classical jurists, he justifies the authority of *Ijmāʿ* on the basis of the Qurʾānic verses 2:143, 3:110, 4:115, 9:100, and 31:15. But verse 4:115 finds a significant place in his reasoning. He remarks that the verse in question constitutes a threat for those who depart from the Sunnah of the Prophet, from the Sunnah instituted by the caliphs after him, and from the believers' way. In his view opposition to the Prophet and departure from the believers' way are identical. In other words, one who opposes the Prophet deviates from the believers' way and vice versa. The agreement of the Muslims on a certain point is like a clear ruling

[85] *Ibid.*, pp. 154-159.

(*manṣūṣ*) given by the Prophet. Hence opposition to the agreement of the believers is opposition to the Prophet, just as opposition to the Prophet is opposition to God.

Ibn Taymiyah believes that *Ijmā*ʿ is always supported by an evidence, patent or assumed. What distinguishes him from Ibn Hazm is the fact that whereas Ibn Hazm stipulates textual evidence (Naṣṣ) for *Ijmā*ʿ, Ibn Taymiyah requires absolute evidence. After making a survey of the questions agreed upon by the Muslims, he found that all such points were supported by the traditions of the Prophet. But sometimes it happens, he says, that the evidence remains latent, and only *Ijmā*ʿ is known to the people. Hence, they argue from *Ijmā*ʿ as they argue from a clear text (Naṣṣ). *Ijmā*ʿ is a secondary proof along with the text corresponding to the similes mentioned in the Qur'ān. Hence the Qur'ān, the Sunnah, and *Ijmā*ʿ are juxtaposed in legal reasoning. Each one of these principles of law (*Uṣūl*), concomitant as they are, leads to the truth, as what is established by *Ijmā*ʿ, is established by the Qur'ān and the Sunnah. Every question established by *Ijmā*ʿ is supported by some text of either of them.

Ibn Taymiyah seeks to remove the misunderstanding that some questions, like *mudārabah* (sleeping partnership), were established by *Ijmā*ʿ, but were not supported by the textual evidence. He says that this is not fact. The practice of *mudārabah* was already prevalent and well-known among the Arabs before Islam. The Prophet himself traveled to other countries with the commercial goods of Khadijah. The caravan in which Abū Sufyan himself journeyed contained mostly the goods of *mudārabah*. The Prophet retained this practice after the advent of Islam. The Companions used to make journeys in his day carrying commercial goods of other people on partnership to foreign countries. This practice continued before the eyes of the Prophet and he never forbade it. The Sunnah, by its very definition, applies to his word, deed, and silent approval. When he kept silent on this practice, this shows that it became legally valid by his

Sunnah. According to *Muwatta'* of Mālik, the practice of *mudarabah* was prevalent among the Companions. This was indeed an. old practice, like husbandry or carpentry, not introduced in the Prophet's time. A number of scholars were ignorant of the textual evidence in support of many cases based on *Ijmā'*. Hence, they decided them on the basis of their opinion, though the textual evidence was known to others. It should not be supposed, he says, that all the jurists were acquainted with the textual evidence and they reported it like the traditions. He cites a number of examples where the Companions decided cases on the basis of their opinion, but later on they were supported by the text. Sometimes the jurists decide cases by general principles or analogy, and they do not know that there exists textual evidence in support of the same case. Some cases are disputed because a group of jurists apply one textual evidence, and others a different one. Sometimes the text is clear, but the scholars neglect it because of some expediency. The Companions were more acquainted with the behaviour and practice of the Prophet than others. They argued from the text in a large number of cases by virtue of their wider knowledge. But this could not be done by the later scholars who argued from *Ijmā'* or *Qiyās* (analogy) on account of their shallow knowledge.

The view prevailing in the classical period that *Ijmā'* is a major source of the *Shari'ah* indicates the lack of knowledge of the Qur'ān and the Sunnah. The classical jurists had recourse to analogy to solve a number of problems presuming that there existed no text relevant to them. This shows their scanty knowledge of the Qur'ān and the Sunnah. Ibn Taymiyah criticizes the view that *Ijmā'* should be given priority to the Qur'ān and the Sunnah in the course of reasoning. According to him, the text (Naṣṣ) should be given priority in all circumstances. In case the text contradicts the *Ijmā'* on a particular question, it will be presumed that *Ijmā'* must have had a well-known text in its support which abrogated the other text. It should not be presumed that the community neglected an exact (*Muhkam*) text and retained only an abrogated one. This is because the agreement of the community is infallible. Sometimes it is. of course, difficult to be acquainted with the *Ijmāʿ* on a certain question, because one cannot remember all the statements of the jurists. But this is not so in the case of the text. The acquaintance with the text is more convenient and easier than that of *Ijmāʿ*. The Companions had resort to *Ijmāʿ* when they could not find an answer to a given question in the Qurʾān or the Sunnah.[86]

We have previously discussed his point of view about the *Ijmāʿ* of the Companions when we analyzed the views of Ibn Hanbal. He thinks if the Companions hold two opinions about a certain question, the one nearer to the Qurʾān shall be adopted. If the Successors agree on one of them, the disagreement on that question shall continue.[87] He believes in the universal *Ijmāʿ* of the community and criticizes those who advocate the *Ijmāʿ* of the Prophet's family, of his early four Successors, and of the people of Medina.[88]

XI

Al-Shawkānī (d. 1255 A.H.), a well-known Zaydī jurist, looks askance at the doctrine of *Ijmāʿ*. He considers the Qurʾān and the Sunnah self-contained authorities. He gives no weight to *Ijmāʿ* in the presence of the text. In his *Irshad al-Fuhūl*, he wrote a lengthy chapter on *Ijmāʿ*. But this is replete with the statements and opinions of his predecessors on *Ijmāʿ* without any comments from him. In the course of his discussion about the justification of *Ijmāʿ* he makes sporadic remarks which imply that he is not convinced of the arguments advanced in favour of *Ijmāʿ*. The answers given by the classical jurists to the objections raised by the opponents are weak

[86] Ibn Taymiyah, *Maʿārij al-Wuṣūl*, Cairo, 1345 A.H. pp. 196-217.
[87] Idem, *al-Musawwadah*, *op. cit.*, p. 325.
[88] *Ibid.*, p. 333.

and incredible to him. The whole argument to substantiate *Ijmāʿ* is nothing but pedantry. We give presently a summary translation of his criticism.

Commenting on the argument from verse 4:115 he remarks that it is striking that the jurists substantiate *Ijmāʿ* on the authority of the Qurʾānic verses and traditions. They agree that a person who rejects by his interpretation a doctrine established on the basis of the generality of meaning of the text is neither unbeliever nor impious. Still, they maintain that the rule supported by *Ijmāʿ* is decisive, and one who opposes it is unbeliever and impious. By this, they seek to make the derivative (*farʾ*) stronger than the original (*aṣl*). The verse in question does not fulfill their objective.

Verse 3:110 too does not prove the authority of *Ijmāʿ*. By the quality that Muslims command what is good and forbid what is evil is not meant that individual opinion of the scholars is a legal authority binding on the whole community. All that the verse means is that they command what is established as good in the *Shariʾah*, and forbid what is established as evil in it. It is the Qurʾān and the Sunnah which declare what is good and evil in the *Shariʿah*, and not *Ijmāʿ*. *Ijmāʿ* at most may serve as an indication to the fact that the point agreed upon by them is supported by the Qurʾān or the Sunnah. The verse in question, however, does not show that *Ijmāʿ* is an independent authority. *Ijmāʿ*, according to the classical theory, means the agreement of the jurists in a certain generation. The word *ʾUmmah* (community) occurring in this verse stands for the whole Muslim community *vis-a-vis* other religious communities of the past. Hence there is nothing in the verse which proves their hypothesis.

Verse 2:143 is also irrelevant. It does not throw light on *Ijmāʿ*. The meritorious character and reliability of the people of *Ijmāʿ* do not presuppose that their individual opinion is a recognized legal authority (*ḥujjah sharʾiyyah*) applicable in all matters. This is a matter to be decided by the lawgiver and not by anyone else. This verse at most indicates that the report of these reliable persons is acceptable if they give a report about something. It never shows that their agreement on a religious point becomes sacrosanct on religious ground, binding eternally on them as well as on others.

As to the tradition 'my community will not agree on an error and similar other traditions, it should be noted that the Prophet in these traditions had predicted that a section of his community will continue to hold to the truth, and prevail over other opposing groups. This tradition is not relevant to *Ijmāʿ*. The other traditions emphasize the unity and condemn separation from the community. They do not show that *Ijmāʿ* is in itself an independent legal source in the presence of the Qurʾān and the Sunnah. The Qurʾān is a comprehensive source that should be consulted in all legal matters vide verse 16:89. Verse 4:59 shows that in the case of disagreement, the Muslims should refer to God, i.e. the Qurʾān, and to the Prophet, i.e. his Sunnah. From this, it is evident that the Qurʾān and the Sunnah are the original sources of law. If at all the arguments advanced in favour of *Ijmāʿ* are accepted, they at most imply that the unanimous agreement of the Muslims is a truth and reality. If a thing is true, it does not presuppose that it should necessarily be followed, especially when the well-known dictum goes: 'Every competent jurist is right (in his interpretation). It cannot be binding on other jurists.[89]

[89] Al-Shawkānī, *Irshād al-Fuhūl*, Cairo, 1347 A.H., pp. 67-69.

Chapter XIII: A Comparative Study of *Ijmā'*: *Sangha*, Sanhedrin, And Church

I

Religion, like many other terms, cannot be precisely defined. The term has been defined variantly but none is a standard definition.[1] We may adopt the one given by Emile Durkheim, an eminent sociologist, as a working definition to show that religion cannot be separated from the idea of a church in the sense of an organizing institution. Durkheim defines religion as follows:

"A religion is a unified system of beliefs and practices relative to sacred things, that is to say, things set apart and forbidden beliefs and practices which unite into one single moral community called a Church, all those who adhere to them."[2]

Religion has some fundamental institutions carrying intrinsic value; church and community, *inter alia*, stand prominent among them. A religion starts from the idea of sacred and culminates in a moral community by degrees through a unifying unit called the church. Faith and doctrine in religion are displayed through order and community- 'a body of individuals who have a common method of deciding questions.'[3] Whether the group is the subject of religion or the individual is disputed among the sociologists. In primitive religions, however, the group, i.e. tribe and its sub-division, is certainly the hub of social activity. The individual was meant for

---

[1] R.R. Marett, art. Religion, *Encyclopaedia Britannica*. London, 1951, XXIX, 103; E.E. Kellet, *A Short History of Religions*, Bungay Suffolk, n.d. Chapter I. esp. note I, p. 9.
[2] Emile Durkheim, *The Elementary Forms of the Religious life* (tr. Joseph Ward Swain), New York: Callier Books, 1961, p. 62.
[3] Lucas, J.R. *The Principles of Politics*, Oxford, 1966, p. 10.

family and its derivatives.[4] However important a position the individual may hold in the civilized and revealed religions, it (religion) initially starts from a small group of believers who share the same faith and doctrine. These faithfuls have a natural tendency to unite themselves with others and thus gain strength and encouragement. Such a small group when united together through the common bond of faith develops into a community to demonstrate its will.[5]

A prophet himself plays an important part in unifying the community. Beliefs, rituals, and practices too contribute profoundly towards the integration of the religious community. In this respect, the functions of a prophet are different from those of priests. A prophet integrates the community on the basis of "value-position" with a view to simplify the relationship of man to the world.[6] The structure of faith and doctrine on which the founder of a religion unites its believers is very simple and rudimentary. At this stage, such a group of believers can hardly be called a purely religious community in the strict sense of the term. This is but natural because the movement which a prophet launches undergoes the process of breakthrough. He grapples with the stubborn and inveterate past tradition. He introduces a system of thought, beliefs, and doctrines of his own, thus brushing away the past practices by virtue of the force of truth and argument. He originates the nucleus of the religious community. The priests, on the contrary, enlarge, strengthen, and standardize the tradition founded by a prophet. They organize this sacred tradition by their rational interpretation, making it adaptable to the changing conditions of life and society

---

[4] Wach, Joachim, *Sociology of Religion*, Chicago: The University of Chicago Press, 1964, p. 30.

[5] *Ibid.*, pp. 142, 332-33.

[6] Max Weber, *The Sociology of Religion* (tr. Ephraim Fischoff), Boston: Beacon Press, 1967, p. 69.

and immersing it in their own thought.[7] The systematization brought about by the priests gives rise to schism and polemics in religion. And, indeed, at this point, the religious community feels the need for a system which protects it from disintegration. Here lies the significance of the church. The role of church in a community is twofold. It saves the community from schism and develops the religion by fresh interpretation of faith, thus enabling it to march with the time. This unifying unit or church is found almost in all kindred religions. The *samgha* (or *sangha*), the ecclesia, the Sanhedrin, and the *'Ummah* are a few examples of such bodies in Buddhism, Christianity, Judaism, and Islam respectively.[8]

The unifying bodies in every religion claim to be the final authority, like a prophet, in religious matters. Disagreement with their decision is considered heresy. They distinguish themselves from laymen by their quality of charisma. Even a prophet appeals to the people by virtue of this merit which inheres in his person.[9] After his death, the whole community or the body of priests takes the place of the prophet. Now, charisma is found in the whole body instead of a single person. The decisions of this sacred body are considered sacrosanct and infallible as those of the prophet. The conception of infallibility in fact springs from the notion of charismatic leadership. Survival of this quality in this unifying body is necessary because religion develops with its fresh statements and decisions. No religion can survive if it fails to answer the new problems of life. Though the scriptures are closed against any further accretions after the death of a prophet, their interpretation, clarification, and amplification are never closed. Hence the necessity of a charismatic body or community for the development of religion.

---

[7] *Ibid.*,

[8] Wach, *op. cit.*, p. 33.

[9] Max Weber, *op. cit.*, pp. 47, 78.

II

Before we dilate on the nature of the church, its definition, and its functions in religion, we shall throw light on the idea of charisma on which the concept of the church stands. This term was introduced by, though not originated with, Max Weber in his Sociology of Religion.[10] It is derived originally from the Greek N.T. Charisma (gift of grace) formed from *charizesthai* (to show favour, give freely). The plural *charismata* meaning 'grace gifts' is used in a technical sense "to denote the extraordinary gifts bestowed on Christians for special service."[11] The term may be peculiar with the Bible, but the phenomenon is common to all religions. The primitive religions have the concept of *mana*, which represents the idea of charisma.[12] The term *hvarnah*, glory, applied by the Persians to the religious or political leader, carries the same connotation.[13] In general, charisma means "a designation for specific power postulating and exercising authority over others."[14]

Max Weber divides charisma into two genres, namely inherent and acquired or personal and official. Personal charisma is a natural gift endowed by God. This cannot be acquired by official means. Official charisma is produced through some extraordinary means, but only in those persons who already carry a germ by nature. This germ, according to Weber, is developed into an extraordinary quality when evoked internally by some force.[15] Explaining these two types, Professor Wach remarks:

---

[10] Talcott Parsons, Introduction to Weber's "*The Sociology of Religion, op. cit.*, p. XXXIII; Wach, *op. cit.*, p. 337.

[11] Putman, W.G., art. Spiritual Gifts, *The New Bible Dictionary* (ed. G.D. Douglas), London, 1962, p. 1212.

[12] Wach, *op. cit.* p. 337, Durkheim, *op. cit.*, pp. 79, 216, 228.

[13] *Ibid.*, p. 337.

[14] *Ibid.*

[15] Max Weber, *op. cit.*, p. 2.

"Charisma of personal character appeals more to the emotions; official charisma is more rational. Whereas the former claims complete loyalty, even personal surrender, the latter usually demands a circumscribed or tempered obedience. This difference, however, is more of a practical than theoretical nature."[16]

After the death of a prophet, official charisma takes the place of personal charisma. This qualification was first attributed to the disciples, like the apostles in Christianity and the Companions in Islam. They had a direct association with the founder of the religion. This was further extended to the priests individually as well as to the whole body. Hence the conception of immunity from error in the case of the decisions taken by a Council or the Pope. Such unifying bodies, being the ultimate deciding authority, are reinforced by the notion of charisma. The *Sangha* in Buddhism, Sanhedrin in Judaism, Church in Christianity, and *'Ummah* in Islam derive the concept of infallibility from the same root, i.e. the official charisma. The charismatic gifts in Christianity aim at "primarily the edification of the whole church and secondarily the connection and conversion of unbelievers."[17] It is worthy of note that a church or an organizing body develops by degrees. It starts from 'circle', then 'brotherhood', then 'community', and finally 'church.' 'Circle' and 'brotherhood' unite the believers as long as they remain small in number. But when the religion spreads widely and culminates in a vast community, it is controlled by a systematic organization which we may call by any name indicating the very concept.[18]

III

We may now analyze the nature, definition, and role of the church in religion as shown by the sociologists. To bring home the

---

[16] Wach, *op. cit.*, p. 337.
[17] Putman, W.G. *op. cit.*
[18] Wach, *op. cit.*, pp. 141-42.

distinctive idea of church we have defined it as an organized religious body formulated to unify the community. But though this definition may be true in common parlance, it is not hard and fast definition. Church is not a descriptive term to be spelled out as a body, an organization, a council, a congregation, or even an ecclesia. It is a normative term containing definite doctrine and referred to as an ideal. This is not peculiar, as we pointed out earlier, with Christianity. Church has two principal features, namely its normative ideality and comprehensiveness. Sometimes it breaks up into several denominations but each one claims to represent the same ideal.[19]

Emile Durkheim has discussed the idea of the church at length. We quote his definition verbatim:

"The really religious beliefs are always common to a determined group, which makes a profession of adhering to them and of practicing the rites connected with them. They are not merely received individually by all the members of this group; they are something belonging to the group, and they make its unity. The individuals which compose it feel themselves united to each other by the simple fact that they have a common faith. A society whose members are united by the fact that they think in the same way in regard to the sacred world and in relation to the profane world, and by the fact that they translate these common ideas into common practices, is what is called a Church. In all history, we do not find a single religion without a Church. Sometimes the Church is strictly national, sometimes it passes the frontiers; sometimes it embraces an entire people (Rome, Athens, the Hebrews), sometimes it embraces only a part of them (the Christian societies since the advent of Protestantism); sometimes it is directed by a corps of

---

[19] *Ibid.*, p. 145.

priests; sometimes it is almost completely devoid of any official directing body."[20]

The anchoring point in this definition is that a religious group has a common bond of faith and practices and that it is a directing body in religion. Sometimes it manifests itself in a body with an external official equipment and sometimes remains invisible having only a directing ideal pattern, like the doctrine of *Ijmāʿ* in Islam.

Besides, Durkheim compares religion with magic and distinguishes it from magic because of the unifying force of religion. He conceives that a magician has no interest in uniting his clientele, nor have they any communion with each other. But religion and church are inseparable. He confutes the prevailing notion that the church is a 'fraternity of priests.' He takes it as "a moral community formed by all the believers in a single faith, laymen as well as priests." Magic is devoid of any such community.[21] The existence of a moral community is a *sine qua non* profoundly stressed by the sociologists to build up an organization like church.[22]

Since the church comes into existence as a binding force in a religious community, its principal function is to create unity by its direction in different ages in doctrine and practice. A religious community substantiates its existence by and demonstrates its will through the church. Religion becomes dogmatic after the final development of the church. Polemics and apologetics grow out of the prerogative of orthodoxy held by the church. Joachim Wach dwells on the functioning of the church in dogmatizing religion. He remarks: "There follows with continued reflection and discussion, systematization, and elaboration of doctrine, the careful and comprehensive formation of a rule of faith or creed, the

---

[20] Emile Durkheim, *op. cit.*, p. 59
[21] *Ibid.*, pp. 60-61.
[22] Talcott Parsons, loc. cit., p. XXXVII.

standardization of forms of collective worship, and eventually the establishment of a constitution to sustain the new stable organization. The oral tradition is written down, the written tradition is collected and standardized, and the doctrine is redefined and hereafter all deviations and opinions at variance with the officially accepted teachings are classed as heresy."[23]

IV

With the rise of this unifying body and directing authority, there emerged the idea of consensus of opinion through which the church functions. Sociologists attach supreme importance to opinion, public or private, in a society. The opinion is sometimes called 'authority, sometimes 'source of authority', and even authority is suspected to be the 'daughter of opinion.' Authority is rather derived from opinion.[24] Public opinion carries more weight than the individual one. It is considered a social force. An individual or a group which has public opinion in its favour receives the whole force of society. Hence the significance of public opinion or the agreement of people in general on a certain matter.

Important matters in the past history were decided in a twofold way, (i) by consulting an individual, say king, priestly divines, or oracles, (ii) by agreement of the body of elders in the community. These methods were applied in the case of the points not answered in the scriptures or by the founder of religion. Instances are frequently found in the early Greek civilization. Cicero remarks: "The Athenians, for instance, in every public assembly always had present certain priestly diviners, whom they called mantis. The

---

[23] Wach, *op. cit.*, pp. 142-43.
[24] Emile Durkheim, *op. cit.*, pp. 238-39.

Spartans assigned an augur to their kings as a judicial adviser, and they also enacted that an augur should be present in their Council of Elders, which is the name of their senate. In matters of grave concern, they always consulted the oracle at Delphi, or that of Jupiter Hammon or that of Dodona."[25] Further, talking of "offices" Cicero lays great stress on consulting, in important matters, men of opinion and persons of extraordinary merits. He thinks one is apt to be misled in one's affairs if one ignores consultation. Referring to Aristippus and Socrates, he remarks that these sages advise in certain matters to do against established rules and customs and one should follow them because of their eminence in wisdom.[26]

The idea of consensus is present in the teachings of the Stoics of Rome as an authority. Both Cicero and Seneca substantiate their point of view in a number of problems on the basis of consensus of opinion. It appears that consensus has been regarded as a criterion of truth from the very beginning in history. Custom and tradition are in fact the manifestation of the consent of the people in general. These must have carried the sanction of the unanimous consent of people in their early stages to become an authority. Hence Cicero considers 'the common consent of people' a law of nature.[27] To prove the existence of gods he argues on the basis of agreement of people. He adds: "You see that the foundation (for such it is) of our inquiry has been well and truly laid. For the belief in the gods has not been established by authority, custom or law but rests on the unanimous and abiding consensus of mankind; their existence therefore is a necessary inference since we possess an instinctive or

---

[25] Cicero, *De Divinatione* (tr. William Armistead Falconer), London: the Loeb Classical Lib., 1953, p. 327.
[26] Cicero, Offices, *Essays and Letters*, London: Everyman's Library, 1949, p. 65.
[27] Cicero *Tusculan Disputations*, in the Basic Works of Cicero, ed. Moses Hadas, New York: The Modern Library, 1951, pp. 77.

rather an innate concept of them; *but a belief which all men by nature share must necessarily be true.*"[28]

At another place, Cicero calls universal agreement (*ominum consensus*) the voice of nature and insists on strict adherence to the agreement of those who passed away from life.[29]

Seneca too attaches great importance to the general agreement on a certain point. He puts his reliance on a thing not because of the agreement of philosophers before him, but because of the general agreement of people in the past. He remarks:

"I myself do not hold the same view, that I judge that our philosophers have come down to this argument because they are already bound by the first link in the chain and for that reason may not alter their definition. People are wont to concede much to the things which all men take for granted; in our eyes, the fact that all men agree upon something is a proof of its truth. For instance, we infer that the gods exist, for this reason among others that there is implanted in everyone an idea concerning deity, and there are no people so far beyond the reach of laws and customs that it does not believe at least in gods of some sort. And when we discuss the immortality of the soul, we are influenced in no small degree by the general opinion of mankind, who either fear or worship the spirits of the lower world. I make the most of this general belief."[30]

Law in every society as a principle is formulated with the consent of the people. Roman law was also founded on popular consent. It was basically customary law because most of the institutions like the

---

[28] Cicero, *De natura Deorum Academica* (tr. H. Rackham), London: the Loeb Classical Lib. 1933, BK. I, XVII, 45, 46.

[29] Cicero, *Tusculan Disputations*, tr. J.E. King, London: the Loeb Classical Lib. 1927, BK.I, XV, 35, pp. 41-42.

[30] Seneca, *Ad lucilium*, Epistalae morales (tr. Richard M. Gummere), London: the Loeb Classical Lib., 1952, III, 341. (Epist. CXVII, 117, 6).

authority of a head of a family, monogamy, and certain other formal ceremonies exist before there is any law in the strict sense of the term. The sources of Roman law were as follows: *custom, lex, plebiscitum, magistratuum edicta, senatusconsulta, principum placita,* and *responsa prudentium. Lex* was a statute formulated on the proposal of the king or magistrate ratified by the vote of the people in a meeting called *comitia.* The king or the magistrate had no authority to legislate on important matters, like declaring war or modification of a custom. Before any lex became binding it had to seek the approval of the senate. The Senate was an important advisory body on legislation. It was the body of elders earlier consisting of only patricians and later on senior magistrates. Roman senate had no final powers. The king was the ultimate authority. Yet it had executive powers. Its official name was the senate of the Roman people which indicates its official designation. It had control over the magistrates, influence over finance, religion, and foreign policy. Under the Empire, the senate became entirely subservient to the Emperor, though vested with more powers. The Emperor had direct control, and most of the legislation was derived from him and his advisers. With the second century A.D. the *senatusconsultum* was recognized having the force of *lex* and modifying *ius civile.* About this period, the Emperor had full legislative powers. After 282, the senate became a town council.

Responsa prudentium consisted of the opinions and decisions of the jurists who were empowered by the Emperor Augustus to give their legal replies on public legal problems (*ius publice respondendi*) to the judges. Their decisions had the statutory force if they were unanimous; the judge could choose any opinion which he liked if they differed. In contrast to the previous practice, the legal opinion was delivered to the judge in writing before it was enforced. By the time of Vespasian, the leading jurists were salaried by the Emperor and subsequently, they became his advisers. The whole legal system was now actually controlled by them. Up to the end of the classical period the jurists gave their legal replies, but by the time of the Emperor Augustus, their main function was to advise the Emperor and to draft laws and constitutions. *Responsa prudentium* in the age of dictatorship was a step in the direction of democracy. Roman law being religiously characterized was mostly influenced by the Jewish law and had the popular consent.[31]

V

Now we return to the church in religion. Only for the sake of illustration we have chosen *sangha*, *Sanhedrin*, and the church as the final directing authority in religious matters. To begin with, Buddhism like other religions, has a concept of community. The community has been divided into *sangha* (monkish church) and the laity. *Sangha* does not constitute the priesthood as in Christianity. The stress on the monkish way of life in Buddhism is a Vedic influence. Such a reference to a muni or monk is found in Regveda (X. 136).[32] The Buddha had not laid down all the 150 rules of the *Sangha* in his lifetime. He gave the reason that if he laid down all the rules at once, people would be afraid of entering the Order and would not trust in his words. Hence, he decided to formulate the rules whenever the necessity arose.[33] Gotama came actually to give "the first wheel of the law" and not the minutiae. He is reported to have said, "Receive initiation from me you shall obtain the place of Nirvan."[34]

It is certain, as the modern researches show, that the *sangha* was founded by the Buddha himself. The Buddha's disciples had some

[31] Prichard, A.M., *Leage's Roman Private Law*., London, 1964, pp. 13-17, 30-32, and 45-46.
[32] Saunders, K.J., art. Buddhism, Enc. of Social Sciences, New York, 1959, III, 36.
[33] *Vinaya Texts* (The Sacred Books of the East), ed. Max Muller, Delhi: Motilal Banarsidass 1965, XXXVI, 110.
[34] *Mahayana Texts*, ed. Max Muller, XLIX, 172.

sort of formal union "through their common reverence for their Master and through a common spiritualism." Their organization started as a brotherhood. This monkish organized body was called Sakyaputtiya Samanas. The appellation was given in the earliest times to the community by the people. *Patimokkha* and *Kammavakas* are the oldest liturgical formularies.[35]

Historically speaking, five Brahman ascetics first joined the Order who listened to the sermon of the Buddha and welcomed his teaching. They wore the yellow robe as their distinguishing dress. The next member was Yasa, a noble youth of *Benares*; then *Sariputta* and *Moggallana*, two Brahman youths, became members of the *Sangha*. They were honoured with high rank in the Buddhist church. Inside the Order, the distinction of caste was eliminated. All lived lives of immense austerity, chastity, and poverty. For a long time, Buddha was reluctant to allow women to enter the Order. But at last, he yielded to the entreaties of his foster mother and permitted women to become nuns.[36]

The formation of *Sangha* started with the simple words of the Buddha "*Ehi bikkhu*" (come, be my monk) with which he invited people of all social ranks to join him. This was then replaced by *upsampada*, an ordination ceremony with the declaration of faith in the three Gems Buddha, Teaching and Order-confession of sin, tonsure, and other requirements.[37] From the sayings of the Buddha it appears that he laid great emphasis on the church, i.e. unity of the monks, and condemned division and schism in the *Sangha*.[38] We can imagine the significance of the church in Buddhism from the following remarks of Buddha:

---

[35] *Vinaya Texts*, Introduction, XIII, XI-XII (11-12).
[36] Art. Buddhism *in Encyclopaedia of Religion and Religions*, London, 1951, pp. 71-74,
[37] Saunders, K. J. *loc. cit.*
[38] Vinaya Texts. *ed. Cit.* XIII, 316; XX, 266-69

"Happy is the arising of the awakened,

happy is the teaching of the true law,

happy is the peace in the church,

happy is the devotion of those who are at peace."[39]

A Bhikkhu is required to take refuge in the Venerable Gotama, in the *Dhamma*, and the assembly of Bhikkhus.[40] There are five kinds of spiritual barrenness; doubt in the brotherhood (*Sangha*) is one of them. One who has no faith and confidence in *Sangha*, his mind is not inclined towards zeal, exertion, perseverance, and struggle.[41] The *Sangha* is a supreme authority to decide disputed points in Buddhism. It appoints the monks, expels them, and formulates rules. The official acts are performed by the *Sangha* in the presence of the entire body. The consent of a sick monk, if he is not present, is necessary for the validity of its acts.[42] The *Sangha* appoints a man as a Bhikkhu who must possess five qualities, namely that he is not involved in lust, in the evil course of hatred and fear, and that he knows what has been received and what has not.[43] The *Sangha* can expel a Bhikkhu only in case he declares himself belonging to another communion, and he refuses to see or atone an offence committed by him, or renounce a false doctrine. In no case can a guiltless monk be ousted by the *Sangha*.[44]

To perform official acts the *Sangha* has been divided into five groups, viz. (1) the Bhikkhu *Sangha* consisting of four persons, (2) five persons, (3) ten persons, (4) twenty persons, and (5) more than twenty persons. The *Sangha* which consists of four persons is a

---

[39] *Dhammapada* (the Sacred Books of the East), *op. cit.*, X, pt. 1, 52.
[40] *Sutta-Nipata* (The Sacred Books of the East), *op. cit.*, XI, 223-25.
[41] *Ibid.*, XI, 223-25.
[42] *Vinaya Texts*, *op. cit.*, XIII, 227.
[43] *Ibid.*, XVII, 200.
[44] *Ibid.*, pp. 260, 272, 273, 291.

perfect body, and is entitled to perform all official acts except three, i.e. *upasampada* ordination, *paurana,* and *abbhama.* The next group consisting of five persons cannot perform two acts *upasampada* ordination in the central countries and abbhama. The third group is competent to perform all official acts except one, namely *abbhama.* The last two groups are empowered to perform all kinds of official acts.[45] Matters are settled by the *Sangha* through taking votes. There are ten definite cases in which the taking of vote is valid.[46] A Bhikkhu possessing certain requiste qualifications is appointed by the *Sangha* for taking votes.[47] The votes are taken in three ways: secretly, by whishpering, and openly. The Bhikkhu who is the teller of votes has voting tickets of different colours. He asks each voter to choose any colour he likes and forbids him to disclose his opinion. If he ascertains that those whose opinion agrees with the Dhamma are in a majority, he validates the voting. But in case those whose opinion is opposed to the *Dhamma* are in a majority, he invalidates the voting. If the in charge of votes tells in the ear of each Bhikkhu that a particular ticket indicates a particular opinion, and asks him to take anyone he likes, this is known as the whispering method. In case he is sure that those whose opinion agrees with the Dhamma are in a majority, the votes are taken openly.[48]

Four kinds of legal questions are settled by *Sangha.* They are dispute, censure, offence, and business. Under dispute fall quarrel, strife, controversy, difference of opinion, contradiction, opposition, and the like. The category 'censure' covers any fault of morality, conduct, means of livelihood, making excuses for a person, or making fun of him. The five groups and seven groups of offence are subject of legal questions of offence. By the term, business is meant

---

[45] *Ibid.*, pp. 268-69.
[46] *Ibid.*, XX, pp. 26-27.
[47] *Ibid.*, pp. 25-26.
[48] *Ibid.*, pp. 56-57.

a matter which ought to be done, an obligation, a matter for which leave ought to be formally asked, the proposal of resolution, etc.[49] These legal questions are settled in the meetings of the *Sangha* by the proceeding in the presence and proceeding by majority of the *Sangha*.[50]

Sangha came into being to bring about integration in the Buddhist community. Hence, we find tremendous emphasis on creating concord in the *Sangha*. One who causes schism and creates division in the *Sangha* has been severely condemned. Schism, concord, and division in *Sangha* have been fully discussed in the Buddhist scriptures.[51]

Laymen are admitted to the *Sangha* though they become backsliders. It was objected by the king Milanda. He suggested not to allow laymen to join the *Sangha* unless they attain the Fruit of the First Path (primary stages of monasticism). But it was pointed out to him by giving a number of illustrations that laymen, however degenerate, would be purified by the Order and their moral debasement would do no harm to the *Sangha*.[52] The members of the *Sangha* are required to be free from breach of ordinary moral law and breach of the rules of the *Sangha*.[53]

The first three Buddhist Councils held soon after the death of the Buddha were most important in the formation of the Buddhist doctrine. The first Council was held in 483. B.C. at Rajagaha under the chairmanship of Kassapa. In this Council, *Vinaya* and *Dhamma* were recited in order to formulate their standard version. The existence of this Council has been debated by the scholars; yet

---

[49] *Ibid.*, pp. 35-37.
[50] *Ibid.*, pp. 45-47
[51] *Ibid.*, pp. 254-55, 266-69.
[52] *Ibid.*, XXXVI, 63, 70.
[53] *Ibid.*, pp. 99-100.

Professor Kern observes that "it is by no means credible that the disciples after the death of the founder of their sect come together to an agreement concerning the principal points of the creed and of the discipline."[54] A century later in 383 B.C. a second Council was held at Vesali to settle certain disputed points regarding food and conduct of monks.[55] The third Council was held in about 247 B.C. at Pataliputta in the reign of Asoka. It is said that due to the prosperity of the monks in the reign of Asoka some heretics who were non-Buddhists came to live with the monks. Asoka assembled all the monks on the earth and asked them questions about the teaching of the Buddha. He turned out all those who wrongly answered the questions. A Council of the true doctrine is also reported to have been formed in this meeting. consisting of a thousand monks, learned and well-versed in Buddha's teaching. The *Dhamma* Council was completed in nine months by the thousand monks. Mrs. Rhys Davids severely criticizes the recorded accounts about this Council. She holds that it was a Congress rather than a Council and that the collection of the Dhamma was the gigantic task of revision and that the judges were not one thousand but only eight. It is, however, certain that a Council was held during the reign of Asoka for the same reason and purpose for which the two previous Councils were held.[56]

In short, *Sangha* came into being to give a sense of community to Buddhism. It developed from certain aspects of the conception of *dhatu* (solidarity based on mutual service and loyalty) to a directing and deciding body. For its high ideals, it is called the "harvest field of merit" (*punnakhetta*). It was the nucleus of the Buddhist community in its embryonic stage. The fundamental ideas of

---

[54] Edward J. Thomas, *The History of Buddhist Thought*, London, 1963, p. 29.
[55] *Ibid.*, pp. 30-33.
[56] *Ibid.*, pp. 33-37. cf. art. Buddhism in *Encyclopaedia of Religion and Religions*, *op. cit.*

the Buddhist faith found actual embodiment in the formation of *Sangha*.[57]

VI

Judaism has a similar religious body known as Sanhedrin. The term has been derived from a Greek word *sunedrion* meaning council. From the earliest times this had been the highest tribunal, for the Jews met at Jerusalem to decide their political as well as religious matters. In the Bible, the term refers to the supreme Jewish court, body of elders, senate, and to any court of justice.[58] Josephus uses this term in connection with the edict of the Roman Governor, Gabinius (57-55 B.C.) who abolished the constitution and the Government of Palestine. He divided the kingdom into seven provinces, each of which was placed under a *sanhedrin*. He uses this word for the first time while giving the account of summoning the young Herod before this council for his misbehaviour.[59] The council to which the Gospels and Josephus refer was the highest political authority and the supreme court. Only this body was authorized to decide criminal cases and to give capital punishments. The other council held in the hall of hewn stones in the corner of the Temple was the supreme religious authority dealing with religious affairs and Jewish law. This also imparted religious instructions to the people.

The early history of *Sanhedrin* is obscure. It appears from the extant literature on the subject that the idea of Sanhedrin was based on the O.T. Nu. II: 16-24. It took its threads from the seventy elders who were asked to assist Moses. Later Ezra recognized this body after

---

[57] K.J. Saunders, *op. cit.*, p. 34.

[58] For Bible references see J.A. Thompson, art. Sanhedrin, The New Bible Dictionary, London, 1962.

[59] *Ibid.*, cf. J.Z. Lauterbach, art. Sanhedrin, *The Jewish Encyclopaedia*, New York, 1905, XI, 41-45.

Exile when the Persians allowed the Jews to look after their affairs. In the time of the Greeks, this body was known as Gerousia (assembly). Antiochus alludes to this council in his epistle which he wrote to the Jews in 203 B.C. The origin and development of this body are not known in detail. It seems, however, certain that it was mainly a political body composed of members drawn from aristocracy who represented the nation. The high priest presided over this council. During the Maccabean revolt, Gerousia played a vital role. Under the Romans, this body was invested with extensive powers. The appellation Gerousia continued till the first century B.C. With the close of the century, this body was subsequently called synderion. Julius Caesar extended the powers of Sanhedrin at Judea and the same continued under the Procurators. In Judea, there existed a number of local courts to decide the petty cases. In small towns, these courts had seven elders and in large towns twenty-three. The political Sanhedrin was abolished in 70 A.D. after the fall of Jerusalem. This was then replaced by the *Beth Din* (court of Judgement) which met at Jabneh, Usah, Shafran, Sepphoris and Tiberias at intervals. This was composed chiefly of scribes whose decisions had practically no value.

The Sanhedrin was composed of seventy-one members drawn from noble families and priesthood. Secular rulers were also added. In N.T. times the Great Sanhedrin consisted of the high priest, members of the noble families, and the legal experts. The high priest who was also the head of the state from the time of Simeon presided over the body. He was called nasi (prince). Later on under the procurators, his powers were curtailed. The body could not be convened without their permission. The political Sanhedrin had extensive powers of deciding civil and criminal cases. The cases which involved capital punishment were settled by it after obtaining confirmation of the Roman procurator, although under the Jewish law, it was empowered to impose the sentence of capital punishment. The well-known cases of trials are recorded in the New Testament. Jesus Christ was charged with blasphemy. Peter and John were tried on the charge of preaching the resurrection of Christ (Acts 5:27). St. Stephen was charged with the blasphemy against the Temple and the Law (Acts 6:12). St. Paul was accused of transgressing the Mosaic law. When he was brought before the Sanhedrin, there arose a dissension between the Pharisees and Sadducees, and the body was divided.[60]

A detailed account of Sanhedrin is found in the tractate Sanhedrin in *Mishnayoth*. It dealt with the cases brought before a court of three, twenty-three, and seventy-one judges, the rights of high priest, money suits, ineligible judges, examining witness, four types of punishment, stoning, hanging, burning, strangling, etc. The Great Sanhedrin was composed of seventy-one, and a small Sanhedrin of twenty-three, members. The cases were decided by majority vote. In property cases, a judge could withdraw his opinion, no matter whether he argued for acquittal or conviction. But in capital cases, he could withdraw only if he argued for conviction and not in the case of acquittal. In the cases of acquittal, a simple majority was sufficient, but in the case of conviction, a two-thirds majority was required.[61]

The religious Sanhedrin was different from the political one. It is said to have existed from the time of Moses. But originally it was not a regular body. It was just like a synod whose meetings were held from time to time to decide questions relating to religious life. It was subsequently replaced by an organized body under the name of the 'Great Synagogue', and finally by Sanhedrin or Beth Din. The

---

[60] *Ibid.*, Stanely Wood, *The Life and Teaching of Christ*, London: George Gill & Sons, Ltd., 1939, I, 49-51.

[61] *Mishnayoth*, (ed. Philip Blackman), New yark: The Judaica Press, Inc., 1963, IV, 235-97 (tract. Sanhedrin, Mishna 1: 1, 2, 6; 4:1); cf. J.A. Thompson, *loc cit.*

functions of this body enumerated in the *Jewish Encyclopaedia* were as follows:

1. "It had supervision over the Temple service, which was required to be conducted in conformity with the law and according to pharisaic interpretation.

2. It decided which priests should perform the Temple service.

3. It supervised especially important ritual acts as the service on the day of atonement.

4. It had in charge the burning of the Red Heifer and the preparation of the water of purification.

5. When the body of the murdered person was found, members of the Great Bet Din had to take the necessary measurements in order to determine which city, as being the nearest to the place of murder, was to bring the sacrifice of atonement.

6. It had also to decide as to the harvest tithes.

7. It sat in judgment on women suspected of adultery and sentenced them to drink the bitter water.

8. It arranged the calendar, and

9. Provided correct copies of the Torah roll for the king and probably for the Temple also.

10. In general, it decided all doubtful questions relating to the religious law and rendered the final decision in regard to the sentence of the teacher who promulgated opinions contradicting the traditional interpretation of the Law."[62]

---

[62] J.Z. Lauterbach, art. Sanhedrin, *op. cit.*

The president of the religious *Sanhedrin*, like that of the political one, was called *nasi* and the vice-president *ab bet din*. Five pairs of scholars, collectively known as *zugot*, are also said to have been at the head of Great Sanhedrin at the time of the Second Temple. They were eminent scholars and the representatives of the Jewish tradition belonging to the Pharisaic school. The procedure of deciding the cases was as follows: When a question was raised, any member who knew the tradition relating to the point under discussion, proffered it before the assembly for decision. If no decisive tradition was found, discussion followed and the matter was settled by ballot.[63]

After the abolition of the Great Sanhedrin, the academy of Jabneh was formed to replace this body. This was considered to be the continuation of the Sanhedrin. The later academies down to the close of the 5th century A.D. were also regarded as the highest religious body. The Jewish law continued in the later Rabbinic literature owes it development to these academies.[64]

The Great Sanhedrin was revived in 1807 by Napoleon I to utilize its decisions for his legislation. This was principally convened to determine the relations of Jews to the state. The twelve questions submitted to the assembly of the notables are recorded in the *Jewish Encyclopaedia*. They are enumerated below:

1. "Is it lawful for Jews to have more than one wife?

2. Is divorce allowed by the Jewish religion? Is divorce valid although pronounced not by courts of justice but by virtue of laws in contradiction to the French code?

---

[63] *Ibid.*

[64] *Ibid.*, I, Abrahams, art. Sanhedrin, *Encyclopaedia of Religion and Ethics*, Edinburgh, 1958, XI, 184-85.

3. May a Jewess marry a Christian or a Jew-Christian woman? Or does Jewish law order that the Jews should only intermarry among themselves.

4. In the eyes of Jews are the Frenchmen not of the Jewish religion considered as brethren or strangers?

5. What conduct does Jewish law prescribe toward Frenchmen not of the Jewish religion?

6. Do the Jews born in France and treated by the law as French citizens acknowledge France as their country? Are they bound to defend it? Are they bound to obey the laws and follow the doctrines of the civil code?

7. Who elects the rabbis?

8. What kind of police jurisdiction do the rabbis exercise over the Jews? What judicial power do they exercise over them?

9. Are the police jurisdiction of the rabbis and the forms of the election regulated by Jewish law, or are they only sanctioned by custom?

10. Are there professions from which the Jews are excluded by their law?

11. Does Jewish law forbid the Jews to take usury from their brethren?

12. Does it forbid or does it allow usury in dealings with strangers"?[65]

The decisions taken by the Sanhedrin were:-

1. "Polygamy is prohibited.

---

[65] Samuel Mannheimer, art Sanhedrin-French, *The Jewish Encyclopaedia, op. cit.*, XI, 46-48.

2. Divorce is valid after the previous permission of the civil authorities.

3. A civil contract is necessary before the marriage on the basis of religion.

4. Marriages contracted between Israelites and Christians are binding.

5. Every Jew should consider a non-Jewish fellow citizen as his brother and help him like his coreligionist.

6. The Jews should regard the land of their birth as their father land and should love and defend it accordingly.

7. There is no ban on any kind of handicraft and vocation in Judaism.

8. The professions preferable for the Jews are agriculture, manual labour, and the arts.

9. The exacting of usury by a Jew from a Jew or a Christian is forbidden."

The notables prepared an official report in the last meeting and presented it to the Government. The assembly was then dissolved for good.[66]

In modern times, there is no common religious body of the Jews like the Great Sanhedrin. The need of forming such a body is being felt immensely in various circles of Judaism. This gave birth to a great controversy over the creation of a synod among the rabbis of U.S.A.[67]

It is worthy of note that Judaism in the past recognized the sovereignty of the people which manifested itself in the Great

---

[66] *Ibid.*

[67] Art. Synod, *The Jewish Encyclopaedia*, XI, 643-46.

Sanhedrin. One can imagine the strength of this body by the fact that even the Jewish king ascended the throne by its election. R. Issac, an ancient teacher, once declared: "One must not appoint an elder over a community except after consultation with that community."[68] The king could not impose any doctrine, however sacrosanct it might be, on the people without the consent of the whole Jewish community.[69] In short, sanhedrin played an important part in the formation of the religious life of the Jewish community. Even today the middle paragraphs of the daily *amidah* contained a prayer, among others, for restoration of the Sanhedrin[70] - an allusion to the significance of this body in the Jewish community.

VII

Christianity, too, as a religion has a similar unifying and directing body known as a church. This body is a continuation of the Jewish synagogue, established independently under a separate name when Christianity had broken with Judaism completely. The word is derived from the Greek adjective *kyriakos*, as *kyriakon doma* or *kyriake oikia*, meaning the "Lord's house." In Greek, *ekklesia* is originally applied to the building, but not to 'organization' or 'community'. In Christianity, the term ecclesia applies both to building and to community. Its counterparts in different languages are *kirk* in Scot., *kirche* in Germ., *kirka* in Swed., *kirke* in Dan., *tserkov* in Russ., *cerkova* in Bul., *cirkev* in Czech., *kirkko* in Fin. Two Hebrew words *edah* and *kahl* in the O.T. have been rendered ecclesia. In Pentateuch, they signify people of Israel during wanderings. Ecclesia there meant the people itself, especially in its relation to God. But the word

[68] Baron, S.W., *A Social and Religious History of the Jews*. New York/London, 1962, V. 75.
[69] *Ibid.*
[70] Louis Finkelstein, *The Jews - their History, Culture and Religion*, New York, 1960, 11, 1769.

synagogue in Judaism survived in the sense of local congregation.[71] Since synagogue was reserved for Jews, ecclesia was adopted by Christianity, as it had a more ideal conception. Synagogue was a local community and visible congregation, but ecclesia was ideal congregation having full-fledged official structure.[72]

The foundation of the church was, in fact, laid by Jesus Christ himself when he chose the twelve disciples out of the multitude to preach his teaching. This was 'the first act of organization done by Jesus Christ.[73] The institution of the church derives its authority from the N.T. The most significant of the verses is the one which shows the presence of Christ in the gathering of the believers. It reads: "For where two or three are gathered together in my name, there am I in the midst of them (Matt. 18:20). Since the local *ekklesia* was characterized by this trait, it was identified with the ideal church founded by Christ. 'Church of God, the appellation of the original or early church repeatedly referred to in the Bible, has a long history. It is, however, true that an individual local church was called the 'Church of God'. The name is derived from the verse, "Take heed therefore unto yourselves, and to all the flock, over which the Holy Ghost hath made you overseers, to feed the Church of God, which he hath purchased with his own blood" (Acts 20:28).[74] The church in its present form, which is the result of a long-chequered history, was not in existence in the early days of Christianity. The term has different meanings in the N.T. Sometimes, and most probably originally, it means building (Matt. 16:18); sometimes it connotes 'body', being Christ at the head (col.

---

[71] Robinson, D.W.B., art. Church, *The New Bible Dictionary*, *op. cit.*; T.A. Lacey, Art. Church, *Encyclopaedia Britannica*, London, 1951, V, 669-71.

[72] John Oman, art. 'Church, *Encyclopaedia of Religion and Ethics*, Edinburgh, 1958, III. 617-24.

[73] Stanely Wood, *op. cit.*, p. 65.

[74] Robinson, D.W.B., *op. cit.*, For 'Church of God' see N.T. Acts 20:28, 1 Cor. 1:2, 1 Cor. 10:32, 1 Cor. 11:22, 1. Cor. 15:9, Gal. 1:13, 1 Tim. 3:5.

1:18), and at other times it conveys the sense of authority (Matt. 18:17), and finally, it stands for a council or a general assembly (Heb. 12:23). In the N.T. it generally connotes 'local congregation of Christians. These local congregations are collectively called the N.T. Church or the Early Church, but no such usage is traceable in the early times. Ecclesia, from which the church takes its origin, was an assembly. The term was used for "the public assembly of citizens" outside Judaea (Acts 19:39). For Jesus ecclesia meant congregation of Israel formulated before the appearance of Jesus. This congregation met at annual feasts attended by the male representatives of Israel (Acts 7:38). Whether Christianity borrowed this term from Gentiles or Jews is disputed. It seems definitely certain that the term implied a meeting rather than an organization or society.'[75]

Christianity started as reformed Judaism. St. James and St. Peter wanted Christianity only to this extent. But St. Paul, to widen the circle of the nascent community, removed the condition of circumcision and the following of the Mosaic law.[76] The church in the Christian sense begins from the ascension of Jesus Christ at Jerusalem. The disciples of Christ and those who followed them by their preaching emerged in a new community, which separated itself gradually from the Jews. They did not use the word ecclesia for them all at once but called themselves 'the elect remnant of Israel. They tended to seek salvation in Zion and to build the tabernacle promised by Jesus. The character of this Jerusalem church was essentially Jewish, as they followed the law and worshipped the Temple. But they distinguished themselves by their faith in the messiahship of Jesus, his crucifixion as a redemption for Israel, his resurrection by God, the visitation of calamity after his death at

---

[75] *Ibid.*

[76] Bertrand Russell, *History of Western Philosophy*, London: George Allen and Unwin Ltd., 1969, p. 325.

the cross, and its culmination in the appearance of Messiah to establish judgment and glory.[77]

The idea of 'one church' or 'Catholic church,' according to Bertrand Russell, crept in Christianity by the influence of the Roman Empire. The Romans had in their minds the notion of empire worldwide, taking inspiration from the teachings of Stoics who believed in the brotherhood of man. In the Middle Ages, after Charlemagne, the church and the Empire were universal in idea, which resulted in the conception of "one human family, one catholic religion, one universal culture, and worldwide state."[78] The Catholic church, Russell presumes, was influenced by foreign elements. Its history was Jewish, its theology was Greek, and its government and canon law were mostly derived from the Romans. The Reformation retained, indeed. strengthened, the Judaic element and rejected others.[79] Christianity could not escape the influence of the Jewish discipline even after its complete break with Judaism. The new community came into existence by the process of substitution: the conceptions were the same; the doctrines, sacraments, and organizational structure were formulated afresh following the pattern of Judaism for further developments. Judaism was anchored in racial pride. "the chosen people of God.' Therein prevailed the idea of collective sin, for which the whole Jewish nation suffered tribulation. Christianity substituted Church for 'chosen people; it differed from Judaism in respect of sin. The Jewish nation sinned and it suffered collectively, but the church being grounded in spiritualism could not sin. Those who commit sin in Christianity lose their communion with the church. This gave rise to the idea of individualism in Christianity most probably through the teaching of the Roman Stoics. The Christian theology had now two parts: one

[77] Robinson, D.W.B., art. Church, *op. cit.*
[78] Bertrand Russell, *op. cit.*, p. 287.
[79] *Ibid.*, p. 20.

was related to the church and the other with the individualism of the Protestants. Church, according to the Catholics, was an intermediary between man and God, as none could get salvation without baptism and without being a member of the church. Church is in fact a developed form of the original 'elect remnant of Israel,"[80]

After the failure of the national ideals of the Jews, the religious bond proved an integrating factor of the Jewish community. It received impetus by exile and reached its acme among the Hellenistic Jews in the time of Jesus Christ. The spiritual conceptions of God and salvation were crystallized, and the Jewish religion became more patient and missionary in the later days of Judaism. The national creed of the Jews was thus transformed into a spiritual creed embodied later in the institution of church. With the vigorous teaching of Jesus regarding the establishment of the kingdom of God, people were anxiously looking forward to its appearance. His death at cross, as it is believed, intensified the idea of unity among his followers. Their belief in the resurrection of Jesus gave birth to church. Moreover, the idea of the church was reinforced by their belief that a new divine order was going to break through the world. The early or the apostolic church was constituted of prophets, apostles, and saints and the Catholic church was founded on bishops who represented Jesus and Peter after him.[81] After the execution of St. Stephen by the Sanhedrin, Christianity had broken completely with the Jewish law and the Temple. The new community now appeared with its own temple, altar, church and sacraments.[82]

With the emergence of the new community, the need for a final religious authority whose decisions should be infallible was immensely felt in Christianity. The Roman church established a

---

[80] *Ibid.*, pp. 345, 311.

[81] John Oman, art. Church, *op. cit.*

[82] Nixon, R.E., art. Stephen, *The New Bible Dictonary*, *op. cit.*, p. 1216; cf. T.A. Lacey, art. Church, *op. cit.*

doctrinal office of bishops with the idea that God would not allow the congregation to fall into error.[83] The Bible being a final authority now came in question. In Catholic doctrine revelation was not confined to the Bible; it perpetuated from age to age through the church. The Protestants, on the other hand, rejected the church and sought the truth only through the Bible. In case of dispute in the interpretation, there was no decisive authority. Every man could interpret for himself. They did not believe in any intermediary between man and God.[84] In the Middle Ages, the political powers of the church increased and the scripture became subservient to it. As time went on, the dogma developed that the Bible held no normative value outside the church. It is the church which constituted canon law and not vice versa. Scripture, according to the orthodox belief, is a part of the living tradition of the church. Without church, the Bible is 'a branch cut off from the tree.' Church is the 'criterion of truth, the ultimate court of appeal, and the final authority.[85] Church was declared to be the decisive authority on religious affairs. Even the Bible owes its authority to the church because it decided which books should be included in the scripture and which not. Church's interpretation of the Bible is final. One who interprets the Bible in isolation from the church runs the risk of falling into error.[86] The exaggeration exercised in vesting all authority in the church by the Catholics produced a sharp reaction as in Chillingworth's dictum: "The Bible, and the Bible only, is the religion of Protestants." This principle was not approved even by Calvin and Martin Luther.[87]

---

[83] Max Weber, *op. cit.*, p. 74.
[84] Bertrand Russell, *op. cit.*, p. 20.
[85] Joseph L. Hromadka, art. Eastern Orthodoxy, *The Great Religions of the Modern World.* ed. Edward J. Jurji, Princeton, 1946, pp. 290-91.
[86] Timothy Ware, *The Orthodox Church*, Bungay Suffolk (Penguine Books), 1963, pp. 207-8.
[87] J.G. Cazenov, art. Church, Encyclopaedia Britannica, Ohio, 1907, V, 664.

Orthodox Christianity attaches supreme importance to the council in the life of the church. Making decisions by a common mind' constitutes an authority by itself. In a council, there is harmony in thinking, unity in love, and faith. There is no dictatorship in mutual consultation. People are free to cast their opinions with open minds. "A council is a living embodiment," it is believed, "of the essential nature of the Church." Believers can claim an authority when gathered together, but not when isolated. Jesus is himself with those who gather in his name (Matt. 18:20). Hence the appellation 'the Church of the Seven Councils' generally applied to the orthodox in Christianity.[88]

We find reference to the first council in the life of the Christian church in the Bible (Acts XV). The apostles met at Jerusalem to decide how far the law of Moses was applicable to the Gentiles. When they arrived at a certain decision with a common mind, they remarked: "It seemed right to the Holy Spirit and to us..." (Acts XV:28).[89] Hence the conception that the decisions made by the church through the councils have the approval of the Holy Spirit. The councils are assisted by the Holy Spirit in their deliberations. The Pope, being the head of the Church, has, therefore, been declared infallible. The early apostolic council had not determined the status of these councils. No such council as representing all the churches of Christendom is traceable in history till the Council of Nicaea held in 325. A.D. By Cyprian's time it became customary to hold local councils of bishops in different provinces of the Roman Empire. But these councils cannot he regarded as the general councils speaking in the name of the entire church. The general or ecumenical councils have their starting point in the Council of Nicaea. These Seven Holy Ecumenical councils were official

[88] Timothy Ware, *op. cit.*, pp. 23, 24, 43.
[89] *Ibid.*, p. 24.

gatherings, held from time to time, to remove controversy in dogma, to define the orthodox teaching regarding the Trinity and Incarnation, to purify creed, and to establish the authoritative version of the Bible, and for similar other purposes.[90] The orthodox church stands on the decisions arrived at in these councils.

Christian orthodoxy believes that ecumenical councils cannot err because their decisions are made with the assistance of the Holy Spirit. The truth and falsehood of doctrine are determined by the "collective wisdom of the councils" and not by the individual thought. The Protestants, on the contrary, maintain that even universal councils may err; hence their decisions are not infallible. Truth, according to them, is not confined to the ecumenical councils. An individual can attain the truth by his self-thinking and interpretation. Protestantism denies the hierarchy of knowledge.[91] The principal function of the church in the eyes of the Protestants is to bear witness to God. It keeps vigil on the adherence to the teaching of the Gospel, the good news of salvation through Jesus Christ. If the church thinks independently of the Gospel, and functions ignoring the central position of the scripture, it diverges from its primary goal.[92]

The Catholic church claims to be the authority in religious matters and to have spiritual power alone. It leaves the temporal power to the state and the political authorities. Its primary objective is to give instructions and guidance to the faithful for salvation. It attempts to achieve this end by establishing the seven sacraments. They are: baptism, communion, anointment or confirmation, ordination into the clergy, marriage, extreme unction, and penance. These are

---

[90] *Ibid.*, pp. 23, 24, 25, 42, 43; cf. Augustin Fliche, art. Religious Institutions, Christian-Roman Catholic, *Encyclopaedia of Social Sciences*, New York, 1962, XIП, 246-248.

[91] Bertrand Russell, *op. cit.*, p. 579.

[92] Joseph L. Hromadka, *op. cit.*, pp. 355-56.

designed to enliven the teaching of Christ, to maintain the morale of the faithful in the light of the Gospel, and to safeguard against heresy.[93] The Catholic Church lays great stress on strict adherence to the teachings of Christ. The more its followers owe their allegiance to Christ, the more perfect they are. It seriously follows the dictum "Ubi Christus ibi Ecclesia (Where Christ is, there is the Church)."[94]

Christianity laid more stress on the relationship of man to God than on his relationship to the state. This was probably due to the influence of the teaching of the Stoics who believed that a man could live a virtuous life in any environment he might be. The relation of man to God was of more importance to them than the relation of citizens to the state. They were as unpolitical in thinking as Christianity was during its early phase. The Stoics had no concern with the creating of a good state, but instead, with the creation of a virtuous man in this unhappy world. People by the Stoic teaching became individualistic in their thinking until Christianity evolved the doctrine of individual salvation which relatively contributed to the creation of the Church. From its very inception it preached individualism by saying: "Render therefore unto Caesar the things which are Caesars,' and unto God the things that are God's (Matt. 22:21). "The conflict between duty to God and duty to the State," says Bertrand Russell, "which Christianity had introduced, took the form of a conflict between church and king."[95]

After the official recognition of Christianity in 313 A.D. Christianity came closer to the state. of separation between the church and the state. there was complete cooperation between the two by the Roman Empire There was no rigid line In Byzantine history Both

---

[93] Augustin Fliche, *op. cit.*
[94] Joseph Z. Hromadka, *op. cit.*, pp. 365-66.
[95] Bertrand Russell, *op. cit.*, pp. 15 16, 240, 579.

were independent but cooperative, and neither was subordinate. By this time the things of Caesar were more closely associated with the instrument of the secular administration.[96]

Orthodox Church is undoubtedly a true custodian of the Christian tradition with a progressive outlook. In Christian orthodoxy tradition. means the heritage handed down from Christ to the apostles and from apostles to the Church. The church is determined to remain loyal to the past. It keeps the tradition just as it received from the ancestors. Bible, creed, and doctrinal definitions as set by the ecumenical councils are absolute and inflexible. Despite this unshakable loyalty to the past, the concept of fidelity to the tradition is dynamic. Tradition is construed not as a "dead acceptance of the past, but as a living experience "of the Holy Spirit in the present." It is not a conservative principle, but "the principle of growth and regeneration." Tradition is the constant abiding of the spirit and not only the memory of words. With this progressive attitude towards tradition, the orthodox church can invite the ecumenical councils to meet in modern times and add to the tradition by its fresh interpretation of creed and doctrine.[97] But it is worthy of note that the church had not started with the same machinery, objectives, and functions which developed in later times. This whole body in its modern form has little resemblance to the early church. This is true not only of the church in Christianity but also of all parallel institutions of other religions of the world. Of such institutions, Bertrand Russell rightly remarks: "Organizations have a life of their own, independent of the intentions of their founders. Of this fact, the most striking example is the Catholic Church."[98]

---

[96] Timothy Ware, *op. cit.*, pp. 50, 98.
[97] *Ibid.*, pp. 203-207.
[98] Bertrand Russell, *op. cit.*, p. 374.

VIII

In the foregoing, we briefly discussed the origin, development, nature, and purpose of unifying bodies in religion. We chose *Sangha*, Sanhedrin, and Church to provide an illustration for our proposition. We have seen that these three institutions started with the intention of unifying the group of believers bound by the ties of faith. These institutions developed in their later life into huge organizations with full-fledged machinery and multifunctions. They derived their authority from the scriptures and ultimately became themselves the source of authority. These unifying institutions, as we pointed out at the very outset, are part of the very religion required essentially for the direction and development of religion. This is true also of the doctrine of *Ijmāʿ* in Islam. We have previously discussed in detail its origin, nature, development, and its theory expounded by the classical jurists. It must have beyond doubt its germ in the lifetime of the Prophet. The Qurʾān emphasizes mutual consultation (*Shūrā*) and even asks the Prophet to consult his Companions in important matters. We are told that the Prophet consulted responsible persons on important matters. But his whole activity of consultation in his day was purely informal. There was no formal machinery, official council of the elders, membership by franchise, or persons nominated for this purpose. The decisions arrived at through consultation were sometimes corrected by divine revelation.

This institution became quasi-formal after the demise of the Prophet. With the beginning of the Caliphate, it took a new turn because there was no longer any ultimate source of authority, like a revelation, to realize the truth in moot questions. In this situation, the council of elders emerged in the time of the early Caliphs. In an earlier chapter, we dwelt on *Shūrā* in the early Caliphate and portrayed how it functioned. The decisions. taken by the council of *Shūrā* were later considered the *Ijmāʿ* of the Companions. But unfortunately, the system of *Shūrā* could not continue indefinitely owing to the civil wars, political upheavals, and above all kingship which struck at the root of this whole system. Henceforth people lost their trust in the caliphs and consulted the individual Companions or scholars. With the individual efforts of the scholars and specialists a doctrine developed in the classical period in Islam known as orthodoxy (*Ahl al*-Sunnah *wal-Jamāʿah*). Of this we have spoken in detail earlier. Doctrine, law, and dogma in Islam were not settled by the council of elders in a certain period of history like other religions. The Qurʾān and the model behaviour of the Prophet had ever remained the basis for further interpretation and legislation. *Ijmāʿ* emerged through the individual opinions of the scholars in the Medieval period and not through the consensus of the whole community except in a few points. Orthodoxy, as based on such a type of *Ijmāʿ* (i.e. by silence), could not satisfy the intelligentsia at all times. There are still a large number of points relating to various aspects of religion which should be decided by the Muslim community as a whole with a "common mind."

Ijmāʿ has a resemblance to its counterparts in other religions in respect of infallibility, but not in respect of machinery and official organization. The classical definition of *Ijmāʿ* indeed implies the gathering of the jurists, but the conception remained purely theoretical throughout history. The questions believed to have been approved by *Ijmāʿ* are in fact based on the tacit *Ijmāʿ* which emerged by the individual thinking of the scholars, and not based on formal *Ijmāʿ* by verbal expression as in other religions. The Qurʾān occupies a central position in religion, yet its meaning is determined by *Ijmāʿ*. Any interpretation not in consonance with *Ijmāʿ* is considered heresy. Thus *Ijmāʿ* resembles its parallels in respect of theory and conception, but not in respect of structure. Here we may quote Professor H.A.R. Gibb to show how far the decisions by *Ijmāʿ* are analogous to the procedure of the Councils of Church. He remarks:

"There is a certain analogy between this settlement of doctrine by 'consensus' in Islam and the Councils of the Christian Church, in spite of the divergences of outer form; and in certain respects, the results were very similar. It was, for example, only after the general recognition of *Ijmāʿ* as a source of law and doctrine that a definite legal test of 'heresy' was possible and applied. Any attempt to raise the question of the import of a text in such a way as to deny the validity of the solution already given and accepted by consensus became a *Bidʾah*, an act of innovation, that is to say, heresy."[99]

---

[99] H.A.R. Gibb, *Mohammedarism*, London, Oxford University Press, 1961, pp. 98

Chapter XIV: Modern Trends in *Ijmāʿ*

Ijmāʿ played a vital role in the process of integrating the Muslim community. With this quality inherent in *Ijmāʿ* orthodoxy utilized it for the stability of dogma and doctrine, and for safeguarding the structure of Islam. But *Ijmāʿ* never became an institution. It was a sort of general will of the community. The absence of hierarchy and loose machinery of *Ijmāʿ* proved to be a safeguard against accretions, except those recognized by the conscience of the community. The classical theory of *Ijmāʿ* aimed primarily at conserving the past heritage of Islam, and secondly at standardizing the religion. Hence rejection of *Ijmāʿ* was considered heresy. During the classical period, differences arose as to the period of *Ijmāʿ*. Ibn Hazm and Ibn Taymiyah penned it to the corner. They restricted it not only to the generation of the Companions, but also stipulated the existence of textual evidence in support of *Ijmāʿ*. Further, the condition of totality and strict unanimity in consensus turned it into a mere theory which could hardly be put into practice. Above all, the retrospective concept of *Ijmāʿ* affected its efficacy, i.e. legislation on current problems. This ultimately resulted in liberalism. Liberal orthodoxy and mostly the modernists utilized this doctrine as an instrument to bring about change. Some interpreted and defined *Ijmāʿ* in a liberal and rational way over against the classical definition; others suggested a machinery to settle fresh cases immediately. According to them, the classical doctrine of *Ijmāʿ* does not serve the purpose of solving the ever-changing problems of the Muslim Community in the modern age. In the following paragraphs we shall analyse the views of some modern thinkers on *Ijmāʿ* starting with Shah Wali Allah (d. 1176. A.H.).

I

One might wonder why we include Shah Wali Allah among the modernists. By modernists, in this context, we mean those thinkers, in the post-classical period and in our own day, who sought to interpret Islam on rational grounds in such a way as to bring it up to date, so that it might adapt itself to the changing conditions of the modern world. Shah Wali Allah was a celebrated thinker of Islam. He was a prolific writer who produced a wealth of literature on various topics. His writings mirror his enlightened thought and progressive outlook on various problems. We call him a modernist or more correctly a liberal orthodox on account of his logical and enlightened interpretation of Islam. He expressed his opinion on almost all important doctrines. *Ijmāʿ* is one of them. He differs with orthodoxy on *Ijmāʿ* in two points, namely its justification and definition. His views on *Ijmāʿ* are summarized below.

The well-known tradition 'my community will not agree on an error' does not mean *Ijmāʿ*. What it means is that a section of the community will continue to follow the truth and adhere to the Sunnah of the Prophet and perform obligatory duties of Islam. It does not indicate the *Ijmāʿ* of the community, though it is construed to mean so. The meaning of this tradition can be determined in the light of another tradition reported by Muslim. It says: 'A section of my community will continue to obey God's command, and those who desert or oppose them shall not be able to do them any harm, they will be dominating the people until God's command is executed. This tradition defines the meaning of the tradition, "my community will not agree on an error." Traditions that emphasize the unity of the community and condemn separation and disagreement imply two important points, viz. establishment of the caliphate and protection of the Shari'ah from schism. *Ijmāʿ* can be justified on the basis of all such traditions as implying integration of the community.[1] *Ijmāʿ* is also substantiated by the tradition which says: "Adhere to my Sunnah (practice) and the Sunnah of the rightly-guided Caliphs who would follow me."[2] Traditions like "follow the overwhelming majority" also support this doctrine.[3] The Companies agreed on the caliphate of Abū Bakr. The agreement of the Companions is an authority by itself. He remarks that Ibn Masʿūd is reported to have said at the time of his death, "What the Muslims consider good is good in the eyes of God, and what they consider evil is evil in His eyes."[4] The statement of Ibn Masʿūd, which is also described as a tradition, refers to the caliphate of Abū Bakr, and justifies *Ijmāʿ* by implication.

Shah Wali Allah, in point of fact, entwines *Ijmāʿ* with the caliphate. From his emphasis on eliminating disagreement from the community by a caliph, it can safely be inferred that what constitutes *Ijmāʿ* in his view is the "soundness of opinion." The soundness of opinion" is found in *Ijmāʿ* more patently and strongly than in an individual opinion. This is because *Ijmāʿ* is arrived at after consultation with men of opinion. A matter which is settled through the process of *Shūrā* must be immune from error, and must have the divine support. Secondly, a caliph is elected by the whole community. He possesses an independent mind and wisdom in religious affairs, and gifted with acumen bestowed upon him by God. *Ijmāʿ* overarches all individual opinions by virtue of its twin qualities, namely agreement of experts recognized by the community and its enforcement by a caliph. He believes that the individual opinion of the caliph, the agreement of the jurists not enforced by the caliph, the individual opinion of Abū Bakr, ʿUmar,

---

[1] Shah Wali Allah, *Izalat al-Khafa'* (urdu tr. by ʿAbd al-Shakūr), Karachi, a.d. 1, 266; idem, *al-Tafhimāt al-llākiyah*, Bijnor, 1936, II, 118.
[2] Shah Wali Allah, *Izalat al-Khafa'*, *op. cit.*, I, 72.
[3] *Ibid*, p. 262.
[4] *Ibid.*, p. 267.

ʿUthman, and of some other celebrated Companions like Ibn Masʿūd, Ubayy b. Kaʿb, ʿAlī, and Zayd b. Thabit can be followed for soundness. Such opinions are inferior to *Ijmāʿ*, yet they can be recognized as sound and mature though not countenanced by *Ijmāʿ*.[5]

As regards the definition and interpretation of *Ijmāʿ*, Shah Wali Allah holds an independent view. To begin with, he severely criticizes the classical definition of *Ijmāʿ*. By *Ijmāʿ*, it is not meant that the community in toto agrees on a point, and not a single person disagrees with this decision. Such a type of *Ijmāʿ* is impracticable, indeed impossible. This happened neither in the past nor can happen in the future. Whenever an agreement was reached in the past on a certain issue, disagreement was also reported on the same issue. *Ijmāʿ* means an agreement which can easily be held in every place and time. It is a consensus of opinion of the men in authority and of the jurisconsults of various towns. This sort of *Ijmāʿ* is found in the legal problems settled during the caliphate of ʿUmar. *Ijmāʿ* in the early phase includes the opinions on a problem given by the overwhelming majority of the jurists, by the people of Mecca and Medina, and by the pious Caliphs. The *Ijmāʿ* on various legal questions was established without making any effort and without issuing any legal verdict by ʿUmar. *Ijmāʿ* was reached on the question of taking a bath on account of *iksal* (*invit sed non emist*) and on uttering four Takbīrāt in funeral prayer.[6]

Elucidating his point of view about *Ijmāʿ* Shah Wali Allah states that *Ijmāʿ* is reached in the community when a caliph issues his edict after consulting the men of opinion. This edict should be enforced in such a way that it spreads widely and is established in the entire Muslim world.

---

[5] *Ibid.*, pp. 266-67.
[6] *Ibid.*, I, 72; II, 144.

In support of his standpoint, he quotes a tradition from the Prophet which stresses obedience to the caliph.[7] *Ijmāʿ* does not mean that every layman gives his opinion according to the dictates of space and time, not basing himself on an evidence from the *Sharīʿah*. To illustrate his point of view he cites the example of *Ijmāʿ* on the validity of the caliphate of the first four Caliphs. The establishment of *Ijmāʿ* on their caliphate means that every Companion proved the validity of their caliphate on the basis of some legal evidence, i.e. explicit or implicit Sunnah of the Prophet. After thinking over this evidence every Companion was convinced and then recognized their caliphate as valid. When the jurists of the first generation, i.e. the Companions, agreed on their caliphate, the *Ijmāʿ* was finally reached. With the establishment of their *Ijmāʿ* there remained no room for opposition.[8]

Shah Wali Allah gives a great weight to the *Ijmāʿ* of the early Caliphs, especially of Abū Bakr and ʿUmar. The reason is that the Prophet himself used to consult them on important matters and accept their opinion. Further, he quotes the tradition of "follow the overwhelming majority," adduced by al-Shāfiʿī in support of *Ijmāʿ*. The meaning of this tradition is disputed. Some interpret it to mean that obedience to the caliph is obligatory provided he does not command the commission of a sin. Others take it to mean the *Ijmāʿ* of the community. This tradition signifies both obedience to the caliph and authority of *Ijmāʿ*. The opinion of the caliph is authoritative when it is diffused among the community and recognized by it. The early Caliphs had deep insight in the affairs of the community by nature. They received divine help and guidance in their actions. Hence there was little chance for committing an error in understanding the injunctions and realizing the interests of

---

[7] *Ibid.*

[8] *Ibid.*, p. 130.

the community. Further, the infallibility of the *Ijmāʿ* of the community is a divine grace. When a rule of law is enforced by the command of the caliph, and it is followed by the community, such a rule would beyond doubt become authoritative in religion.[9]

Shah Wali Allah extends the period of the Prophet to the period of the first four Caliphs. The tenure of the mission of the Prophet was fifty-three years. He lived for twenty-three years in his own age and for thirty years in the time of pious Caliphs. The difference between these two periods is that in his own age he imparted the teachings of Islam with his tongue, while during the time of the early Caliphs, he kept silent, but signalled now with this hand and now with his head. Some realized these signals and reached the goal, while others committed a mistake.[10] He thus considers the age of the orthodox Caliphs a continuation of the Prophetic age, and a remnant of the Prophetic mission. The reason for attaching importance to the age of the early Caliphs is that the *Ijmāʿ* in its real sense was reached only in the age of the first three Caliphs, Abū Bakr, ʿUmar, and ʿUthman. After this age disagreement and schism arose in the community, and *Ijmāʿ* could never be established. *Ijmāʿ* was established during this age by the will and command of these Caliphs.

He expatiates on the procedure of *Ijmāʿ* during the time of the early Caliphs. In this early age preaching and the pronouncement of verdicts on legal problems was confined to the Caliph. He performed these duties either himself or appointed some competent person as his deputy. No one could preach or give an opinion on a legal question without his permission. This procedure was changed in the later days of Islam. Whenever the Companions were faced with a new situation or had a fresh problem for which they could not find any tradition of the Prophet, they decided it on the basis of their

---

[9] *Ibid.*, p. 262.
[10] *Ibid.*, p. 72.

own opinion and agreed on it. In fact, truth is what these Companions took for truth on a certain question by their agreement. There arose no difference of opinion in the legal sphere until the time of 'Uthman. If there was any disagreement on a legal point. they consulted the Caliph. The disagreement was thus ironed out by his decision. The Caliph generally decided the disputed points by consulting the men of opinion. His decision ultimately took the form of *Ijmā'*. After the rise of *fitnah* (perversion and civil wars) in Islam every learned man began to give legal verdicts which resulted in chaos in the community.[11] Shah Wali Allah applies the tradition which predicts the good of the first three generations (*Khayr al-Qurūn*) to the age of the first three Caliphs closing with the caliphate of 'Uthman. In his opinion, disagreement, schism, and perversion permeated the community after the caliphate of 'Uthman.[12] He seeks to prove that this age was an ideal and likens it with the age of the Prophet. He believes that the four orthodox schools of law were founded on the *Ijmā'* reached during the time of the first two Caliphs, particularly in the reign of 'Umar. We shall dilate on this point presently.

As already noted, in the opinion of Shah Wali Allah the *Ijmā'* reached during the caliphate of the first three Caliphs was the only right type of *Ijmā'* in Islam, though theoretically, he believes that *Ijmā'* is the agreement of the jurists when reinforced by the consent of the caliph. But such a kind of *Ijmā'* was never reached in Islam except in the age of Abū Bakr, 'Umar and 'Uthman. He does not take into account the regime of 'Alī and the later years of 'Uthman, because this period was one of instability. According to him, *Ijmā'* is reached on a certain point when the caliph issues his ordinance after mutual consultation with the men of opinion and it is recognized by the

[11] *Ibid.*, p. 314.
[12] *Ibid.*, p. 270.

community in toto. Abū Bakr, 'Umar, and 'Uthman had an opportunity to decide problems through the process of *Shūrā* and enforced them. But 'Alī could not have such an opportunity due to continuous civil wars and turmoil during his caliphate. He failed to consult the learned and men of opinion on legal problems in a formal manner. Hence the legal knowledge possessed by the jurists of his time could not spread throughout the community through the process of *Shūrā*. Therefore *Ijmā'* could not take place in the reign of 'Alī.[13]According to his theory Shah Wali Allah might be correct, as 'Alī, in fact, could not get a chance to establish an ijmã' through its established procedure. Nevertheless, we find that some change essentially came over the problems settled during the Caliphate of 'Umar. He placed a ban on the sale of a slave-mother and announced it to the people. People might have followed his instructions during his reign. In the beginning 'Alī was in agreement with 'Umar on this point. Later on, he changed his opinion and lifted the ban placed by 'Umar. Finally, according to some jurists, *Ijmā'* was reached on the prohibition of the sale of a slave-mother, and according to others it remained disputed.[14] As the history of the legal activities of the early Caliphs is obscure, it would be tendentious to assert conclusively that no *Ijmā'* was reached during the caliphate of 'Alī.

Shah Wali Allah thinks the four orthodox legal schools are based on the *Ijmā'* reached during the caliphate of Abū Bakr and 'Umar. The legal problems well known and agreed upon among the Sunnis are those which were decided during the reign of the first two Caliphs. After Abū Bakr and 'Umar there was little agreement.[15] The questions settled and agreed upon during the reign of 'Umar became

[13] Shah Wali Allah, *Qurrat al-'Aynayn fi tafdil al-Shaykhayn*, Peshawar, 1310 A.H., p. 133.

[14] Al-Sarakhsi, *al-Mabṣūt*, Cairo, 1324 A.H., VII, 150; 'Abd al-Aziz al-Bukhari, *Kashf al-Asrār*, Istanbul, 1307 A.H., II, 968.

[15] Shah Wali Allah, *Qurrat al-'Aynayn, op. cit.*, pp. 134-35.

most authenticated. He compares *Ijmāʿ* with the knowledge of the Prophet with respect to certainty and exactitude. Certainty in disputed legal questions can be achieved only through *Ijmāʿ*. No quality of the Muslim community is more important than its agreement on a certain point. He contends that if the agreement reached in the reign of ʿUmar is totally ignored, most of the doctrines may lose their authenticity. There are many problems which remained obscure and disputed during the time of the Prophet and Abū Bakr, but ʿUmar decided them finally by means of *Ijmāʿ*. Whatever was left unsettled and disputed during his caliphate was never settled through *Ijmāʿ*. Had ʿUmar not endeavoured to establish *Ijmāʿ* on moot questions, the Muslim scholars would have fallen into chaos, and the way to *Ijtihād* and truth would not have been revealed.[16] To justify the proposition that the four orthodox schools of law are based on the *Ijmāʿ* reached during the pious caliphate he argues that all the basic legal manuals of these schools contain original reports mostly from ʿUmar and not from ʿAlī except in a few cases. Works, like Al-Muwaṭṭa', Musnad al-Shāfiʿī, *Kitāb* al-Athar by al-Shaybani, and Musnad Abi Hanifah support his point.[17]

Finally, he agrees in principle with the orthodox view that *Ijmāʿ* is the agreement of the jurists. A layman has no say in *Ijmāʿ*. If laymen (*Ahl Taqlīd* conformists) give a different opinion on the same point, the opinion of the jurists will be binding. The opinion of laymen, whether it agrees with the opinion of the jurists or not, has no worth. He thinks disagreement precedes *Ijmāʿ*. Whenever any problem is brought for discussion, the scholars express different opinions. By degrees, the disagreement is reduced and *Ijmāʿ* is finally

[16] *Ibid.*, pp. 42, 55, 142, 143.
[17] *Ibid.*, pp. 149, 150, 169.

established. The *Ijmāʿ* reached during early generations went through the same process.[18]

In brief, Shah Wali Allah, despite his agreement with the classical theory, stipulates the enforcement of *Ijmāʿ* by the caliph and its recognition by the community. This is a novel idea which we do not find in the discussions of *Ijmāʿ* made by his predecessors. *Ijmāʿ*, in his view, can be reached theoretically in every generation, but practically it took place in the reign of the first three Caliphs and was never reached afterward.

II

Sir Sayyid Ahmad Khân (d. 1315 A.H.) was an eponym of modernism in Indo-Pakistan sub-continent. He was essentially a rationalist. Any doctrine of Islam that contradicted reason was interpreted by him rationally. According to him, harmony between the work and the word of God is essential. He opposed orthodoxy on a large number of problems listed in Hayat-i-Jawid.[19] His controversies over some accepted doctrines with the *ʿUlamāʾ* actually centered around his theory that Islam does not teach anything which conflicts with reason. In his early life, he was himself an orthodox believer. By degrees, as his field of study widened, he had misgivings about most of the traditional doctrines and practices which he either rejected or harmonized by his rational interpretation. *Ijmāʿ* is one of them. He validated it in his early career, but rejected in the long run. In point of fact, he rejected the *Ijmāʿ* as defined and theorized by the classical jurists. He gave his own definition of *Ijmāʿ* controverting the one enunciated in the classical period.

Sayyid Ahmad Khan differentiated *Ijmāʿ* from custom (*riwāj*). He believed that *Ijmāʿ* was confused with custom by the masses who

---

[18] *Ibid.*, pp. 202-3.

[19] Hali, Altaf Husayn, *Hayat-i Jawid*, Lahore, 1957, p. 604 r.

were following the custom in the name of *Ijmāʿ*. Hence, he explained the definition of *Ijmāʿ* and distinguished it from the latter. Defining custom, he remarks that sometimes a new practice in society starts for unknown reasons. The masses keep on following it for a long time. This practice becomes binding on the people so much so that one is maligned in the society if one abandons it. But when evidence in support of that practice is searched in the *Shariah*, it is found nowhere. The prevalence of such an unfounded practice among the society is called custom (*Riwāj*). It carries no authority at all. To regard such a practice as an *Ijmāʿ* of the community is heresy. But *Ijmāʿ* is something different. Sometimes a fresh problem emerges in the society. The scholars attempt to find out its answer from the Qur'ān, *Ḥadīth* and practice of the Companions after deep consideration. When the rule of law about any fresh case is known to all, the evidence in support of the rule is also widely known. The rule is then followed by the people in general after realizing the evidence from the *Shari'ah*. Searching for an injunction or deriving a rule about a fresh situation from the Qur'ān or the Sunnah and practising it generally is called *Ijmāʿ*. After the passage of the first three generations of Islam, any new practice which is not founded on the *Shari'ah* is a religious innovation (*Bid'ah*). On the contrary, any point which is agreed upon by the community through the process of *Ijmāʿ* becomes a part of the Sunnah. The Qur'ān states that anything which the Muslims follow as a prescript of religion is right. He adduces the Qur'ānic verse 4:115 in support of the authority of the 'way of believers'. The authority is due to its Islamicism and not for any other reason. The edict of a king or the decision of a judge means the edict or the decision issued by them as king or judge and not for some other quality. Similarly, the 'way of soldiers' or the 'way of saints' indicates the way which they adopted for their soldierly qualities or for their saintliness. Hence the authority of the 'way of believers' is due to their Islamicity. This is supported also by a tradition which says: 'What the Muslims consider good is good in the eyes of God,' implying that what the Muslims consider good for them is good with God, too. Finally, all that is agreed upon by the Muslims is a part of the Sunnah, and all that is practised as a custom among the Muslims but has no basis in the *Sharīʿah* is innovation (*Bidʿah*).[20]

In this interpretation of *Ijmāʿ* Sayyid Ahmad Khân does not deviate from the orthodox point of view. All that he stresses is that *Ijmāʿ* must have some evidence and support from the Qurʾān or the Sunnah. He regards the practice of the Muslims in the first three generations of Islam, i.e. the Companions, Successors, and followers of the Successors, as the Sunnah and ideal practice. But he condemns the customs and practices of the later generations as innovations. He quotes the tradition 'my community will not agree on an error' to substantiate *Ijmāʿ*. Even in the presence of this tradition, he does not take anything as *Ijmāʿ* unless it is supported by the Qurʾān or the Sunnah.[21] But in his later writings he looks askance at *Ijmāʿ*[22] Sometimes he rejects it totally and sometimes he considers it a secondary source or a confirmatory principle.[23] This led his critics and biographers to describe him as an opponent of *Ijmāʿ*.[24] It appears that there is some confusion in the assessment of his point of view about *Ijmāʿ*. In fact, he did not reject its authority. Where he does so he means that *Ijmāʿ* is not an authority by itself, independent of the Qurʾān and the Sunnah. According to one point of view, supporting evidence is not necessary for the validity of *Ijmāʿ*. It is recognized without evidence taking its existence in good faith, that might be known to the early generations. But Sayyid Ahmad Khan validates *Ijmāʿ* provided it is supported by some

---

[20] Sayyid Ahmad Khan, *Taṣnīfāt Aḥmadiyyah*, Aligarh, 1883, I, 126-27.
[21] *Ibid*, pp. 125-26.
[22] Muhammad Ismaʿil Pānipati, ed. *Maqālāt Sir Sayyid*, Lahore, 1961, I, 296.
[23] *Ibid.*, XIII, 35.
[24] *Ibid.*, Hall, *op. cit.*, p. 604; Bashir Ahmad Dar, *Religious Thought of Sayyid Ahmad Khān*, Lahore, 1958, pp. 275-76.

evidence. We reproduce below his rejoinder to the criticism of Sayyid al-Hajj on his belief about *Ijmāʿ*.

"Sayyid al-Hajj states that my belief is that *Ijmāʿ* of the community or adherence to the way of believers in general, or to argue on the basis of the opinion of an *ʾalim* (learned) carries no weight, and that *Ijmāʿ* is no authority. In fact, there is no truth in ascribing this belief to me. What is true is that the *Ijmāʿ* of the community, or adherence to the way of believers in general, or the *Ijmāʿ* which has no evidence in its support from the Qurʾān or the Sunnah, is not an authority. The community or Muslims never agreed, or *Ijmāʿ* was never reached, on a question which lacked evidence from the text (of the Qurʾān or the Sunnah). Rather all questions not founded on the Qurʾān or the Sunnah are disputed."[25]

This statement of Sayyid Ahmad clearly refutes the presumption that he rejected the authority of *Ijmāʿ*. We find that his views were shared in the past by men like Ibn Hazm and Ibn Taymiyah. They were not opponents of *Ijmāʿ* but in fact, they emphasized the necessity of evidence.

Sayyid Ahmad Khan actually held that the doctrine of *Ijmāʿ* was a progressive concept. It should march with the time to solve fresh problems. Hence sometimes he invalidated even the *Ijmāʿ* of the Companions on a certain point contending that a fresh *Ijmāʿ* should be substituted for it in view of the change of circumstances. The *Ijmāʿ* reached by the scholars in the past is not binding if the situation changes. He argues that the *Ijmāʿ* of certain scholars in the past might have taken place in a different situation which does not obtain now. With the change of situation, their *Ijmāʿ* lost its force, indeed, validity.[26] Professor Aziz Ahmad rightly observes, "He tried

---

[25] *Maqalat Sir Sayyid*, *op. cit.*, XIII, 35.
[26] Bashir Ahmad Dar, *op. cit.*, pp. 275-76...

to resolve the difficulties inherent in our traditional sources of Muslim law by a dialectical rationalist exegesis of the Qur'ān; by historical skepticism in scrutinizing the classical data of the *Ḥadīth*; by an almost unlimited emphasis on *Ijtihād*, as the inalienable right of every individual Muslim; and finally rejecting the principle of *Ijmāʿ* in the classical sense which confined it to the *ʿUlamāʾ*."[27]

His colleague and associate Muhsin al-Mulk Mahdi ʾAlf Khān (d. 1325 A.H.) wrote a detailed article on *Ijmāʿ* published in *Tadhib al-Akhlaq*. In this article he fully explains the point of view presented by Sayyid Ahmad about *Ijmāʿ* and refutes the classical stand. He demurs that the Muslims regard the practices and customs prevalent among the society as *Ijmāʿ*. He refutes the idea that by faith is not meant adherence to the custom, but to the Qur'ān and the Sunnah. The only authority to be followed in religion is the Qur'ān because it is established by *Tawātur* and agreed upon by the Muslims en masse. *Ḥadīth* is inferior to the Qur'ān in respect of certainty and decisiveness. *Ijmāʿ* is therefore no authority by itself. It constitutes an authority when supported by an evidence from the Qur'ān or the Sunnah. Rejection of this type of *Ijmāʿ* is heresy. *Ijmāʿ* is the agreement of the Muslims on rules established by the text of the Qur'ān or of the Sunnah directly and not on rules derived from these sources indirectly. The text, for instance, may be ambiguous, and if *Ijmāʿ* is reached on its meaning, such an *Ijmāʿ* is no authority. *Ijmāʿ* should not indicate more than what the text indicates. In this sense *Ijmāʿ* is a confirmatory and secondary source of law. Further, he contends that when the jurists are not infallible in their individual interpretations, how can they be immune from error in their collective agreement? They might have agreed on an error in the past, and this error can be removed in subsequent ages when it comes to light. Finally, he criticizes the *ʿUlamāʾ* by saying that the

---

[27] Aziz Ahmad, *Islamic Modernism in India and Pakistan*, London, 1967, p. 54.

doctrine of *Ijmāʿ* was formulated by these jurists to justify their wishes and whims. As a matter of fact there is no *Ijmāʿ* on points of detail derived from the Qur'ān and the Sunnah.[28] It is not correct to say that this principle was formulated to fulfil the wishes of the *ʿUlema*. In fact, it came into being to integrate the community.

III

ʿUbayd Allah Sindhi (d. 1363 A.H.), although influenced in no small degree by Shah Wali Allah, gave his own interpretation of *Ijmāʿ*. Shah Wali Allah had narrowed down *Ijmāʿ* to the Caliphate of Abū Bakr, ʿUmar, and the early phase of the Caliphate of ʿUthmān because in his opinion no disagreement was found during this period.[29] But ʿUbayd Allah Sindhi extended it to the rule of the Umayyads. He describes the agreed practice and legal decisions of the Companions as Sunnah, and the agreed practice and decisions of the Successors until the end of the Umayyad regime as *Ijmāʿ*. The Sunnah, according to him, means the by-laws derived from the Qur'ān by the Prophet and the first four Caliphs and the Companions. The Qur'ān is the basic law of Islam and therefore it is immutable. The Sunnah is the subsidiary law framed from time to time in the age of the Prophet and the Companions. The Prophet and the Companions formulated certain by-laws through mutual consultation during the period closing with the death of ʿUthman. The Prophet himself, being commanded to consult the Companions, described by the Qur'ān as 'the first to lead the way of the Muhajirin and the Anṣar, formulated these by-laws known as the Sunnah. According to the Hanafi jurists, the Sunnah is the practice and model behaviour of the Prophet and of the pious Caliphs. This Sunnah, i.e. the by-laws, has been derived from the Qur'ān itself. It corresponds to the Indian Penal Code and its criminal laws. The

---

[28] *Tahdhib al-Akhlāq*, Lahore, 1894, I, 186-91.

[29] ʿUbayd Allah Sindhi, *Shah Wali Allah awr unka Falsafah*, Lahore, n.d. p. 97.

former is the fundamental law, while the latter are its details and derivatives. Hence the Sunnah, being the by-laws of Islam, is flexible.[30]

ʿUbayd Allah Sindhi draws a sharp distinction between Sunnah and *Ijmāʿ*. The by-laws formulated by the first category of the Companions are known as Sunnah, while the by-laws framed by their followers, described by the Qurʾān as 'those who followed them in goodness' are *Ijmāʿ*. The difference between the two is that whereas Sunnah signifies the behaviour of the Prophet, *Ijmāʿ* denotes the agreement of the Muslims alone. Further, it is worthy of remark that agreement is necessary for both Sunnah and *Ijmāʿ*. Sunnah is not an isolated decision or practice.[31]

ʿUbayd Allah Sindhi has analyzed his point of view about *Ijmāʿ* in detail. We present a summary translation of his discussion. By *Ijmāʿ* is meant the agreement reached through the process of mutual consultation, majority opinion, and debate. The Qurʾān, being the fundamental (source of) law of Islam, was strictly followed by the first category of the Companions, the Muhajirūn and the Ansar. Every word and deed of this body was appreciated by God. The period of this generation ended with the death of ʿUthman. The way that this generation of the Companions acted upon the Qurʾān, and the laws derived by them from the fundamental source book of Islam became binding on the later Muslims. The strict adherence in letter and spirit to the decisions made during this period, i.e. "epoch of agreement," is known as "following in goodness" in the Qurʾānic terminology. This body, "the followers in goodness," like the previous generation, is duty-bound to formulate laws keeping in view the changing conditions of the society with the passage of time. The decisions agreed upon by this body will be called the *Ijmāʿ*

---

[30] *Ibid.*, pp. 99-101.
[31] *Ibid.*, pp. 100-101.

of this generation. These decisions will be binding on the people. In a word, *Ijmā'* denotes the decisions agreed upon by the body of Muslims in toto or by majority. This sort of *Ijmā'* can be reached in modern times and will continue for good. This is not confined to a particular age. The condition for this sort of *Ijmā'* is that this agreement should be reached by the body which bears the quality of those who "follow in goodness." In other words, this body should consider the decisions of the Prophet, and those taken during the period of agreement of the Muhajirūn and the Anṣār to be an authority in addition to the Qur'ān. In fact, their decisions are not something separate from the Qur'ān; they are the by-laws which explain the Qur'ān. If this body is not allowed to frame laws in fresh situations, then no developing order and no progressive body can survive for long. 'Ubayd Allāh Sindhi repeatedly emphasizes that *Ijmā'* is not an independent authority. This is indeed the agreement of the body which rules by the Qur'ān. The Qur'ān is the basic law of Islam acted upon by the first category of the Companions. Sunnah is the *Ijmā'* of the first generation of Islam and *Fiqh* is the *Ijmā'* of the later generation who "followed their predecessors in goodness."[32]

'Ubayd Allah Sindhi considers *Muwatta* of Mālik the most sound and authoritative work in *Ḥadīth* and *Fiqh* literature. For this, he gives the reasons that disagreement arose among the Companions after the death of 'Uthman. But Medina remained immune to schism during the civil wars because 'Alī shifted his capital from Medina to Kūfa. The heritage of learning at Medina also remained intact during the Umayyad regime because they had their capital at Damuscus. Mālik's *Muwaṭṭa'*, therefore, contains the agreed decisions made during the period beginning from the orthodox Caliphate until the end of the Umayyad regime. The seven jurists of

[32] *Ibid.*, pp. 100-104.

Medina preserved this agreed practice and decisions of the early generation now recorded in *Al-Muwaṭṭa'*.[33]

Finally, he adduces another argument in favour of *Ijmā'*. Following the line of argument advanced by Shah Wali Allah he also contends that the legitimacy of Abū Bakr's caliphate and of the authenticity of the recension of the Qur'ān prepared in the reign of 'Uthman depend on the legitimacy of *Ijmā'*. If *Ijmā'* is no authority, the legitimacy of both would be challenged. He explains the meaning of *Ijmā'* in modern terminology. In modern times the term 'ordinance' of the central (ruling) body is used instead of *Ijmā'*. What is called the ordinance of the central ruling authority today was called *Ijmā'* in the past. No political movement can succeed without recognizing the decisions of central authority.[34]

IV

Another celebrated thinker on juristic problems of our day was Dr. Muhammad Iqbal (d. 1357 A.H.). He was himself a lawyer and had a keen interest in the reconstruction of Islamic law on modern lines. He was not out and out a modernist, but a liberal orthodox like Shah Wali Allah. Having studied the Muhammadan Thoeries of Finance by Aghnides he had misgivings about the juristic principle that *Ijmā'* could repeal the Qur'ānic injunction, as stated by the author. This moved him to ask Sayyid Sulayman Nadawi (d. 1373 A.H.) a series of questions about Islamic jurisprudence, particularly about *Ijmā'*. Sulayman Nadawi replied that the author had misinterpreted the orthodox point of view on this question. *Ijmā'* cannot abrogate any Qur'ānic injunction, but can only particularize or generalize it as an explanation of the text. Iqbal again asked him whether this sort of particularization was confined to the Companions or if every jurist

---

[33] *Ibid.*, pp. 146-48.

[34] 'Ubayd Allah Sindhi, *Shah Wali Allah awr unki Siyasi tahrik*, Lahore, 1965, p. 241.

could do it. Further, he enquired him if any decision of the Companions had contradicted the Qur'ānic text, and if so, did it mean that they had some other text which abrogated this text, and which remained obscure? The point in question is whether there exists any decision of the Companions which conflicts with the Qur'ānic text on the presumption that they must have had some evidence from the Qur'ān. Is this presumption a "legal fiction" based on good faith? He pointed out to Nadawi that Al-Āmidī's discussion of this problem shows that the *Ijmā'* of the Companions could override a Qur'ānic injunction a view that supports Aghnides's point of view. The evidence possessed by the Companions must have been a tradition of the Prophet, if not the Qur'ānic verse. From this, it follows that a tradition can repeal the Qur'ānic injunction as generally held by the classical jurists. But Iqbal rejects the principle that a tradition can repeal a Qur'ānic text.[35] We have quoted these questions asked by Iqbal to show that he was not a rigid thinker on such problems. He was a staunch critic of those classical doctrines which contradicted reason or became obsolete with the passage of time. He interpreted Islamic doctrines in a liberal and rational way that could be applied to the modern Muslim society.

Let us give a few more examples of his liberalism. Iqbal agrees with Ibn Taymiyah who criticized the Hanafi principle of reasoning by analogy and *Ijmā'* as he thought that agreement was the basis of all superstition.[36] He holds that the purpose of the state in Islam is to transform 'spiritual' and 'ideal principles into practice and to embody them into a definite human organization. The state in Islam is not headed, according to him, by the representatives of God on earth, as the classical doctrine says.[37] He is profoundly impressed by the views of the grand vizier of Turkey who advocates the freedom

[35] Shaykh 'Aṭā Allah (ed.), *Iqbal Nāmah*, Lahore n.d., I, 131-35.
[36] Muhammad Iqbal, *Reconstruction of Religious Thought in Islam*, Lahore, 1962, p. 152.
[37] *Ibid.*, pp. 154-55.

of *Ijtihād* to rebuild the law of *Shari'ah* in the light of modern thought and experience.[38] He agrees with Turkey's *Ijtihād* that a caliphate or *imamate* can be vested in a body of persons or an elected assembly. He considers this measure to be 'perfectly sound'. He believes that the republican form of government is consistent with the spirit of Islam.[39] He admires Turkey for its intellectual and religious awakening and the consequent attempt to reconstruct Islamic society on modern lines and exhorts the Muslims of the world to follow them. He courageously puts forward the idea that Islamic law is 'capable of evolution.' He had a longing to reorient the Islamic law on the basis of the Qur'ān. This is implied from his remarks: "....... provided the world of Islam approaches it in the spirit of 'Umar, the first critical and independent mind in Islam, who, at the last moments of the Prophet, had the moral courage to utter these remarkable words, "The Book of God is sufficient for us."[40] By his liberal interpretation of the *Shari'ah* law he was working for the renaissance of Islam as in Turkey.[41]

The revision of Islamic jurisprudence in the light of the modern situation prevailing in the Muslim world is the principal aim of Iqbal. He thinks a deeper study of Islamic law will frustrate the advocates of the view that Islamic law is stationary. The classical *Fiqh* of Islam requires critical discussion, though this will offend most of the orthodox Muslims,[42] *Fiqh* should be changed in view of the change of circumstances. The founders of *Fiqh* never claimed the finality of their views. The fundamental legal principles are to be interpreted in the light of the experience of the modern Muslim generation.[43] Summing up his reasoning to revise the Islamic law he

---

[38] *Ibid.*, pp. 156-57.
[39] *Ibid.*, p. 157.
[40] *Ibid.*, p. 162.
[41] *Ibid.*, p. 153.
[42] *Ibid.*, p. 167.
[43] *Ibid.*, p. 168.

remarks, "The result is that while the people are moving, the law remains stationary."[44]

In order to reorient the *Fiqh* of Islam, Iqbal had to give a new meaning and fresh interpretation to the doctrine of *Ijmāʿ*. The classical theory of *Ijmāʿ* portrays it as an ideal and a principle of deciding the disputed cases by the unanimous consensus of the community or of the *ʿUlema.*' It does not suggest any machinery for *Ijmāʿ* which may function in the form of an institution like the church in Christianity or similar other bodies in other religions. *Ijmāʿ* is a doctrine, a principle, a vital source of law, and a process of deciding cases with an avowed authority according to the Islamic jurisprudence. But it is not an institution. It remained amorphous throughout history. Modernists criticize *Ijmāʿ* for its looseness of organization and seek to turn it into an institution. Iqbal is one of them. He is of the view that *Ijmāʿ* is an important legal notion, but it remained merely an idea and did not assume the form of a permanent institution. This might be due to the opposition of the monarchy after the pious caliphate. Individual *Ijtihād* was more in keeping with the wishes of Umayyad and ʿAbbasid caliphs than those of the permanent assembly. But in modern times new world forces and political experience of European nations are justifying the idea and value of *Ijmāʿ*.[45] He believes that the transfer of power of *Ijtihād* to a Muslim legislative assembly is the only possible form of *Ijmāʿ* in modern times. This will also secure contributions from laymen who possess insight into affairs. But there are difficulties for assembly consisting of non-Muslims, as was the situation in India before the partition. This is because a non-Muslim legislative assembly can hardly exercise *Ijtihād.*[46]

---

[44] *Ibid.*, p. 169.
[45] *Ibid.*, pp. 173-74.
[46] *Ibid.*,

Iqbal remained a firm believer in the idea of a Muslim national state in India which appeared later in the name of Pakistan after his demise. He therefore poses a question about the function and activity of a modern Muslim legislative assembly. He is opposed to the view that such an assembly should comprise purely laymen or the *'Ulamā'*. He suggests that both the elite and the *'Ulamā'* should be present in the assembly. Rather the *'Ulamā'* should form a vital part of the assembly for guidance on matters relating to religious law. Furthermore, he expresses the opinion that in order to remove the erroneous interpretation of Islamic law steps should be taken to reform the legal education in the Muslim countries combined with the intelligent study of modern jurisprudence.[47]

He thinks a separate ecclesiastical committee of the *'Ulema* is a dangerous arrangement. Such a committee constituted under the Persian constitution in 1906 might be useful in Persia, as the *Shī'ah* held that the king was a custodian. The *Imām* exercises supreme authority in religious affairs. The *'Ulamā'* as representatives of the Imam supervise the life of the community. Nevertheless, he doubts whether the *'Ulamā'* can represent the Imam in the absence of an apostolic succession. Such an arrangement is dangerous, but can be introduced as an experiment in Sunni Islam.[48] He considers this arrangement dangerous because Sunni Islam is democratic in character. There is no one single authority like the infallible *Imām*. Hence both the *'Ulamā'* and the laymen play an equal role in the legislative assembly.

We have stated earlier that Iqbal asked Sayyid Sulayman Nadawi some questions about *Ijmā'*. In his lectures, he has discussed these points at length and replied to them. He refutes the opinion of Aghnides that *Ijmā'* can repeal the Qur'ānic injunction by saying that

---

[47] *Ibid.*, p. 176.
[48] *Ibid.*, pp. 175-76.

he was confused by the term *naskh* which carried a wider meaning and did not mean annulment exclusively. He discusses another point whether the *Ijmā*ʿ of the Companions is binding on the later generations even in the altered circumstances. To this, he replies that *Ijmā*ʿ of the Companions is binding on later generations in some cases, and not in all cases. He draws a distinction between questions relating to point of fact, and those relating to point of law. In the former case, the *Ijmā*ʿ of the Companions is binding because the Companions alone possess the knowledge of those questions. Such questions cannot be answered by analogy and individual interpretation. In the latter case, the *Ijmā*ʿ of the Companions is not binding because such questions relate to interpretation which is a right of every competent person. In support of his point of view, he quotes al-Karkhī about the Sunnah of the Companions. He remarks, "The Sunnah of the Companions is binding in matters which cannot be cleared up by *Qiyās*, but it is not so in matters which can be established by *Qiyās*."[49]

It can be inferred from his discussion on *Ijmā*ʿ that he wants to convert it into a viable and living institution with full-fledged machinery to put its decisions into practice. The Muslim legislative assembly is the best organization for this purpose. That *Ijmā*ʿ should be converted into an institution is a point in dispute between the scholars of our day. Some are opposed to this idea. We give presently the views of Dr. S.M. Yusuf, the critic of Iqbal's views on *Ijmā*ʿ.

Iqbal was mistaken in holding his view about *Ijmā*ʿ as a permanent institution for the lack of organization in Islamic legislative activity. In fact, this shows his superficial knowledge about the nature and growth of Islamic society. *Ijtihād* and *ijma*ʾ were diffused among the whole community. They were never a privilege of a particular class or body. To organize them into permanent 'rigid' mechanical

---

[49] *Ibid.*, pp. 174-75.

institutions is dangerous. It will lead to "rigging and regimentation." *Ijtihād* is the 'non-transferable right' of any competent scholar to exercise his mind to find out a solution to fresh problems which crop up in the wake of the march of time. According to the classical theory of *Ijmāʿ* the number of Mujtahids varies with the change of education and culture. A *Mujtahid* is recognized by the community by virtue of his personal qualities and merits as known during his whole lifetime, and not through the election campaign or the award of certificates. No machinery is employed for the recognition of their qualities. The process of arriving at *Ijmāʿ* in Islam is entirely different from that of legislation in the modern elected assemblies. When the Mujtahids give their opinions on a certain point, it passes through the process of 'conflict' and 'survival of the fittest.' The process of *Ijmāʿ* is identical with that of the natural selection in the physical world-a process that cannot be measured by the yardstick of Mathematics. It is very slow and sometimes takes a generation for its completion. Unlike the procedure in the legislature, no effort is made to silence the opposition or to defeat the minority in the process of *Ijmāʿ*. On the contrary, opposition is tolerated patiently until the *Ijmāʿ* is established. Once *Ijmāʿ* after a long time is achieved, their remains almost no 'disagreeing' minority waiting for its turn to enforce its point of view. An *Ijmāʿ* is established, after long patience, endurance, and stability. There is no *Ijtihād* for the sake of *Ijtihād* in Islam. It is resorted to in the wake of a certain persisting need in an unprecedented situation.

The reason for closing the door of *Ijtihād*, says Dr. Yusuf, was that the Islamic culture and civilization in the medieval period reached their zenith. The corpus of Islamic law developed to the extent that it could cater for all the needs of the time from the family life to the problems of war and peace. The law became static because the society in the medieval times was static. It was not moving as rapidly as in our day. This was a period of decline for Muslims. The Muslims of those days were more aware of their needs than the Muslims of today. In fact, there was more need of codification rather than that of the 'forward movement of *Ijtihād*. Nevertheless, some work was done in India and Turkey in this field.

Theoretically, the door of *Ijtihād* is open today. But it is the privilege of competent scholars and not of laymen. Modern legislative councils would violate this privilege. Iqbal's anxiety for an organization of legislation led him to compromise. Further, his suggestion that both *ʿUlamāʾ* and laymen should take decisions in a legislative assembly is not reasonable. Such a combination is impossible, rather 'a contradiction in terms. In the West, a layman has freedom of opinion in all social and political matters because legislation there stems from the will of the people. But in Islam, it is based on the Qurʾān and Sunnah which can best be judged by a competent scholar alone.

Ijtihād precisely means 'individual effort' which is neither independent nor free. It is grounded in the direct guidance of the Qurʾān and Sunnah. Pure reason will result in an "interpolation into the *Shariʿah.*" Iqbal is impelled to use the term "free *Ijtihād*" in view of the weak position of Turks relating to the recognized principles of *Fiqh* and *Uṣūl*. In the sphere of physical sciences, there is no room for 'free science' (science based on the opinions of laymen). Similarly, on religious plane in Islam, there is no room for free *Ijtihād* (*Ijtihād* based on pure reason and opinions of laymen). Free *Ijtihād* really means freedom of the conscience of a *Mujtahid* from political authority. How can it be achieved in the presence of an organized and permanent institution? It is easier to win over a limited and defined body than an unlimited and undefined body of scholars recognized by the community for their personal qualities, qualifications, experience, and competence.

Dr. Yusuf differs with Iqbal on the point that the Umayyad and the ʿAbbasid caliphs had not organized a legislative assembly because they feared lest the assembly should become too powerful for them. History refutes this idea. The Mujtahids themselves resisted the caliphs in their move to recognize their legislative status. Ibn al-Muqaffa' could not succeed in his attempts to influence the caliphs to eliminate the individual judgments, sometimes conflicting, of the Mujtahids for fear of public opinion led by the *ʿUlamā'* against him. Power politics failed to blackmail the conscience of the community which manifested itself in the form of *Ijmāʿ*. "Thanks to the absence of rigid organization", says Dr. Yusuf, "no one is able to lay his hands on Islam; when anyone tries to hammer Islam, he ultimately finds to his chagrin that he has only been beating in the air."[50]

Dr. Yusuf could not probably understand Iqbal's view on *Ijmāʿ* correctly. He is not granting right of *Ijtihād* to a layman. *Ijtihād* in his opinion will be exercised by the Mujtahids and competent persons, but in cooperation with specialists in other fields. *Ijtihād* today cannot be exercised in isolation. Modern conditions demand that it should be exercised collectively. A *Mujtahid* may be an expert in Islamic learnings, but he cannot claim to be perfectly acquainted with the social conditions of a country and the diverse nature of its problems. All that is stressed by Iqbal is to make a collective endeavour for *Ijtihād* in modern times. The right place for this purpose is the legislative assembly. Legislation is meant for society and not for the individual. The opinion of a *Mujtahid* will no doubt carry weight in the assembly due to his expertise in religious matters.

He seems to be opposed to a regular organization for *Ijmāʿ*. In a sense, he may be correct in his view. We must however ask him: *Ijmāʿ* takes a generation, sometimes rather more, for its establishment.

---

[50] Yusuf, S.M., *Studies in Islamic Culture and History*, Lahore, 1970, pp. 212-18.

What would be the method of finding an answer to the immediate questions in the absence of an organized machinery?

V

Mufti Muhammad Abduh of Egypt (d. 1323 A.H.) is another modern thinker who interprets *Ijmāʿ* in a liberal and progressive manner to make it practicable in the Muslim society. He criticizes the classical theory of *Ijmāʿ* in respect of (1) its evidence, (2) its definition, and (3) its rigidity of character. He thinks *Ijmāʿ* is not based on the Qurʾānic verse 4:115 nor on the tradition "my community will not agree on an error," and similar other verses and traditions adduced by the classical jurists. He believes that *Ijmāʿ* is not the agreement of the jurists, as generally defined, but the consensus of the men in authority (*Aulī al-Amr*), as supported by verses 4:59 and 4:83. *Ijmāʿ* of the previous generations can be repealed by a subsequent *Ijmāʿ* if it is not practicable in the changed circumstances. We shall elaborate on these points in the following paragraphs.

Verse 4:115, *inter alia*, is generally adduced by the classical jurists to substantiate the doctrine of *Ijmāʿ*. *Ijmāʿ* is identified by them with the "way of believers." But ʿAbduh disagrees with them. He contends that according to the classical definition, *Ijmāʿ* means the agreement of the jurists after the death of the Prophet in any generation. But the verse in question was revealed in his lifetime and not after him. How can the "way of the believers" of the Prophet's generation be identified with the *Ijmāʿ* of the Muslims after him.[51] Here, ʿAbduh appears to be subjective in his criticism because he seeks the truth of *Ijmāʿ* on the basis of verses 4:59 and 4:83 which enjoin obedience to the men in authority. One might tell him that these verses too were revealed during the time of the Prophet. How can the agreement of men in authority of the later days be valid after the

---

[51] Muhammad ʿAbduh, *Tafsir al-Manār*, ed. Muhammad Rashid Rida, Cairo, 1367, A.H., V, 201, 714.

demise of the Prophet? In fact, all such verses in the Qur'ān do not refer to such doctrines as *Ijmā'*, as 'Abduh himself admits,[52] but speak in general of the unity of Muslims and condemn schism and disunity among them.

As regards the well-known tradition about *Ijmā'*, 'my community will not agree on an error,' 'Abduh thinks it does not speak of *Ijmā'* at all. He contends that *Ijmā'* is arrived at after the exercise of *Ijtihād*. An error in *Ijtihād* cannot be taken as straying from the right path and truth (*Dalālah*). A *Mujtahid* performs his duty by exercising *Ijtihād* which might be right or wrong. His mistake in *Ijtihād* is parallel to the mistake of a person who misses the right direction of prayer despite his best efforts. (From this he concludes that *Ijmā'* is revocable). He, therefore, refutes the view that the tradition in question means the *Ijmā'* of the community.[53]

He states that the word *Ijmā'* is not found in the Qur'ān or Sunnah in its technical sense. Instead, the word *Jamā'ah* has been frequently used in the Prophet's traditions which imply the same meaning as contained in the term *Ijmā'* i.e. agreement and unity of Muslims. In contrast to the term *Jamā'ah* the terms *ikhtilaf* (disagreement) and *tafarruq* (disunity) are found in the Qur'ān and Sunnah. There are a number of traditions which exhort the Muslims to remain united and to abstain from disagreement. He then cites many Qur'ānic verses advanced by the jurists in support of the unity of the community (*Jamā'ah*) along with their interpretation. He remarks that some of these verses and traditions signify the unity of Muslims and others speak of the agreement of the "men in authority." But none of them means *Ijmā'* in its technical sense.[54]

---

[52] *Ibid.*, III, 9, 12; V, 213-14.
[53] *Ibid.*, V, 209-10.
[54] *Ibid.*, pp. 213-14.

As regards the classical definition of *Ijmāʿ*, ʿAbduh considers it erroneous. He contends that the classical definition, i.e. the agreement of all jurists, does not conform to the point of view that *Ijmāʿ* is the consensus of *Ahl Al-Hall wal-ʾAqd*. The jurists, as they are defined in classical *Fiqh*, are not conversant with the socio-political interests of the community such as the problems of peace and war, finance, administration, and others. These jurists can be relied upon at most in respect of their deep knowledge of classical *Fiqh* and the procedure of deciding legal cases. But in modern times the genre of these problems has completely changed; hence the knowledge of classical *Fiqh* cannot be sufficient for becoming a competent *Mujtahid* today.[55] Further, the decision taken on the basis of *Ijmāʿ* is said to be infallible. But it is worthy of note that the consensus of jurists cannot be immune from error, particularly when they are two or three in number. Some jurists have rather exaggerated the infallible character of *Ijmāʿ* stating that it is as infallible as the decision of the Prophet. Others have remarked that the action agreed upon by the jurists is identical with the action of the Prophet. Deriving the idea of infallibility from the tradition "my community will not agree on an error" they make a tall claim that there is no possibility of error in the agreement of jurists. On the other hand, if there is no jurist in the community, and the agreement is reached by laymen, the whole community might agree on an error. Some invalidate the classical theory of *Ijmāʿ* and consider it impossible. Its definition is disputed among the scholars, whether it means the consensus of the Companions, or the agreement of followers of the Companions, or the agreement of the members of the Prophet's family, or the practice of the people of Medina in the first generation. Some stipulate *Tawātur* for its validity and others

---

[55] *Ibid.*, p. 205.

support of the public consent. How can the definition of *Ijmāʿ* be correct when it has so many differences?[56]

ʿAbduh says that literally *Ijmāʿ* means 'putting the things together,' 'determining upon an affair, and 'resolving or deciding upon a matter. *Ajmaʾu al-amr wal Raʾy* means 'they composed and settled a thing or opinion which has been decomposed and unsettled. or 'they determined, resolved or decided upon an affair so as to make it firmly settled. Such a determined and settled decision is reached after mature thought and reflection, and close study in *Shūrā*. The Qurʾānic verse 10:71 implies that *Ijmāʿ* is followed by necessary measures for its enforcement. Verses 2:15, 12:102, and 20:64 indicate that *Ijmāʿ* on a certain point can be reached by the opinion of a single person or a body. He presents a number of prophetic traditions and Arabic maxims to substantiate that *Ijmāʿ* means "firm determination" and "putting the things together." Broadly speaking, it connotes to bring in order what is in disorder.[57] By all this discussion he tends to prove that *Ijmāʿ* substantially does not mean the agreement of people or of a body on a certain point; it stands for making an unsettled and confused matter abundantly clear. It is not necessary that the opinion of all and sundry be sought to arrive at an *Ijmāʿ*. This can be done by one or more than one person. Referring to the statement of ʿUmar, Ibn Masʿūd, and Ibn Hanbal, he says that the word *Ijmāʿ* occurring in these statements does not mean the agreement of the jurists, but carries its non-technical meaning, i.e. firm determination on a matter. Moreover, he remarks that there were thousands of Mujtahids in the early period of Islam. How could it be possible to count them and assemble them for the sake of *Ijmāʿ*?[58]

---

[56] *Ibid.*, pp. 205-6.
[57] *Ibid.*, pp. 207-8.
[58] *Ibid.*, p. 208.

Really speaking, ʾAbduh observes, *Ijmāʿ* means the consensus of the whole Muslim community in a particular generation. Since gathering the whole community is not practically possible, the representatives of the community, i.e. *Aulī al-Amr* (men in authority) in the broader sense of the term, will be assembled and their agreement will serve as the agreement of the whole community. In fact, the classical theory of implicit and explicit *Ijmāʿ* of *Mujtahidūn* is not traceable in early Islam.[59]

He gives much weight to the term *Aulī al-Amr* (men in authority) which occurs in the Qurʾānic verse 4:59. This verse contains four important fundamental principles of the *Shariʿah*. The whole doctrine of *Ijmāʿ* anchors on the term *Aulī al-Amr*. Opposing the traditional meaning of the term, he interprets it in a wider context. *Aulī al-Amr* (men in authority) in every nation, in every town, and in every tribe are well-known people. They are the men in whom all people place their reliance in respect of their religious and temporal affairs by virtue of their wider knowledge and sound opinion. There existed such a group of people in the lifetime of the Prophet. This body existed in Medina before the conquests of Islam; they spread later on throughout the Islamic world. People consulted them on the occasion of taking an oath of allegiance (*bayʿah*), in *Shūrā*, in political, administrative, and judicial matters. At the time of electing a caliph in medieval times, military commanders and chiefs from among the people were sent to seek their consent.[60]

The term *Aulī al-Amr* is sometimes construed to mean kings and despots. But it should be noted that the verse in question was revealed. during the time of the Prophet when no kings and despots existed in Islam.

---

[59] *Ibid.*, pp. 208-9.
[60] *Ibid.*, p. 195.

It is implied from this verse that there must always exist in the community men of opinion who possess acumen in social and political affairs, and are competent for deriving rules from the Qur'ān and Sunnah. This body was known as *Ahl al-shurā* and *Ahl al-hall wal-'aqd* in medieval times. Their significance lay in the fact that even the general *bay'ah* (oath of allegiance) for the caliphate was not valid without their consent. By the existence of this body in Muslim countries disagreement can easily be eliminated and the community can be saved from its perils. By means of this institution judiciary, administration, and politics can be organized on the right lines in the changing Muslim society. As regards dogma and rituals, they should be followed in the light of the agreement of the past generations (*Salaf*) without making any change therein.[61]

He expresses the opinion that men in authority (*Aulī al-Amr*) in modern times are the eminent (religious) scholars, commanders of the army, big tradesmen, peasants, people working in public service departments, directors of companies and societies, leaders of political parties, celebrated writers, physicians, advocates, managers and editors of the dignified journals people in whom the community places its confidence in important affairs, and consults them about the problems of daily life. People of every town perfectly know the person who is reliable and whose opinion is respected among them. Besides, the men in authority, being well-known and distinguished persons, should be in such a position that the ruler is able to recognize them and assemble them for consultation.[62]

He suggests that the men in authority should be elected by the people themselves from the community. But it is doubtful whether the elected members would bear the requisite qualities. He answers that the community should be fully acquainted with the purpose of

---

[61] *Ibid.*, ПI, 11-12.
[62] *Ibid.*, V., 187, 198-99,

the election and the qualities of the members. It would certainly then elect reliable, competent, and sincere persons suitable for the task. In case the community is ignorant of the purpose and significance of the election, it would certainly not elect the right men. It is not necessary to elect all men in authority from the community. They should be elected according to the requirements. If they are, for instance, one thousand in number in all, spreading in different towns of the country, one or two hundred would be sufficient, or whatever number might cater to the need. These members should be elected with the consent of the remaining competent members, but not elected formally. People may consult these remaining members in their judicial and administrative matters for their competence and qualifications.[63]

He holds that obedience to the men in authority is binding on the people as well as on the government, provided they are honest in their dealings and do not oppose what is established on the basis of the Qur᾽ān. Sunnah, and *Tawātur*, and decide cases by mutual and free discussion. The questions dealt with by them must relate to public interest. They have no say in questions relating to dogma and rituals. These matters will be decided directly on the basis of the Qur᾽ān and Sunnah. This power of deciding cases, for which there exist no clear injunctions in the Qur᾽ān or Sunnah, has been vested in them spontaneously by the people and not by any external force or temporal authority. Hence it is correct to say that their agreement on a certain point is infallible.[64]

He supports his interpretation of *Aulī al-Amr* by the statement of al-Nishapuri who holds the view that the term means reliable persons, men of opinion, and men in authority persons upon whom the

[63] *Ibid.*, pp. 200-201.
[64] *Ibid.*, p. 191.

whole community relies. He criticizes Fakhr al-Din al-Razi for interpreting the term in a narrow sense.[65]

The system of *shurā*, according to ʿAbduh, in the Muslim community varies in method with the change of time and space. The Prophet predicted that Islam would spread far and wide and the nations of the world would be subdued by the Muslims. This prevented the Prophet from laying down once for all a concrete, permanent, and inert methodology of *Shurā* to be followed by the Muslims of all times. The reason is that the principles of *Shūrā* compatible with the seventh-century Arabia with its simple and unsophisticated culture could not suit the shura of the coming ages. Hence, he gave the community the right to choose and devise any method and principles of *Shūrā* in accordance with the needs of the time. Had he prescribed definite principles of *Shūrā* in accordance with the situation of his time, the Muslims of the future generations would have taken them as a part of religion and applied them in every space and time. In fact, *Shūrā* is essentially a temporal affair. That is why the Companions are said to have remarked at the moment of the election of Abū Bakr, "The Prophet was satisfied with him for our religious affairs, why can we not be satisfied with him for our temporal matters?" This tradition clearly indicates that Muslims are better acquainted with their worldly affairs and they should manage them according to the existing situation.[66]

He is of the view that *Ijmā*ʿ of the previous generations is revocable. He rejects the classical theory that the *Ijmā*ʿ reached in one generation, especially the *Ijmā*ʿ of the pious Caliphs and the Companions, is eternally valid. He criticises the classical theory that *Ijmā*ʿ is the consensus of the jurists. A jurist may err in his individual interpretation (*Ijtihād*) but this error cannot be called straying from

---

[65] *Ibid.*, p. 187.
[66] *Ibid.*, IV, 201-2.

the right path. Hence the tradition 'my community will not agree on an error' does not refer to *Ijmāʿ*. Furthermore, the mistake in searching for the direction of prayer is no mistake; the prayer is valid. By the same analogy. and also according to another tradition, the *Ijtihād* of a *Mujtahid* is valid: indeed he is rewarded for this endeavour. When the rules of prayer and other rituals which bear permanent value can be changed in changing circumstances, why can the rules concerning political and judicial matters not be changed, particularly when they are based on *Ijtihād*, *Ijmāʿ*, and public interest?

Secondly, adherence to the previous *Ijmāʿ* is due not to its infallible character but to its utility, advantage, and public interest (*Maslahah*). The interest is sometimes visible and sometimes invisible because it too changes with the change of circumstances. Hence there is no reason for sticking to the *Ijmāʿ* of the past. Further, he remarks that al-Shāfiʿī advocates a similar kind of *Ijmāʿ* in his *Kitāb Al-Risālah*. Ahmad b. Hanbal also believed in the same type of *Ijmāʿ*. ʿAbduh also adduces the opinions of Abū ʿAbd Allah al-Baṣri and Ibn ʿAqil al-Hanball in support of his view that previous *Ijmāʿ* is open to modification if conditions change.[67]

VI

Ziya Gökalp, (d. 1343 A.H.), the eminent Turkish poet and sociologist, devised a novel method of reinterpreting the Islamic law. He made a distinction between the traditional and social elements in the Shart ah law. In his opinion the social elements are based on *ʾUrf* (mores) and not on tradition. His following statement shows that the social aspect of the *Shariʾah* is flexible:

"The sources of *fikh* are two: traditinal (*nāqiṭ*) *Shariʾa*, and social *Shariʾa*. But the social *Shariʾa* is in a continuous process of 'becoming,

[67] *Ibid.*, V, 208-10.

like all social phenomena. It follows, then, that part of *fikh* is not only liable to evolution in accordance with social evolution. and also has to change. The fundamentals of *fikh* related to Naṣṣ are eternally constant and unchangeable, whereas the social applications of these fundamentals which are based on the *ʿUrf* of the public and on the *Ijmāʿ* (consensus) of the scholars of *fikh* have to adapt themselves in accordance with the necessities of life."[68]

He distinguishes *ʾurf* (mores) from *ʿĀdah* (custom). *ʾUrf* is generally confused with custom, but this is not the real case. There is a partial general-particular relationship between *ʾUrf* (mores) and custom. Customs are not *ʾurf* (mores) because they are sometimes accepted and sometimes rejected by the community. Rejected customs are also transmitted from previous generation to the present one. But there can be no rejected *ʾurf* (mores). *ʾUrf* contains those rules which are accepted by the community. *ʾUrf* means 'the by-product of its (community's) real legal life, which constitutes the living law of the community,' and it stands for 'the norms living in the consciousness of the people who interpret, and apply to the actual, the formulae written in the law books. [69]Public opinion, mores, customs, usages, consensus of the scholars, and the negative decisions of the *Shariʿah* are all forms of *ʾUrf*.[70] There is a maxim already recognized in classical jurisprudence that "action according to *ʾUrf* is like acting on the Naṣṣ."[71] From this, he infers that "under necessity *ʾUrf* may take the place of Naṣṣ."[72] Generally speaking, *Ijtihād* is not permissible in questions where Naṣṣ exists. But according to some scholars, if Naṣṣ is the outcome of *ʾUrf*, then *Ijtihād* is permissible

---

[68] Ziya Gokalp, *Turkish Nationalism and Western Civilization*, tr. and ed. Niyazi Berkes, London, George Allen and Unwin Ltd., 1959, p. 196.
[69] *Ibid*., p. 197.
[70] *Ibid*., p. 198.
[71] Al-Sarakhsi, al-Mabsūṣ, Cairo, n.d., XXVI, 23; idem, *Sharh al-Siyar al-Kabir*, Hyderabad, Deccan, 1335 A.H., I, 194; IV, 23.
[72] Ziya Gokalp, *op. cit*., p. 194.

there. By referring to such principles he seeks to expand the scope of *'Urf* neglected in classical times.[73]

It may be noted that Ziya Gökalp was mistaken in understanding the meaning of the legal maxim "action according to *'urf* is like acting on the Naṣṣ." In this maxim, the word Naṣṣ does not mean the text of the Qur'ān or Sunnah. Here it means the provisions and conditions contained in an agreement, written or verbal, reached between two parties. This maxim means that if a condition has not been mentioned in the agreement, but that is understood and generally practiced by the people as a custom, that condition will also be applicable like the other conditions mentioned in the agreement. If either of the parties violates that condition, that will be considered the violation of the agreement. The condition required by custom and general practice, though not mentioned in the agreement, will be taken into account as if it were mentioned in the agreement. For example, a man concludes an agreement with a tailor for sewing a certain number of clothes. In the contract, no mention has been made as to which party will supply the thread and buttons. Now if there is a custom prevailing in that locality that the tailors generally supply this material themselves, the contracting tailor too shall supply the material.[74] This maxim therefore cannot be a basis of the argument advanced by Ziya Gokalp in support of *'Urf*.

He lays great emphasis on *'Urf* because it constitutes the living law of the community. A law, according to him. which in itself is not alive and does not provide life cannot regulate the life of the community. Hence, he divides *Fiqh* into 'social fundamentals' and 'dogmatic fundamentals." The former is flexible and the latter is

[73] *Ibid.*, p. 196.
[74] Munir al-Qadi, *Shark al-Majallah*, Baghdad: Matba'ah al-'Ani, 1949, 1, 106-108.

inflexible.[75] Therefore, laws based on *'Urf*, i.e. the value judgments of a people or of a given community, are subject to modification if the situation demands, according to the 'collective opinion' or 'national conscience,' i.e. *Ijmāʿ* of the community.[76]

Being essentially a sociologist, Ziya Gökalp applies the sociological values and principles to Islam. He distinguishes between 'religious' and 'secular' in Islamic law. This is indeed a departure from the existing view that Islamic law provides rules for every act of life, both temporal and religious. It should be noted that Ziya Gökalp is not alone in classifying the *Sharīʾah* into flexible and inflexible elements. ʿAbduh, too, like him, distinguishes between rituals and other social, political and administrative matters. The former, in his opinion, are unchangeable, while the latter are open to change with the change of circumstances. Apart from variance in terminology and way of expression, both have projected the same point of view. Criticizing Ziya Gökalp H.A.R. Gibb observes: "Obviously, however, this attempt to distinction is purely subjective; and the setting of customary law on an equal footing with the revealed law, even if it is regarded as the deposit of the historical experience or the character of a given nation, is irreconcilable with the bases of Islamic thought."[77]

It is worthy of remark that Ziya Gökalp's approach to the problem is not purely secular. *'Urf*, according to him, is not equivalent to customary law as Gibb presumes. He has explained this term in greater detail and identified it more or less with mores a sociological term used in a wider sense. Moreover, he seeks to substantiate his proposition on the basis of the Qur'ān and the Sunnah. We find in the classical jurisprudence classification of the *Sharīʾah* law into laws

---

[75] Ziya Gokalp, *op. cit.*, p. 198.
[76] Gibb, H.A.R., *Modern Trends in Islam*, Chicago, Illinois, 1950, p. 92.
[77] *Ibid.*

based on revealed texts (manṣūṣ) and laws based on individual interpretation (*mujtahad fih*). The former are certain (*Qaṭʾī*) and inflexible, and the latter speculative (*zanni*) and open to change. Besides, there is a difference of opinion among the jurists on the question of abrogation of *Ijmāʿ* reached in the past. The abrogation of a rule based on *Ijmāʿ* is valid, according to the exponents of this theory, in case the situation demands. This implies that they recognize in the *Shariʾah* elements which are open to review. Ziya Gökalp calls such elements *ʾUrf* according to the Qurʾānic terminology. This can well be reconciled with the basis of Islamic thought.

VII

Professor H.A.R. Gibb has dealt with the doctrine of *Ijmāʿ* in greater detail in his different works especially in *Modern Trends in Islam*. He has traced its origin, its development, justification, and the part it played in the integration of the community. He believes that absence of hierarchy, looseness of organization, and tolerance of difference are the characteristic features of *Ijmāʿ* which Islam advocates. To convert it into an organized institution, in an elected legislative assembly, in a council of *ʿUlamāʾ* or a synod, like Christianity, is against its nature. He describes it as 'conscience of the community,' 'voice of the people' and a 'general will' which emerges after the lapse of generations. He vindicates the informal decisions of *Ijmāʿ* arrived at through the toleration of differences and imperceptible slow progress of the general will by the pressure of public opinion. With this realistic approach to *Ijmāʿ* he proffers a moderate outlook which is neither conservative (i.e. *Ijmāʿ* of the *ʿUlamāʾ*) nor modernistic (elected legislative assembly). We summarize his discussion of the subject in the following paragraphs.

Ijmāʿ was originally introduced as a doctrine to substantiate the political structure in the second century of the Islamic era. The whole classical religious structure on different levels owes its rigidity and in turn stability to this principle. The emergence of the class of *'Ulamā'* was a natural and inevitable development. Although theoretically there is no clergy in Islam, the *'Ulamā'* played an important role in providing guidance to the community and thus acquired the high prestige and religious authority. They were recognized as the representatives of the community in faith and law, particularly against the authority of the state. In the second century, *Ijmā'* (especially *Ijmā'* of the learned) was regarded as a binding force. As tradition came to integrate the Qur'ān, *Ijmā'* came to integrate the tradition.

Ijmā' gives the final validity to the "imposing structure of Islam." It guarantees the authority of the text of the Qur'ān and of the tradition. *Ijmā'* determines the authoritative way of reading of the Qur'ān, its correct interpretation, and its right application. *Ijmā'* tampers with every branch of the *Shari'ah*. Though it cannot directly abrogate the Qur'ānic text or tradition, it may indicate that the rule is obsolete. It may throw away strict logical conclusions relating to the authenticity, meaning, and application of a text: it may approve a tradition which strict criticism rejects.

Ijmā' played a vital role in closing the gate of *Ijtihād*. The agreed decisions of the second and third centuries were irrevocable. *Ijtihād* was exercised on points not yet settled by *Ijmā'*. This continued in every generation; the scholars of subsequent generations commented on or explained the decisions of the early generations. Henceforth the gate of *Ijtihād* was closed, though some scholars at various times claimed to be *Mujtahid*. There is a certain analogy between the decisions taken on the basis of *Ijmā'* and those taken by the councils of the Christian church. *Ijmā'* in Islam became the touchstone of heresy.

Islam is both authoritarian and democratic, provided the political sense of the term 'democracy' is not stressed. In religious matters all Muslims are equal and the ultimate control rests with the conscience of the people, i.e. *vox populi*, expressed will of the community. This is not measured by the counting of votes or majority, but manifests itself "by the slow accumulating pressure of opinion over a long period of time." Some have tried to limit *Ijmā*ʿ to the consensus of the scholars. But it proved futile against the public opinion in the case of coffee-drinking held unlawful like wine-drinking by the *ʿUlamā*ʾ of Egypt.

There has been a controversy between the conservatives and the modernists over the character of *Ijmā*ʿ. *Ijmā*ʿ is not a liberal principle; it is a principle of authority. It provides authority for the things not covered by the rules in the Qurʾān and the tradition. The classical theologians and the Wahabis sought to confine *Ijmā*ʿ to the first generation. The modernists, on the other hand, considered it a liberal and progressive principle and attempted to justify it in all ages. Being a principle of authority, *Ijmā*ʿ used to narrow the range of faith and practice, and being a principle of toleration it rests upon the consensus of the whole community. It has done a great deal to minimize divergence among the Muslim community.

Islam is sometimes called a totalitarian religion. In fact, all religious ideas which have their bearing on outlook, human mind, and human will are totalitarian. They seek to impose their standards, values, and rules upon all social activities and institutions. But it is remarkable that the totalitarianism of religion is "an easy yoke." The religious authorities recognize the value and personality of individuals and allow a considerable range of liberty. The liberty in Islam is further extended by the looseness of its organization, the absence of hierarchy, and toleration of differences. It sought to curb the communication and spread of dangerous thoughts to the individual to the purity of doctrine and to the salvation of the community. Dangerous thought cannot dominate in a society which recognizes *Ijmāʿ* as normative.[78]

VIII

To sum up, Shah Wali Allah, being a liberal orthodox and enlightened progressive thinker, rejects the orthodox theory of total *Ijmāʿ*. He regards a law sanctioned by the shura and enforced by the caliph as *Ijmāʿ*. Sayyid Ahmad Khān throws doubts on the classical theory. He validates *Ijmāʿ* provided it is supported by the Qurʾān or the Sunnah. In other words, he considers it a secondary or confirmatory source. Ubayd Allah Sindhi has projected almost the same view as held by Shah Wali Allah. He sharply distinguished between the Sunnah and *Ijmāʿ*. Muhammad Iqbal regards the decisions of the elected legislative assembly as *Ijmāʿ* of the Muslim community. He desires to make it a permanent and well-organized institution. Muhammad ʿAbduh holds the same view. He considers the elite of the Muslim society competent for *Ijmāʿ*. They represent the community in the elected legislature and the agreement on a certain rule amounts to the *Ijmāʿ* of the community. Ziya Gökalp classifies the *Shariʾah* into dogmatic and social. *ʾUrf* (mores) represents the social aspect which is subject to change. *Ijmāʿ* falls under this category. The former is rigid and permanent. Gibb considers *Ijmāʿ* an agreement of the whole community. It emerges spontaneously in the form of general will after the lapse of time.

Change in the classical theory of *Ijmāʿ* is a feature common to all fresh interpretations.[79] Change, of course, is a pressing need of the

---

[78] *Ibid.*, pp. 85-86, 95-98; cf. Detlev H. Khalid, The Problem of defining Islam and modern accentuations, Islamic Studies, Autumn 1977 (Vol. XVI. No.3), pp. 224-27, 260-61, note 58.

[79] Dr. Fazlur Rahman considers *Ijma* of the community 'essentially an ever-expanding press, utterly democratic in temper," "a process and something

Muslim society in modern times. Modernists are utilizing *Ijmāʿ* as an instrument for bringing about change in society. This indeed can be done by degrees through the process of *Ijmāʿ* in the course of time. But kaleidoscopic change cannot be related to *Ijmāʿ*. The change to be brought about by *Ijmāʿ* is slow and imperceptible. Modernists may Islamicize some secular institutions borrowed from the West through *Ijmāʿ* modernism theory, but that would not be an *Ijmāʿ* in its true sense. Professor Leonard Binder has minutely examined this question showing its subsequent dangers to Islamic tradition.[80]

---

forward-looking', and not 'something static and backward-looking, *Islamic Methodology in History*, Lahort, 1965, pp. 6, 20, 24; Kemal A. Faruki takes *Ijmāʿ* as prospective and makes certain suggestions to make it practicable and efficacious in the modern age. *Ijma and the Gate of Ijtihād*, Karachi, 1954, pp. 19-20, 27-28, 30-33, and 37-38.

[80] Binder, Leonard, *Religion, and Politics in Pakistan*, Berkeley and Los Angeles, 1961, p. 69.

Conclusion

In the preceding chapters, we have reviewed at length the doctrine of *Ijmāʿ* in Islam. The classical theory portrays it as a total agreement of the community or of the scholars. The classical jurists dilated on it with all its implications. They raised important questions with regard to its conception, definition, and competence. period, procedure, and applicability, and sought to present the theory in its complete form.

There are, however, a number of points that are lacking in the classical theory. The most significant of them is the absence of a machinery for its practical functioning. The classical theory presents *Ijmāʿ* as a purely informal activity of the scholars in their private and individual capacity with no definite organization and specific procedure. Further, it is content to describe certain qualifications for the competence of *Ijmāʿ*; it does not identify the persons in whom these qualifications were actually found and who could be considered competent for it in its true sense. The condition of 'total agreement' of the scholars has again been condemned by the opponents. The unanimous agreement of the community is confined to the essentials of religion. The consensus of the scholars has been presented as the *Ijmāʿ* of the community. This has also not been universally recognized. Those who defined it as an agreement of the whole community, like al-Ghazali, were severely criticized by the classical jurists. A large number of questions concerning points of detail are said to have been covered by *Ijmāʿ*. Such questions are, in fact, supported by tacit *Ijmāʿ* communicated verbally. The validity of the tacit *Ijmāʿ* is already disputed. The most objectionable point that strikes the modern mind is that the classical theory neglects in *Ijmāʿ* the intellectual elite and the masses which constitute the bulk of the community. In certain situations, the masses and the public opinion practically bypass the agreement of the scholars, and the scholars themselves recognize it with the passage of time by their practice. Can it be characterzied as *Ijmā*ʿ? The objections raised by the exponents of *Ijmā*ʿ themselves, let alone the opponents, indicate that the classical theory of *Ijmā*ʿ was not recognized in full even during its formative period. Because of its purely theoretical nature and perhaps for want of some definite practicable machinery, it could not be utilized to reform the Muslim society.

The doctrine of *Ijmā*ʿ, of course, played a fundamental and significant role in conserving the past heritage and formation of institutions in Islam. It served as a unifying force, like some parallel institutions in other religions, in the Muslim community. It engendered unity and solidarity in the whole system of law, dogma, and rituals. Creating unity in diversity was the principal function of *Ijmā*ʿ in the medieval times. And probably for this purpose this principle, though forward-looking and progressive in its early stages, was theorized in a retrospective manner and it went a long way towards the fulfilment of this objective.

It seems that the concept of *Ijmā*ʿ originally began as a theory of the will of the community. This theory continued for a certain period of time until the rise of scholars as a pressure group in the Muslim society. With their dominance in the religious sphere, and with the separation of religion from politics in practice, the scholars were regarded as representing the will of the community. Another reason may be that the *ʿUlamā*ʾ in the medieval times almost constituted the whole of the educated class and the intellectual elite of the society. The masses mostly relied on them in different matters, especially in religious affairs. The consciousness of common men in the affairs of society, whether religious, political, or social, grew fast in modern times. Allegiance to a single authority, a chief characteristic of the medieval period, was replaced by allegiance to the public will. Hence the modern mind is not convinced of the classical definition of *Ijmā*ʿ which shows the hierarchy of the scholars in Islam. Modernists seek to employ it as a 'tool of reform.' Influenced by the universal democratic trend in thinking, they identify public opinion, public will, opinion of the intellectual elite of the society, and the enactments of representative assemblies of the Muslim countries with the *Ijmāʿ* of the community. There are of course people who take it only as a unifying and conserving authority. They see little hope of reform through *Ijmāʿ* in view of its classical definition.

We think the *ʿUlamāʾ* or the specialists provoke public opinion to form a consensus on a given question by their expert opinion. And if they are agreed, it certainly constitutes *Ijmāʿ*, though only tentatively, unless it is confirmed by the will of the community, i.e. by practically recognizing or rejecting it in the course of time. The classical theory recognizes the opinion of the masses and intellectuals only in respect of essentials or questions directly relating to them. But it recognizes the consensus of the scholars alone on questions of purely academic and technical nature. The masses do not come into the picture. We are of the view that even on such questions the *Ijmāʿ* of the scholars may be accepted in a tentative manner to be finally approved of by the will of the community at large.

In the present political situation, the division of the Muslim community into a number of national states has created fresh problems for the formation of *Ijmāʿ*. There are problems which are of purely religious nature and require the assent of the universal community. Others relate to a local situation obtaining in a Muslim country. What should be the procedure of reaching *Ijmāʿ* on both these types of questions? We are of opinion that questions of universal nature may be discussed on an international level in a meeting of experts who represent different Muslim countries. The consensus arising out of their deliberations may form a tentative *Ijmāʿ* of a functional nature. It will be regarded as permanent when confirmed by the universal community. As to the *Ijmāʿ* on questions of parochial nature, the specialists or elite of the society, as the case may be, of a particular Muslim country may form a consensus, by their mutual discussion, say in a national assembly, which will be of a temporary nature. This can be confirmed or rejected in course of time by the will of the local community. It is worthy of remark that both types of *Ijmāʿ*, local and universal, will function as a temporary measure, subject to the acceptance or rejection by the universal or local community in the long run.

Ijmāʿ, it may be noted, is not retrospective by nature, as the classical theory depicts it. Originally it started as a forward-looking and prospective phenomenon. Modern researches of the early period show that *Ijma* in the pre-Shāfiʿī period was an ongoing process, liable to be changed with the change of conditions. It exercised a check against the fallibility of the new content which emerged in the wake of *Ijtihād Ijmāʿ* activity. With the cessation of original thinking in law and suspension of the activity of *Ijtihād*, it became inert by degrees, and ultimately a custodian of tradition. But it can be utilized for the benefit of Muslim society by taking it back to its original conception.

Bibliography

1. Arabic Sources

ʿAbd Allah b. ʿAbd al-Hakam, *Sirat ʿUmar b. ʿAbd al-ʿAzīz*, Cairo, 1927.

ʿAbd al-ʿAzīz al-Bukhārī, *Kashf al-Asar ʾala Uṣūl al-Bazdawī*, Stanbul, 1307 A.H., Vol. III.

ʿAbd al-Jabbar, *al-Mughnī fi Abwab al-Tawhid wal-ʾAdl*, Cairo, 1382 A.H., Vols II, XV, XVII.

"Abduh, Muhammad, *Tafsir al-Manar*, (ed.) Rashid Rida), Cairo, 1367 A.H., Vols, III, V

Abū Dāwūd, *Sunan*, Cawnpur, n.d., Vols. I, II.

Abu'l Qasim al-Qummi, *Kitāb Qawānin al-Uṣūl*, Tehran, 1304 A.H.

Abū Riḍā, *Ibrāhīm b. Sayyār al-Naẓẓām*, Cairo, 1946.

Abū Yūsuf, *Kitāb al-Kharāj*, Cairo, 1302 A.H.

Abū Zahrah, *Muḥammad*, Ibn Ḥanbal, Cairo, 1947.

Al-ʿAjlānī, *Kashf al-Khafāʾ*, Cairo, 1351 A.H., Vol. I.

ʿAlī ʿAbd al-Rāziq, *al-Ijmāʿ fil-Shariʾah al-Islamiyyah*, Cairo, 1947.

ʿAlī al-Muttaqī, *Kanz al-ʾUmmāl*, Hyderabad, Daccan, Vols. III, IV.

Al-Āmidī, al-Iḥkām fi Uṣūl al-Aḥkām, Cairo, 1914, Vols. I, IIII.

Al-Asfarāʾinī, *Al-Tabṣīr fil-Dīn*, Cairo, 1955.

Al Ashʿari, *Maqālāt al-Islamiyyīn*, Cairo, 1950, Vols. I, II.

Idem, *Kitāb al-Lumaʿ*, Beirut, 1953.

Idem, *al-Ibānah*, Hyderabad, Deccan, 1948.

Atfish, Muhammad b. Yūsuf, *Shāmil al-Aṣl wal-Farʿ*, Cairo, 1332 A.H. Vol. I.

Al-ʿAyni, *ʿUmdat al-Qārī*, Istanbul, 1310 A.H., Vol. II.

Al-Azdi, Muhammad b. ʿAbd Allah, *Futūḥ al-Shām*, Calcutta, 1854.

Al-ʿAzizi, *al-Sirāj al-Munīr*, Cairo, n.d. Vol. I.

Al-Baghdadi, *ʾAbd al-Qāhir, Kitāb Uṣūl al-Dīn*, Istanbul, 1928.

Idem, *al-Farq bayn al-Firaq*, Cairo, 1948.

Al-Baji, Abuʾl-Walid, al-Ishārah fī Uṣūl al-Fiqh, MS. Escorial, I.R.I. Lib. 130 (Photo).

Al-Baṣri, Abuʾl-Husayn, *Kitāb al-Muʾtamad*, Damuscus, 1965, Vols. I, II.

Al-Bayhaqi, *al-Sunan al-Kubrā*, Hyderabad, Deccan, 1355 A.H., Vol. X.

Al-Bazdawī, *Kitāb Uṣūl al-Dīn*, Cairo, 1963.

Al-Bazdawī, *Kanz al-Wuṣūl ila ma rif-t al-Uṣūl* or (*Uṣūl al-Bazdawī*), Karachi, 1966.

Brūjirdi, Muhammad, *Mukhtalif al-Usūl*, Tehran, 1341 A.H.

Al-Bukhari, *al-Jāmiʿ al-Ṣaḥīḥ*, Leiden, 1962, Vols. I-IV.

Burhan al-Din al-Marghinānī, *al-Hidāyah*, Deoband, 1380 A.H., Vol. II.

Al-Firawzābādi, Majd al-Din, *Sifr al-Saʾadah*, Cairo, 1347 A.H.

Al-Ghazali, *Al-Mustaṣfā min ʿIlm al-Uṣūl*, Cairo, 1937, Vols. I, II.

Idem, *al-Tafriqah bayn al-Islām wal-Zandaqah*, Bombay, n.d. Idem, al-Mustazhirt, Leiden, 1956.

Idem, al-Mankhūl min Taʿlīqāt al-Uṣūl, Damuscus: Maktabah Dår al-Fikr, n.d.

Al-Haythami, *Majmaʿ al-Zawāʾid*, Cairo, 1353 A.H., Vol. V.

Husain, S.M. e.d., *Muntakhab min Kitāb al-Khiyārayn*, Delhi, 1938.

Al-Husayni, Muhammad al-Mahdi, *al-Wuṣūl ilā Kifāyat al-Uṣūl*, Najaf, n.d. Vol. III.

Ibn Abi Dawūd, *Kitāb al-Maṣāḥif.* (Arthur Jaffery, ed.), Cairo, 1936.

Ibn Ab'il-Hadid, *Sharḥ Nahj al-Balāghah*, Cairo, n.d. Vol. I.

Ibn ʿAsākir, *Tahdhīb al-Tārīkh al-Kabīr*, Damascus, 1329, A. H., Vol. I.

Ibn Hajar al-ʿAsqalani, *Fatḥ al-Bārī*, Cairo, 1329 A.H. Vol. XIII.

Ibn Hanbal, *Musnad*, Cairo, 1313 A.H., Vols. I, II, IV, V, VI.

idem, *al-Risālat al-Saniyyah*, in Majmūʿah al-Ḥadīth al-Najdīyah, Qatar, 1383 A.H.

Ibn Hazm, *Al-Iḥkām fī Uṣūl al-Aḥkām*, Cairo, 1347 A.H. Vol. IV.

Idem, *Marātib al-Ijma*, Cairo, 1357 A.H.

Ibn Hishām, Sīrat al-Nabī, Cairo, n.d. Vol. II.

Ibn al-Humām, *al-Taḥrīr fī Uṣūl al-Fiqh*, Cairo, 1351 A.H.

Ibn Kathīr, *al-Bidāyah wal-Nihāyah*, Cairo, 1932, Vols. VI, XI.

Ibn Khaldūn, *Muqaddimah*, Beirut, 1900.

Ibn Majah, *Sunan*, Lucknow, 1315 A.H.

Ibn al-Malak, *Sharḥ al-Manār*, Istanbul, 1306 A.H.

Ibn Manẓūr, *Lisān al-ʿArab*, Beirut, 1955.

Ibn al-Murtada, *Ṭabaqāt al-Muʿtazilah*, Beirut, 1961.

Ibn Qayyim, *Iʿlām al-Muwaqqiʿīn*, Delhi, 1313 A. H., Vols. I. II.

Idem, *Zād al-Maʿād*, Cairo, 1950, Vol. III.

Ibn Qudamah, *al-Mughnī*, Cairo, 1367 A.H., Vol. I.

Ibn Qutaybah, *Taʾwīl Mukhtalif al-Ḥadīth*. Cairo, 1326 A.H.

Idem, *Al-Imāmah wal-Siyāsah*, Cairo, n.d. Vols. I. II.

Ibn Rushd, *Kitāb Faṣl al-Maqāl*, Leiden. 1959.

Ibn Saʿd, *al-Ṭabaqāt al-Kubrā*. 1957, Vol. 111.

Ibn Taymiyah, *Majmūʿat al-Rasāʾil wal-Masāʾil*, Cairo, 1354 A.H., Vol. II.

Idem, *Ma'ārij al-Wuṣūl*, Cairo, 1323 A.H.

Idem, *Ma'ārij al-Wuṣūl*, Cairo, 1964.

Al-Isnawī, *Nihāyat al-Sūl fī Sharḥ Minhāj al-Wuṣūl ilā 'Ilm al-Uṣūl*, Cairo n.d., Vol. II

Al-Jahiz, *al-'Uthmāniyyah*, Cairo, 1955.

Idem, *al-Nābitah*, Cairo, 1937.

Idem, *Thalāthah Rasā'il*. Leiden, 1903.

Al-Jalal Al-Maḥallī, *Sharḥ Jam' al-Jawāmi'*, Cairo, 1927 A.H. Vol. II.

Al-Jaṣṣāṣ. *Kitāb Uṣūl al-Fiqh*, MS. 229 Uṣūl, Dar al-Kutub al-Miṣriyah. Cairo.

Idem, *Aḥkām al-*Qur'ān, Istanbul, 1335 A.H. Vol. III.

Al-Juwayni, Imam al-Haramayn, *al-Burhän fi Uṣūl al-Fiqh*, MS. 714, Dar al-Kutub al-Misriyah, Cairo.

Idem, *Kitāb al-Irshād*. Cairo, 1950.

Al-Karkhi, *Risālah al-Karkī*, Cairo, n.d.

Al-Khayyat, *Kitāb al-Intiṣār*, Cairo, 1925.

Al-Kulini, *al-Uṣūl min al-Kāfī*, Tehran, 1382 A.H., Vol. I, V.

Lane, E.W. *Arabic-English Lexicon*, London, 1963.

Al-Mahallawi, *Taḥṣīl al-Wuṣūl ilā 'Ilm al-Uṣūl*, Multan, 1961.

Mahmūd al-Hasan, *Mu'jam al-Muṣannifīn*, Beirut, 1344 A.H. Vol. II.

Mālik, *Al-Muwaṭṭa'*, Cairo, 1951, Vols. 1, II.

Al-Mawardi, *Al-Aḥkām al-Sulṭāniyyah*, Cairo, n.d.

Al-Mufaḍḍal al-Ḍabbī, *Al-Mufaḍḍaliyyāt*, Cairo, n.d.

Muhammad A'lā al-Thanawi, *Kashshāf Iṣṭilāḥāt al-Funūn*, Calcutta, 1862, Vols. 1, 11. Mulla 'Alī al-Qari, *Sharh al-Fiqh al-Akbar*, Karachi, n.d.

Muslim, *Ṣaḥīḥ*, Delhi, n.d., Vols. I, II.

Mustafa Zayd, *al-Maslaḥah fī al-Sharīʿah al-Islāmiyyah wa Najm al-Dīn al-Ṭuffī*, Cairo, 1964.

Al-Muzani, *Mukhtṣar*, on the margin of K. al-Umm. 1321 A.H.

Al-Nasāʾī, *Sunan*. Delhi, 1335 A.H., Vols. I, II.

Al-Nawawi, *Sharḥ al-Ṣaḥīḥ li Muslim*, Delhi, 1376 A.H.. Vol. II.

Al-Nawbakhti, *Kitāb Firaq al-Shīʿah*, Istanbul, 1931.

Al-Qadi Adud al-Din, *Sharḥ Mukhtaṣar al-Muntahā*, Istanbul, 1307 A.H.

Al-Qarafi, *Sharḥ Tanqīḥ al-Fuṣūl*, Cairo, 1306 A.H.

Qurʾān

Al-Qurtubi, *al-Jāmiʿ li-Aḥkām al-Qurʾān*, Cairo, 1940, Vol. X.

Al-Razi, Fakhr al-Din, *ʿItiqād Firaq al-Muslimīn wal-Mushrikīn*, Cairo, 1938.

Idem, *Mafātīḥ al-Ghayb*, Cairo, 1308 A.H., Vols. III, VI.

Al-Ṣadoq, Abū Jaʿfar, *al-Hidāyah*, Tehran, 1377 A.H.

Idem, *al-Mughnī*, Tehran, 1377 A.H.

Idem, *Waṣf Dīn al-Imāmiyyah*, 1377 A.H.

Sabnūn, *al-Mudawwanah al-Kubrā*, Cairo, 1322 A.H., Vol. I.

Al-Sarakhsi, *Uṣūl al-Sarakhsī*, Cairo, 1372 A.H., Vols. I, II.

Idem, *al-Mabsút*, Cairo, n.d. Vol. XXVI.

Idem, *Sharh al-Siyar al-Kabir*, Hyderabad, Deccan, 1335 A.H., I, IV.

Shah Wali Allah, *Al-Tafhīmāt al-Ilāhiyyah*, Bijnor, 1936, Vol. II.

Ṣadr al-*Shariʿah*, ʿAbd Allah b. Masʿod, *al-Tawathu*, Cairo, 1957, Vols. I, II.

Al-Shafiʿi, *Kitāb al-Umm*, Cairo, 1321 A.H. Vol. VII.

Idem, *Ikhtilāf al-Ḥadīth*, on the margin of K. al-Umm, Vol. VII.

Idem, *Al-Risālah*, Cairo, 1312 A.H.

Idem, *Jima al-'Ilm*, ed. Shakir, Cairo, 1940.

Al-Shahid al-Thani, Hasan b. Zayn al-Din, *Ma'alim al-Uṣūl*, Tehran, 1370 A.H.

Al-Shahrastānī, *Kitāb al-Milal wal-Nihal*, Cairo, 1921.

Al-Shāṭibi, *Kitāb al-I'tiṣam*, Cairo, 1914, Vol. III.

Idem, *al-Muwāfaqāt*, Tunis, 1302 A.H.

Al-Shawkāni. *Irshad al-Fuhūl*, Cairo, 1327 A.H.

Al-Shaybani, Muhammad b. al-Hasan, *Al-Muwaṭṭa'*, Deoband, n.d.

Al-Shirāzi, Abū Ishaq, *al-Luma' fī Uṣūl al-Fiqh*, Cairo, n.d.

Siddiq Hasan Khān, Muhammad, *Ḥuṣūl al-Ma'mūl min 'Ilm al-Uṣūl*, Istanbul, 1296 A.H.

Al-Suyūṭi, *al-Jāmi' al-Ṣaghīr*, Cairo, 1954, Vol. I.

Al-Tabari, *Ta'rīkh al-Umam wal-Mulūk*, Cairo, 1336 A.H., Vol. V.

Idem, *Jami al-Bayan fi Tafsir al-Qur'ān*, Cairo, 1336 A.H. Vols. XII, XIV.

Al-Tabatabai, Muhammad Kazim, *al-'Urwah al-Wuthqā*, Tehran, n.d.

Al-Taftāzāni, *Sharḥ al-'Aqā'id al-Nasafiyyah*, Cairo, n.d. pp. 7-8.

Idem, *Talwīth*, Cairo, 1957, Vol. II.

Al-Tabawi, Mukhtaṣar al-Ṭaḥāwī, Cairo, 1370 A.H.

Idem, *Sharḥ Ma'ānī al-Athār*, Deoband, n.d.

Al-Tirmidhi, *al-Jami*, Cawnpur, n.d. Vols. I, II.

Al-Tasi, *'Uddat al-Uṣūl*, Bombay, 1312 A.H., Vol. II.

Idem, *Al-Tibyān fi Tafsir al-Qur'an*, Najaf, 1957, Vol. II.

Idem, *al-Istibṣār*, Najaf, 1956, Vol. III.

Idem, *Tahdhīb al-Aḥkām*, Najaf, 1959, Vols. II, VIII.

Walī al-Dīn al-Khaṭīb, *Mishkāt al-Maṣābīḥ*, Delhi, 1350 A.H.

II. Non-Arabic Sources

ʿAbd al-Rāhīm, *Awl wa Taʿṣīb*, Tehran, 1382 A.H.

Ahmad Hasan, *The Early Development of Islamic Jurisprudence*, Lahore, 1970.

Idem, The Concept of Infallibility in Islam, *Islamic Studies*. March, 1972.

ʿAtā Allah, Shaykh, ed., *Iqbal Namah*, Lahore, n.d.

Aziz Ahmad, *Islamic Modernism in India and Pakistan*, London, 1967.

Barker, Ernest. *Principles of Social and Political Theory*, London, 1961.

Baron, S.W. *A Social and Religious History of the Jews*, New York/London, 1962, Vol. V. The Holy Bible

Binder, Leonard, *Religion and Politics in Pakistan*, Berkely and Los Angeles, 1961.

Blackman, Philip, ed., *Mishnayoth*, New York, 1963, Vol. IV.

Cicero, *De Divinatione*, (tr. W. Armstead Falconer), the Loeb Classical Lib., London, 1953.

Idem, *Offices, Essays, and Letters*, London 1949.

Idem, *Tusculan Disputations*, ed. Moses Hadas, New York, 1951. Coulson, N.J.; A History of Islamic Law, Edinburgh, 1964.

Dar, Bashir Ahmad, *Religious Thought of Sayyid Ahmad Khan*, Lahore, 1958.

Doughlas, D.H., ed. *The New Bible Dictionary*, London, 1962.

Durkheim, Emile, *The Elementary Forms of the Religious Life* (tr. Joseph Ward Swain), New York, 1961.

Faruki, K.A., *Ijmāʿ and the Gate of Ijtihād*, Karachi, 1954.

Fazlur Rahman, *Islamic Methodology in History*, Lahore, 1965.

Fazlur Rahman, *The Impact of Modernity on Islam*, Islamic Studies, V, 2 (June, 1966)

Finkelstein, Louis, *The Jews their History, Culture and Religion*, New York, 1960, Vol.

Gibb, H.A.R. *Mohammedanism*, London, 1961.

Idem, *Modern Trends in Islam*, Chicago, Illinois, 1950.

Goldziher, Ignaz, *Le dogme et la loi de l'Islam*, Fr. tr. Felix Arin, Paris, 1958,

Grunebaum, G.E. Von, *Islam*, London, 1961.

Idem, *Medieval Islam*, Chicago/London, 1966.

Guillaume, A. *The Life of Muhammad*, London, 1955.

Hali, Altaf Husayn, *Hayat-i-Jawid*, London, 1957.

Hourani, George F., *The Ethics of 'Abd al-Gabbar*, Oxford, 1971.

Iqbal, Muhammad, *Reconstruction of Religious Thought in Islam*, Lahore, 1962.

Jurji, Edward J., ed. *The Great Religions of the Modern World*, Princeton, 1946.

Kellet, E.E., *A Short History of Religions*, Bungay Suffolk, n.d.

Khadduri, Majid, *Islamic Jurisprudence*, English tr. of al-Shāfiʿī's Risalah, Baltimore, 1961.

Khalid Masʿūd, Muhammad, Taʾrīkh al-Islām mayn abli ball wa ʿaqd kā taṣuwwur, *Fikr-o-Naẓar*, I, 7, 8, (Jan., Feb. 1964).

Lyall, C.J. *English translation of the Musaddaliyāt*, Oxford, 1918.

Lucas, J.R. *The Principles of Politics*, Oxford, 1966.

Madina, M.Z., *The Classical Doctrine of Consensus in Islam*, unpublished Ph.D. thesis No. 3872, submitted in 1957 to the Department of Political Science, the University, Chicago, Illinois

Marie Bernand. Ligma' chez 'Abd al-Gabbar et'l'objection d'an-Nazzām, *Studia Islamica*,

Max Miller, ed., *Vinaya Texts*, Delhi, 1965, Vols. XIII, XX, XXXVI,

Idem, ed., *Dhammapada*, Delhi, 1965, Vol. X.

Idem, ed., *Sutta-Napata*, Delhi, 1965, Vol. XI.

Idem, ed. *Mahyana Texts*, Delhi, 1965, Vol. XLIX.

Muhammad Ismā'il Panipati, ed., *Maqālāt Sir Sayyid*, Lahore, 1961 Vols. I, XIII.

Pellat, Charles, *The Life and Works of Jahiz*, Eng. tr. D.M. Hawkes, London, 1969.

Prichard, *A.M. Leage's Roman Private Law*, London, 1964.

Rosenthal, E.L.J. *Political Thought in Medieval Islam*, Cambridge, 1958.

Russell, Bertrand, *History of Western Philosophy*, London, 1969,

Sayyid Ahmad Khan, *Taṣnīfāt Aḥmadiyyah*, Aligarh, 1883, Vol. I.

Idem, *Tahdhīb al-Akhlāq*, Lahore, 1894, Vol. L

Schacht, Joseph, *The Origins of Muhammadan Jurisprudence*, Oxford, 1959.

Seneca, *Ad Lucilium, Epistalae Morales* (tr. Richard M. Gummere) London, 1952.

Simon Van den Bergh, *Averroe's Tahāfut al-Tahāfut*, London, 1954, Vols. I, II.

Sindhi, 'Ubayd Allah, *Shah Wali Allah awr unka Falsafah*, Lahore, n.d.

Idem, *Shah Wali Allah awr unki Siyast Tabrik*, Lahore, 1965.

Shah Wali Allah, *Izālat al-Khafā'*, Urdu tr. by 'Abd al-Shakor, Karachi, n.d. Vols. I, II.

Idem, *Qurrat al-'Aynayn fī Tafḍīl al-Shaykhayn*, Peshawar, 1310 A.H.

Tamanna Imādi, *Ikhtilāf al-Ummat Raḥmat Hay yā Zaḥmat*, Karachi, n.d.

Thomas, E.J., *The History of Buddhist Thought*, London, 1963.

Timothy Ware, *The Orthodox Church*, Bungay Suffolk, 1963.

Tritton, A.S., *Muslim Theology*, Bristol, 1947.

Wach, Joachim, *Sociology of Religion*, Chicage, 1964.

Watt, W.M. *Islamic Philosophy and Theology* (Islamic Surveys 1), Edinburgh, 1962.

Idem, *Islamic Political Thought* (Islamic Surveys 6), Edinburgh, 1968.

Idem, *What is Islam?*, London, 1968.

Idem, *Islam and the Integration of Society*, London, 1961.

Weber, Max, *The Sociology of Religion*, (tr. Talcott Parsons), Boston, 1967.

Wensink, A.J. *The Muslim Creed*. Cambridge, 1923.

Wood, Stanely. *The Life and Teaching of Christ*, London, 1939.

Yusuf, S.M., *Studies in Islamic Culture and History*, Lahore, 1970.

Zoya Gokalp, *Turkish Nationalism and Western Civilization*, London, 1959.

III. Encyclopaedias

Encyclopaedia of Islam, Leiden, 1913, art. Idjmä

Ibid., New edition art. ldjmä

Shorter Encyclopaedia of Islam, Leiden, 1961, arts. Din, Pikad, Shariʿa.

The Encyclopaedia of Religion and Ethics. Edinburgh New York, 1959, arts. Binding and Loosing, Church, Infallibility, and Sanhendrin.

Encyclopaedia Britannica. London, 1951, arts. Church, Religion.

The Jewish Encyclopaedia, New York/London, arts. Sanhedrin, Sanhedrin-French, Synagogue the Great Synod.

Encyclopaedia of the Social Sciences, New York, 1959, arts. Buddhism, Religious Institutions: Christian Roman Catholic.

Encyclopaedia of Religion and Religions, London, 1951, art. Buddhism.

www.ingramcontent.com/pod-product-compliance
Ingram Content Group UK Ltd.
Pitfield, Milton Keynes, MK11 3LW, UK
UKHW021404190726
13845UKWH00028B/870

9 789366 086712